Teaching Mental Health

Teaching Mental Health

Edited by

Theo Stickley
University of Nottingham, UK

and

Thurstine Basset
Consultancy Ltd, UK

John Wiley & Sons, Ltd

Other Wiley Editorial Offices

John Wiley & Sons Inc., 111 River Street, Hoboken, NJ 07030, USA

Jossey-Bass, 989 Market Street, San Francisco, CA 94103-1741, USA

Wiley-VCH Verlag GmbH, Boschstr. 12, D-69469 Weinheim, Germany

John Wiley & Sons Australia Ltd, 42 McDougall Street, Queensland 4064, Australia

John Wiley & Sons (Asia) Pte Ltd, 2 Clementi Loop #02-01, Jin Xing Distripark, Singapore 129809

John Wiley & Sons Canada Ltd, 6045 Freemont Blvd, Mississauga, ONT, L5R 4J3

Wiley also publishes its books in a variety of electronic formats. Some content that appears
in print may not be available in electronic books.

Anniversary Logo Design: Richard J. Pacifico

Library of Congress Cataloguing-in-Publication Data

Teaching mental health / edited by Theo Stickley and Thurstine Basset.
     p. ; cm.
  Includes bibliographical references and index.
  ISBN-13: 978-0-470-03029-5 (pbk. : alk. paper)
  1. Mental health services – Study and teaching.   I. Stickley, Theo.   II. Basset, Thurstine.
  [DNLM: 1. Allied Health Personnel – education.   2. Mental Health Services – organization & administration.
  3. Education, Professional – methods.   4. Teaching – methods. WM 18 T2528 2007]
  RA790.8.T43 2007
  362.2071 – dc22

                                                                                2006038744

British Library Cataloguing in Publication Data

A catalogue record for this book is available from the British Library

ISBN 978-0-470-03029-5

Typeset in 10/12pt Times by TechBooks, New Delhi, India
Printed and bound in Great Britain by Antony Rowe Ltd, Chippenham, Wiltshire

This book is printed on acid-free paper responsibly manufactured from sustainable forestry
in which at least two trees are planted for each one used for paper production.

Contents

About the Editors

Theo Stickley trained in counselling and mental health nursing and practised in both professions for many years. Theo now teaches mental health at the University of Nottingham and has published widely in the nursing and mental health press. The focus of his research is mental health and the arts and has led on a number of research projects in collaboration with people who use mental health services. Theo is a keen gardener, motorcyclist and artist (but has not yet found a way to combine all three simultaneously).

Thurstine Basset trained as social worker and worked as a community worker and social work practitioner, mostly in the mental health field. He is now an Independent Training and Development Consultant and runs his own company which is based in Brighton. He works for national voluntary agencies, such as Mind, Together and the Mental Health Foundation. With the Richmond Fellowship, he is the joint course leader for their Diploma in Community Mental Health, which is accredited by Middlesex University. He has written mental health learning materials, many of which are published by Pavilion Publishing, with whom he works in an advisory role. He likes to walk and watch cricket.

Contributors

Jill Anderson
Senior Project Development Officer, Mental Health in Higher Education

Russell Ashmore
Senior Lecturer, Sheffield Hallam University

Jacqueline Atkinson
Senior Lecturer in Psychology at the University of Glasgow

Ian Baguley
Professor of Mental Health and Director of the Centre for Clinical and Academic Workforce Innovation, the University of Lincoln

Janet H. Barker
Associate Professor, School of Nursing, University of Nottingham

Thurstine Basset
Independent Training and Development Consultant

Peter Bates
National Development Team

Alan Beadsmoore
Senior Lecturer, Middlesex University

Paul Bickerstaffe
Lecturer, Mental Health and Learning Disabilities Directorate, Cardiff School of Nursing and Midwifery Studies, Cardiff University

Chris Blackmore
Research Associate, Centre for the Study of Conflict & Reconciliation, University of Sheffield

Alison Blank
Senior Occupational Therapist, West Sussex Health and Social Care NHS Trust

Jayne Breeze
Nurse Lecturer, Faculty of Health and Wellbeing, Sheffield Hallam University

Hilary Burgess
Senior Lecturer, Social Work, University of Bristol and Project Director for Mental Health in Higher Education

Neil Carver
Senior Lecturer, Sheffield Hallam University

Ron Collier
Research Associate, Lecturer, School of Nursing, University of Nottingham

Esther Cook
Training and Staff Development Co-ordinator, East Suffolk Mind

Joan Cook
User Involvement Development Worker School of Nursing, University of Nottingham

Carol Cooper
Lecturer in Mental Health Nursing, University of Sheffield.

Peter Ferns
Independent training consultant

Allan Foreman
Teacher and service user

Dawn Freshwater
Professor of Mental Health and Primary Care, Bournemouth University

Bill Fulford
Professor of Philosophy and Mental Health University of Warwick

Melissa Gunasena
Service user activist

Sue Gunstone
Nurse Lecturer, University of Sheffield

Ben Hannigan
Senior Lecturer, Mental Health and Learning Disabilities Directorate, Cardiff School of Nursing and Midwifery Studies, Cardiff University

Mark Hayward
Academic tutor at the University of Surrey and Clinical Psychologist, West Sussex Health and Social Care NHS Trust

Philip Houghton
Clinical Psychologist, Nottinghamshire Healthcare NHS Trust

Peter Lindley
Visiting Academic, Middlesex University

Paul Linsley
Senior Lecturer in Nursing, University of Lincoln

Liam MacGabhann
Lecturer in mental health nursing, Dublin City University

Rachel Nickeas
Trainer and researcher with Making Waves, a service user research and training organisation

Madeline O'Carroll
Lecturer, City University, London

Clare Ockwell
Training and Development Co-ordinator, CAPITAL Project Trust

Alan Pringle
Lecturer, School of Nursing, University of Nottingham

Lorraine Rayner
Lecturer, School of Nursing, University of Nottingham

Julie Repper
Senior Research Fellow, University of Sheffield

Sharon Roberts
Managing Director, Vision Community Training Ltd, Nottingham

Brenda Rush
Associate Professor, School of Nursing, University of Nottingham

Becky Shaw
Trainer and researcher with Making Waves, a service user research and training organisation

William Spence
Research Fellow, National Health Service Education for Scotland

Chris Stevenson
Professor of mental health nursing, Dublin City University

Theo Stickley
Lecturer, School of Nursing, University of Nottingham

Digby Tantam
Clinical Professor of Psychotherapy and co-Director of the Centre for the Study of Conflict and Reconciliation at the University of Sheffield

Emmy van Deurzen
Professor of Psychotherapy at Schiller International University, Dean of the School of Psychotherapy and Counselling, and Honorary Reader in the University of Sheffield.

Yolanda Wasylko
Clinical Development Manager, Lifestyle Care plc

Steve Wood
Lecturer/Practitioner, Mental Health and Learning Disabilities Directorate, Cardiff School of Nursing and Midwifery Studies, Cardiff University and Cardiff and Vale NHS Trust

Kim Woodbridge
Until recently, Kim led the programme for values in mental health at the Sainsbury Centre for Mental Health and is co-author of Whose Values? A Practical Guide for Developing Values-based Practice in Mental Health

Norman Young
Consultant Nurse for Serious Mental Illness, Complex Needs, Cardiff and Vale NHS Trust

Preface

This book aims to encapsulate good practice and innovation in mental health training and education at the beginning of 21st Century. As editors of this book, our collaboration is closely linked to a mental health training and education conference. This annual conference that takes place in mid-September in the UK, brings together trainers and educators from across the mental health field. Sponsorship from the Mental Health Foundation, The Richmond Fellowship, Together, the National Institute for Mental Health England (NIMHE) and others has resulted in a strong presence of service user/survivor trainers and educators at successive conferences. Service users/survivors do not attend as passive observers, but also lead workshops, parallel sessions and speak on the main platform. In editing this book, we wanted to capture some of the innovation and creativity that we have been fortunate to encounter through involvement in this process over the years. A number of the chapters are written by service users, others are co-authored. A number of chapters are written by nurses, others from medical, social work or other professional disciplines. Hopefully, as the book is read, what stands out more than anything else, is that traditional barriers are challenged and in places removed. There is much talk of *service user involvement* and *inter-professional learning* and this book makes a significant contribution to these subjects and more besides. It is our hope that what is offered here will inspire and encourage teachers and trainers in the mental health world so that they may in turn encourage and inspire those who they teach. Ultimately of course, the people that will benefit the most from developing good practice will be those who will be on the receiving end of mental health services in the future.

CHAPTER 1

Setting the Scene

Theo Stickley and Thurstine Basset

Massive changes have taken place in mental health services in recent years. In the UK, when the NHS came into being after the conclusion of the Second World War it inherited many large mental hospitals. These hospitals were nearly all built in the 19th Century. They were also very full and overcrowded. Government policy to close these hospitals and move to community care may have started in the 1960s but most hospitals didn't actually close their doors until the 1990s.

The "Modernisation Agenda" was very welcome when it arrived but it came rather late in the day with the National Service Framework for Mental Health (Department of Health 1999) emerging in the very last months of the last year of the 20th Century. Our experience of mental health training and education in the second half of the 20th Century was that it was mostly very institutional, with the large psychiatric hospitals holding sway at the centre of much of the training and education. The main professions in mental health work: nursing, occupational therapy, psychiatry, psychology and social work, tended to learn and train in isolation from each other. As the large hospitals closed, so many staff had to learn new skills in order to work in multi-disciplinary teams in the community (Muijen, 1997). It was a difficult shift to make and there was always the chance that staff would merely transplant their institutional practices from the large hospitals to the community setting.

The Sainsbury Centre for Mental Health published *Pulling Together* (1997) in an attempt to make some sense of a muddled and confusing situation and begin to make plans for the future roles and training of mental health staff. It was clear that the overlap of roles between professional staff was significant. Concentrating on the work that needed to be done, rather than the profession of the worker, the Sainsbury Centre produced the *Capable Practitioner* (2001) and this explored the generic knowledge and skills needed for mental health work. Specialist work was then looked at in terms of both interventions and the service setting in which the intervention would take place. Subsequent work led to the development of the *Ten Essential Shared Capabilities* (Department of Health, 2004).

Alongside the professionally qualified mental health workers, attention has also been paid to those who work in mental health with no specific professional background, and indeed, often very little training. *More than a Friend* (Sainsbury Centre, 1997) examined the role of the support worker in mental health and found them to be highly valued by service users. These workers had been employed to fill gaps left by the professionals, who were increasingly spending less time in face-to-face contact with service users. The

Teaching Mental Health. Edited by Theo Stickley and Thurstine Basset.
Copyright © 2007 John Wiley & Sons, Ltd.

"Modernisation Agenda" has spawned an increasing number of new workers (in primary care, working with carers, working with black and ethnic minority communities amongst others). Indeed, we counted up to 21 new roles in the National Mental Health Workforce Strategy (NIMHE, 2004).

The professions have responded to the 'Modernisation Agenda' with various reviews and reports (for example Department of Health and Royal College of Psychiatrists, 2004). The review of mental health nursing (Department of Health, 2006) recommends that mental health nurses should "take a holistic approach, seeing service users as whole people and taking into account their physical, psychological, social and spiritual needs". The overlap between the professions still remains and there is now a tendency for all professions to head for the same ground. They are moving back towards listening to service users, respecting their perspective, acknowledging their strengths and engaging with them in meaningful therapeutic relationships. This reflects the broadening out of mental health work away from the pre-occupation with medication as the only effective treatment.

A further welcome facet of the "Modernisation Agenda" has been the acknowledgement of past failures and the will to improve mental health services for significant and important parts of society–for example, women and black and ethnic minority people. Another key factor that has influenced training and education has been the emergence of an increasingly potent service user voice. In less than twenty five years, we have moved from the patient as an exhibit (Basset, 1999) to the active involvement of service users as trainers and educators (Basset et al., 2006).

We must also acknowledge the contested nature of what is being taught and learned. Whilst there is a consensus in mental health about such things as respect for service users, there are many different schools of thought about what causes mental ill health and how it can be treated. It is often this difference of opinion and approach that makes the mental health field such an interesting arena for teaching and learning.

It is not entirely clear what direction teaching and learning about mental health will take in the future. Nevertheless, we are confident that mental health workers will always be learning from service users, together with a strong component of learning from each other. The key topics that we explore in this book are unlikely to go away and teachers will always need an array of teaching and learning methods to get the message across. This introductory chapter sets the context for the book and outlines the contents of the chapters, which are presented in three parts.

PART ONE: LEARNING FROM ONE ANOTHER

Service-user involvement is seen as a key component of contemporary mental health training and education. The first two chapters explore the development and achievements of two broad projects–PINE (Participation in Nurse Education) and CAPITAL (Clients and Professionals in Training and Learning). The PINE project (Chapter 2), describes a model for meaningful service user involvement in mental health nurse education. The overall outcome of the development has been a number of teaching sessions written and delivered by service users and now mainstreamed into nurse education in a UK university. In Chapter 3, Ockwell charts the activities and achievements of the CAPITAL project since its first meeting in 1997. She raises and explores some of the dilemmas and difficulties that CAPITAL has encountered. Chapters from individual trainers follow with Nickeas (Chapter 4) and

Foreman and Pringle (Chapter 5). Nickeas gives, from her own experience, both good and bad examples of service-user involvement in education, as she argues for partnership not paternalism for the future. Foreman and Pringle reflect on the successful involvement of a service user trainer and the importance of acknowledging the skills of the trainer. The key transition for this trainer was a move from being seen as a service user trainer who does some teaching to a teacher who has spent some time using services. Allan Foreman trained as a teacher but became extremely debilitated, not necessarily from the effects of mental illness, but more from the effects of medication causing irreversible damage to his central nervous system. This has not, however, prevented him from teaching mental health students.

Gunasena (Chapter 6) explores how her personal experience of mental health services led to her producing the influential film 'Evolving Minds–an exploration of the alternatives to psychiatry and the links between psychosis and spirituality'. Gunasena operates as an activist as she seeks to both explore and discuss alternatives to the conventional services that she found to have very little relevance to her.

Atkinson (Chapter 7) explains how a service user perspective is included in the training of doctors through a voluntary sector inspired module "Consumer Perspectives of Mental Health". There is a strong emphasis in the module on learning from visits to mental health services and engaging with service users in these services. Breeze and Repper (Chapter 8) describe the development of a module that is planned, delivered, assessed and evaluated in partnership with service users and carers. Working with carers/relatives as well as service users is a key innovation of their approach.

It has long been accepted that an inter-professional approach is necessary within education and training in order to break down professional barriers and hierarchies and to adopt a more generic approach to learning about mental health. Baguley, Basset and Lindley (Chapter 9) explore how the Ten Essential Shared Capabilities have been developed and then incorporated into mental health training and education. The chapter contains some illustrative material from a learning pack for mental health practice.

Anderson and Burgess (Chapter 10) use their experiences of coordinating the "Mental Health in Higher Education" project to reflect on how people learn to teach about mental health and how their professional development is supported. Spence (Chapter 11) explores inter-professional action research and discusses the rationale for inter-professional working.

PART TWO: KEY TOPICS IN MENTAL HEALTH EDUCATION

Here the book gives examples of how key topics for contemporary mental health have been incorporated into the training and education agenda. Fulford and Woodbridge (Chapter 12) describe the principles of values-based practice and give examples of approaches used in workshops to incorporate values-based practice into day-to-day working practices. Getting the value-base right is an important foundation, which if overlooked can result in getting lost, stuck and frustrated. Links are drawn to the *National Framework* of values for Mental Health (NIMHE, 2005). Freshwater and Stickley (Chapter 13) examine the concept of emotional intelligence and explain how emotional intelligence can be appropriately integrated into professional education and practice through a transformatory learning programme. Cook (Chapter 14) describes a number of initiatives as part of "Recovery" training across East Anglia in the UK. Bates (Chapter 15) describes his experience as a "social inclusion" trainer and outlines an in-depth training programme on social inclusion developed by the National Development Team. He raises some interesting issues and dilemmas for trainers and educators.

Ferns (Chapter 16) describes initiatives to train mental health staff in race equality and cultural capability, drawing on his work for a national training programme for NIMHE. Rayner, Young and O'Carroll (Chapter 17) review the position of training and education in relation to psychosocial interventions. They examine how academics/teachers can influence and improve the implementation of psychosocial interventions in the workplace. Carver and Ashmore (Chapter 18) examine how student mental health nurses can learn about the pharmaceutical industry so that they understand some of the ethical dilemmas when they come into contact with them as part of their training.

PART THREE: A VARIETY OF APPROACHES

In this part of the book a variety of different learning methods are explored as we seek to ensure that mental health training and education is not too reliant on "talk and chalk" or "power-point presentations". Hayward et al. (Chapter 19) describe their experience in delivering an experiential workshop, which examines new ways of looking at psychosis. Cooper and Gunstone (Chapter 20) and Bickerstaffe et al. (Chapter 21) both explore problem-based learning. Cooper and Gunstone (Chapter 20) explore the philosophy of problem-based learning and then describe how they incorporated this approach into pre-registration mental health nursing education. Bickerstaffe et al. (Chapter 21) focus on the development and use of problem-based learning trigger materials, the approach to working with students, the student experience and incorporating problem-based learning into assessment strategies.

Freshwater (Chapter 22) outlines the methods and processes of reflective practice in training and learning, examining in detail the strategies available to promote deep reflection on action and reflection in action. MacGabhann and Stevenson (Chapter 23) and Rush and Barker (Chapter 24) both discuss "learning from enquiry". MacGabhann and Stevenson (Chapter 23) explore ways and give examples of how "learning from enquiry" can be used to bridge the theory-practice gap. Rush and Barker (Chapter 24) explain how they have involved service users in mental health education through "enquiry-based learning". Wasylko and Stickley (Chapter 25) advocate the use of drama in mental health education, giving examples from their own experiences.

Beadsmoore and Basset (Chapter 26) describe a work-based learning approach with examples of how this has been used in practice and its relevance to lifelong learning. They stress the accessibility and flexibility of a work-based learning approach through examples of partnerships between voluntary organisations, service user groups, NHS Trusts and Universities on accredited learning programmes. Linsley (Chapter 27) explores the increasing use of information technology and e-learning in health and social care. He calls for a collaborative approach that involves service users. Blackmore, van Deurzen and Tantam (Chapter 28) examine the role of the internet in mental health training and education. They present the learning from the experience of SEPTIMUS, an E-based psychotherapy training programme. They raise interesting challenges for the role of the teacher and trainer. In the concluding Chapter, the editors consider the relevance of philosophical roots of education and examine some of the future challenges for mental health training and education in the 21st Century.

REFERENCES

Basset T. (1999). Involving service users in training. *Care: the Journal of Practice and Development.* **7**(2), 5–11.

Basset T. Beales A. Beresford P. Hitchon G. and Westra A. (2006). *Service-users Together–a guide for involvement.* Brighton: Pavilion.

Department of Health (2006). *From values to action: The Chief Nursing Officer's review of mental health nursing.* London: Department of Health.

Department of Health and Royal College of Psychiatrists (2004). *Guidance on New Ways of Working for Psychiatrists in a Multi-disciplinary and Multi-agency Context.* London: Department of Health.

Department of Health (1999). *The National Service Framework for Mental Health.* London: Department of Health.

Department of Health (2004). *The Ten Essential Shared Capabilities – A Framework for the Whole of the Mental Health Workforce.* London: Department of Health/NHSU/Sainsbury Centre/NIMHE).

Muijen M. (1997). The Future of Training. *Journal of Mental Health,* 6(6), 535–538.

National Institute for Mental Health England (2004). *Mental Health Care Group Workforce Team– National Mental Health Workforce Strategy.* London: Department of Health.

National Institute for Mental Health England (2005). *The National Framework of Values in Mental Health.* London: Department of Health.

Sainsbury Centre for Mental Health (2001). *The Capable Practitioner Framework: A framework and list of the practitioner capabilities required to implement the National Service Framework for Mental Health.* London: Sainsbury Centre for Mental Health. Available to download from *www.scmh.org.uk.*

The Sainsbury Centre for Mental Health (1997). *Pulling Together. The Future Roles and Training of Mental Health Staff.* London: The Sainsbury Centre for Mental Health.

The Sainsbury Centre for Mental Health (1997). *More Than a Friend: The Role of Support Workers in Community Mental Health Services.* London: The Sainsbury Centre for Mental Health.

Learning From One Another

CHAPTER 2

Making Waves in Nurse Education: The PINE Project

Sharon Roberts, Ron Collier, Becky Shaw and Joan Cook

INTRODUCTION

The Nottingham PINE Project (Participation In Nurse Education) is a collaborative educational development and research endeavour. The partners in the project are: a service user organisation called Making Waves, an independent training consultancy, Vision and the Nottingham University School of Nursing. The PINE project directly involves service users in mental health student nurse education. Making Waves is an organisation containing a group of people who live with mental distress. It campaigns, teaches and undertakes development work to improve mental health services for the people who use them. Members of Making Waves are very keen to bring about meaningful change in nurse education. Many of the service users have experienced not only the effects of mental health problems but have also felt what it is like to be in hospital. They therefore know how important the role of the nurse is. While there are indeed some skilled and compassionate nurses, service users also know there is plenty of room for improvement. Having the opportunity to influence nurses before they qualify through the PINE project was a welcome opportunity to do this.

The School commissioned Making Waves to design and deliver teaching sessions. To facilitate the development of the sessions, Making Waves employed a professional trainer, Sharon Roberts. Sharon begins the chapter describing the development process. The professional researcher then explains the research method and philosophy. One of the service users involved, Becky Shaw, then focuses upon values in research and examines some of the research processes. Joan Cook, School of Nursing User Involvement Development Worker offers some reflection on the implementation from an organisational perspective.

PART ONE: SERVICE USERS AS EDUCATION FACILITATORS FOR STUDENT NURSES

Sharon Roberts

In 2005 I was commissioned by Making Waves as a development consultant to identify through consultation with mental health service users, areas of the School of Nursing

Teaching Mental Health. Edited by Theo Stickley and Thurstine Basset.
Copyright © 2007 John Wiley & Sons, Ltd.

curriculum where service user facilitation might take place. The idea was to develop the appropriate educational materials to support this and to train service users to be able to facilitate teaching sessions. Between us we developed the philosophy behind the project:

- To educate student mental health nurses from a service user's perspective.
- To make sure all service users and relevant staff understand the project's goals and aims.
- Putting a face on the issues and the development of the teaching materials.
- The sessions stress the importance of student nurses' potential impact on service users' lives.
- All development sessions should be a welcoming place for service users to attend.

The overall aim of the development sessions is to involve and actively support service users in the process of developing teaching materials. In order to achieve this; certain first stage issues had to be realised:

- Develop a relationship with existing service users who have delivered training sessions within the mental health curriculum.
- Make contact with new providers and service users who wish to take part in the development and training process.
- Select four key educational/development areas.
- Develop a realistic timescale.

We organised an open day. Service users were invited to attend and have their experiences and knowledge used to highlight the ways in which the four educational themes could be further developed. Sixteen service users attended and the four educational themes were decided upon:

- Strategies for Survival.
- Professionals on Tap not on Top.
- Diagnose This.
- Living on an acute ward.

PROJECT DEVELOPMENT

Service users were arranged into four work streams to develop the teaching sessions. The number of service users assigned to each of the teaching areas were as follows:

- Strategies for survival (nine service users).
- Living on a acute ward (six service users).
- Diagnose This (ten service users).
- Professions on Tap not on Top (seven service users).

Each educational theme had at least 12 hours devoted to the development of the specific theme identified and the teaching sessions were designed to last two hours each.

HOW THE IDEAS, EXPERIENCE AND KNOWLEDGE BECOME A SCHEME OF WORK

It became clear, that in order to develop the ownership of the themes the vital element was to listen to the service users, their needs and their wants. It was agreed, at an early stage of the development process, that service users would prefer the term "facilitator" rather than "service user". The consensus was that service users felt they were often just "wheeled" in when requested, whereas the term "facilitator" put service users on an equal footing with the professionals. In order to have a clear focus of the teaching material's aim and objectives, eleven service users took part in a focus group looking at:

"What do We Mean by Teaching Materials?"

The focus group decided that before any development of teaching materials could take place, a discussion should focus on what service users felt were the most effective methods of delivery, so that student nurses were made as aware as possible of the views of service users.

Therefore, a workshop was convened in order to arrive at agreed methods of delivery. After evaluating a large number of possible modes of delivery the following six styles were agreed upon as the most effective for service user facilitation with combined information sharing with interactive learning.

- **Audio.** Projecting your voice, the use of instruments, the use of music.
- **Visual.** Role-play, video, printed masks.
- **Digital images.** Powerpoint presentations, overhead-projection, computer equipment.
- **Audience participation.** Group and individual exercises, questions and answers, personal experiences.

After deciding on the appropriate means of communicating a session, the next question which service users addressed and needed answering was:

"What do We Want to Achieve Through Our Teaching?"

Again, a session was dedicated to this question and the following "Facilitating a session" was developed by the service users as a guide for facilitation:

Box A   Facilitating Teaching Sessions

- Passing on knowledge.
- Being able to impart wisdom from experience.
- Encouraging students to learn and being the vehicle to do this.
- Making relevant information memorable.
- To deliver a message.
- Getting people to understand what it is like to be a service user.
- Gaining confidence through facilitating.
- To change thought process.
- Imparting knowledge to others.

The next question was about delivering a message.

"What do We Want to Say?"

A) The First Theme to be Developed was "Strategies for Survival"

This theme developed materials around the following points:

• As service users how do we manage our lives and relationships?
• What has aided service users in their recovery?

Nine service users took part in the development process of materials. There was a clear need to challenge some of the perceptions and attitudes towards employability and the recovery of service users with mental health problems.

How the Theme Took Shape and a Structure Formed

The service users were divided into two groups. Group 1 decided to use the lyrics of the song "Mad World" by Tears for Fears as their teaching aid. The lyrics would be used as a point of reflection for student nurses, by means of providing the students with the lyrics of the song and by playing a section of the video of the film "Donnie Darko". The section of the video used is where the song is played in a disturbing setting. Group 1 concluded that they would deliver the setting based around the song by means of de-construction and analysis of the lyrics, verse by verse. This they felt would encourage the student nurses to find hope in certain lines and then reflect on how service users might feel in that situation and relate this back via feed back in order to develop coping strategies. The possible coping strategies included service users writing their own lyrics to help them express their feelings, to just listening to various kinds of music in order to help service users find their safe place to be.

Group 2 developed their ideas and thoughts more on how the lyrics made them feel from the past to the present especially regarding their feelings, memories and thoughts. With this in mind an idea emerged to provide student nurses with an A–Z of helpful nursing skills. This developed the main teaching resource for strategies for survival.

Training Resources:

(i) Lyrics were handed out with blank spaces for the nurses to complete and discuss.
(ii) A–Z of helpful nursing skills.

Delivery Aims (From a Service User Perspective):

(i) What was going on for you? What does survival strategies mean to a service user?
(ii) How can student nurses understand survival strategies?
(iii) How can student nurses help with the recovery process?

Service users paired off and came up with ideas for future survival strategies. These were some of the things, which worked best:

Role play: In a pair, one person played a patient, and the other a nurse. The patient held up a mask with a big smiley face on it. The nurse asked the patient how she was. The patient replied: (said in a flat, depressed voice), "Oh, I'm ok, yeah I'm doing alright, you know . . . coping". The nurse then said, "Oh good, would you like a cup of tea?"

Teaching point: to not take at face value what people say to you. Read between the lines. Don't be misled by a cheerful appearance. Also, a little more questioning by the nurse would probably have revealed the patient's true feelings.

Coping mechanisms: ask the students to write down on post-it-notes their top three coping skills when facing difficulties or feeling stressed. Take the most common ones and write them on flip chart.

Teaching point: to understand that what works really well for one person (e.g. drawing) can be another person's worst nightmare! So when suggesting coping mechanisms to a patient, don't impose your own ideas. Also, make them aware that more ill you become, the less able you are to carry out the more positive methods, and can succumb to the more negative ones, such as drugs/alcohol, self harming, isolation, etc.

"Mad World" song: ask the group to read the lyrics and say how many different people are involved with the person in crisis. Then get people to stand in different parts of the classroom, representing each group, e.g. school teachers, friends, family, etc. Then the person in crisis asks each group in turn, help me, what should I do?

Delivery: it is expected that students will come up with different opinions on what this person should do. This exercise can illustrate how confusing it can be receiving all this conflicting advice; wanting to please everybody; then often retreating into isolation.

Recovery: ask student nurses what they think are the signs that someone is recovering from their illness.

Teaching points: to challenge some perceptions, and encourage them to think laterally. A positive sign of recovery for one person is not necessarily the same for another.

ABC of skills handout: at the end of the session give out this handout, explaining that it was devised by a group of service users. They looked at key nursing skills important to ensure the development of an individual's survival strategies.

Teaching point: encourage the students to observe on their next mental health placement how much of the skills listed are actually being practiced. What effects do they have on patients? And what effects can be observed when they are not practiced?

Chain Letter/song: ask a person to write on A4 paper how the song made them feel. Then they fold over the paper and pass it on to the next person to do the same. Pass it round the whole classroom.

Teaching point: to encourage them to empathise with the writer, and hence mental health patients. Explain the nature of depression. Was the writing of this song a coping strategy for the writer?

"Ask it Basket": encourage students to put any further questions in the "Ask it Basket". Students may want to ask questions of a more personal nature and not want to ask in front of their peers. Or you may simply run out of time, or just not know the answer. Ask them to put an e-mail address on so that their queries can be answered this way. Bring it to their attention at the beginning of the session so that they can write down any questions that arise for them throughout the session.

B) The Second Theme to be Developed was "Diagnose This"

- Its key theme developed teaching resources relating to receiving psychiatric diagnosis.
- It looks at the reality of being on psychiatric medication. Ten service users took part in the development process for "Diagnose This".

How the Theme was Structured

The service users involved in "Diagnose this" were divided into two groups of five. One group would attend every week to develop their ideas and knowledge in a basic format. The second group were to develop Group One's materials further by adapting educational resources for student nurses. It became delightful to witness the unique partnership between both groups and to see the progress made day by day. The development of the teaching materials also gained a greater perspective with a clear focus from each group, and the support each group showed one another.

The Main Points Service Users Wanted to Portray Within the Teaching Materials

- Treat the cause not just the symptoms.
- Show a level of respect for the person and the illness.
- Develop an open mind to have a holistic view of the patient.

The service users who took part in the diagnose theme came to the sessions with so much energy, motivation and ideas. They produced various handouts and began to develop a *snakes and ladders* game. The game is designed for service users and student nurses to work on together. It helps put into practice social and personal issues that affect mental health patients and professionals. There are many other resources that need to be developed for further "Diagnose this" teaching sessions. Due to the short time scale for the development of materials and other constraints relating to this project it was unrealistic to develop all the ideas for teaching resources. However, it is hoped that these will be developed at a future date.

Materials to be Refined Further for "Diagnose This"

- Real life case studies provided by service users attending the session.
- Family matters. Does having a diagnosis make the family feel better?
- Top tips for nurses, dealing with a person who has a diagnosis that is new to the nurse.

C) The Third Theme to be Developed was "Living on an Acute Ward"

Objective of the Session

"Living on an Acute Ward" looked at service users' experiences in relation to life on the wards. Do they work? How could service user involvement improve them?

Attendance

Six service users took part in the development of the teaching materials. This area was seen as the most difficult to develop. Some individuals who attended the sessions felt very uncomfortable reliving memories and feelings of being compulsorily detained and the trauma associated with acute wards.

How the Theme was Structured

Due to the nature of these sessions, being aware of people's feelings and the recovery stages they were at, this theme explored and reviewed past acute care experiences. This was in order to raise the awareness of student nurses and how, consequently, they can develop their future personal skills on acute wards.

The Main Points that Were Developed into the Sessions

- Providing positive care in a safe environment.
- The shadow side of helping. What could student nurses learn in order to help future patients on an acute ward
- Develop true and false questionnaires in order to make teaching sessions more interactive for student nurses.

Further Materials to be Refined for This Theme are as Follows

- Making the environment safe (handout).
- Honest answers for family and friends (but you have so many good things in your life why are you so unhappy?).

Living on an Acute Ward

The following teaching resources were developed by service users

---

Box B   Helping People on Acute Wards

1. Explain advance agreements (pets, bills etc).
2. Explain the security of my property.
3. Take religious/dietary requirements into consideration.
4. Respect patients barriers.
5. Help me stop being harassed.
6. Personal safety and listen to my concerns.

---

7. Talk about family and friends visiting (private room).
8. Explain why I have the right to accept or refuse treatment.
9. Think about proper discharge package and diary included for future appointments.
10. Explain individually tailored Occupational Therapy package.

Box C   Understanding Professional Role

1. Explain about rights and welcome packs, don't just give out information.
2. Be professional.
3. Keep confidentiality regarding the patient.
4. Explain your policies.
5. Think about your attitudes.
6. Communicate with patients and other staff.
7. Do you require supervision?
8. Do you have support of your management team?
9. Provide crisis support contacts.
10. Always consider boundaries.

Effective Nursing Management Skills
Being an effective nurse means more than being a good listener (although this is obviously important).

In Small Groups Discuss the Following Points:
• Confusion
• Language
• Perceptions
• Scape-goating
• Resources
• Activities
• Power
• Understanding

Student Action

List six or more skills/qualities which you think would make a difference.
   When supporting a service user through a crisis consider the above points.

D) The Fourth and Final Theme Developed was "Professionals on Tap Not on Top"

Objective of the Session

"Professionals on Tap not on Top" looked at what service users want from mental health professionals and, consequently, developing an understanding of how service users are affected by professional power.

Seven service users took part in the development process of "Professionals on Tap not on Top". Service users who had taken part in previous sessions now began to see the benefits of their knowledge and ideas being put into practice. Because this was the last theme to be developed, many people felt excited and sad because the development sessions were coming to an end. Additionally the task of delivering the sessions to student nurses was fast approaching for those service users who had volunteered to deliver teaching sessions. The panic and excitement worked well and had a positive effect. The service users were now mentoring and supporting each other through various stages of the development process.

The group was asked about how professionals make you feel and responded:

- Acutely embarrassed and awkward.
- Depressed and apathetic.
- Worthless, useless and insignificant.
- Physically sick and tense.
- Frightened and powerless.
- Resentful and embittered (due to various wrong diagnoses).
- Misunderstood.
- Guilty and to blame (I should feel well).

It was clear from the feedback that there was a sense of feeling let down and misunderstood. With this in mind those attending the sessions were encouraged to develop positive teaching resources to be used to challenge the students' positive change.

The main points service users wanted to portray within the teaching materials were:

- Working with the professionals not against them.
- Supporting service users in a crisis.
- Encouraging professionals to promote user involvement in care plans.
- How professionals help can support patients and family members.
- Knowing your rights; understanding your rights when planning advanced agreements, etc.

EVALUATING THE TEACHING SESSIONS AND SUPPORTING PARTICIPANTS

The four teaching themes raised the importance of service user involvement. In developing teaching materials for student nurses; all service users who took part in the development process gave 100 %. Some service user led organisations claim that service user involvement in this way is difficult if not impossible. However, this project had no problems recruiting service users to attend the development sessions. Not only did the sessions have a clear focus but they also supported the growth, personal development and self-awareness of those that took part in the development process. Service users were paid for the time they contributed to the development.

For some service users it takes a tremendous amount of time to establish trusting relationships with other service users and staff. Making Waves supported service users who went on to deliver teaching sessions by means of developing a support group for facilitators.

PERSONAL DEVELOPMENT WITHIN THE DEVELOPMENT PROCESS

This was tackled in various ways, i.e. practical, theory and a combination of both. This allowed individuals the time to look at what they have learned from the experience and put into practice what they have achieved. This was especially true for those who plan to undertake the next stage, facilitating sessions through progressive learning.

EMBEDDED AREAS COVERED WITHIN THE DEVELOPMENT SESSIONS

Although there were four clear themes to be developed. There were also other areas which were implemented within the development sessions. These were:

- Developing teaching materials.
- Delivering teaching sessions.
- Developing presentation skills.
- Dealing with difficult questions when facilitating.
- Supporting and networking with other mental health agencies.

SOME PROBLEMS

The project was successful with 40 service users taking part in the whole development process. As with all projects there were lessons to be learned. The following points raise a few of the problems the project came across.

Open Door Policy

The recruitment of service users was so successful that word of mouth did become a problem. At various stages of the session individuals would just arrive expecting to be asked into the session, without any prior contact with Making Waves.

Advertising Payment for Attendance

The majority of individuals who attended the sessions did so because they wanted to help others learn from their experience. However, it was felt that two service users only wanted to attend the sessions to receive payment for their personal use. The first service user was asked to leave. The second service user was asked only to attend one development theme. This did cause frustration and anger for the service user. This information, with agreement from the person concerned, was passed on to the service user's key worker, who provided extra support when required.

Development Sessions not a Support Group

Although the development sessions enabled service users to express their thoughts and feelings, the sessions were not developed to be a support group. It became clear that some service users were having difficulty in taking part in group participation in this way. Various amounts of anger were expressed to other service users and myself as the facilitator of the sessions. This resulted in one service user being asked to leave and not attend future sessions. On a positive note, this service user has since identified that their behaviour was inappropriate and part of their illness.

POSITIVE PROGRESSION

The development sessions created a strong foundation for Making Waves to recruit volunteers and future facilitators. It is hoped that Making Waves will continue to develop its services and the service users it continues to recruit. Many service users who attended the development sessions felt a sense of relief, knowing that Making Waves existed and could provide support and advice on a range of issues.

A MESSAGE FROM THE SERVICE USERS

Over the duration of the programme, 22 evaluations were collected in from service users. The following comments are taken from those evaluation forms.

What did You Enjoy Most Within the Sessions?

- Working in small groups.
- Using our ideas to develop teaching materials.
- Learning from others.
- Group exercises were fun and thought provoking.
- Discussions in small groups.
- Developing my confidence skills.
- Talking out problems to develop solutions.
- Original views on reality teaching points.
- Everything – thinking alone, group work, delivery of the sessions.
- Learning what to do in certain teaching scenarios.
- Challenging professionals.
- It has helped me discover a way of dealing with my illness in so many ways.

What did You Think of the Information and Assistance Given in Sessions?

- Good
- Brilliant

- Excellent
- Good–enjoyed it all
- Very good

What did You Think of the Teaching Given in the Sessions?

- Good
- Extremely good
- Excellent
- Top standard
- Though provoking
- Different
- Informative
- Brilliant
- Challenging

Would You Like to Take Part in Further Learning?

All evaluation forms received said "yes".

If Yes What Would You Like to Do?

- Learning how to use various software programmes, when delivering teaching sessions.
- Extended delivery of training sessions.
- Practical teaching practice skills.
- Confidence building course.
- Developing role play techniques.
- More teaching sessions.
- Teacher training course.
- Facilitating different sessions.
- Health awareness course.
- Co-supporting each other, when delivering sessions.
- Develop more work streams.
- Psychosis.
- Advice on listening.

Service users were asked "Would you like help and advise on future progression routes?". Seventeen people requested they would like future advice and support. Twenty-two service users said they would like to take part in further training.

The overall feedback from the sessions was very positive. As a result nine service users took part in a cooking course with Making Waves and two service users are now completing their teacher-training certificate.

PART TWO: EXPERIMENTAL RESEARCH AS SOCIAL INQUIRY

Ron Collier

Leading up to and overlapping with the setting up of PINE, the Department of Health published a number of papers that focus on issues of co-operation and understanding between users and providers of health services (1990, 1991, 1994, 2001, 2004). These attempt to create a climate for change in the relationship between providers and receivers of health services.

A pivotal aspect of the PINE project aims at collaboration and partnership between service users, tutors and student nurses. This is in a field of human activity (the professional education of mental health nurses) that, until more recently, has largely excluded the input of service users. I was drawn to become involved as a research associate because of the social justice implications of the project. My previous work as an approved social worker in mental health, in community development and in education with families and teachers had highlighted for me the importance of social justice issues in fields of human interaction.

The Toronto Group's report on "Research as empowerment?" (Hanley, 2005) points out an inevitable conflict between mainstream evidence based research and research aimed at bringing about social change. Users as researchers are, inevitably, caught up in this. Hanley proposes that some form of emancipation is required for effective collaboration to take place between all those with an investment in a particular piece of mental-health research: service users, tutors and student nurses. She poses a question about the nature of such research: is it to bring about change or to gain more knowledge? Accepting Hanley's premise, what are the implications for the approach to research that PINE needs to adopt? Can a form of emancipation be incorporated in such a way as to address issues of change and social justice? And will this be able to supply evidence that contributes to new knowledge?

THE PHILOSOPHY UNDERPINNING THE RESEARCH

The 18th century Scottish philosopher, David Hume argued that all possible connections we make about the world around us derive from our habits of reasoning and not from what we observe (Hume, 1962). His argument still appears to be sound and its significance for researchers is that we cannot draw conclusions from what we observe. This is as true for research in the natural sciences as it is for social research (Russell, 1961). We are left with the conclusion that we do not know if our ways of making sense of the world around us coincide with how it really is or not.

Ethnomethodology is rooted in this concept and is related to the subsequent philosophical speculations of Husserl (1970) and its sociological application by Schutz (1972, 1980). Garfinkel (1967) developed this research approach and it is the study of methods used by people to account for and give meaning to their social world. It proposes that our social reality cannot be separated from our accounts and interpretations of it and the object of research is to explain the methods and accounting procedures that people use to construct their social world.

So we are left with the conclusion that the things we know about are constructions of the human mind that we project onto the world around us. For the ethnomethodologist this is social reality. Fair enough as far as it goes; however, subsequent research and theoretical speculation on my part lead me to question the limitations of this definition of social reality. Additionally, ethnomethodology does not help us to understand the processes involved in the development of communication between us and how we deal with differences as members of groups or as individuals—and this is crucial if we are to understand what is going on between service users, students and tutors, who bring different cultural agendas to the field of mental health education.

My own argued position (Collier, 2001) confirms that we are indeed involved with the creation of our own realities but that these realities are culturally based and constructed between people (i.e. not confined to a single person's consciousness). They are also dynamic in nature and formed at the unpredictable interface between our knowledge about things, our beliefs about the world and our sensory experiences. They contain areas we neither control nor understand. Moreover, the language we have constructed and use to communicate aspects of our social reality reflects both the extent and the limitations of our state of conscious awareness.

THE IMPLICATIONS FOR RESEARCH OF ADOPTING THIS PHILOSOPHICAL PREMISE

Since we all start from the basis of belief, all accounts of the social world are equally valid. An outside researcher can bring technical know-how, mentoring and critical friendship (and this is my rôle within the PINE project) but her/his account has no more validity than that provided by inside researchers and can give a misleading and spurious impression of objectivity. The PINE research, therefore, is undertaken by the service users and professionals (and maybe, in the future, students) involved in developing the project.

Attempting to establish common ground between the varying research processes, we will be assessing how far these are able to accept difference in aims and approach between the various contributors and, thus, expand or restrict the development of that common ground. In this way the research approaches are mirroring the educational approaches (user and professional) of the contributors to this project and the research should be able to provide a contribution to knowledge within the field of social development.

THE RESEARCH STRATEGY EMPLOYED

At the time of writing there are three strands to the PINE research programme: one undertaken by three user researchers interested in exploring the perceptions of those involved in this educational project, including themselves; one by a professional tutor focusing on an analysis of student attitudes; the third by a professional development administrator who is analysing the very detailed project steering group minutes. In the future, student participation in research may well form an additional element. The strategy employed is action research (Denscombe, 2003) because we anticipate that the research being undertaken will reflect on the current involvement of the participants themselves and will be used to inform and influence future development of this educational project; the process of research and action will thus be integrated. The methods of social research employed will include questionnaires, focus groups, interviews and participant observation.

Additionally, the researchers engaged in the various strands will observe and comment on their working relationships as a means of noting the extent and the limitations of common ground achieved between researchers with different agendas.

Some colleague researchers will now outline their approaches.

MY BACKGROUND

Becky Shaw

I was training to be a teacher and had nearly finished my course before I had mental health difficulties. The service from the mental health sector of the NHS was not good and although there were areas of good practice mixed in, overall it disempowered me, took away my autonomy, took away my hope and future. I was not seen as an individual but a label of which I have had at least seven or eight so far. All was not lost though, through this struggle I had learnt a great deal. I learnt who my real friends were and the ones that stayed and the ones I have now are the best. I also learnt that I have an enormous amount of inner strength and resources and that I could achieve. This was encouraged by a few great members of staff who saw my potential and through the many other recipients of the mental health service.

Opportunities were created for me and others to teach in the school of nursing and other areas of the NHS. I also undertook a research course of which I had always been interested. My research previously had been in quantitative research, number crunching, but I felt there was more to research than this and found qualitative research far more meaningful, helpful and informative but, however, not seen as mainstream (yet!). Although there is a place for quantitative research, qualitative research I believe is far more valuable when it comes to looking at people's experiences, their values, beliefs etc.

I recognised that if I was going to teach about mental health I needed a fuller perspective from not only a service user perspective but also as a worker, trainer and researcher. I am now midway through a degree in mental heath care.

What motivates me to research the impact of service user led involvement in nurse education? I am by definition a peer researcher and trainer. Undertaking peer research has its conflicts and also many benefits. I feel deep down that people who have used the mental health service have a lot to offer when it comes to delivering training. Previous feedback from training has given mainly a positive response but this has never been researched. PINE gave me this opportunity to research a part of this from not only the students' perspective but also from my peer facilitators and trainers.

VALUES UNDERLYING THE RESEARCH

From the perspective of service users, the PINE Project (whether teaching, researching or taking part in forum-type activities) is about taking control of our lives and having an impact on nurse training that results in service users being treated with respect, valued and needed by professionals.

MY VALUES BEHIND THE RESEARCH

I do have my values and interest in the outcome of the research and I always will do but then so does every single researcher whatever kind of research they are carrying out. I would like to see a change in perception of service users in the staff in a positive way so that they can see and treat us as individuals not as labels or objects. However I don't know yet if service user facilitation will do this or not, whether our input will be positive or negative or the other questions that will arise and themes that will develop. I am intrigued to find out and this is what motivates me to do the research. As well as all this will my perceptions change in light of this research and through delivering training? There are so many questions and this research is evolving as it goes along, as it should do. I am not saying it will be easy and I am not always well enough to put my all into it but with support and time anything is possible.

There is the question that service user research is not valid. But what is valid research if it's not brought about from the hearts and minds of the people it concerns? Is this not more valid a reason to be involved; to have a passion and help make a difference through research? I might not have a lifetime of research study behind me but I do have passion and given the right tools, information and support I can do research as valid and robust as anyone else. I believe it is valid, can be reliable and is useful in changing attitudes and perceptions of those working in and running the services as well as the public and ultimately in developing services and challenging the stigma and discrimination inside and outside the service.

WHAT WE HAVE DONE SO FAR

We started by looking at what area we wanted to research. What was it that we wanted to find out? Why were we doing this research? Starting with the values that lay behind my own personal motivation for doing the research and incorporating my colleagues' motivations we began by discussing what we all ideally wanted to research. Then coming back to reality we looked at what we all had in common, the core themes and ideas that emerged and also what was practical to achieve. Having advice from our research associate on the process we were going through proved to be a valuable resource although we guided the sessions ourselves and directed the study.

Perceptions affect the attitude of an individual and also the behaviour of that individual; we therefore decided to look at the change, if any, in the perception of students. We came up, after long discussions, with the research question: *From an emancipatory service user perspective, in what ways does user involvement in nurse training affect the perceptions of the student nurses and service users involved?* We decided to take a two-pronged approach. We wanted to look and see if the perceptions of the students changed during the study but also we wanted to look at the perceptions of the service user facilitators themselves. Would we ourselves change the way we perceive the students?

The reason we have focused on perception is that perception affects attitudes and behaviour. We could not possibly look at all three areas and so had to focus on only one. We decided the best way to find out the initial perception of students was to carry out a focus group before the students had any contact with service user facilitators or researchers. We have now carried out two initial focus groups one in Nottingham and one in Lincoln both where the PINE teaching was taking place. We also devised a questionnaire for the students after each session delivered by service user facilitators. To find out the initial perception of the service user facilitators we carried out an interview with three questions and also a simple self-reflective questionnaire post the delivery of a session.

The hard part of this process is keeping to the research question and keeping the questions focussed on perceptions. So many more questions and ideas for research have already come from this process and you can easily become swamped by ideas and lose track and focus, although I am personally keeping note of ideas as they arise for possible future areas of study and interest. We also ideally want to incorporate students into the research process and look at what they also feel is important to research just as we, the service user facilitators and the academic staff, have been doing. As yet we have only a few contacts with students and are not sure yet in what way we are going to incorporate them. We have found one difficulty in that students are limited to the time on the course whereas we have a longer time span to play with.

THE VIEW OF A PROFESSIONAL DEVELOPMENT WORKER

Joan Cook

I am employed by local voluntary organisation Self Help Nottingham to work with the School of Nursing as "User Involvement Development Worker". This work goes across the different nursing branches and courses. I joined the PINE steering group in Spring 2004, not long after it began to meet, and very early on in my time at the School of Nursing. My work background is mainly in the voluntary sector and in disability access work. I think my main contribution has been to make links between PINE and service user and carer involvement going on in other parts of the School, and as one of the people who took and sent out minutes of the steering group. I haven't used mental health services, but some of the issues covered in the teaching sessions really hit home with my childhood experiences as a long stay in-patient, and as an adult disabled person. I am now working on the organisational strand of the research, using the steering group minutes as the source.

The steering group met every four to six weeks over two years, with a membership of service users, university and other staff connected with the project. This part of the research looks back at the issues discussed in these meetings, where regular agenda items included ethics, reports from Making Waves, teaching and research groups, financial and administrative issues, project management, and dissemination. Two particular areas of interest are the group's wide interpretation of ethics, which touched on most aspects of the project, and the way in which steering group meetings became a focus for wider networking and exchange of information on service user involvement in education and research.

The minutes also show connections with other developments going on at the same time: these include changes in services, the work of a new School of Nursing Service User and Carer Advisory Group, public consultations as part of reviewing the Diploma in Nursing course which have recently helped to integrate PINE sessions into the new curriculum, and a research project where people using mental health services are involved with assessing student nurses during their practice placements.

This strand of the research will also identify administrative barriers encountered and some of the solutions found–for me this is particularly important to learn from in developing further service user and carer involvement with other areas of the School of Nursing.

THE FUTURE...?

This is a glimpse in time of an educational development project and research experiment in the early stages of its development. We have plenty of ideas for how the project can develop in the future. What we are constantly aware of however that in spite of service user involvement being demanded in policy, there is very little money available to make this mainstream. In order to develop teaching and training ethically and meaningfully, service users need to have the support, time and money to do this. Service users are not short of vision, ideas and enthusiasm, however they may be short of funding to carry out ambitious projects in the future.

We will be happy to receive any feedback from you, the reader, to work collaboratively with you in the process of bringing about lasting change in mental health education in the future.

Please feel free to contact the authors of this chapter:

Making Waves: info@makingwaves.org.uk
Sharon Roberts: Sharon@Visionconsulttraining.co.uk
Ron Collier: ron.collier@tiscali.co.uk
Becky Shaw: bshawmh@inbox.com
Joan Cook: joan@selfhelp.org.uk

REFERENCES

Collier, R. (2001). *Some working-class families and their struggles over education: How can we know what is real?* Ph.D. Thesis, University of Nottingham Trent.
Denscombe, M. (2003). *The Good Research Guide.* Maidenhead: Open University Press.
Department of Health (DoH). (1990). *The NHS and Community Care Act.* London: HMSO.
Department of Health (DoH). (1991). *The Patients Charter.* London: HMSO.
Department of Health (1994). *Working in partnership.* London: HMSO.
Department of Health (2001). *Involving Patients and the public.* London: HMSO.
Department of Health (DoH). (2004). *The Ten Essential Shared Capabilities.* London: HMSO.
Earl-Slater, A. (2004). *Lay Involvement in Health and Other Research.* Abingdon: Radcliffe Medical Press.
Garfinkel, H. (1967). *Studies in Ethnomethodology,* Englewood Cliffs: Prentice-Hall.
Hanley, B. (2005). *Research As Empowerment? Report of a series of seminars organized by the Toronto Group,* York: Joseph Rowntree Foundation.
Hume, D (1962). *A Treatise of Human Nature. Book One.* D.G.C. Macnabb, (ed.), Glasgow: Fontana/Collins (first published 1739).
Husserl, E. (1970). *Cartesian Meditations,* The Hague: Nijhoff.
Making Waves (2003). *Carry on Nursing?* Limited circulation paper, available on request.

Repper J., Hanson B., Felton A., Stickley, T. & Shaw T. (2001). One small step to equality. *Mental health today.* December, 24-27.

Roberts, S. (2006). *Participation in Nurse Education.* Limited circulation paper.

Russell, B. (1961). *A History of Western Philosophy.* London: Routledge.

Schutz, A. (1972). *The Phenomenology of the Social World.* London: Heinemann. (first published 1932).

Schutz, A. (1980). The Social World and the Theory of Social Action. *International Quarterly of Political and Social Science, 28,* Summer.

CHAPTER 3

Learning from Experience: The CAPITAL Project

Clare Ockwell

During the mid 1990's in West Sussex, in the UK, Andrea Linell, a social services training officer recruited a few people from local drop-in centres to talk to social care workers about what it was like to use services. These volunteers had neither training nor support. I was one of those people. What normally happened was that we worried beforehand, went in and told our life stories, then went home and recovered from the ordeal. The money was useful but the work was emotionally draining. We persisted in doing this work out of the conviction that if we did not tell people how it was then no-one else would.

However as time went on, Andrea began to wonder about better ways of involving people. She was aware of that lack of training and support and decided to raise money to rectify this. Eventually she secured a grant and recruited Veronica Dewan to co-ordinate the project. So it was that "Users as Trainers" came to be advertised all over West Sussex to recruit service users to be involved. The advertisement invited people to join a course possibly leading to NVQ level 3 in training for trainers. People from the county's day centres, consumer groups and drop-in centres were encouraged to come along.

In late August 1997 a disparate collection of unconfident and uncomfortable individuals assembled at Billingshurst Village Hall in the heart of the Sussex countryside for the introductory training day. It is fair to say that none of us had much idea of what we were doing there. Some admit that their original motives for coming were nothing more than a day out and a free lunch. Others were more idealistic, wanting to make a difference or hoping to gain a qualification, even perhaps a new career. Motivation did not matter, from the very beginning it was accepted that everyone brought their own perspective to the group and that was enough. To this day people contribute as much or as little as they want to. There have been occasions when someone has attended for months on end without saying a word finally to come out with something amazing.

One of the first things we did was to formulate some basic group agreements (ground rules). We re-visited these frequently in the course of our training. At times it felt like overkill but with hindsight we realised how crucial this process was to our bonding together as a group. We remain a very disparate collection of individuals in terms of age, social class, education and life experience. The only thing all CAPITAL members have in common remains our experience of using mental health services and a desire to input into mental

Teaching Mental Health. Edited by Theo Stickley and Thurstine Basset.

health education. The extensive work on our group agreements helped us to develop a collective identity. They still evolve with the group but the core principles of confidentiality, respect, inclusion and the freedom to behave in any way you like as long as it does not interfere with others remain to this day.

The first phase of our training dealt with mental health issues. Topics covered included treatments, benefits and the Mental Health Act. Inevitably looking at topics like these with a group of people experiencing mental distress will, at times, stir up uncomfortable memories. Initially we were very much dependant on Veronica to support us through these times and without that support many of us would almost certainly have fallen by the wayside. Gradually we became far more aware of our need and ability to support each other. This mutual support remains crucial. The majority of members could be described as having severe and enduring mental health problems. At times something will crop up that can upset even the most experienced of us. The support and care we give each other is the one thing that makes these occasions safe, as well as reinforcing our group identity.

We also needed to find a name we could identify with. An exercise on our first day showed that the thing we least liked to be called was "user" although there was no real consensus about what we preferred. Our general principle is that we are people first and using services is just one facet of our lives. Unfortunately this principle does not lend itself to snappy titles and our unanimous dislike being called "Users as Trainers" could not channel into unanimous enthusiasm for anything else. Several suggestions were thrown into the ring. Our newly selected members' steering group finally settled on CAPITAL, Clients And Professionals In Training And Learning. The reference to professionals was intended primarily to point out that we approach our work professionally. This has blurred through the mists of time and is more often taken to mean that we work with professionals. While both are true our approach to our work remains the more important.

The commitment to equal opportunity has heavy financial implications. West Sussex is a rural county and public transport is, in many places, limited at best. Nowhere is easily accessible from all parts of the county. Therefore providing transport to meetings in the form of lifts, minibuses or taxis as necessary has been vital. Arguing the case for this with commissioners and other funders has taken a lot of courage on the part of CAPITAL's successive leaders but the policy of providing transport opens the door for many people who could not access other groups. Even where public transport is readily available actually coping with using it can feel impossible for many people with mental health problems to use it. I joined CAPITAL unable to leave my home unaccompanied. My enthusiasm to get out and do training enabled me gradually to overcome my agoraphobia and I am now confident in travelling alone all over the country. Offering transport can change lives.

The founder members progressed from mental health issues to training for trainers. The focus of our course was clear. We were all being specifically trained as trainers. This almost certainly cost us some very skilled people who felt that standing in front of a group and teaching was not for them. As time went on we partly relaxed that emphasis. Training is still a core function but we recognise that people come with talents and experiences to contribute. Those who do go out and train can do so with a collective experience far richer than any individual perspective.

Our first training course ended in uncertainty. There was money for the group to continue but Veronica had only been contracted for one year and was moving to another job. At this point we were at serious risk of pulling ourselves apart. Some members felt we should carry on meeting as we were with no paid co-ordinator and no expansion. CAPITAL was ours and should stay that way. On the other side were those who argued for expansion, it would be hard to sustain ourselves as we were. CAPITAL was too precious just to keep to ourselves and we would need another co-ordinator to help us expand. Ultimately this argument prevailed and by Christmas 1998 some of us were not sure what had hit us. We had our new co-ordinator, Anne Beales.

The impact Anne had on CAPITAL was huge. At the beginning we needed nurturing but now although many of us did not realise it we were ready to be challenged and Anne's sweeping vision of our potential for expansion was nothing if not challenging. She saw a potential in us that we could not see in ourselves and had the energy and determination to help us reach that. The beginning of 1999 saw us going out to the same sorts of places Veronica had visited single-handed and telling people why they should come and join CAPITAL. It worked! A new intake began that spring embarking upon training for one day a month along the same lines as we had been trained. Our group continued to meet separately for the next year and then we merged. This proved difficult as for a long time the two groups held onto separate identities. Nowadays members in training are encouraged to join in meetings with the wider membership at the same time so we retain one collective identity.

All this time demands for our services were growing. In our first year we did four outside events, by 1999 our annual tally was ninety-one. The expansion was difficult to keep pace with as members found themselves increasingly busy and far more de-briefing was required. This need was partially met by our policy of never sending members out alone and providing the opportunity for people to wind down together afterwards. We also tried to ensure that whoever commissioned our work would be available at the end of a session both for informal feedback and to offer support if necessary. However while some people take this obligation very seriously and provide excellent support, others forget about it, meaning all support falls back on the organisation. This was a big problem when there was only a part-time co-ordinator, as the staff group expanded it became easier.

In January 2001 we hosted the David Goodey Memorial Conference (named after a founder member who had died in the previous year) for people who access mental health services across the county. Our task for the day was to produce a Charter for Service User Involvement, detailing both why we should be included and offering an extensive list of dos and don'ts. The key premise about why people should be involved is that:

> Being employed by services carries an obligation to consult with service users.
> To acknowledge service users' expertise.
> To promote ownership and empowerment.
> To address discrimination.[1]

Key comments about how to involve people included giving timely, appropriate, under-standable information, acceptance of our right to be listened to at all levels and above all treating us with respect. All of these things were also negatively reflected in the don'ts list as well but here people referred particularly to not being patronised, further stigmatised or treated with tokenism. The Charter was adopted as policy by West Sussex Health and Social Care Trust and has been widely used in training as well as by other service user groups as a guide to developing their own charters for involvement.

Another key issue on the Charter was provision of travel expenses on or before the session they are supposed to attend. Payment both of expenses and appropriate fees for our work

---

[1]   Charter for Service Users Involvement, CAPITAL (2001).

probably remains one of the biggest barriers to involving people properly. As an organisation we have the absolute principle that our time is as valuable as any other expert's and should be paid for accordingly. However the benefits system often makes payment to individuals more stressful than it is worth. In the early days of CAPITAL there were some pieces of work for which individuals were paid which became highly divisive as some people became highly possessive of the paid work while opportunities were denied to others who may have been more appropriate for the work in question. Ultimately the membership decided that it was better that nobody should be paid for occasional work for the following reasons:

1. Some pieces of work offer payment while others do not. It is unfair to pay for one and not the other.
2. How would we choose people for paid work?
3. Some people might volunteer for a piece of work just because it is paid.
4. Different people are on different levels of benefit therefore payment could not be equal.
5. The Benefits Agency regards people doing some work as more likely to be fit for work.
6. People who go out as CAPITAL members take with them the work of the wider group therefore either everyone should be paid or no-one. Payments made regularly to 50+ members would cripple a much larger organisation.
7. Money paid into the organisation can be used for the benefit of all the members providing transport, training and support.
8. Most members feel safer working as volunteers, if we are not well there is less pressure.
9. When possible CAPITAL should create part-time posts that are paid well enough for people to be able to afford to come off benefits.

This is a debate members revisit about once a year and as yet the majority has always voted to remain working voluntarily and all fees go into maintaining the project. Being paid properly is still a sticking point.

Payment for some of what we do comes out of our core funding. This was prone to being stretched to include whatever the Trust and commissioners wanted us to do at the time. Recently we have worked with our funders to detail far more precisely what is covered by the grant we are given. While there are some very switched on people we work with in universities, the bureaucracy of the establishment often lags behind. They and we have put in a great deal of time persuading the powers that be what resources are necessary for proper service user involvement. Some universities have only budgeted one lecturer's fee for a service user slot that up to four people may be expected to fill, while their finance departments took a lot of persuading that an invoice from an organisation was an acceptable way of paying visiting lecturer's fees.

Love her or loathe her (and CAPITAL members definitely came to love her) Anne Beales was not someone who could easily be ignored. Her energy and drive rubbed off on us, developing the collective mutual confidence that has enabled us to speak with an authority that makes people sit up and listen. She also helped us carve out new roles, diversifying into research and audit work, consultations and videos.

This was not always plain sailing. There is always the temptation to say "yes" to every interesting piece of work that comes in and there were occasions when people were not as supported as they should have been, particularly on some of the first research projects we did. There was a tendency to under-estimate the emotional effect some of the information we heard would have on us. Our support systems for people doing research have been strengthened with every project we undertake. Now our research teams are always trained to sit and debrief each other post interview as well as having a staff member on call and access to an outside supervisor if necessary. However since this has been available no-one has actually felt the need to call on an external supervisor, knowing someone is there can often be enough in itself.

Another problem that arose from some of the research we undertook was that the powers that be did not always like the outcome and a couple of reports were very efficiently buried. So we learnt to be more forthright in seeking assurances that the work we undertake will be put to good use. We are also wary being used to give a veneer of respectability to a tokenistic consultation. Any service user group is vulnerable to such manipulation and needs to be clear and uncompromising about the ways in which it is prepared to be involved. We require a contract for any long-term work to ensure both sides are clear about their obligations.

The business side of things is something that has had to be developed sensitively. First and foremost CAPITAL belongs to its members and maintaining the personal touch as the membership continues to grow has been of prime importance. The training course in Billingshurst has become an annual event. Alongside this members old and new now meet in three separate localities once a month with gatherings for the whole membership held only quarterly. This helps everyone to feel part of a group that is not too big and intimidating while still being able to feed their views into the direction of the whole. CAPITAL became a charitable trust in July 2001 with its board of trustees drawn from the membership across the localities and informed by the membership both formally through consultations at meetings and informally over those all important cups of coffee.

The staff group developed slowly and today there is a full-time director and an administrator and a collection of part-timers equivalent to about another 1.5 full-time posts. The majority of these are also members and receive as much support from the wider membership as they give in return. As one staff member put it: "CAPITAL is not so much a job as a way of life". It is not a workplace where traditional boundaries can be applied; we are all in this together. Almost all the time this works well because everyone respects the group agreements. On the rare occasions it does not the group agreements provide the framework to work through any difficulties.

In autumn 2004 Anne Beales left CAPITAL to take on a national post with Together (formerly known as MACA). The organisation she left behind had evolved almost beyond recognition from the one she had six years before, it was bigger, bolder and far more confident to stand up for itself. In this last year we have for the first time put our underpinning values and philosophy into writing and I am confident that as long as we remain true to those CAPITAL will continue to grow in influence and respect both locally and nationally and in the words of our first co-ordinator Veronica Dewan:

I very much hope that the strong foundation, upon which CAPITAL builds, will be an inspiration to others to develop similar opportunities around Britain.[2]

---

[2] "'More than just a learning experience' Clients and Professionals in Training and Learning" Veronica Dewan and Jim Read, The CAPITAL Project/West Sussex Social Services, (1998).

CHAPTER 4

The Highs and Lows of Service User Involvement

Rachel Nickeas

In this chapter, I will explore some key issues and dilemmas through my involvement as a service user trainer who is active in education and training. We all know the government have made it known that they want service users to be involved in education and training. We know that involving service users can provide professionals and students with a real insight into the experiences, feelings and problems that service users encounter when confronted by the services put at their disposal. If we all know this and subscribe to it then what is going wrong? Why is the overall picture of involvement so inconsistent and variable in quality? It would be easy to put the blame firmly in the arms of the professionals but I believe that service users have to hold their hands up and take some of the responsibility for this–although the lion's share rests with the professionals.

SERVICE USERS AS TRAINERS

I shall begin with us the service users and our part of the responsibility. Service users, independently or through voluntary organisations are often willing to get involved in training and education but, as with the rest of the population, many are unskilled in providing training and education sessions. People with mental health problems often have low self esteem, lack confidence or are so grateful to the professional staff for the care they received that they are completely compliant to the wishes of the professionals. Despite this many will try and get involved but not always successfully.

We all have our story to tell and our own gripes about how things have not gone our way or that we have been on the receiving end of poor services. For many it is enough just to tell their story–but without a purpose. They have a point to make and hope that will help professionals to change services for us. Many can also ramble on in planning meetings about their own issue, which has nothing to do with the task in hand. They believe that they are talking for all service users where as they are only really talking for themselves. Some do not choose to tell anyone, other service users or professionals, that they may have a period of "unwellness" that may affect their thinking. Medication can make us think less clearly for periods or affect short-term memory, which in meetings and teaching sessions can be a real disadvantage.

Teaching Mental Health. Edited by Theo Stickley and Thurstine Basset.

Some service users seem to be delivering education sessions because it is therapeutic for them. This, I believe, is not the primary reason for delivering such sessions. The purpose is to educate staff and students in order that services improve. If providing sessions also proves to be therapeutic then that is a wonderful additional benefit.

PROFESSIONALS AS TRAINEES

Now let us turn to the professionals. Although some professionals treat service user trainers with the same respect they would treat anyone else providing a training session many professionals do not seem to know how to treat and work with us. Often professionals over-compensate. Everything we say is listened to politely, noted down, if notes are being taken, but never ever challenged. Points we make are not discussion points. Service users can't possibly be wrong or "off task"–or if we are no professional "dares" to say so. We are permitted to just ramble about something completely inappropriate. I consider this to be patronising and no one will learn anything from it. Nor will it be a good experience for either service user or professional.

Professionals, of course, need to be aware of and take account of the fact that we may be vulnerable to challenge and see challenge as rejection. However, the lack of challenge and real debate between us will not produce the valuable education and training sessions, we are all looking for. I say all–but I really mean some professionals are looking for. I am not normally cynical but have been pushed to this by some of the education planning meetings I have been to. Undoubtedly some professionals are just ticking the box, saying "yes" to service user involvement.

What dilemmas! But surely, these can be overcome! Service users are people. Our skills and abilities reflect those of the general population. Our past jobs and experiences are valid even though we have a mental illness/disorder. We, like professionals, aren't right all the time.

HOW TO MOVE FORWARD TOGETHER–SUPPORT AND TRUST

I believe that at any initial planning meeting all the cards need to be laid on the table by both professionals and service users. There should be discussion about support mechanisms for service users, which includes support that could be needed both during planning meetings and when providing a session. For example, a lecturer and myself discussed what support I would need if I dissociated/switched at any stage. I had to acknowledge that I do dissociate and the lecturer had to be willing to work with this probability.

Let me explain here what I mean when I say I dissociate/switch. I had to admit that I have Dissociative Identity Disorder (DID). According to the ICD10, DID exists when an individual has two or more identities or personalities, each with its own way of being– relatively enduring patterns of perceiving, relating to and thinking about the environment and self. At least two of these identities or personality states recurrently take control of the person's behaviour and there is an inability to recall important personal information that is too extensive to be explained by ordinary forgetfulness. Also the disturbance is not due to direct physiological effects of a substance or a general medical condition.

I am still fragile and vulnerable to "switching" personalities/alters. When I dissociate a different one of my alters/personalities emerges. This can be another adult state or a child alter state. This seems to happen for no apparent reason and is beyond my control [at present].

It can be difficult for people to cope with this and it can mean I am unable to participate in the meeting for a period. I have no memory of what has happened to me during these periods–to me only a second has passed. There have in fact been two or three times over the last three years when I have dissociated/switched. The lecturer has taken me out, talked to me and when I am ready we have gone back in together to continue the session. Although I would rather I didn't switch during these times it is a reality for me [at present]. If we want "live" service users as well as those who have recovered then these sorts of happenings need to be worked with. There has never been a suggestion that I should not be providing any teaching sessions–indeed I am frequently asked to provide sessions by that particular lecturer and by others.

In order for this level of trust and respect to develop both the lecturer and I had to talk about the possibility of dissociation and about my possible needs and what support I might want. Then both of us had to put this into action. This particular agreement has never stopped the lecturer or me from challenging each other over the contents of sessions. I feel we have a mutually respectful and equal relationship. For an explanation of DID and how I have coped with living with this condition please see Stickley and Nickeas (2006).

Service users need to feel comfortable about disclosing any needs they have for support. Trust is vital here. How does that develop? It does not always take a long time. You know as a human being when someone is truly actively listening to you and respects you enough to have an honest discussion. This does not mean that service users need to disclose their diagnosis if they do not want to–support needs are different. The question to be asked and answered here is not "what is your diagnosis?" but "do you have any specific support needs that will need to be met for your session to be as good as it can be". This is basic good practice and applies to all teachers/lecturers. In any good professional culture people's needs will be taken into account.

This approach can also be very liberating for professionals, who can work with service users often for the first time in a situation where diagnosis is just not relevant. Indeed, I recently spoke to a professional trainer, who informed me that in nine years of working together with a service-user training group, the diagnosis of co-trainers has never remotely been an issue. He is also of the opinion that once co-trainers and indeed learners start thinking in terms of the diagnosis of the service user trainer, then all attempts at equality and partnership go straight out the window.

HOW TO MOVE FORWARD TOGETHER–STAYING "ON TASK" AND FOCUSSING

We can all be guilty of rambling and being "off task" on occasions but we all need to be brought back "on task". Not all people are aware that they are rambling and service users who are not particularly well that day may not be aware at all. I have known an entire teaching session be hijacked because a service user was unwell. No one, professional or service user went to her rescue. We were all too embarrassed or afraid. What should have happened? We all need to agree a contingency plan for this sort of event. We as service users must acknowledge the possibility and professionals must have it as a regular item on the agenda. We are providing sessions to future professionals as well as additional training to professionals – we are all working in the field of mental health. Surely we can be open about the possibility of "an episode", cope with it and get on with things all without making us feel less valuable or "too ill to work with".

As I said earlier we all have a story to tell. Often, but not always it is a story about poor and inadequate services. What happens is the story gets retold as it happened. There is not any talk of what was good about the experience, what was bad and what in the future needs to happen to improve on the experience. Most service users will not have experience of teaching. That is no criticism just a reality. So some help is needed–particularly help in the planning stages. Yes, professionals have to listen to the story because there will be some valuable teaching points within the story. What is needed is to tease out the key points of the story from the service user–not put words into our mouths–but actively listen and reflect back and come to some agreement on the point that needs to be drawn out for teaching. I'm sorry but work of this kind with service users will normally take longer than when you are working with just professionals.

HOW TO MOVE FORWARD TOGETHER–TRAINING FOR TRAINERS AND CO-TRAINING

We need training for service users in teaching skills to build confidence and to overcome the natural nerves of talking to a group of people when we may lack teaching experience! Many service users will need training in how to deliver an effective teaching session–voice projection, timing, making the teaching points clear. With the Nottingham University post-graduate mental health workers project, we, as a group of service users, provided many teaching sessions. We provided the training as a group. We planned the sessions with a lecturer, agreed the teaching points and the amount of time we had. We noted the points down as a reminder to ourselves. The lecturer led the sessions as a type of group discussion. He raised questions and we gave our experiences/views. The lecturer led but he did also try his best to get one of us to lead. However, we stated that we were happy with him leading as this gave us the confidence to open up and really give the students/workers our true experiences and views. By working as a group, people felt confident enough to talk when they would not have done so as the only person providing. We had also agreed in advance to meet with the lecturer for a short time after each session as we were very honest and open in our giving to the workers and it could sometimes cause one or other of us a little distress. These short sessions helped us to be able to give our all as we knew we were there for each other and time had been particularly set aside for us. Several of us gained the confidence from group work to go on and provide individual sessions.

HOW TO MOVE FORWARD TOGETHER–PRACTICAL ARRANGEMENTS

Transport to and from training venues is crucial. Many service users do not have cars. So a suitable teaching venue is vital–one that is easy to get to. Also someone to meet you is important. Due to my disorder often I cannot find my way around places, even though I have been there frequently. Getting the right venue may mean moving your students–but you are preparing them for work and meeting the simple needs of service users will help prepare them.

We also need frequent breaks. Many of us are on medication that decreases our ability to concentrate. Just not being well is tiring, repeating your very personal story is exhausting! Sometimes repeating your own story can be frightening so we need a support system in place in case of distress.

Water, tea, coffee are vital! Do you know how many medications make you thirsty and how many service users would not want to ask for a drink? Remember the low self-esteem and also the inability some of us have to ask for our needs to be met.

Payment–what a big issue! Do you know how embarrassing it is to have to ask for payment when it is not offered? When I first started to do this work it did not occur to me that I would be paid. Fortunately for me my first piece of work was with a lecturer/practitioner who told me how much I would be paid. The payment was the same as any other lecturer. [I was talking to the final year degree student nurses.]

I have been in planning meetings where no reference to payment was made. This simply is not good enough! We, like anyone else need to be paid for our work–budgets should be found before any professional embarks on work with service users. Pay can vary from area to area and job to job but please be open about it. In the Graduate Mental Health Workers project we had several rates of pay: one rate for planning meetings, another for delivering a session as part of a group and a higher one for delivering a session on our own. Of course we also got travel expenses. Many of us have had to give up work and live on benefits and the money for travel simply is not there. Also childminding costs should be taken into consideration. The experiences of young mothers with mental health issues is vital but it would be very difficult to work if the children were there–so child minding costs have to be met and/or sessions be held during school hours so mums/dads can drop their children off and collect them from school.

LIMITS TO INVOLVEMENT–TAKING RISKS–GOOD AND BAD EXAMPLES

I feel I have covered most of the points I want to talk about except one very contentious one. This involves the limitations that both service users and professionals put on the involvement of service users. When talking about acute ward experiences or about the details and experiences of a particular diagnosis it is most valuable to hear it from someone experiencing it at that time.

However, whenever I have suggested asking someone on the wards, just discharged, or someone in the acute stages of their illness everyone throws their arms up in the air and says "no". In this case, they do not ask service users what they think but answer for them. I recognise that we should not be pressuring anyone but working closely with key workers, nurses and care coordinators may give us a different picture occasionally. I will cite my own situation to stress this point:

• I had been in touch with a nurse lecturer/practitioner about an arts project I was interested in. At that time I was in the acute stage of my illness–attending a psychiatric day unit three–five days a week and had an enhanced CPA. However when well [ish] I wanted something to do. I had until a few months earlier had a full time and demanding job. I am not sure how it happened but we got around to discussing my diagnosis and he asked if I would be willing to talk to a group of final year degree nurse students about my disorder. I agreed and we had several planning meetings. The date to deliver the session was set for a few months away so there was plenty of time to prepare. I asked about what he wanted the content of the session to be and added things I wanted to say. I was also preparing a handout for the students to take away with them after the session. It is important to say that I had done a lot of training when I was working. However I had lost a lot of confidence and was nervous about this session. We were both very open and honest with each other and a respectful and trusting working relationship developed.

- Unfortunately ten days before I was due to deliver the session my mental health deteriorated [absolutely nothing to do with the teaching session]. I was admitted to an acute ward and was put on observation.
- I knew I was to deliver the teaching session and would still be in hospital. I got my husband to contact the lecturer/practitioner to let him know I was in hospital. I believe he talked to my key worker first but next he asked me if I still wanted to deliver the session or to postpone it.
- I explained that I was dissociating a lot and could not guarantee delivering the session without dissociating. He said that would not worry him if we worked out a plan of action to cover that eventuality.
- I thought carefully about it and decided that I did want to deliver the session. My husband got the teaching sheets off our computer. I read them through, practiced the session–which certainly allayed the boredom of being on the ward.
- At the appointed time the lecturer/practitioner came to escort me to the teaching room. I gave a talk and answered questions over one and a half hours. I do not think I dissociated. The students listened well and asked questions sensitively.
- I was escorted back to the ward where I slept off the tiredness. It was a good experience for me. Although on the ward and acutely ill I could still teach a session. It helped my self-esteem and my mental health was not adversely affected by the experience.

They have asked me back each year to do the same talk–so I couldn't have been too bad despite the acuteness of my health at that stage. It took a brave person to take the risk to ask me to go ahead with the talk. The students certainly got a real up-to-date and live experience, of my disorder. I believe he took a considered risk that paid off for all of us! My key worker was very supportive of it and provided additional support.

I am not saying that everyone in that situation should be asked/could be asked–but do not assume that something cannot be done. We need to be improving continually on service user involvement and looking at what may seem impossible in a more positive light.

In contrast to the positive experience above, I want to cite a particularly bad one I had that highlights for me many of the points I have made in this chapter:

- I was asked to join a training and development group. It was the third meeting of the group. There were four or five professionals and as many service users. They talked about the role of the training section and how much they wanted our involvement. We also talked about the need for support for service users–a buddy system. I was quite excited about it–it all seemed very positive.

- The next meeting was a real disappointment. Only one of the professionals turned up. There were four service users. It seemed we were to be "allowed" to look at a module and see if the wording could be changed. We were not to be allowed to add things to the module. I bit my tongue and did what was asked.
- After a couple of meetings like this my patience wore thin. We had got onto who should deliver this module. I began to realise that the professional person was indicating that I could not deliver. I couldn't work out why at first–then the penny dropped. I was able to have discussions on an equal footing. I had worked for 25 years before all my coping skills broke down completely. I was a senior manager in Education, Social Services and in a forensic mental health environment where designing, delivering and evaluating training sessions was a significant part of my role. I believe he felt threatened by me. In my view I was merely drawing on my experience from past work and as a present service user to ensure the training we were discussing would be of the highest quality. I hadn't considered he could be threatened by me. Also I had been "well" during all the meetings of this group. When I am well I come across as any other well person. I don't show any signs of mental illness. I don't think he thought I "really" had a significant mental illness. We hadn't talked about our diagnosis or about what our support needs might be. This meant he was going on what he was "seeing". He was seeing mental illness as he thought it should be seen. Therefore if I was "well" how could I deliver as a service user?
- At my first meeting with this group I had given the group the information that I was on an enhanced CPA and attended an acute psychiatric Day Unit three–five days a week. I thought this gave them an idea where I was at in my mental health–clearly not. I think this information got lost once I started functioning on an equal footing.
- So two things were at play here. First, he felt threatened as I was demonstrating I had at least the same experience and knowledge he had in developing training sessions and second I was not displaying any signs of mental illness that he was used to seeing which meant I was not "ill enough" to be asked to deliver as a service user. I wouldn't be seen to be "ill". I didn't fit the model of service user and therefore had little experience of mental health to pass on in training.
- I couldn't decide at first what I thought. I was desperate to be well; I didn't want to "act" ill. I wanted to hold it together in planning meetings. Yet the fact that I was ill was being denied. I was really distressed. Was I to argue that I was ill–that seemed an odd thing to do. It was also difficult as I had already spent a long time in the mental health services having to argue for the correct treatment for my disorder. Managers had said DID is an unusual disorder and one they hadn't met before so they needed second opinions. This took a while and was distressing at the time. All has turned out well with my care/treatment but it took a long time to get there. Here again my unusual mental illness seemed to be causing problems. It is a very uncomfortable position to be in as well as extremely confusing.
- However my disorder took over in a positive way. I became very clear and was able to tell the professional in clear terms that people were not what they always seemed, that mental illness comes out in a variety of ways, that each person experiences things uniquely and no-one, least of all a professional, should make assumptions.
- He took it very well. In fact he apologised and said he had made the classic mistake of assuming through seen behaviour what someone's experience of mental illness was.
- The meetings improved slowly and the brief widened. I think he was the only person in his section that was willing to put the time into working with service users.

- It was a hard experience for both of us
- Positively–payment was discussed openly, travel expenses paid as well. He asked me to talk about the group–at a conference so we must have moved on!

I have chosen two opposite examples of my own involvement in training and education. As can be seen it is very varied. Throughout this chapter I have tried to highlight some of the key issues and dilemmas in connection to service user involvement in training and education. There is room for negotiation and improvement from service users and professionals. I firmly believe that if we all learn from experiences and really want to make a difference to services then it is worth all the hard work.

REFERENCE

Stickley. T & Nickeas R. (2006). Becoming one person: living with dissociative identity disorder. *Journal of Psychiatric and Mental Health Nursing, 13,* 180–187.

CHAPTER 5

"I am the Visual Aid": A Teacher Who is also a Service User, not a Service User Who Used to be a Teacher

Allan Foreman and Alan Pringle

More and more organisations involved in health care are including service users in the planning, delivery and evaluation of their work. This may be in response to Government demands that all NHS Trusts and Primary Care Teams involve patients and carers in evaluation of services and engage with them when constructing policies (Department of Health, 2000). In recent statements the Government has emphasised the importance it says it places on user and carer involvement in mental health services (Department of Health, 2001) and cites, as an example, the National Service Framework for Mental Health which states that 'Service users and carers should be involved in planning, providing and evaluating training for all health care professionals' (Department of Health, 1999). Daykin et al. (2002) applaud the developments in UK health policy that seek to place the service user at the centre of service delivery and suggest that they are a positive step in the right direction. Edwards (2000) goes further, suggesting that these moves are the foundation of a fundamental philosophical change and an expression of a new emerging order.

The move to involve service users has also been seen in a range of developments in some universities where service users are seen as valuable members of teaching teams in health-care areas where staff are attempting to overcome the age old question of how best to link theory to practice. If done well the involvement of service users in education programmes can help foster what Wood and Wilson-Barnett (1999) call a "two-way relationship" between service users and education or clinical professionals. Felton and Stickley (2004) claim that, presently, service user involvement is playing an increasingly bigger part in the health arena generally and applaud the fact that growth in service user involvement in health care has extended to include professional training in the UK. Masters et al. (2002) are clear that service users and carers should be involved where practicable not only in teaching but also in the development, delivery and evaluation of the curriculum whilst Anthony and Crawford

(2000) go so far as to call the involvement of service users in the planning, delivery and evaluation of care an "essential component of healthcare philosophy".

One potential problem in this overwhelmingly positive move towards the involvement of service users in education and practice, however, is the potential to focus on defining the service user primarily in terms of their current or previous symptoms. This chapter focuses on how one service user, Allan Foreman, was able to move beyond the confines of the service user label and rediscover, and use to great effect, his skills as a qualified teacher in working with a University's Diploma in Nursing programme. This process led to Allan also becoming a founder member of a Practice Development Steering Group that guided four departments in his local mental health unit to successful accreditation as recognised Practice Development Units. The key feature here is the focus on Allan as a skilled teacher who had time as a service user, not on Allan as a service user who used to be a skilled teacher. Although this emphasis may initially appear as no more than a question of semantics it is much more important than that, and is the cornerstone on which genuine partnership can be built. If we are serious about such concepts as respect and inclusion then this order of things becomes the foundation of a philosophy that must underpin our approach to the teaching and delivery of mental health care.

WHO IS ALLAN?

Allan's professional background is in education. He trained as a school teacher in the 1970's and found himself at ease in what would now be classed as special educational needs teaching. In the 1970's this area was known colloquially as "bad lads" education and catered mostly for pupils whose disruptive behaviour had resulted in their expulsion from mainstream schools. Allan describes his time in this environment as generally happy but certainly stressful. An increasing workload, and reluctance to ask for help and support, resulted in what would now be classed as burnout and Allan found himself suffering from symptoms including anxiety, depression and extreme agitation.

Allan recalls how he was admitted to a mental health unit in what he describes as a disturbed state and how he was treated with medication. Interestingly the concept of informed consent was not an issue Allan considered at this time. Allan recalls how he was told to take the medication that would make him better with no information about how this process was supposed to work and or any potential effects or side effects to the medication. The dugs prescribed to Allan included Chlorpromazine and Haloperidol and according to his medical notes of the time these began to produce side effects such as stiffness, akathisia, tardive dyskinesia and dystonic movements. What neither Allan nor the staff at the time were to realise, until much later, was that these features would prove to be permanent in Allan's case and leave him with a virulent form of dystonia that would completely transform his life.

After being discharged from hospital Allan continued to take his medication as prescribed and was reassured that the symptoms would settle and become less pronounced as time progressed. For Allan this was simply not the case and the profundity of the uncontrolled and uncontrollable movements associated with his condition led to his being registered disabled, unable to drive, unable to work and to him living apart from his wife and son.

USING SKILLS

During the 1980's and 1990's Allan had two short admissions to hospital but the overwhelming amount of his time was spent living on his own in a small flat. Allan became involved in local organisations, notably MIND and the Dystonia Society, where his skills were valued and began to think about how his talents could be used in other areas. Allan was primarily interested in working to help educate people about mental health problems and about the stigma that surrounds the whole field.

Allan describes himself as having a unique perspective on such questions as drug induced dystonia and the effect they have on a person's life. It is, of course, true that everyone has their own unique perspective on every aspect of life but the ability of most staff and students to understand issues in Allan's life is perhaps limited by their lack of experience of the condition.

The important area of expertise in Allan's case was not just his life experience *but his skills, knowledge and experience, built up over years of teaching practice in communicating this experience* to staff and students, as well as his ability to link his personal experiences to the wider experience of people who use the service in general.

INVOLVEMENT IN NURSE EDUCATION

Allan first brought the skills he has to the field of nurse education in 1997 when he was invited to address a group of mental health branch students on the Diploma in Nursing course at the University of Nottingham. Hanson and Mitchell (2001) outline the value and importance of preparing service users for involvement in nurse education by training them to become trainers themselves. In Allan's case the actual knowledge and skills required to teach effectively were already present. Although the setting (teenage students in a school compared to adult learners in a university) was different the fundamental skills of how to teach were transferable.

Simpson (1999) feels that users becoming involved in the training of mental health workers can help to increase the understanding of students about users' views of mental health services and their needs from the perspective of the users themselves. In discussions between Allan and the lecturer organising the module it became clear that this was something that Allan could bring to the educational field that was hugely important. In this case it was felt that this perspective could offer three distinct things were crucial in this area:

1. Sharing the actual experience of mental health care in the local area.
2. Sharing the experience of drug induced dystonia.
3. Sharing the experience of extreme stigma due to the effects of accepting prescribed medication.

The lecturer involved, having been a teacher/practitioner in the clinical areas Allan had been admitted to was able to explain to students from a clinician's perspective the three areas noted above but this, of course, was only one point of view. Allan's high level of expertise, in these areas, offered him an opportunity to use his teaching skills and personal narrative to help students make clear connections between theory and practice from the client's point of view. This involved Allan taking the major role in the planning and delivery of the session rather than having a "walk on" part in the process.

1. The Actual Experience of Mental Health Care in the Local Area

In this area Allan was able to discuss with students their experience on placement and provide a complimentary perspective for them. Subjects like what it actually feels like, as a human being, to be restrained and medicated, how victimising detention can feel, how frightening mental health units can be and the effect that being an inpatient has on relationships with a spouse or child were all able to be addressed in a constructive way with Allan dealing with discussion in an honest forthright manner. Forest et al. (2000) suggested that nurses who had been educated and professionalised through the hospital based mental health "system" ended up perceiving and interacting with users as "text book cases", rather than individuals with unique experiences of distress. Allan's sessions offered an alternative to this process with the unique experience of distress being made accessible to students through their access to Allan face to face. The impact of the process on students of these sessions was very powerful. Allan always makes a definite point of stating, early in his presentations, that he is "not a vendetta man" and that his purpose is not to use the sessions to help put a human face on the text book descriptions of such issues as dystonia, stigma and social exclusion. He is, however, very clear about the sequence of events that unfolded through his particular admission, detention, taking of only prescribed medication and dystonia. Much of Allan's interactions with students are marked by a frank, honest exchange of views that are of great value not only at the point of contact but also when students and teaching staff present reflect on the exchanges later.

2. The Experience of Drug Induced Dystonia

This area of Allan's teaching focused on the development of his dystonia, and the subsequent impact on his life. This part of Allan's teaching always evaluates well due, in some part, to his innovative teaching methods. An example of this is his "bag of tricks", a bag from which he would produce several everyday household objects that had been destroyed due to his uncontrolled muscle spasms and movement. Examples included watches, cameras, headphones and most markedly for some (often older!) students, a copy of a first pressing of a 1967 Pink Floyd single, "Arnold Layne", which would be a valuable collector's item was it not for the large portion missing after it had been smashed against the record player.

Characteristically Allan opens this session with the quip "no need for overheads for this session . . . I am the Visual Aid"

3. The Experience of Extreme Stigma Due to the Effects of Accepting Prescribed Medication

Allan's work with MIND had seen him become involved extensively with their anti-stigma campaigns. He brought this experience and knowledge to the classroom and was able to inform students about the most current developments of various campaigns and about

MIND as an organisation in general. As with his other subjects, however, it was the real life, locally based, examples that Allan could provide of how stigma is visible in a community that helped the students focus their minds on the issue and see the subject from a different perspective.

What all of this meant in essence was that Allan was involved not as a token service user but that he had to contribute to the sessions from the perspective of a visiting lecturer rather than a curiosity to be exhibited. Allan was employed as a visiting lecturer to run joint sessions with a health lecturer on the Diploma in Nursing course. Allan's degree in teaching and his experience in the classroom meant that although this was a task that challenged him it also helped him both be seen and see himself as a teacher with mental health problems rather than a service user "doing a bit of teaching".

All three areas of Allan's input evaluated very well in formal evaluations during the modules and Allan became an integral part of the module as it was delivered in this particular curriculum. For Allan evaluation was a matter of professional pride. He came as a paid visiting lecturer, followed the lesson plans he had written for the sessions and used props and teaching aids that he had devised himself to enhance the sessions and the students' learning.

INVOLVEMENT IN PRACTICE DEVELOPMENT

Through his work at the University Allan became more confident and this was reflected in his acceptance of an offered place on the Practice Development Steering Group of the local mental health unit. This unit was applying for the nationally recognised Practice Development Unit (PDU) accreditation for four of its areas. Part of the process involved the formation of a steering group to help oversee the process and work closely with the university of Leeds who were the accrediting body. Reflecting on this process Allan observed that although he found the initial idea daunting he had developed enough confidence, through the re-use of his skills and knowledge in the university setting, to accept the offer and as such Allan became a founder member of the PDU steering group and helped guide the unit through six successful accreditation visits during which all four areas achieved the Stage I and Stage II (advanced) accreditation awards.

Throughout this process one of the features that Allan outlines as being of paramount importance is the inclusive nature of the relationship with the rest of the accreditation team, a group made up of consultant psychiatrists, senior nurses, ward based clinicians and staff from practice development and audit areas of the Trust. He cites examples of this inclusiveness as including being funded to present work he had been involved with at national conferences and on occasion being the unit's sole representative at meetings with the accreditation team from Leeds. This, more than anything else, suggested to Allan that he was actually in a relationship with others that was based on trust, partnership and respect.

Another such example can be found in Allan's involvement in the Mental Health Collaborative (MHC) in the Northern & Yorkshire and Trent regions of the English National Health Service. This initiative involved service users in mapping the patient journey to help professionals build insight into the impact of "taken-for-granted" routines (Robert et al., 2003). While it was seen as important that the final "mapped process" was credible and representative, it was felt that the discussion and sharing of perceptions between users and professionals was where the "real learning and potential for service improvement took place" (Roberts et al., 2003). As with other aspects of practice development at Millbrook it was the backing that Allan received to represent the unit in his own words that helped develop the sense of partnership and respect he felt whilst engaged in this process.

Allan continues to be involved in education, in MIND, and with staff at the local mental health unit and he remains an example of how service user involvement can be a valuable integral part of the design and delivery of both services and education. What becomes important here, however, is that although the process has been very positive and productive for all concerned, (i.e. Allan, the university and the Millbrook mental health unit) reflecting on the process brings into sharp focus some issues that need to be addressed around some of the fundamentals of Allan's involvement in both organisations in terms of genuine partnership. The most significant amongst these is power.

POWER

Poulton (1999) suggests that although the rhetoric of user involvement has featured in health policy documents for over a decade, there is mixed evidence as to the extent to which it is actually being achieved. Warne and Stark (2002) propose that this is because the prevailing mental health care culture remains steeped in a discourse of treatment and care, control and compliance and professional expertise. Croft and Beresford (1995) go so far as to suggest that user; involvement in some areas is merely a process by which providers co-opt users' views to legitimate their own agenda whilst Hanson and Mitchell (2001) observe that although there is evidence of involvement of service users in education, there has been little evidence of any challenge to existing power structures as service users have been involved on stakeholders' terms. They go on to suggest any that meaningful service user involvement in education inevitably requires a shift in power.

Felton and Stickley (2004) argue that to be in any way meaningful service user involvement in education inevitably requires a shift in power away from the traditional power bases. It is proposed by Warne and Stark (2002) that this is because although as long ago as 1996 the ENB in their Document *Learning from Each Other* made it clear that user and carer involvement is "more than slotting people into the curriculum," it appears that very little has changed in general. Warne and Starke (2004) conclude that is that there needs to be a shift from rhetoric to reality at all levels, from governmental to individual practitioner, if true user involvement is to be achieved.

Service user involvement in education continues to be about service users being used as "front line" staff to deliver sessions but with only limited input into the design and construction of the modules on which they offer teaching input. Masters et al. (2002) argue that this typifies a traditional view of education, with only professionals viewed as having the legitimate and appropriate expertise to be involved at all levels of curriculum design and delivery. Allan's experiences of the changing power structures in education and in PDU work reflect in the literature with things, in his view, progressing in the right direction but at a pace that can sometimes be frustrating.

Anthony and Crawford (2000) suggest that the mindset of "only professionals know best" is changing in practice areas where service users utilising the power of charities such as MIND and the National Schizophrenia Fellowship have begun to generate a powerful influence on policy and service development. Davidson and Perkins (1997) highlight the fact that the increasing "voice" and influence of service users is also evident in organisations such as The Sainsbury Centre for Mental Health, which promotes literature and research generated by mental health service users, and the Pathfinder Trust in London, which recruits staff who have themselves been mental health service users.

User involvement is a central principle of the Mental Health National Service Framework and is also evident in initiatives like the Expert Patient Programme, which explicitly acknowledges the expertise of people with experience of chronic illness. Robert et al. (2002) suggest that a major contribution that can be made by involving service users as experts is in mapping the patient journey where they can be valuable in building insight into the impact of "taken-for-granted" routines. Allan's contributions in this area were invaluable when the unit was constructing such things as the rapid tranquilisation protocol and the Millbrook ECT Care Pathway.

Allan's involvement with the PDU process at the mental health unit was characterised by feelings of empowerment at both the planning and design stages and the front line delivery stages of the process. His input into educational issues, however, was restricted initially to slotting into pre designed modules to deliver a self standing portion of teaching that dovetailed with the overall aims and objectives of the module in question.

Le Var (2002) claims that new partnerships need to be developed between users and providers, the hallmarks of which are respect, acceptance and sensitivity with no room for barriers caused by traditional professional "distance". Allan's view that this was visible in the PDU process and has begun to be replicated in the University of Nottingham where the university's close working with service users in mental health education through such organisations as Making Waves, and through such initiatives as the PINE project, is producing a structure where service users are becoming an integral part of the fabric of nurse education.

RECOVERY

All of the steps in Allan's journey that have been outlined in this chapter have been, Allan says, steps on his road to recovery. Allan's view of recovery is encapsulated in an address he gave, in February 2000, to a "survivors as workers" conference. It was at this time he started to call himself "a fully qualified survivor" (a phrase coined by singer/songwriter Michael Chapman in an album of the same name) but, he went on, "even to be a partially qualified survivor of the mental health system needs others to help". In the area of help Allan stated "I've always considered continuity to be an important idea but unfortunately, due to restraints in relationships and changes in careers, continuity is in short supply. Continuity and inspiration are important and, one should add, hope too". Allan concluded his address to this gathering with the observation that with encouragement, support, a sense of continuity and relationships built on trust and respect, recovery is not merely a buzz word for the mental health service networks but a real state of health to be achieved.

If "fully qualified survivor" is the end of the journey, the starting point on this road is presented in Allan's teaching as a state of being "cracked and broke" . Labelled as mentally ill, unemployed and seemingly unemployable, he uses the smashed Pink Floyd single to illustrate this. "There it is, cracked and broke, and there was I . . . cracked . . . and broke". The analogy of the journey from cracked and broke to being a fully qualified survivor is of huge importance and the response from those being taught by Allan is often a strong, immediate and emotive one. "My recovery", Allan states, "has been a lot to do with self image and continuity, especially continuity of opportunity". Given the opportunities, Allan concludes, service users can make massive contributions rather than token gestures in all fields of mental health care. This can, of course, only be true if, rather than using service users for short projects and then leaving them out in the cold again, organisations offer this "continuity of opportunity" that has been a hallmark of Allan's involvement in the fields of both service provision and education.

THE FUTURE

Whilst it is clear that, as Edwards (2000) suggests, the past decade has witnessed the beginning of the end of the era of the passive patient, the decentralisation of power from a professionally led service to one that is based on power sharing can be both challenging and threatening for all involved. Le Var (2002) suggests that new partnerships between users and providers are the way forward but this is easier said than done. The fact that these changes can be difficult to achieve does not, of course, mean that we should shy away from achieving them.

Throughout the country the beginnings of these moves are clearly visible in some initiatives whilst, it must be said, in others they are merely illusionary. Allan's story shows some clear steps in the right direction but there is still a long, long way to go if as mental health service providers and educators we are to move towards a genuine partnership with service users at all levels. Maslin-Prothero (2003) suggests that collaboration and partnership are key words used by the UK Government, practitioners, users and policy-makers when discussing the way forward but these pretty words must be accompanied by what Poulton (1999) calls a shift from rhetoric to reality at governmental and practitioner level if true user involvement is to be achieved. Allan's story is being echoed in pockets throughout the country and there are clearly the beginnings of a strong foundation on which to build.

The Government's acknowledging of the fact that involving users of healthcare services in provision and planning will lead to improved access, better services and subsequently improved health outcomes is further progress in the right direction. Although the confidence displayed by Edwards (2000) that "the old order within mental health services, characterized by hierarchies, authoritarian structures, promotional cultures and the concept that length of service constitutes a reason for conferring "expertise" on individuals, is breaking down and that the collaboration of users is an expression of the new emerging order" may appear a somewhat optimistic view of the present, it reflects a tide that is inexorable.

CONCLUSION

This chapter has outlined the importance of user involvement in education and practice development in clinical areas using one man's journey to recovery as an example.

The recognition of skills, the opportunity to use them and ultimately the rewards, both financial and social, associated with the good use of them has been a key factor in Allan developing the confidence to go from strength to strength in finding his way back from being "cracked and broke" to recovery as what he terms "a fully qualified survivor". Direct contributions in lectures offer the opportunity for service users to genuinely educate and inform future mental health nurses in areas that are unique to them and if service users can deliver them with confidence they can have a profound impact on the audience who hear them.

In Allan's case this confidence has also been visible in other areas of his life, most notably in sport. Allan's dystonia makes a bicycle impossible but Allan is a familiar local figure on his tricycle as he trains for races regularly. In the 2004 world tricycle association championship event Allan won the champion handicapped trophy (handicapped as in horse racing not as in disabled!) and has used the subsequent publicity to highlight the problems of those who suffer from dystonia and Tardive Dyskinesia.

When reflecting on the journey to recovery Allan suggests that "together we can" is not a cliché. With support characterised by respect and honesty and a continuity of opportunity service users both past and present can make a massive contribution. The key factor of respect for Allan, he says, can be summed up clearly in the shift of emphasis from seeing him as a service user who does some teaching to a teacher who spent time as a service user.

REFERENCES

Anthony P. & Crawford P. (2000). Service user involvement in care planning: the mental health nurse's perspective. *Journal of Psychiatric & Mental Health Nursing, 7(5)*, 425–434.

Crawford M. J., Aldridge T., Bhui K., Rutter D., Manley C., Weaver, T., Tyrer P. & and Fulop N. (2003). User involvement in the planning and delivery of mental health services: a cross-sectional survey of service users and providers. *Acta Psychiatrica Scandinavica, 107(6)*, 410–414.

Croft S. & Beresford P. (1995). 'Whose empowerment? Equalizing the competing discourses in community care' in Jack, R. (ed.) *Empowerment in Community Care*, London: Chapman & Holt.

Davidson B & Perkins R. (1997). Mad to Work Here Nursing Times, *93(31)*, 26–30.

Daykin N., Rimmer J., Turton P., Evans S., Sanidas M., Tritter J.& Langton H. (2002). Enhancing user involvement through interprofessional education in healthcare: the case of cancer services. *Learning in Health and Social Care, 1(3)*, 122–131.

Department of Health (1999). *The National Service Framework for Mental Health*. London: Department of Health.

Department of Health (2000). *The National Plan: a plan for investment, a plan for reform*. London: The Stationery Office Ltd

Department of Health (2001). *Involving Patients and the Public in Healthcare: A Discussion Document*. London: Department of Health

Edwards K. (2000). Service users and mental health nursing. *Journal of Psychiatric & Mental Health Nursing, 7(6)*, 555–565.

ENB (1996). *Learning from Each Other*. London: ENB.

Felton A. & Stickley T. (2004). Pedagogy, power and service user involvement. *Journal of Psychiatric & Mental Health Nursing, 11(1)*, 89–98.

Forrest S., Risk I., Masters H. and Brown N. (2000). Mental health service user involvement in nurse education: exploring the issues. *Journal of Psychiatric & Mental Health Nursing, 7(1)*, 51–57.

Hanson B. & Mitchell D. (2001). Involving mental health service users in the classroom: a course of preparation. *Nursing Education in Practice, 1*, 120–126.

Le Var R. M. H. (2002). Patient involvement in education for enhanced quality of care. *International Nursing Review, 49(4)*, 219–225.

Maslin-Prothero S. (2003). Developing user involvement in research. *Journal of Clinical Nursing, 12(3)*, 412–421.

Masters H., Forrest S., Harley A., Hunter M., Brown N. & Risk I. (2002). Involving mental health service users & carers in curriculum development: moving beyond 'classroom' involvement. *Journal of Psychiatric & Mental Health Nursing, 9(3)*, 309–316.

Pilgrim D. & Waldron L. (1998). User involvement in mental health service development. How far can it go? *Journal of Mental Health, 7(1)*, 95–104.

Poulton, B. C. (1999). User involvement in identifying health needs and shaping and evaluating services: is it being realised? *Journal of Advanced Nursing, 30(6)*, 1289–1296.

Robert G., Hardacre J., Locock L., Bate P. & Glasby J. (2003). Redesigning mental health services: lessons on user involvement from the Mental Health Collaborative. *Health Expectations, 6(1)*, 60–71.

Simpson A. (1999). Creating alliances: the views of users and carers on the education and training needs of community mental health nurses. *Journal of Psychiatric & Mental Health Nursing, 6(5)* 347–356.

Wallcraft J. with Read J. & Sweeney A. (2003). *On Our Own Terms.* London: The Sainsbury Centre for Mental Health.

Warne T. & Stark S. (2004). Service users, metaphors and teamworking in mental health. *Journal of Psychiatric & Mental Health Nursing, 11(6)*, 654–661.

Wood J. & Wilson-Barnett J. (1999). The influence of user involvement on the work of mental health nursing students. *NT Research, 4*, 257–270.

CHAPTER 6

The Evolving Minds Experience: Using Video for Positive Change, Education and Empowerment

Melissa Gunasena

EXPERIENCES OF PSYCHIATRY AND THE MAKING OF A VIDEO FILM

In the early 1990s whilst working for an environmental charity, I became a video activist with Undercurrents, an alternative media production company using video as a tactical tool for environmental protection and positive social change. The biased reporting and misrepresentation of the non-violent road protest movement in the mainstream media, as well as the violence towards protesters by police and security guards had convinced campaigners of the need to create films documenting the campaigns and of reporting news themselves. After only one hour's training, filming ducks on the pond in the park, I went off to video my first assignment, a protest about homelessness and the right to squat empty buildings. The police arrived and started being violent, and although I was scared, I tried to recall what I had been told about using a camcorder, and carried on filming. I remember hiding the tape from the police, feeling that I had something incredibly precious, and a record of what had actually happened. My footage was later used by the defence lawyers to help acquit some of the protestors of the charges against them. This experience was extremely empowering, as it demonstrated to me not only what a powerful tool for social justice video could be, but also how someone like me with no video experience and little training could make a real difference. I then went on to make films on topics such as women only direct action groups, squatted community centres and children's health in the Ukraine after the Chernobyl accident, and taught video and media skills to young women campaigners in Eastern Europe. A few years later, after being diagnosed with chronic fatigue syndrome, I became convinced of my need for personal healing, specifically the need to release and process pent up trauma and grief. This journey took me to many places, both geographical

---

Teaching Mental Health. Edited by Theo Stickley and Thurstine Basset.
Copyright © 2007 John Wiley & Sons, Ltd.

and spiritual. One of those was a locked ward in a psychiatric hospital where I was put under section.

Prior to being sectioned myself, I had, like most people sparse knowledge about psychiatric hospitals. In my mind, they were vague shadowy places, grim and intimidating, something like the film "One Flew Over The Cuckoo's Nest". References to them are few and far between in the mainstream media and it is extremely rare to hear a person describing their experiences of being an inpatient. In a 2001 survey by Mental Health Media, only 6.5% of press articles with a mental health interest contained the views and voices of survivors, and Mind determined in 2000 that 60% of people with mental health problems blamed media coverage for the discrimination they experience in their daily lives. In 2004 a MACA survey of journalists found out that whilst 84% thought that the general public would benefit from reading about personal accounts of living with mental problems, most of those questioned (73%) said they would approach a medical professional first for background information on a story involving a mental health angle (Macmin, 2001). This discrepancy demonstrates the way sufferers are marginalised in society and made to feel that their views are not taken seriously. Added to this is the sensationalist way in which murder stories involving someone with a mental illness diagnosis are reported, creating fear amongst the public that to have such a diagnosis means to be dangerous.

My experience of the medical model of mental illness has been generally disempowering, disabling and often terrifying. I made the video, "Evolving Minds"; an exploration of the connections between psychosis and spiritual experience and the alternatives to psychiatry, in order to enable others to have access to the information that enabled me to recover from it. This information was totally unavailable through the psychiatric system, both in and out of hospital. The only "help" given to me was enforced heavy medication, which not only made me feel physically ill, but also increased my distress. I was told I had a serious mental illness, and would probably have to take medication for the rest of my life to suppress the symptoms of my so-called "disease". My prior history of chronic fatigue had led me to seek healing through nutritional therapy, herbal medicine and spiritual practice and I had become aware of the ways in which food sensitivities and poor nutrition can affect our physical and mental health. Coming from a holistic perspective, I believe that all so called mental illness is actually a combination of malnutrition, unresolved trauma and the involuntary access of spiritual realms or non ordinary reality familiar to shamans, spirit mediums, clairvoyants, takers of psychedelic drugs and spiritual seekers. My refusal to believe in the validity of the diagnosis I was given enabled me to reject the medication and seek alternative solutions. This process took me on another journey, one of research and self-empowerment leading to the production of the video. I do not call myself a service user and find the title derogatory and misleading. I am someone who has been forcibly sectioned against my will on several occasions and therefore forced to undergo compulsory "treatment".

In my view, psychiatry is often used as a tool of state control and suppression rather than of genuine healing, where the aim is to maintain the status quo and silence disturbed and disturbing people; rather than deal with the causes of their distress. To this end the concept of illness is stretched somewhat to include experience or behaviour that is seen as irrational or abnormal, and, in the great tradition of patriarchy, emotional expression and bizarre behaviour can be seen as part of that illness. Instead of seeing the whole person, their lifestyle, history and beliefs, the medical model sees only a set of presenting symptoms. The diagnostic system is only useful for professionals to categorise people, and for the pharmaceutical industry to sell drugs, and along with all allopathic medicine treats the symptoms rather than the causes, blocking emotions and creative expression. Psychiatric medication has been described as chemical lobotomy and its use under compulsion as medical rape. Prolonged use of the drugs can lead to depression and even brain damage, causing conditions such as tardive dyskinesia. Peter Breggin in his book "Toxic Psychiatry" (Breggin, 1994) believes that these "miracle" drugs have actually "caused the worst plague of brain damage in medical history". Once a person becomes dependent on psychotropic medication, withdrawal can produce symptoms which look identical to many of the symptoms labelled as mental illness; mania, anxiety, depression and hallucination. Amongst medical professionals, this is usually seen as a return of the "illness", but is often the brain and body adjusting to normality after being suppressed. It is therefore wise to come off the drugs slowly and with appropriate nutritional and emotional support.

Social exclusion is inherent in the structure and philosophy of the medical model. By labelling and separating psychiatric patients from "normal" society through incarceration and mind numbing drugs, it sends a message to the rest of the populace not to cross the "normality" line. This detention is why sectioning is so often viewed as punishment both by patients and the general population. Added to the damaging effects of the medication, such as depression, apathy, panic, hallucination, muscle spasms, pain, inability to keep still and brain damage, are the dehumanising, brutalising and traumatising effects of effectively being kidnapped by strangers and kept prisoner against one's will. Much of the efforts of the staff are directed towards trying to control the patients and limit their emotional expression through the use of sedation, restraint and solitary confinement. Mental health staff who are interested in alternative healing methods, often find their efforts are limited by the modern psychiatric system, the origins of which can be found in the torture experimentation of the Nazi concentration camps. Much psychiatric treatment is reliant on the use or threat of force, as is any fascist government. Rudin, a Nazi psychiatrist whose theories on eugenics influenced Hitler's genocide policies was partly responsible for the mass murder of over 200,000 mental patients on grounds that they were "genetically defective". Many of the Nazi psychiatrists were never brought to trial and allegedly continued to practice both within Germany and in the countries they emigrated to such as the USA, where they were given asylum in the scientific establishment. The chief of research at New York State Psychiatric Institute and professor at Columbia University after WW2, Kallman, was trained in Germany in the 1930s, and called for the sterilisation of every family member of anyone labelled with schizophrenia or showing signs of eccentricity. His theories were widely studied in the 1950s and '60s, and gave continued credence to biological, genetic and racist theories of mental illness in the USA. The spectre of eugenics is not relegated to our past however but is becoming increasingly widespread in a different guise, as can be seen in the genetic screening of foetuses and the continued use of ECT. Compounding these ideologies is the strong influence the pharmaceutical industry has on the medical establishment. It appears that drug companies are constantly inventing new syndromes and symptoms to increase sales; one just has to look at the rapidly expanding market in psychiatric medication targeted at children. There is documented research demonstrating how Ritalin and other amphetamines used in the treatment of ADHD can actually cause drug induced behaviour problems, psychosis, hyperactivity, inattention, lethargy, depression and permanent neurological damage. Feeling a bit shy at a party? Don't worry; it is now possible to get medication for that disorder.

Currently in the UK, the Mental Health Act states that one must be at risk of harming oneself or others to be sectioned. Contrary to popular belief most "psychotic" people are not violent. This view has been created by the sensationalist media coverage, surrounding the rare occasions when someone with a mental health label is responsible for murder. This then reinforces the idea that mental patients are violently out of control and gives credence to the current system of incarceration and forced drugging. According to Government statistics, you are thirteen times more likely to be murdered by a "sane" person than by someone with a psychiatric diagnosis. However the Government wants to bring in new laws increasing compulsory detention and introducing forced medical treatment in the community; a gross violation of human rights demonstrating the current political ideology that our existence is owned by the state. If the medical system actually cured mental illness, people would be admitted once only and would go on to lead happy and successful lives. Sadly, psychiatric hospitals are full of people who are admitted repeatedly, spending their lives on the mental health treadmill, and more people are being diagnosed with mental illness every year.

In my experience, the medical model of mental health is not only of no help in treating mental distress it is actively harmful and if any healing does occur it is despite, not because of medical intervention. Diagnoses are made with limited knowledge of the patient's history and beliefs, often by doctors who have only met the patient briefly for a few minutes, a couple of times, and refusal to take drugs orally will result in forced injection whilst under restraint. The diagnoses of mental illnesses are actually a collection of observed behaviours and moral judgments and there are no scientific tests. For example, in a report written about myself it was seen as a symptom of mental illness that I maintained "too much" eye contact with the assessors. In my mind, however it was important to maintain eye contact with these people who had such power over my life. A patient then often carries this label with them for the rest of their life, affecting their job prospects, relationships and self-esteem. Psychiatry has however, had excellent results in the field of political oppression, with the use of medication to suppress political dissidents by causing apathy and memory loss, notably in the former USSR and currently in China.

VIDEO AS A TOOL FOR TEACHING

I had wanted to video my experiences as an inpatient in hospital but was refused permission by the hospital staff. At the time, I was told it was to protect the privacy of the other patients, despite the fact that many patients are under constant surveillance or "observations" and CCTV is everywhere. I felt it was more to protect the staff. One of the reasons why mental hospitals can be such scary places and such a mystery to the general population, is that so much happens behind locked doors, seen only by the staff, who may be afraid of losing their jobs if they speak out, and the patients, who if they try to complain or intervene on another's behalf may be told that they are imagining things as part of their illness and given even more medication.

Although I believe it is important to expose mistreatment and abuse, bombarding people with horror stories about how awful things are without offering positive solutions, only leads to apathy, hopelessness and despair. I decided to make the video for training purposes as I felt it was vitally important to pass on the information and techniques that had helped me lead a happy, successful and medication free life, to others. Digital camcorders and simple editing programmes have unleashed the potential for anyone with access to a camera and computer to make a film on a remarkably low budget, thus democratising the media in a way that was completely unforeseen a couple of decades ago. Streaming films on the Internet has enabled quick and easy distribution of footage considered too radical to be shown on mainstream TV. Film-making was traditionally seen as something done only by experienced professionals and specialists with qualifications and on high salaries; some people are still surprised when I tell them I have never been to film school, and my initial training in documentary film-making lasted for just one hour. In broadcast television, each stage of the filmmaking process i.e. research, production, editing and distribution, is carried out by different people. In activist filmmaking, most if not all of these tasks are done oneself, making the whole experience extremely empowering. I made "Evolving Minds" with Paul O'Connor, one of the founders of Undercurrents, who continue to train hundreds of people in how to use video as an effective campaign tool, make activist videos, and who now run a video activist festival Beyond TV, and make educational programmes for school and university students.

Video is a useful teaching medium for a variety of reasons.

- My experiences of filmmaking and direct action have convinced me of the power video has to inform, empower and motivate individuals to make positive change.
- The use of music, lighting and other effects can add interest to a subject and help to convey different realities and moods.
- The persons featured can share a personal and possibly painful story without having to retell it again and again or feeling emotionally exposed to the audience.
- The process of making a video; thinking, planning, researching, filming, editing and distribution allows one to clarify thoughts, arguments and ideas and to present them in a way that not only inspires, but also entertains.
- Ease of communication and dissemination of information; as one doesn't need to be physically present for one's information to reach people, and I can reach a far wider audience than by just doing talks and lectures and workshops.
- It is possible to include many different perspectives in a presentation in a way that would be logistically hard if all the people featured in the video had to be physically present at each workshop.

Before I embarked on making the film I had to consider several questions; why I was making the film, what my audience would be and how they would benefit from it, how it would effect change, and how I would distribute it. I decided I wanted to make it for two main reasons, to empower others by giving them information and to empower myself by transforming pain into something positive. My audience would primarily be those experiencing mental distress, their friends and families, mental health professionals, students and the public. I wanted it to be entertaining and funny as well as informative, easy to understand, cheap and easily available. Initially I thought I would distribute it on the Undercurrents network but once the film was made its distribution became much wider. My experiences in hospital had left me feeling extremely vulnerable and scared of the psychiatric system and I was concerned that if I made the film I would become a target for even more psychiatric abuse. However, support and encouragement from Undercurrents enabled me to get the confidence to start researching the project. Once I started speaking to others with similar interests I became even more aware of the pressing need for such a film and the storyline began to take shape. The "Evolving Minds" video can be roughly divided into three main topics, spirituality, nutrition, and protest against psychiatric legislation and practice. It consists of personal accounts, interviews with experts about their work and practical self-help techniques.

SPIRITUALITY

There are many people who view what is often called mental illness as a spiritual crisis; an accelerated opportunity for spiritual breakthrough and the resolution of old traumas. I decided to interview psychologist Isabel Clarke, editor of the book "Psychosis and Spirituality" (Clarke, 2001), who divides reality into two states, the ordinary everyday, and the transliminal, in which the part of the mind discriminating along conditioned boundaries is suspended. Both psychosis and spiritual experience fall into the transliminal. The reason why one individual is a successful medium, clairvoyant or shaman, and another is labelled with a mental illness, is largely due to their cultural upbringing and ability to navigate between realities, entering and leaving different realities on volition. The medical model tends to deny the validity of peoples' meaningful spiritual experience by saying it is part of their delusional illness. Isabel rejects this approach and uses the concepts of shared and non-shared reality to enable people to understand what they are experiencing.

Searching for more information on the links between mental illness and spirituality I came across a website entitled "Schizophrenia and Shamanism" and decided to interview its founder, Sam Malone. She had previously been sectioned, diagnosed with schizophrenia and put on anti psychotic medication against her will. Rather than risk being sectioned again and having to endure another stay in hospital, she ran away and spent time alone with nature, developing a set of techniques based on studies of shamans across the world. This enabled her to journey through her experience and back to ordinary reality. Shamanism is another form of spirituality that can resemble the states of non-ordinary reality labelled as psychosis. Historically it was widespread in Britain and across the world, and is still practised by many cultures today. The shaman moves between different realities using techniques such as drumming, fasting and hallucinogenic drugs, to effect change in ordinary reality, generally for healing purposes. For this reason they are valued and revered by their societies as powerful healers; their ability to enter different states of being is nurtured through rigorous training rather than suppressed or persecuted. People around the world have always experienced alternate states; going into trance, communicating with, or being possessed by spirits, hearing voices or having visions. In the UK, the fact that this can be considered deviant or even illegal, is due to the Christian witch-hunts of the 16th and 17th Centuries, when practitioners of traditional shamanism and the pagan goddess worshipping religions were almost completely exterminated, and any extra-ordinary, supernatural or spiritual experience became criminalised as devil worship. Practitioners of paganism, traditional healing, magic, midwifery and even politically troublesome peasants were persecuted and murdered. Thomas Szasz in "The Myth Of Mental Illness" (Szasz, 1984) likens the treatment of contemporary psychiatric patients to the witch-hunts, and the DSM ("Diagnostic And Statistical Manual Of Mental Disorders") has been called the equivalent of the "Malleus Maleficarum", a book used in the Middle Ages to identify and exterminate witches. Herbal medicine, with its holistic approach and tradition of wise women was thus superseded by the male dominated medical profession.

In modern Britain however, it is still considered acceptable to talk to god, but what if God talks back? Some people find the voices they hear to be useful, others harmful, but people have been hearing voices since time immemorial; some famous voice hearers include Jesus, Joan of Arc, Teresa of Avila and Carl Jung. Important factors are the extent to which one identifies with them, the context one hears them in, one's background and beliefs, and whether they have a positive or negative influence, as statistically far more people claim to hear voices than actually come into contact with psychiatric services. Voices can be seen as coming from sources such as goddesses or gods, ghosts, spirits, devils, dead friends, animals, trees, relatives or ancestors, the universe and aliens. They can also represent a part of the person that may have to be left behind in order to heal and move on, and threatening voices can often be a re-run of abuse or trauma with a supernatural tint. It can be helpful to open a channel of communication with the voices, talking back or writing down what they are saying for example or conversely, by refusing to pay any attention to them and simply not giving them any energy they may gradually fade away. Art and poetry can be useful ways of documenting and remembering one's experiences in other realities for future reference.

Some of my family are Buddhists, and according to this philosophy, few people actually experience the true nature of reality, as it is usually obscured by delusions in our minds caused by desires and attachments. Psychosis often involves a feeling of connection with the rest of creation, the ability to communicate telepathically and the dissolution of personal boundaries. This sense of ego loss is also the aim of Buddhist meditation but it is done gradually in controlled environments, usually with the support and guidance of an experienced teacher. I decided to interview a Buddhist priest, Venerable Lodro, who also teaches meditation. He feels it is important not to identify with any mental states, be it mania or depression as Buddhism teaches that everything experienced by the ego is illusory and transitory.

GROUNDING AND RELAXATION TECHNIQUES

Psychosis has been described as dreaming whilst awake and sleep deprivation will cause anyone to hallucinate. Very often insomnia and racing thoughts can be a sign that you are entering the transliminal and it is important to rest and relax even if you can't sleep. The psychotic state often feels magical, mystical and super-meaningful and this state of high arousal can leave a person feeling vulnerable. This feeling of threat, when the mind goes into tunnel vision might be caused by something real, imagined, or out of the memory. One way of relaxing the mind and body, taught by Isabel Clarke, is to breathe out more than you breathe in, long slow out-breaths, relaxing on the out breath, a technique which can allay feelings of anxiety or panic. Massage, aromatherapy, acupuncture and herbal medicine can also be of great benefit in aiding relaxation.

The video also includes a brief introduction to meditation. Many people are aware that meditation can be a useful tool in calming and controlling one's mind, but are reluctant to actually go to a class or read a book about it. Initially aim for ten to fifteen minutes daily. Sit comfortably, close your eyes and focus on the sensation of the breath as it passes through the nostrils, breathing gently and normally. When thoughts come up and the mind becomes distracted, bringing the mind back to its object, the breath, will strengthen concentration. Initially you will find that it is difficult to focus for long but by paying no attention to thoughts and feelings and just focusing on the breath the turbulence will gradually die down and you will be left with a feeling of calmness and spaciousness in the mind.

Making a list of ten things that tend to happen when things go wrong and seeing how many of them need to be in place before you need to take steps to shut yourself down before you are "shut down" officially can be helpful. Another useful technique is to stick up messages around your house to remind yourself what it is you need to do to feel calm, for example "Think you're Jesus; go bang a drum!". Repetitive drumming is very useful for silencing the voices and is an ancient shamanic technique to invoke and ground the trance state; it can be done on hand drums or even just your legs or a tabletop.

In my experience, spending time in nature was fundamental to my recovery, allowing myself to feel at one with the universe. Being away from the demanding and often limiting and frightening world of people enabled me to regain confidence in my own strength. Indeed, a premise of Eco-psychology is that our current addictions to technology and over-consumption, and the consequent disassociation between us and the rest of the natural world, is the primary trauma we are all suffering. Gardening is a great way of healing and grounding as you are literally earthed, and the physical activity can help alleviate both psychotic and depressive types of symptoms. Growing organic vegetables is a wonderful act of self-nurture and empowerment, whether in your garden, on an allotment or simply in a window-box or flowerpot.

ACTIVISM AND DIRECT ACTION

I also found it extremely empowering to be involved in campaigning and protest against mental health legislation. I felt that it was important to include this in the film as it is often sidelined in the mainstream media, and is an important way for people to come together and feel solidarity. For people who have never been on a demonstration, watching a sympathetic account on video can alleviate any fears or prejudices and enable them to participate in the future. Just hearing about the organisation Mad Pride, which campaigns against discrimination and stigmatisation by using direct action, gave me a lot of hope after being sectioned. Mad Pride also puts on events, festivals, gigs and picnics to raise awareness about mental health and have a good time. Many people are also coming together to fight the proposed changes to the Mental Health Act. Whilst filming a march through central London I interviewed campaigner Rufus May, whose experiences of being given a label of schizophrenia as a young man and then going on to train and work as a clinical psychologist within the psychiatric system have given him real insight in how to treat people. He minimises the use of compulsion on wards by giving people feedback about how they are coming across, a range of options about how to control their moods and taking their concerns seriously and acting upon them. The failure of the psychiatric system to deal adequately with people's mental health needs is part of a wider social and environmental global crisis in which compassion and sustainability have been sidelined in favour of corporate irresponsibility.

THE IMPORTANCE OF GOOD NUTRITION

"Let food be your medicine and your medicine be your food". Hippocrates, the so-called "father" of modern medicine, said this over 2,000 years ago. However despite growing amounts of research on the positive impact of a healthy diet, psychiatry largely ignores this and concentrates almost exclusively on chemical medication. In my own experience, realising how the food I eat affects my mood and changing my diet has made an incredible difference to my life. The physical structure of the brain as well as the chemical processes that transmit messages are both dependant on the food we eat, and our brains need the right balance of nutrients to function properly. It is hard to believe that people in the affluent Western world are suffering from malnutrition, but the average diet is deficient in important nutrients for healthy brain function. This is mainly due to our dependence on processed food and the mineral depletion of soil through the use of agrochemicals, and is partly to blame for the rise in "mental illness". Problems diagnosed as being mental health issues can actually be caused by a variety of nutritional factors such as blood sugar imbalances, vitamin, mineral and essential fat deficiencies, food and chemical sensitivities and allergies, and Candida, a fungal overgrowth in the gut.

In "The Food And Mood Handbook", Amanda Geary (Geary, 2001) lists symptoms such as aggression, depression, delusions, ideas of grandeur, confusion and panic attacks as being food related. Although I had self-treated by changing my diet, I felt it would be useful to have the views of a professional in the video and interviewed Lorraine Perretta, a nutritional therapist specialising in the treatment of mental health. In her practice, she successfully treats all types of psychotic symptoms, schizophrenia, depression, bi-polar disorder and obsessive-compulsive disorder using nutritional therapy.

Maintaining an even blood sugar level is fundamental for optimum mental health. The ingestion of caffeine and processed sugar causes blood sugar levels to rise rapidly; the body panics and releases insulin to reduce blood sugar, which then drops rapidly causing people to feel irritable, lethargic, depressed, tearful or panicky; they then eat more sugar to raise blood sugar levels and the whole cycle starts again. In addition most psychotropic medication also has this impact on blood sugar. Cutting out all caffeine, sugar and sugar containing foods and snacking throughout the day on healthy food is an effective way of maintaining an even blood sugar level.

According to Patrick Holford, author of 'Optimum Nutrition for the Mind, and founder of the Brain Bio Institute, zinc is probably the most commonly deficient mineral in the British diet (Holford, 2004). The recommended daily allowance is 15mg, but the average intake in Britain is only 7.6mg and deficiencies can lead to depression and hallucinations. Tests done in 1960's found 52 % of people diagnosed with schizophrenia actually had a stress related condition known as Pyroluria, which depletes the body of vitamin B6 and zinc. A study carried out by Dr Glen of Aberdeen University found that 80 % of schizophrenics are deficient in Essential Fatty Acids, or EFAs (Holford, 2004). Essential fats and oils found in nuts, seeds, vegetables, eggs and fish and, as their name suggests, are essential for the brain to function properly. An imbalance of gut bacteria caused by poor diet, use of antibiotics or stomach bugs can lead to the inability to digest foods properly, also leading to nutritional deficiencies. If you suffer from bloating, diarrhoea or constipation you could have an overgrowth of intestinal candida, a yeast-like organism, and it may be helpful to cut out all sugar, fermented and yeast containing foods, take herbal anti-fungals and beneficial bacteria supplements.

Food sensitivities can also be an important factor for people with mental health problems; a study done by the University of Sheffield found that 60 % of people with depression were intolerant to wheat. A food allergy will cause an immediate and severe reaction, whereas an intolerance may take a few days to appear and can manifest as a variety of symptoms including depression, anxiety, anger, lethargy, hallucinations, bloating, and digestive and skin problems. In a 1981 study published in the Journal of Biological Psychiatry, the foods that caused the most severe reactions were wheat, milk, sugar, eggs and additionally, tobacco smoke, (Holford, 2004). Research was first carried out in the 1950s on the link between schizophrenia and celiac disease, and tests have been carried out in hospitals and penal institutions on how a change in diet can alleviate or produce symptoms.

NUTRITIONAL ADVICE IN BRIEF

• Avoid all stimulants, caffeine, sugar, and sugar containing foods.
• Avoid all dairy and wheat products and any other foods you suspect are causing a problem, slowly introduce them, one at a time every five days or so, to see which ones are the culprits.
• Eat plenty of fresh organic vegetables, fruit, nuts, seeds and free-range eggs.
• Drink plenty of water.

Since 1971 thousands of patients been successfully treated using vitamin and mineral supplements, and making dietary changes; if psychiatric hospitals blanket tested everyone on admission for nutritional deficiencies and food sensitivities the NHS could save millions of pounds and alleviate a lot of unnecessary suffering. Once again, it is the stranglehold that drug companies have on the medical profession creating a situation in which doctors get only very scanty nutritional information whilst in medical school, that is preventing this simple solution to the current national health crisis in the UK.

DISTRIBUTION AND TRAINING

Once the film was completed, I faced the task of screening it. The premiere was at an independent cinema in Brighton, and although I was terrified, the evening was a huge success. The cinema was packed, and the audience discussion afterwards was so lively and intense that I realised I had to do more with the film than simply stick it on a website. Since then, I have used it to run training workshops for survivors, sufferers, students, mental workers, doctors, nurses, carers and the public. I have screened the film in a variety of situations, such as hospitals, festivals, conferences, clubs and universities, and in my experience, it has always generated deep and useful discussion amongst viewers. The mixture of personal history, humour, and radical information encourages others to come forward with their views and experiences. It is now available on a number of mental health websites, and if anyone would like to put it on TV or screen it themselves, let us know! I have become part of a growing network of people interested in promoting alternatives to psychiatry, and have been involved in presenting these ideas to mental health professionals and establishing interest groups.

I generally run two types of training sessions; a screening of the film followed by a group discussion, or a workshop situation in which I ask the participants to split up into two's or three's and share their thoughts and experiences with each other, and I sometimes combine the two. If possible, I get the participants to rearrange their chairs into a circle after the screening as this generates a feeling of inclusiveness, equality and ease of communication. The benefits of a group discussion are that everyone gets to hear everyone's views, new connections are forged between people and the group can be united in a common purpose by discussing a particular theme. The downside is that it is sometimes only the louder people who feel confident enough to speak, although this can be overcome by facilitating the group in such a way that everyone gets an opportunity to have their say. The benefits of breaking the group into smaller units are that people generally feel safe enough to share their ideas and experiences on a deeper level and the discussion topic can remain focused. I usually begin by asking people to tell each other what they think the purpose of being human is, and then develop this into how they can make positive change in their lives and who or what is stopping them, finishing with a short meditation to relax and inspire.

CONSCIOUS EVOLUTION

Psychosis is defined as "any form of mental disorder where the individual's contact with reality becomes distorted", the dictionary definition of reality is "the state of things as they are or as they appear to be, rather than as one might wish them to be". However, much of what we think of as being reality has been created by our cultural, political, economic and religious conditioning and varies across the world and over time. One of the most influential and least challenged concepts we adhere to, is the artificial division of time into the Gregorian calendar and the twenty-four hour clock. These constructs are not only illogical but actually interfere with natural cycles and rhythms such as the thirteen-moon year. That this is so widely accepted as being "real" is just one indication of how absolutely we accept our conditioning. Our schooling, the media and legal systems also heavily influence our reality and are often used to uphold the current economic and political system, based on exploitation and violence.

In the UK, it is currently illegal to be naked in public, and it is often considered a sign of madness or perversion. It is also illegal to take non-prescribed mind-altering drugs, including magic mushrooms, a naturally growing native species with hallucinogenic properties used by our ancestors for thousands of years to enhance spiritual understanding. Both these practices arguably cause no harm to others and are part of our shamanic cultural history. It is however currently legal and therefore "sane" to murder children, as long as one is a member of the armed forces, or to engage in rampant environmental destruction and pollution, conflict or social exploitation, as long as it is done for monetary gain.

The looming ecological crises and consequent social upheaval caused by our over-consumption of resources and reliance on polluting technologies will create unprecedented mental distress on a global scale unless steps are taken now to change the way we relate to the natural world and each other. Unfortunately our current definitions of what constitutes mental illness and our pathologising of emotional distress, partly explains how our society is able to remain in denial about the crisis we are facing. Indeed, it could be seen as a symptom of mental illness for anyone, be it governments, corporations, advertising or the media to be promoting environmentally unfriendly and unhealthy lifestyle choices as the primary goal of human endeavour. To paraphrase Krishnamurti, it is not a sign of sanity to be well adapted to a sick society.

There is a school of thought, which believes that the state of madness is fundamental to human evolution, innovation and creativity, as it is so closely related to the ability to perceive new connections, make new links and invent new objects and concepts. This is borne out by the link traditionally seen between madness and genius, and the high level of creative, intelligent and psychically sensitive people labelled with mental illness. We are still evolving as human beings and I believe that psychiatry is being used to suppress areas of human consciousness and experience that could be drawn on to develop our existence and enhance our reality.

Ultimately however, we are all responsible for defining our reality. Global peace and environmental sustainability will only be achieved by challenging and changing the versions of reality that promote war, exploitation and rampant consumerism. It is our collective responsibility to promote positive, sustainable and peaceful living. Be the change you want to see.

To obtain copies of the "Evolving Minds" video and other radical social, political and environmental documentaries go to the Undercurrents website: www.undercurrents.org.

REFERENCES

Breggin, P. (1994). *Toxic Psychiatry: Why Therapy, Empathy and Love Must Replace the Drugs, Electroshock and Biochemical Theories of the New Psychiatry.* New York: St. Martin's Press.

Clarke, I. (2001). *Psychosis and Spirituality: Exploring the New Frontier.* John Wiley & Sons, Chichester.

Geary, A. (2001). *Food and Mood Handbook: Find Relief at Last from Depression, Anxiety, PMS, Cravings and Mood Swings.* New York: HarperCollins.

Holford, P. (2004). *Optimum Nutrition for the Mind.* London: Piatkus Books.

MACA. (2004). *Reporting Mental Illness.* (MACA is now called Together: Working for Well Being): http://www.together-uk.org/documents.asp?id=111&cachefixer=.

Macmin, L. (2001). *Mental Health and the Press.* Mental Health Media: http://www.mhmedia.com/training/report.html

Szasz, T. (1984). *The Myth of Mental Illness: Foundations of a Theory of Personal Conduct.* New York: Harper and Row.

BIBLIOGRAPHY

Dreaming the Dark and The Spiral Dance–Starhawk.

Ecopsychology–Ed. Roszak, Gomes and Kanner, ISBN 0-87156-406-8
   Revolutionary concepts of mental health redefining sanity on a personal and planetary scale.

Hedge Witch–Rae Beth, ISBN 0-7090-4851-3
   A guide to the ancient craft and traditions for the solitary practitioner.

My Name is Chellis and I'm In Recovery from Western Civilisation–Chellis Glendinning.

Optimum Nutrition For The Mind–Patrick Holford, ISBN 0 7499 2398 9
   A comprehensive guide to nutritional treatment for mental health.

Psychosis And Spirituality–Isabel Clarke,
   A fascinating and useful collection of perspectives, theories, research and experience.

Rising Tides: The History and Future of the Environmental Movement–Rory Spowers, ISBN 1 84195 402 0.

Schnews–weekly direct action newsletter and action update– www.schnews.org.

Shamans, Healers and Medicine Men–Holger Kalweit ISBN 1 57062 712 6.

Spiritual Emergency–Stanislav Grof
   The classic guide to the state of spiritual crisis and transformation.

Stepping Into the Magic–Gill Edwards, ISBN 0 7499 1238 3
   A practical approach to everyday life; blending metaphysics, shamanism and psychology.

Strong Imagination–Daniel Nettle, ISBN 0 19 850876 X
   A look at the links between madness, genius, creativity and evolution.

The Food And Mood Handbook–Amanda Geary, ISBN 0 00 711423 0
  Easy to read, simple and informative, with recipies and cartoons.
The Great Work: Our Way to the Future–Thomas Berry, ISBN 0 609 80499 5.
The Myth Of Mental Illness–Thomas Szasz, Granada Publishing
  A classic challenge to the basic model of psychiatry.
The Places That Scare You–Pema Chodron, ISBN I 57062 921 8
  Tools for overcoming fear and developing compassion.
The Practical Guide To Candida–Jane McWhirter, ISBN 0 952 6286 0 0
  Invaluable resource for those suffering from Candida.
The Video Activist Handbook–Thomas Harding, ISBN 0 7453 1174 1 hbk
  Everything you need to know about making and distributing a video.
Toxic Psychiatry–Peter Breggin, ISBN 0 00 637803 X
  Exposes the harm done by psychiatric medication.

USEFUL CONTACTS

Antipsychiatry Coalition
    www.antipsychiatry.org
Hearing Voices Network
    www.hearing-voices.org.uk
Learning From Psychosis
    www.learningfrompsychosis.com
Listen to The Voices
    www.gingerbeer.co.uk
Mad Pride
    www.ctono.freeserve.co.uk
Madnation
    www.madnation.cc
Mental Health
Mental Health Media
    Promotes peoples voices to reduce prejudice and discrimination
    www.mhmedia.com
Mind
    www.mind.org
No Force Campaign
    www.pages.zdnet.com/cullyd/thenoforcecampaign
Sound Minds
    www.soundminds.co.uk
Successful Schizophrenia
    www.webecom.com/thrive/schizo
Support Coalition International
    www.mindfreedom.org
Survivors Network
    www.survivors.network.ukgateway.net
Toxic Psychiatry
    www.breggin.com

SPIRITUALITY

Friends Of The Western Buddhist Order
    www.fwbo.org
PSI Research Centre
    serenard@compuserve.ocm

Psychosis & Spirituality
    www.scispirit.com
Sacred Hoop
    www.sacredhoop.demon.co.uk
Sacred Trust
    www.sacredtrust.co.uk
Schizophrenia & Shamanism
    www.madness.crowcity.com
Spiritual Crisis Network
    Understanding and support for those going through transformation
    catherine_lucas@hotmail.com
Spiritual Emergency
    www.holotropic.com

NUTRITIONAL THERAPY

Brain-Bio Centre
    www.mentalhealthproject.com
British Association for Nutritional Therapy
    www.bant.org.uk
Food and Mood Project
    www.foodandmood.org
Institute for Optimum Nutrition
    www.ion.ac.uk
Women's Nutritional Advisory Service
    www.naturalhealthas.com

ALTERNATIVE THERAPIES

British Complementary Medicine Association
    www.bcma.co.uk
National Institute of Medical Herbalists
    www.nimh.org.uk
Register of Qualified Aromatherapists
    01245 227957
The Society of Homeopaths
    www.homeopathy

ORGANIC GARDENING

Henry Doubleday Research Association
    www.hdra.org.uk
Organic UK
    www.organicgarden.org.uk
Thrive
    www.thrive.org.uk

Personal Perspectives on Mental Health Problems: An Introduction in the Medical Undergraduate Curriculum

Jacqueline Atkinson

INTRODUCTION

It is a truth universally acknowledged that most undergraduate medical students have little interest in mental health, mental illness or psychiatry (Lambert et al., 1996, Martin et al., 2005). This has been of concern to the Royal College of Psychiatrists and others planning workforce matters (Brockington and Mumford, 2002; Storer, 2002). This is not confined to the UK (Sierles and Taylor, 1995, Weintraub et al., 1999; Malhi et al., 2002; Martin et al., 2005). The focus is, however, almost inevitably on psychiatry as a future speciality rather than looking at different approaches to introducing medical undergraduates to mental health issues. This chapter looks at involving voluntary organisations in the undergraduate curriculum and giving a different perspective on mental health problems.

THE UNDERGRADUATE MEDICAL CURRICULUM AT THE UNIVERSITY OF GLASGOW

A brief background on the course is necessary to understand how this module fits in. A new medical curriculum was introduced in 1997 following a problem based learning (PBL) approach. The focus upon clinical relevance within the core curriculum was explicit from the outset. Alongside the core curriculum, students also get the opportunity for some choice in what they study. This comes in the form of student selected modules (SSMs). Students do seven of these over the last four years. They are intensive periods of study being full time for five weeks. The SSM being described here is Consumer Perspectives of Mental Health and has been offered since the start of the new curriculum in the second year.

Teaching Mental Health. Edited by Theo Stickley and Thurstine Basset.
Copyright © 2007 John Wiley & Sons, Ltd.

BACKGROUND TO INVOLVING VOLUNTARY ORGANISATIONS IN TEACHING

Many voluntary organisations or user groups have been involved in teaching students in all aspects of health care. Most commonly this seems to involve service users or carers describing their experiences. This can be a nerve-wracking experience for those not used to public speaking, although some may find it empowering. Although this can be enlightening accounts which tend to be wholly negative about services and professionals, these accounts may alienate students if they have no real understanding of the context of what is being said.

RATIONALE FOR THIS SSM

The aims of the module are to introduce students to service users' perspectives in mental health and to address their own preconceptions, prejudices and stereotypes of what it means to have a mental illness. From this they should gain an understanding of how having a major mental illness has an impact on all aspects of a person's life, the ways people come to terms with and manage their illness and how they view issues such as stigma, the treatment they receive and other aspects of care. This involves them in seeing people with mental health problems as people first, patients second and a collection of symptoms somewhere far behind. The module comes before any other introduction to mental health in the curriculum.

My long involvement with a voluntary organisation[1] led me to consider that involving them might be the way to achieve these aims. Rather than just have people along to talk to the students it seemed a better idea to send the students to spend time in the voluntary organisation. This would accomplish several aims in that the students:

* would be able to meet informally with people with mental health problems and talk to them;
* would get to meet people over a longer period on time, on their own ground, and a thus gain a more rounded picture of them as people;
* get a better understanding of voluntary organisations, how they are run and what they can provide.

Spending some time in the voluntary organisations themselves means that the students would be entering the user's world, learning something about what this is like and although they retain the status of medical students the usual trappings which support them in this role would no longer be there. They would be guests in someone else's environment. This would also, hopefully, mean that the members of the places they visited would feel more able to speak freely with them and share aspects of their lives.

Since students would have no experience of the NHS psychiatric setting it seemed sensible to include some time there, so that they had more opportunity for comparison.

My local links with voluntary organisations meant that the placements were fairly easily set up on what is an essentially reciprocal arrangement. I had, and continue to support the

---

[1] I am a Director of National Schizophrenia Fellowship (Scotland) and was involved in setting this up as a separate charity in Scotland in 1984.

organisations by, for example, speaking at or chairing conferences and meetings for them, being on a management advisory committee and so forth. Hosting the students does not come cost free to the organisations as staff spend time with them and rotas have to ensure appropriate staff supervision. In discussion with the centres two days in each place were decided on. As some of the material described in this chapter is of a sensitive nature, the actual identity of the centres has been withheld.

THE VOLUNTARY SETTINGS

Centre A

This is a drop-in centre for people with severe and enduring mental health problems. It is part of the National Schizophrenia Fellowship (Scotland) and has been running since 1990. It has a café in the basement, which is open to the public and in which some centre members work. It has rooms over three more storeys for socialising, pool, counselling sessions, groups, a "chill out" space and an art room as well as office space. Members attend as they choose, some attending most days and others only for particular groups or counselling.

Centre B

This is based on the American Clubhouse model and it was originally run through the Glasgow Association for Mental Health (GAMH) but has been independent for several years. There is a café for members, run by members, a large reception/work area, and the second floor is divided into different work area with a small computer room, where classes are held. The numbers in the centre vary as many are out on work placements at different times.

THE NHS SETTING

This has varied more over the years and is organised by a consultant psychiatrist. It usually includes a half-day spent in a "depot clinic" (a clinic for patients on long-acting medication to receive their injections), an inpatient ward, a rehabilitation service, and a visit to someone in their home.

These placements introduce students to people in a variety of settings with a wide range of stages of their illness, ongoing issues and expectations on them in each setting. Although some people attend both Centre A and Centre B, many of those who attend Centre A have continuing problems which would make it difficult for them to be fully involved in the more structured and demanding regime at Centre B.

CONTENT OF THE MODULE

Although the visits are the main learning experience these have to be put in a wider learning context. The module is thus made up of:

Two Introductory Sessions

As well as introducing the student to the module as a whole this also covers what students might expect in the visits. There are many aspects in common between the visits in the NHS and voluntary sector but some differences. Topics covered include: confidentiality; dress, demeanour and disclosure; communication. One session is with the consultant who arranges the NHS visits.

The main difference is in the approach to people. In the NHS settings people are there in the role of patients and are used to being interviewed about their illness. If people agree to talk to the students, they are usually open about their illness, their symptoms and present as "patients" and expect to be asked questions. In the voluntary organisations people are not in the role of patients, and may not want to discuss their condition in the same way, such as focussing on symptoms, but may be more open about other aspects of their life. Students need to understand the different settings and the most appropriate type of questioning and response. In the NHS setting it is more likely to be student led, in the voluntary organisation it is more likely to be member led.

Disclosure is also an important issue as the informality of the setting can lead to inappropriate disclosure, either about themselves or others. They also need to remember they are there as guests and as medical students it is important and that confidentiality is maintained in all the areas.

Six Days in Visits (Two Days per Week for Three Weeks)

The students normally attend in pairs, with a different partner for each visit. Students are expected to take part in whatever centre activities are ongoing which ranges from taking part in different groups, working in the kitchen as well as having individual and group conversations with people.

Staff in the centres can contact me at any time if they have concerns about a student. This has happened only rarely but seems to have been an important safeguard, particularly at the outset when the students were an "unknown" quantity. Staff can also ask a student to leave if necessary, although this has never happened.

Debriefing Sessions Discussing their Experiences

These sessions are held with the students at the end of each week in which they make visits and a final one with the psychiatrist after all visits have been completed. This is an opportunity for students to recount what has happened during their visits, the high and low points, their perceptions of the places and any particular difficulties they encountered. It is made clear to the students that these sessions are confidential and that nothing will be fed back to the organisations without permission. It is a good opportunity for them to learn from each other and to assist each other with any difficulties. The different experiences of two students in the same visit leads to a useful exploration of how they, through their behaviour, may have contributed to their different experiences. This frequently makes very clear the impact gender and dress can have on how people relate to them.

It seems important for the students to share how they felt, their anxieties, for example in walking into an unknown place. On the few occasions a student has had to go somewhere alone the difference is noted and students relate this to the comfort and psychological safety of being in pairs. They consider what it would be like to be recovering from an acute illness, especially for the first time, and to arrive at one of these places alone, not knowing anyone and not being very well. They understand immediately why so many choose to make their first visit with their community nurse or social worker.

These debriefing sessions also encourage the students to discuss the services offered in each organisation, how these are received by members and their views of them, as well as wider issues such as stigma and public education. These sessions then tie in with other teaching sessions.

Reading the Autobiographies of People with Mental Health Problems and Carers

Students are expected to read at least one published first person account from someone with a mental health problem or a carer. These also give the student insight into a range of views and experiences, impact on life, attitudes to treatment and also allow for some discussion of the historical context in which these are set.

Seminars and Tutorials

The students' experiences in the organisations are put in context to help them understand issues more fully. They include:

- background to services, community care and the role of voluntary organisations;
- family and carer issues;
- stigma and recent anti-stigma campaigns;
- media and mental illness;
- service development;
- recovery.

Personal Study on a Particular, Self Chosen Topic

Students pick a topic related to the module on which to carry out a literature search and write an essay. This contributes to the tutorial sessions.

MODULE ASSESSMENT

Assessment is in two parts:

(1) An essay (2,500–3000 words) on a topic of their choice related to the aims of the module SSM title (i.e. they would not be expected to write a very "medical" essay

about medication or similar). Although not formally assessed they present this as a short talk to the group in the last session.

(2) A short reflective piece on their experience of the SSM, with special emphasis on what their preconceptions (prejudices and stereotypes) about people with mental health problems were and how these have been challenged.

Why Students Chose the SSM

Unsurprisingly the main reason students choose the SSM is that they have an interest in mental health problems with a few declaring an interest in wanting to become psychiatrists. Some may also wish to become a GP and are aware of the need to have a good understanding of mental health problems. For others the interest is more general, and a criticism that they have not had anything about mental health in the course thus far. For some, their interest is more personal as they have family or friends who have a major mental illness. Some acknowledge this at the outset of the course, others later in the module. Their reticence to share such personal information stems from anxieties about how such information will be received. This in itself provides a topic for discussion by the students as they reflect on how people in medicine can be as stigmatising as everyone else.

There were a few who chose the SSM for reasons largely unconnected with mental health, such as wanting "patient contact", not wanting to do lab work or science and wanting an opportunity "to get out and about".

What Students Get Out of the Experience

This section focuses on the students' experience whilst on visits. All the students found the visits interesting, illuminating and informative in different ways and almost all said it was enjoyable. A number of themes are evident.

CHALLENGE TO THE STEREOTYPE: THE MOVE TO "NORMALITY"

As had been hoped the main thing the students got out of the visits was a challenge to their preconceptions and prejudices, even if they had not necessarily been aware of them in advance. This in itself was shocking to some students. Almost all were surprised by how much their views had changed over a short space of time.

> When I first met people who had mental health problems I was shocked by how well they were and how normal they appeared. I suppose I was also shocked by the full realisation of what my prejudices were and how totally inaccurate they had been.

Some of the students found it difficult to admit, at first, that their expectations were as negative as they had been. Fortunately most students were not reticent about this and their frank expression allowed most to express their views. There were one or two who did not seem able to engage with this and simply reiterated that it was all much as they expected.

An interesting difference in challenging preconceptions was for the few students who had an "heroic view" of people with a mental illness.

> I had always considered myself as unprejudiced and having a family history of psychiatric service use, I felt a sense of self-satisfaction at my own enlightened attitude... However... I found that I did indeed have many preconceived notions... [previously stated as positive] [which] were no less false.

> I thought by virtue of their suffering a mental illness all the people I was going to see would be inherently good, or at least pitiable. Of course, just as in any other group this was not the case. While many of the people I spoke to were likeable others were not. At first I felt guilty for having such opinions, but looking back I can see just how patronising my previous ideas of the mentally ill patient were.

The change in their attitude was so marked in some cases it caused the students to question what they had believed.

> In retrospect I am frankly ashamed of thinking this way and have begun to doubt whether I really did believe these things as on reflection they seem so absurd. However, on talking to fellow students I believe that they too had been lead to think as I had.

The most common word used to describe the people they met was "normal" (or sometimes "ordinary"), often leading to a discussion about what constituted normality.

> If all you have heard comes form the media you really do expect to see "mad people". Although several members were "mad" in the sense you would call your friend "mad.

Reflecting on a hospital visit that included time on an acute ward, one student commented:

> I learned that the majority of people, although acutely unwell, were friendly and capable of expressing valuable opinions.

The importance of the debriefing sessions in enabling the students to "confess" their former attitudes and to work through the change, including the emotional and psychological consequences was evident. The common words used were that they felt "guilty", "ashamed" or "embarrassed" by their former attitudes and seemed to welcome a non-judgmental place to explore this with others going through the same experience. For a few it challenged their view of themselves as medical students as they seemed to assume that this somehow meant they would automatically be less prejudiced or more aware than "the public".

Awareness of Impact of Mental Illness

Along with challenging their prejudices the other major thing students got out of the visits was an understanding of the enormity of the impact of having a major mental illness.

> I learned how different psychiatry is to other fields of medicine. There are very few others which can so fundamentally alter a person's perception of them and society's views of them.

It was here that being able to sit and talk to people in what amounted to a conversation rather than a clinical interview was so valued. Students spoke of being "moved", "humbled", "astonished", "amazed" or "upset" when people chose to share their life stories or aspects of this. Particularly affecting were conversations with people roughly their age and people who had been forced to drop out of education because of their illness. There was some surprise that a number of members had degrees and/or had professional jobs before becoming ill. One male student had a very intense conversation with another young man his age who described in detail his response to anti-psychotic medication, problems with side-effects and the impact of this on every aspect of his life, in a way which the student believed he "would remember for the rest of my life" and which made him understand "the reality of psychopharmacology in a way that no amount of reading or classes ever would".

The impact of medication was a particularly important area for students to understand and come to terms with, including, as it did, such a contrast to the medical model. Some students struggled to reconcile how medication which they had taken for granted as a positive thing and "prescribed with the best of intentions", could be so resented, unwelcome and have such a devastating effect on those it was supposed to "help". The heterogeneity and confusing aspects of the issue were highlighted when they also spoke to people who felt their medication was positive and of benefit.

The way having a major mental illness affected all aspects of life, lack of having something to do, especially valued and role-related, the impact of stigma and poverty, the impact on social life and personal relationships and increasing isolation made a lasting impression. It could also cause not a little consternation and sense of inadequacy and helplessness. The debriefing session with the psychiatrist seemed particularly important in addressing these feelings and placing them in a wider context of medicine and being medical students.

The visits

Students' previous beliefs led many of them to be "anxious" or "apprehensive" about meeting people with mental illness, which was expressed by some during the introductory session. Often this had to do with concerns about violence or aggression or witnessing "mad" behaviour. For others it was more focussed on simply talking to people who were "mad".

> I was somewhat apprehensive about meeting the patients. Having never met anyone with a severe mental illness I was not sure how to talk to them . . . was genuinely surprised how normal they seemed. I had assumed they would be difficult to speak to and that what they had to say would not be of great value. I soon learned that mental health problems are just one aspect . . . and they can and should be treated just like anyone else.

There were very few negative experiences. Some students complained that they spent time sitting around not doing much. When this was discussed with members their response was "that's because they don't come and talk to us". This might not always be true but emphasised the need for students to be proactive. One student was teased by some members and found this difficult but the other student on that visit did not have problems nor did others. The issue seemed to have to do with the individual student's confidence and social skills.

Sources of Previous Information

For most students the media had almost entirely informed their views. While most of them recognised that this was almost inevitable, a few questioned the fact that 18 months at medical school had done nothing to challenge this. A few also noted that if they, as medical students with an interest in mental health had not critically assessed media reporting, others with less interest could hardly be blamed for accepting this negative portrayal.

For some students, previous knowledge came from having an ill relative or friend. This could lead to some being surprised that despite being "OK" with this they still held negative stereotypes about others. This was a particularly useful insight leading to discussions about the formation and pervasiveness of stigma. Some have said that closeness to a topic reduces negative stereotyping previous, however, this is not necessarily the case in mental illness (Philo, 1996).

Views of Services and Psychiatry

Students were usually impressed by the services on offer in the voluntary sector and the differences between them, including the people they met at the services.

> ...experiencing three completely different aspects of mental health work, which I might not otherwise have become aware of...

The informality of the voluntary organisations and their different ethos, with an orientation to a more social model was often commented on, enabling a more holistic approach to be taken. That staff usually had more time to spend with members in the voluntary organisations than staff in the NHS was also noted frequently, as were the informality of the relationships.

> As I began to question the traditional medical model it became more and more apparent to me just how all pervading it is, in part I found the power relationships of professional and patient were present to some degree in all the settings.

A major challenge to the students, especially those with an interest in a career in psychiatry was the very negative views they encountered about psychiatric services, psychiatrists and GPs.

> I was unaware how unpopular psychiatrists were among users...I now believe this unpopularity stems from the fact that they prescribe medicines, make diagnoses, have the power to hospitalise and have little time to spend with their patients.

> Many of the (members) did not hesitate to warn us away from psychiatry, although one person did say that "someone had to get in there and change things".

A number of students believed this negativity against psychiatrists and statutory services was fostered within the voluntary organisations by both members and staff. This made it difficult for positive experiences to be expressed. Students were surprised to find that on occasion staff and members in one organisation expressed some (modest) "rivalry" towards others, both statutory and voluntary. In some cases students recognised this as perhaps an overzealous "selling" of their service but in others a it represented a lack of appreciation of what other services offered and the type of people who attend. Some of this also had to be set within a context of competition for funding and other scarce resources.

One or two students struggled to understand the purpose of the voluntary organisations' services. The function of the drop-in centre, where "people sit around smoking and talking" was particularly difficult for one student. This seemed to have to do with expectations that everyone could and should be encouraged to return to work, and that it was made too easy for people to opt out of trying to do this.

Challenging Stereotypes in Medicine

A number of students commented on fellow students' surprise at their choice of SSM and the very negative and prejudiced views students had about people with mental illness, including assumptions of violence. They were also aware of similar attitudes amongst some members of staff. They started to question how this could be challenged.

Other Generalisable Benefits

Although becoming more at ease in clinical settings, student often expressed the view that it had been beneficial learning to adapt and adjust to being located in different settings. Communication skills were seen as a special area of development: "it allowed me to develop communication skills which were different from those I have already experienced in medicine".

Although perhaps not strictly relevant to a medical degree there was evidence of other skills improving. The majority of students returned with improved pool playing skills thanks to intensive coaching at the Centre A. A number (notably male students) seemed particularly pleased that they had developed cooking skills at Centre B (and one was delighted he had been able to persuade them to put a new dish, that he could cook, on their menu).

VIEWS FROM THE SERVICES

Limited feedback between staff, a few members and myself takes place each year. The views recorded here were collected from a group discussion held at Centre A with 15–20 members and a meeting with a member of staff and a member at Centre B. The main view was overwhelmingly positive. Although, of course, members who were not happy might have absented themselves. The consensus was that if you did not want to have anything to do with students you did not have to, and even people who might be wary had got used to them. It was summed up as "its good for them and its good for us".

Members were keen to see the students at this early stage in their career, describing it as "seeing them while they are still quite fresh", others hoping they were "impressionable" and there was agreement that it was a good opportunity to "indoctrinate them". Although this was said amid laughter it was clearly a serious point and, indeed, many students had recounted that this had been said to them. It was seen as an opportunity to give students an "insight into everyday life", to see them "as people and not just symptoms", as "personalities", to focus on issues such as benefits rather than medication. Seeing them as individuals also meant that students would realise they would like some of them and not others, and that was fine. The Scottish Executive campaign slogan "See me, not a label" was quoted along with a focus on recovery and seeing people "in different stages of recovery".

Seeing students on the members' "own ground" was appreciated. One person commented that seeing students in hospital, often in a group could "feel like being in a zoo" but that was not the case at the Centre, where they could interact one-to-one. Also people could walk away if they wanted and were rarely asked by staff to talk to anyone so they had more control. It was described as the students "not being in your face" as was sometimes the case in hospital and "it's easier to talk about myself in this environment".

There was some concern expressed about the students' expectations of what people with mental illness were like when they arrived and that many were clearly anxious or apprehensive. Interestingly, some members developed a protective stance towards the students. Some were seen as "shy" and arriving "looking scared". A discussion developed about how much this was due to their negative stereotypes and how much due to them being young and faced with a new experience. Amid laughter one member reminded the others that students were all individuals too and others remembered their anxieties about attending for the first time. The discussion also enabled me to put this in the context of the stage the students were at in their studies. There was a view that the visits "worked both ways, we start seeing them as people too".

The only negative comments concerned the rare student who they perceived as "lazy" or "stand-offish" and not willing to make an effort to engage with them. This was contrasted with the "shy" student with whom many could empathise. There was also an only half-joking comment about students who were "too trendy" which seemed to set up barriers.

There was also interest in learning more about what the students have to do in training and welcome for the insights gained from students sharing this with them. Without irony one member recounted his negative stereotype of lazy, drunken students and how surprised he had been about how much work they had to do. It was particularly appreciated that one student had taken the time to write something about this for the members' Newsletter.

Staff were keen to explain more about the ethos of the organisation, the voluntary sector in general, to get the students to appreciate the social model of disability or an holistic approach and challenge the medical model. One was concerned that voluntary sector staff should be also seen as professionals in their own right.

A few members saw hosting the students in what was their place and talking to them enabled them to feel they were "making a real contribution to making the health service better". Acknowledging them as students one person said "we are planting the seed and watching to see if it bears fruit".

Asking the question if there was "anything which could be done to improve the visits" the only response, from members in both organisations was "they should come for longer".

CONCLUDING THOUGHTS

This approach is positive from both the students' and the service users' perspectives and gets the students thinking more widely about aspects of mental health problems and integrating this into the person's whole life experience. It is, however, fairly demanding on the projects in that staff have to spend some time with the students and have to be willing and able to act in a supervisory capacity. For a project not to be overwhelmed means that probably no more than two or three students can attend at any one time, and this limits the numbers that can benefit. We may need to think about how projects might be paid or otherwise recompensed for their time to enable such links to develop.

REFERENCES

Brockington, I. & Mumford, D. (2002). Recruitment into psychiatry. *British Journal of Psychiatry*, *180*, 307–312.

Lambert, T.W., Goldacre, M.J., Edwards, C. & Parkhouse, J. (1996). Career preferences of doctors who qualified in the United Kingdom in those doctors qualifying in 1974,1977, 1980 and 1983. *British Medical Journal*, *317*, 1429–1431.

Malhi, G.S., Parker, G.B., Parker K., Kirkby K.C., Boyce P., Yellowlees, P. , Hornabrook C. & Jones K. (2002). Shrinking away from psychiatry? A survey of Australian medical students' interest in psychiatry. *Australian and New Zealand Journal of Psychiatry*, *36*, 416–423.

Martin, VL., Bennett, D.S. & Pitale, M. (2005). Medical student's perceptions of child psychiatry: pre-and post- psychiatry clerkship. *Academic Psychiatry*, *29*, 362–367.

Philo, G. (1996). The media and public belief, in (ed.) Philo G. *Media and Mental Distress*. Harlow: Longman.

Sierles, F.S. & Taylor, M.A. (1995). Decline of U.S. medical student career choice of psychiatry and what to do about it, *American Journal of Psychiatry*, *152*, 1416–1426.

Storer, D. (2002). Recruiting and retaining psychiatrists, *British Journal of Psychiatry*. *180*, 296–297.

Weintraub, W., Plant, S.M. & Weintraub E. (1999). Recruitment into psychiatry: increasing the pool of applicants, *Canadian Journal of Psychiatry*, *44*, 473–427.

CHAPTER 8

Consumer Involvement: Collaborative Working in Post Basic Mental Health Education

Jayne Breeze and Julie Repper

This chapter describes the development of a new module that was planned, delivered, assessed and evaluated in partnership with mental health service users and carers and aimed at qualified mental health professionals. It is innovative in that it adhered to the principles of true partnership as advocated by models of participation (e.g. Goss and Miller, 1995; NCMH, 2003) and it included both service users and carers. Whilst policy recommendations include the involvement of both, there is a paucity of examples in the literature of this being applied in practice.

POLICY CONTEXT

The importance of involving consumers in all aspects of health care began to permeate government policy in the 1980's and was firmly ensconced in health policy by the 1990's. The Community Care Act (1990) clearly placed consumerism upon the health care agenda with "choice and independence" as its underlying principles. Subsequent health policy and legislation have confirmed this principle as an essential part of the modernisation agenda (see, for example, "The New NHS: Modern and Dependable" (Secretary of State for Health, 1997); "A First Class Service" (DOH, 1998); "Patient and Public Involvement in the New NHS" (DOH, 1999); "The Expert Patient" (DOH, 2001); and the different National Service Frameworks).

This has resulted in the development of structures for consumer involvement within services (for example: the development of Patient and Public Involvement Forums (PPIF's) in every NHS Trust to seek the views of patients receiving services (DOH, 1999)); in research (for example ethical committees are not merely concerned with protecting patients involved in research but require evidence that consumers have been involved in the development,

Teaching Mental Health. Edited by Theo Stickley and Thurstine Basset.
Copyright © 2007 John Wiley & Sons, Ltd.

implementation and dissemination of research projects (DOH, 1998)) and in education, where education institutions are required to involve service users and carers when designing and delivering training programmes (for example, "Tomorrow's Doctors" (GMC, 1993); "Changing the Culture: involving service users in social work education" (Beresford, 1994); and "Learning From Each Other" (ENB, 1996)).

This policy is reflected in practice development around the country (Le Var, 2002). The literature on user involvement (cf. Repper and Breeze, 2005) describes different ways in which service users have been involved in healthcare education and training including: service users as consultants (Mansfield et al., 1982; Rudman, 1996; Forrest et al., 2000; Greenfield et al., 2001); service users as teaching aids (Mayo-Smith et al., 1992; Stacy & Spencer, 1999; Coleman & Murray, 2002); service user involvement in the classroom (Curran, 1997; Turner et al., 2000; Costello & Horne, 2001); service users assessing students (Frisby 2001) and several papers describe barriers to involvement (e.g. Felton & Stickley, 2004). There is a paucity of examples of carer involvement in education, notable exceptions being Soliman & Butterworth, 1998 and Turner et al., 2000.

In response to policy requirements for healthcare education, educational institutions and workforce confederations have developed guidelines for involving service users and carers in education and training. The Northern Centre for Mental Health, funded by NIMHE (National Institute for Mental Health England), produced a tool to help workforce development confederations to audit user and carer involvement in higher education and inform the commissioning of post-qualification mental health education programmes (NCMH, 2003). An integral part of the tool is the adaptation of the "ladder of participation" offered by Goss and Miller (1995). This comprises five levels ranging from: "no involvement" at level one; through "passive involvement" (e.g. consultation with users via a third party); "token involvement" (e.g. consultation with users through non decision-making forums); "collaboration" (e.g. users' views form basis of decisions); to level five–"partnership" whereby "educationalists and users work together systematically, strategically, and with full support, reimbursement structures and with education and training opportunities available. Users are involved at all stages of the planning, delivery and management processes. Decisions are made jointly" (NCMH, 2003 p. 34).

On reviewing the literature, there appear to be no examples of level five (working in partnership) within healthcare professional education. In 2004 the Department of Mental Health and Learning Disability at the University of Sheffield included, for the first time, a module entitled "Working with Service Users and Significant Others" within its post basic provision. A principle aim of the module was to promote partnership with service users and carers and this partnership approach also underpinned the development and delivery of the module as outlined in level five of the adapted ladder of participation (NCMH, 2003). The module forms part of the "BMedSci Mental Health Practice" degree but it can be accessed by all post basic students.

PLANNING PROCESS

Having determined the basic aim of the module the authors approached the Hull based "Impact Research Team" (comprising four service users), and a carer's group within the Rotherham branch of Rethink. A series of meetings ensued in which the aims, objectives, content and underpinning values of the module were developed. From the onset, whilst the authors facilitated these meetings, the resulting materials were ultimately created and agreed upon by the users and carers. Although there are many common issues between service users and carers, there are also differences in views and priorities (Shepherd et al., 1994) giving potential for conflict. It was, therefore, thought prudent to keep separate days within the module for carer-led sessions and service user-led sessions. These planning and development sessions were likewise kept separate but both groups were kept informed of each other's progress and the management group for the ongoing organisation of the module comprises all parties.

The first step in developing the module was the agreement of a more developed aim for the module. This was discussed by both carers and service users and agreement was achieved without difficulty:

> Promote collaborative working between mental health professionals and service users and their significant others by attempting to break down barriers between "us" and "them" and challenging traditional ways of thinking and working. Whilst module content will include and acknowledge past and present difficulties, the main emphasis will be on examples of good practice to enable the student to develop strategies for working alongside service users and carers.

This aim provided the benchmark for the evaluation at the end of the module.

Whilst there may be situations in which service users and carers independently develop their own training for professionals, this was not the case in the present situation. Rather than a "user-led" module, this exercise exemplifies a partnership approach in which the initial idea and aim was developed by professionals for further amendment and development by users and carers. All parties supported and learned from each other and although discussions were rich and reflective, there was little disagreement.

Once the aim was agreed, service users and carers developed a set of values that would underpin and inform ongoing work. These values prompted reflection and discussion amongst staff, users and carers about relationships, language and the aims and content of the module. Agreement of such principles would appear to provide a sound platform for anyone proposing a similar exercise (see Box 8.1).

Box 8.1   Values Underpinning the Module

Learning from, and valuing, good practice rather than dwelling upon the negative aspects.

Working in partnership with everyone involved in delivering and receiving mental health services.

Valuing and learning from everyone's experience and perspectives: user, carer and professional.

Recognising the skills and strengths that everyone has, whether as consumer or professional.

Service users and carers should have the opportunity for meaningful (not tokenistic) involvement in all aspects of care delivery – from individual care pathways through to strategic planning of services.

> Meaningful involvement can be helped by mutual respect between mental health workers and consumers.
>
> Honest and open dialogue can aid the process of change.

As values were developed, so the list of topic areas that might usefully be covered grew. Both service users and carers had extensive ideas about content: aspects of practice that might illustrate involvement, facilitate partnerships and promote changes in services. Lists were gradually collapsed and refined to a list of complimentary session headings from which service user and carer trainers defined learning outcomes, determined the focus and content of the teaching sessions and selected methods of delivery. A key concern was the application of classroom learning in students' own practice areas, so a set of "homework tasks" was devised to help the students apply theory to practice and consider the barriers through reflection on their own responses and the more practical and structural issues encountered in their day to day work.

A major concern for service users and carers who participate in educating health professionals is remuneration. Appropriate and adequate payment is important as proper remuneration equates with value yet there are very few examples of this in the literature and it can be assumed that many service users and carers involved in the different aspects of nurse training have not been offered adequate payment or even not offered payment at all. The service users and carers here were paid a consultation payment in excess of the standard lecturer fee. The extra money was allocated to cover developmental costs and to show the department's commitment to service user and carer involvement. As the module evolves this will no longer be necessary or feasible but the department will continue its commitment to pay service users and carers the standard fee paid to all visiting lecturers in recognition of their expertise. This type of approach is advocated in guidelines for good practice when involving service users and carers in education (Tew et al., 2004).

A lack of, or limited, preparation prior to participating in education can result in service users feeling uncertain about their involvement, not understanding the purpose and feeling that they lack expertise (Spencer et al., 1999; Turner et al., 2000; Masters et al., 2002). Not surprisingly, therefore, preparation is considered to be an important part of the process (Curran, 1997). This can include structured training on teaching and assessing (Hanson and Mitchell, 2001). The service users and carers involved in this module were all experienced trainers and therefore did not require this level of preparation. In addition they had control over the learning content of the module from the outset as well as full participation in the proposed learning outcomes and teaching delivery and so were always in a position whereby they understood what was expected of them. The planning meetings with the accompanying lecturer support were considered by the service users and carers to be appropriate preparation.

The lecturer also participated fully throughout the planning process but mainly by making use of her experience and expertise in teaching and assessing rather than exerting undue influence upon the content of sessions. This was considered an important element of working in partnership. Lecturers may work with the best of intentions to redress the balance of power but this can be undermined by seemingly normal academic activity such as holding "lecturer-only" meetings and juxtaposing professional views alongside service users' in order to provide objectivity and balance. Unfortunately, these conventional academic approaches may do much to maintain the power imbalance and can damage the credibility of service users (Reynolds and Read, 1999).

MODULE DELIVERY

A variety of topics were delivered, for example: developing strategies for involvement at both micro and macro levels; community care; good practice in in-patient settings; assessment of needs; young carers; being sectioned; advanced directives; risk management; involvement in audits and research. However, some issues were considered to be so integral to working alongside service users and carers that they were used throughout the module to underpin each topic area. These were: support, communication, empowerment, and empathy. This reflects the common themes found in studies that asked service users what they want from health professionals (Mansfield et al., 1982; Fraser et al., 1996; Rudman 1996; Barnes et al., 2000; Crawford, 2003).

Various teaching methods were adopted. The service users' early sessions were tightly structured, being thoughtfully divided between mini "lectures" (aided by OHP acetates and handouts), led equally and in turn by each service user, and student participation by means of group exercises. A homework "task" was set each week, based upon these exercises and subsequent sessions would begin with feedback from these tasks. The sessions were littered throughout with illustrations and examples from the service users' experiences with involvement and monitoring of services.

In contrast, the carers' elected from the beginning to deliver their sessions by means of their individual case studies carefully constructed to meet the agreed learning outcomes. A different case study was focused upon each session, which would comprise two parts. Firstly the case study would be given to the students in written form from which they would elicit questions based upon a group discussion. In the second part the relevant carer would answer questions and would expand upon her "story" further, ensuring that all of the topic areas, decided by the carers' beforehand, had been covered by the end of the session. A final consolidation session, attended by all the carer trainers, was aimed at enabling the students decide how they were going to put what they'd learnt into practice.

The students also visited a project aimed at Asian women who had been diagnosed with, or were caring for someone with, a mental health problem. This enabled the students to appreciate the diversity of service user and carer perspectives.

While the lecturer was present throughout all the sessions, these were led by either the Impact user group or carer trainers. The lecturer's role was that of support for the session leaders and also to help the students to apply what they were learning to their own practice situation. Frisby (2001) argues that professional accountability during sessions involving service users remains with the lecturer and that it is sometimes necessary to challenge ideas in a supportive and constructive way. Failing to do so, he asserts, is to promote tokenist compliance. This was never considered necessary during the delivery of this module and the lecturer by agreement with the user and carer trainers, joined in students' discussions considering implications for practice alternatives to restrictive practice.

Although service users and carers took an active part in the development of assessment, they chose not to take on the role of tutor supporting assignment work so this became the lecturer's role. In order to comply with university regulations as well as ensuring meaningful service user and carer assessment of student learning, the assessment of the module was in two parts. The first was a learning portfolio that was based around the students' progress through the module and included reflections and completion of homework tasks. The service users and carers formatively assessed this at the end of the module. The second part of the assessment followed a more traditional essay format, which was summatively assessed by academic staff.

OUTCOME

The evaluation of the module also reflected a partnership approach. The students completed a standard evaluation form given to all School of Nursing students but in addition completed one designed by the service users. Both forms were supplemented by an informal verbal evaluation. A focus group with service user and carer trainers was facilitated at the end of the module to enable the service users and carers to comment on the process of planning and delivering the module.

The numerical scores of the standard evaluation form were very high indicating a high level of student satisfaction. They were very positive about the design and delivery of the module, "it's a breath of fresh air to be taught by service users and carers". They particularly liked the service users and carers retelling their own experiences. Whilst they certainly found it useful when the service users introduced established tools to aid strategies for involvement, and drew upon empirical evidence to support their advice, it was the individual "stories" that brought these to life. It is a very powerful learning tool to hear what it feels like to screw up courage and knock on the closed door of the ward office in the middle of a busy acute ward (only to hear unrelated laughter and assume its about you) or listen to a carer's story about her sheer desperation for the proper diagnosis and care of her loved one but who had to wait until he was so ill that he harmed himself irreparably, before finally receiving one.

The students appreciated that the sessions were led "by actual service users and carers" enabling them to get the user and carer perspective first hand'. This, it was felt, enhanced their understanding giving them "more awareness of carers' needs" and "seeing patients as people". This may seem surprising when they have the opportunity to hear similar accounts every day whilst working in the practice area. Hutchings (1999) and Forest and Masters (2004) also found this and argue that a shift in the balance of power takes place through the students recognising the expertise of the service users in a classroom setting where the roles are reversed from those in practice: students are the recipients of information and education whereas in practice they perceive themselves to be in the role of information giver.

The students appeared to find the experience uplifting, almost a "tonic for the troops": "getting back to how I used to be", "enabling me to find the old me", "I can be the nurse I set out to be". Service user accounts have suggested that whilst student nurses start out as caring they become "corrupted" by working in the mental health system once they have qualified (Forrest et al., 2000) and seem to lose these caring qualities as they progress through their careers (Rudman, 1996). Accessing the module had enabled the students to regain their positive attitude that, it was felt, had been restrained by the system. "This has been a wake up call–a reminder of what we should be doing".

However, whilst it was important that the students had derived some benefit from under-taking the module, its main aim was to "challenge traditional ways of thinking and working" and to "enable the student to develop strategies for working alongside service users and carers". The students' accounts suggest that changes had already taken place as a result of undertaking the module, which range from: changes in perception and attitude ("its opened my eyes", "now I'm *really* listening to service users", "more awareness of carers" needs and the giving of time and space', "more aware of carers and how they feel when their loved one is admitted"); through to attempts to change other workers' perceptions ("I'm inspired to tell anyone who will listen about user and carer issues", "it has lead to me questioning lots of things in practice", "I feel a sense of responsibility to reflect all this back to my practice area – share it with the team"); to the implementation of user and carer involvement strategies (I have ensured that carers are more involved in the assessment process and I am making users and carers aware of how they can be involved in wider issues', "As a result of one of my homework tasks I have found out there is an NSF standard six group in the area and I have now joined it", "I am now passing on information about Advanced Directives").

As a direct outcome of an exercise facilitated within one of the sessions, one student realised that an information leaflet believed to have been composed with the involvement of carers, was in reality tokenistic. As a result of this she prepared a replacement leaflet that was based upon true collaboration with a carer group. Another student, despite strong opposition from the consultant psychiatrist, set up a carers' group on an Intensive Care Unit. She said that undertaking the module had not only given her the understanding of why this was a useful initiative, but it also gave her the courage to overcome the opposition. She has since set up a further group.

However, not all the students felt empowered to apply theory to practice. One student felt she was thwarted by "the organisational constraints", whilst another felt disempowered "it makes it difficult to think that you can't make a difference". It has been suggested that clinical setting may have an influence over whether nurses engage in empowering practice. For example, whilst service users perceived nurses working in hospital wards to lose their caring qualities, due to being disempowered by poor working conditions, under-resourcing and medical model dominance, they felt that these human qualities were redeemed by nurses who moved to the community resulting in the service users feeling more positive about their contact with community nurses (Rudman, 1996). Nevertheless the students were also able to recognise that "I've learnt that it's the small things that matter", and, "one small stone in the pool can still give a rippling effect".

In keeping with the literature (see, for example, Curran, 1997; Turner et al., 2000; Costello & Horne, 2001) the focus group data suggests that the service users and carers felt positive about their involvement in the module "it felt exciting that we were being given the opportunity to, in our own way, make a difference within the service user involvement field, particularly in education. It was an exciting adventure, and we spent many happy hours, didn't we, sitting down and planning it?". The service users and carers felt that they were working in equal partnership with each other and with the lecturer. They had complete control over the content and method of delivery for their sessions and equal input into the design of the module. This they felt was essential if the aim of the module ("promote collaborative working between mental health professionals and service users and their significant others") was to be achieved, "one of the criticisms in the service user movement is 'whose agenda is it? Whose agenda are we dancing to? Which tune are we dancing to?' And I know we have said it before, it needs emphasising that not only did service users and carers plan it, they delivered it and they are going to evaluate it". However, they also emphasised that they they could only have been done within a framework that enabled preparation and ongoing support.

LEARNING POINTS

The involvement of service users and carers in the education and training of health professionals is gathering momentum, driven by the current policy context and directions for good practice. Whilst there is still a paucity of evidence within the literature, what little there is suggests that this is a positive development. The evaluation of the module "working with service users and significant others" concurred with this. The students, service users and the carers all appear to have found the experience uplifting and, in some cases, productive. However, whilst there is suggestion that some practice has changed as a result of undertaking the module, it is not known how long this will last nor whether this will have significant impact upon future practice. The literature is also lacking evidence in this area. More research is therefore required to examine impact upon practice in order to better guide Institutes of Higher Education on the most effective way to enable students to work alongside service users and carers.

In addition, the student evaluation indicated that not all students were equally placed to apply theory to practice. This suggests that education alone may be insufficient to bring about the desired change. The context of care may therefore require attention as well as adequate student support within the clinical area in order to "promote collaborative working between mental health professionals and service users and their significant others".

In keeping with the literature, preparation was considered to be important. There is some evidence that this can be in the form of structured courses (see, for example, Hanson & Mitchell, 2001) and learning a variety of teaching methods can be very helpful for service users and carers to underpin their delivery as well as building confidence in a classroom setting. However, lecturers should be cautious that this does not over emphasise the academic at the expense of the consumer's lived experience, their personal story. The students undertaking this module found this to be the most powerful method of facilitating the change in their attitude and practice. Whilst this is not to undermine the importance of theory and the evidence gained from the wider movement, this should compliment, not take the place of, shared experience.

It is worth noting, however, that the students found the structured exercises extremely useful for assessing their own practice and enabling them to individualise the suggestions for improvement arising from current models and frameworks within the literature. The actual implementation of strategies identified by the students was as a direct result of undertaking the group exercises and homework tasks.

Remuneration is an important issue for service users and carers. Even when they are paid the going lecturer rate, the method of payment can be problematic in that, due to bureaucracy, there is often a significant delay (up to two months) between delivering the session and receiving payment. Fortunately, the service users and carers in this module were in a position in which they were able to wait without hardship, but many service users do not have this luxury. They may be on low incomes, travel at their own expense and then have to wait an unacceptable lengthy time in order to be re-reimbursed. This is a challenge that departments need to overcome in order to successfully implement service user and carer involvement.

Finally, true partnership cannot be achieved without a shift in the balance of power. This will not be easy given the barriers created by rules, regulations and bureaucracy of academia. This is further compounded by views held by some lecturers as to the wisdom and practicalities of involving service users and carers in curriculum planning and delivery (Felton & Stickley, 2004). However, this small module has shown that it is possible and the experience gained is going to be used to inform a departmental strategy that will be applied to all courses.

This chapter represents the academic perspective. A collaborative view, representing service user, carer and academic perspectives, can be found in Breeze, J., Bryant, H., Bryant, L., Davidson, B., King, S., Morgan, A., Whittall, L. and Richardson, M. (2005) Working in Partnership in Nurse Education *Mental Health Nursing, 25*(3), 4–7.

REFERENCES

Barnes, D., Carpenter, J. & Bailey, D. (2000). Partnerships with service users in interprofessional education for community mental health: a case study. *Journal of Interprofessional Care 14*(2), 189–200.

Beresford, P. (1994). *Changing the Culture: Involving Service Users in Social Work Education.* London: CCETSW.

Coleman, K. & Murray, E. (2002). Patients' views and feelings on the community-based teaching of undergraduate medical students: a qualitative study. *Family Practice 19*(2), 183–188.

Costello, J. & Horne, M. (2001). Patients as teachers? An evaluative study of patients' involvement in classroom teaching. *Nurse Education in Practice 1*, 94–102.

Curran, T. (1997). Power, participation and post modernism: user and practitioner in mental health social work education. *Social Work Education, 16*(3), 21–36.

DOH (1997). *The New NHS: Modern, Dependable.* London: HMSO.

DOH (1998). *A First Class Service.* London: HMSO.

DOH (1999). *Patient and Public Involvement in the New NHS.* London: HMSO.

DOH (2001). *The Expert Patient.* London: HMSO.

ENB (1996). *Learning From Each Other.* London: English National Board.

Felton, A. & Stickley, T. (2004). Pedagogy, power and service user involvement. *Journal of Psychiatric and Mental Health Nursing, 11*, 89–98.

Forrest, S., Risk, I., Masters, H. & Brown, N. (2000). Mental health service user involvement in nurse education: exploring the issues. *Journal of Psychiatric and Mental Health Nursing, 7*, 51–57.

Forrest, S., Masters, H. & Milne, V. (2004). Evaluating the impact of training in psychosocial interventions: a stakeholder approach to evaluation–part 2. *Journal of Psychiatric and Mental Health Nursing, 11*, 202–212.

Frisby, R. (2001). User involvement in mental health branch education: client review presentations. *Nurse Education Today, 21*, 663–669.

General Medical Council (1993). *Tomorrow's Doctors: Recommendations on Undergraduate Medical Education.* London: GMC.

Goss, S. & Miller, C (1995). *From Margin to Mainstream: Developing User and Carer Centred Community Care.* York: Joseph Rowntree Foundation.

Greenfield, S.M., Anderson, P., Gill, PS., Loudon, R., Skelton, J., Ross, N. & Parle, J. (2001). Community voices: views on the training of future doctors in Birmingham, UK. *Patient Education and Counselling, 45*, 43–50.

Hanson, B. & Mitchell, D.P. (2001). Involving mental health service users in the classroom: a course of preparation. *Nurse Education in Practice, 1*, 120–126.

Hutchings, D. (1999). Partnership in education: an example of client and educator collaboration. *The Journal of Continuing Education, 30*(3), 128–131.

Le Var, RMH (2002). Patient involvement in education for enhanced quality of care. *International Nursing Review, 49*, 219–225.

Mansfield, E., Garrard, J., Hausman, W. & Howey, M.K. (1982). Comparison of psychiatric-mental health nursing education objectives: consumers, educators and practitioners. *Journal of Psychosocial Nursing and Mental Health Services, 20*(5), 29–36.

Masters, H., Forrest, S., Harley, A., Hunter, M., Brown, N. & Risk, I. (2002). Involving mental health service users and carers in curriculum development: moving beyond classroom involvement. *Journal of Psychiatric and Mental Health Nursing*, 9, 309–316.

Mayo-Smith, M., Gordon, V., Dugan, A. & Field, S. (1992). Patient participants in a physical diagnosis course: a study of motivations and experiences with a comparison to student and faculty perceptions. *Teaching and Learning in Medicine*, 4(4), 214–217.

NCMH (2003). *National Continuous Quality Improvement Tool for Mental Health Education.* Durham: NCMH.

Repper, J., & Breeze, J. (2005). *Review of the literature on user involvement in the education and training of health care workers* University of Sheffield. Available at www.shef.ac.uk/snm/research/user-involvement-in-training-health-professionals.html.

Reynolds, J. & Read, J. (1999). Opening minds: user involvement in the production of learning materials on mental health and distress. *Social Work Education*, 18, 417–431.

Rudman, M.J. (1996). User involvement in the nursing curriculum: seeking users' views. *Journal of Psychiatric and Mental Health Nursing*, 3, 195–200.

Shepherd, G., Murray, A. & Muijen, M. (1994). *Relative Values.* London: Sainsbury Centre for Mental Health.

Soliman, A. & Butterworth, M. (1998). Why carers need to educate professionals. *Journal of Dementia Care,* 6, 26–27.

Spencer, J., Blackmore, D., Heard, S., McCrorie, P., McHaffie, D., Scherpbier, A., Gupta, T., Singh, K. & Southgate, L. (2000). Patient-orientated learning: a review of the role of the patient in the education of medical students. *Medical Education*, 34, 851–857.

Stacy, R. & Spencer, J. (1999). Patients as teachers: a qualitative study of patients' views on their role in a community-based undergraduate project. *Medical Education*, 33, 688–694.

Tew, J., Gell, C. & Foster, S. (2004). *Learning from Experience: involving service users and carers in mental health education and training* York: Mental Health in Higher Education/NIMHE West Midlands/Trent WDC.

Turner, P., Sheldon, F., Coles, C., Mountford, B., Hillier, R., Radway, P. & Wee, B. (2000). Listening to and learning from the family carer's story: an innovative approach in interprofessional education. *Journal of Interprofessional Care*, 14(4), 387–395.

CHAPTER 9

The Ten Essential Shared Capabilities: Their Development and Application

Ian Baguley, Thurstine Basset and Peter Lindley

INTRODUCTION

In this chapter, we explore how the Ten Essential Shared Capabilities were developed and their initial application in practice as part of the training and education of mental health workers.

Early in the 21st Century we find ourselves in the position whereby it is widely acknowledged that education and training for mental health practice has not kept pace with contemporary service models or the changing needs of service users and carers. There continue to be serious concerns about the utility, relevance and effectiveness of much of our current education and training provision. Although it has long been recognised that there are distinct advantages in multidisciplinary and shared training, much of the coordination and delivery of programmes remains fragmented and uni-disciplinary. Differences between the professional roles of mental health practitioners are difficult to define and the role of nurses and social workers covers much of the same ground. In addition a number of new roles have been created and there are increasing numbers of mental health workers who do not belong to the established professions. Their training and education, whilst generally more modern in its approach, has grown in a very piecemeal way and presents as an interesting, lively but somewhat un-coordinated patchwork of vocational and academic qualifications.

THE TEN ESSENTIAL SHARED CAPABILITIES

The development of the Ten Essential Shared Capabilities (ESCs) was a joint Sainsbury Centre for Mental Health and National Institute for Mental Health England (NIMHE) project, as one of a number of projects to address these issues. Building on the work reported

Teaching Mental Health. Edited by Theo Stickley and Thurstine Basset.
Copyright © 2007 John Wiley & Sons, Ltd.

Box 9.1   The Ten Essential Capabilities for Mental Health Practice-Shared Capabilities for all Mental Health Workers

1. **Working in Partnership.** Developing and maintaining constructive working relationships with service users, carers, families, colleagues, lay people and wider community networks. Working positively with any tensions created by conflicts of interest or aspiration that may arise between the partners in care.
2. **Respecting Diversity.** Working in partnership with service users, carers, families and colleagues to provide care and interventions that not only make a positive difference but also do so in ways that respect and value diversity including age, race, culture, disability, gender, spirituality and sexuality.
3. **Practising Ethically.** Recognising the rights and aspirations of service users and their families, acknowledging power differentials and minimising them whenever possible. Providing treatment and care that is accountable to service users and carers within the boundaries prescribed by national (professional), legal and local codes of ethical practice.
4. **Challenging Inequality.** Addressing the causes and consequences of stigma, discrimination, social inequality and exclusion on service users, carers and mental health services. Creating, developing or maintaining valued social roles for people in the communities they come from.
5. **Promoting Recovery.** Working in partnership to provide care and treatment that enables service users and carers to tackle mental health problems with hope and optimism and to work towards a valued life-style within and beyond the limits of any mental health problem.
6. **Identifying People's Needs and Strengths.** Working in partnership to gather information to agree health and social care needs in the context of the preferred lifestyle and aspirations of service users their families, carers and friends.
7. **Providing Service User Centred Care.** Negotiating achievable and meaningful goals; primarily from the perspective of service users and their families. Influencing and seeking the means to achieve these goals and clarifying the responsibilities of the people who will provide any help that is needed, including systematically evaluating outcomes and achievements.
8. **Making a Difference.** Facilitating access to and delivering the best quality, evidence-based, values-based health and social care interventions to meet the needs and aspirations of service users and their families and carers.
9. **Promoting Safety and Positive Risk Taking.** Empowering the person to decide the level of risk they are prepared to take with their health and safety. This includes working with the tension between promoting safety and positive risk taking, including assessing and dealing with possible risks for service users, carers, family members, and the wider public.
10. **Personal Development and Learning.** Keeping up-to-date with changes in practice and participating in life-long learning, personal and professional development for one's self and colleagues through supervision, appraisal and reflective practice.

in Pulling Together (Sainsbury Centre for Mental Health, 1997) and further developed in the Capable Practitioner Framework (Sainsbury Centre for Mental Health, 2001), the ESCs lay out the capabilities that all staff working in mental health services are expected to achieve during their basic training. In addition, the ESCs explicitly describe the core elements in the curricula of pre and post qualification training for all mental health workers. They have considerable potential to promote education and training that is responsive to the needs of service users and carers and also to produce practitioners with the capabilities required by modern mental health services.

BACKGROUND AND DEVELOPMENT

Mental health care is experiencing a period of change which has enormous implications for the education and training of all mental health workers including those that have become known as "non-professionally affiliated". Mental health currently represents one of the top clinical priorities in the NHS and major reforms have been unveiled to modernise health and social care (Department of Health, 1998a; Department of Health, 2000). A fundamental programme of reform has been outlined in the form of Modernising Mental Health Services (Department of Health, 1998b) and the National Service Framework for mental health (Department of Health, 1999a), which sets standards for mental health care across both health and social care.

The past few decades have also witnessed a shift in the provision of mental health services from the large institutional hospital setting to a range of diverse services in the community, with an increasing emphasis on service-user-centred care, values-based practice and evidence-based practice. Much of mental health provision is moving into partnership trusts and joint health and social care services are being established. In addition a number of mental health trusts have applied for Foundation status and will become masters of their own destiny and subject to less national pressures. A thriving and innovative voluntary and independent sector has also achieved an enhanced role in relation to the provision of services.

The importance of modernising education and training to ensure that the workforce is capable of delivering the new mental health agenda is critical to the process of reform. The "Pulling Together" report highlighted the need to ensure that the skills, knowledge and attitudes of both existing and future mental health staff are appropriate to the demands of this changed environment, and that they are prepared to function in continually evolving services (Sainsbury Centre for Mental Health, 1997).

Research also indicates that many existing and newly qualified staff are currently in-adequately prepared for present day services, with particular shortfalls being identified in training for working with the severely mentally ill (Holmshaw et al., 1999), for roles in primary care (Department of Health, 2001a), and for acute care (Department of Health, 1999b). Current courses are often inappropriate and not relevant to support the implementation of the National Service Framework (Brooker et al., 2002; Department of Health, 2001b).

In addition, there are a raft of new workers whose roles are directed by the needs of service users who have previously been poorly served; Community Development Workers for the Black and Minority Ethnic Community (Department of Health, 2002d), Graduate Workers for Primary Care Mental Health (Department of Health, 2003a) Support, Time and Recovery (STR) Workers (Department of Health, 2003b).

To support new workers and new ways of working, a large number of guidance documents have been published addressing the roles and education needs of the existing workforce in relation to:

- Breaking the Cycle of Rejection: the personality disorder capabilities framework (NIMHE, 2003c).
- Women's Mental Health (Department of Health, 2002f and 2003d).
- Modernising Mental Health Services for People who are Deaf (Department of Health, 2001c).
- Developing Positive Practice to Support the Safe and Therapeutic Management of Aggression and Violence (Department of Health 2002e).
- Acute Inpatient Mental Health Care (Department of Health, 2002a, Clarke, 2004).
- Dual Diagnosis (Department of Health, 2002b).
- Community Mental Health Teams (Department of Health, 2002c).

Also, concerns have been expressed about the competency of the current mental health lecturer workforce to deliver these radical new approaches, and a need identified for them to update their own skills and knowledge in line with the competencies expected of the workforce (Ferguson, Owen & Baguley, 2003; Sainsbury Centre for Mental Health, 1997). Many practitioners consider that academics lack robust recent clinical experience, are not regarded as clinically credible, have little experience in the skills and interventions they are required to teach, and have training needs of their own (Brooker et al., 2002, Department of Health, 1999b, 2001a).

The current ambitious changes to modernise health and social care services have necessitated a far-reaching rethink regarding the education and training of the future workforce. Recent reviews (c.f. Department of Health, 1999b, 2001a, Gourney, 1998, Holmshaw et al., 1999, Sainsbury Centre for Mental Health, 1997) and mapping exercises (c.f. Brooker et al., 2002, Department of Health, 2001b) have highlighted the gaps in educational provision for the mental health workforce. They have also questioned the ability of Higher Education Institutions to prepare practitioners with the capabilities required to implement the National Service Framework for mental health.

Box 9.2   A treasury of resources to inform every aspect of education and training for mental health practice

- The Ten Essential Shared Capabilities – fundamental building blocks of training – the minimum requirements for everybody working in mental health services
- The Capable Practitioner Framework – capabilities required to implement the National Service Framework
- The National Occupational Standards for Mental Health – detailed competencies to support the Knowledge and Skills Framework
- The Knowledge and Skills Framework – generic and not mental health specific – designed to assist pay progression in the NHS

With such a plethora of guidance and policy initiatives being introduced within a culture of rapid change, it is little wonder that the values that should drive service activity, those of service user centred care, often get lost. The development of the Ten ESCs is an attempt to put these service user centred values back at the heart of mental health activities. The ESC were developed through consultation with service users, carers, managers and practitioners. They are explicitly and deliberately centred upon the needs of service users and carers, emphasising the essential capabilities required to provide the kind of care that they deserve and that everyone working in mental health services aspires to deliver.

The ESC are designed to be complementary to the Capable Practitioner Framework, the National Occupational Standards and the Knowledge and Skills Framework, and together with them provide a set of powerful resources for every aspect of training programme design, delivery and evaluation.

DEVELOPMENT OF LEARNING MATERIALS

In 2005, NIMHE collaborated with the NHS University and the Sainsbury Centre for Mental Health to produce learning materials. (Basset, Lindley & Barton, 2005). These materials are aimed at all staff, but particularly those who are open to new ways of thinking about service provision and support, including both people who are new to mental health work and those with more experience.

In these materials the immediate challenge was to describe the ESCs and how they broadly relate to mental health work. The materials are available on CD ROM and as hard copy. They are designed so that they can be used flexibly on an individual basis or as a group learning experience. However, the group approach is recommended. The materials illustrate each ESC through current practice, research findings and reflective activities. A summary with some example material will give a feel for how this was achieved in the module that introduced the ESCs.

Working in Partnership (ESC 1)

> This capability concerns the engagement of all those involved in receiving or providing mental health care in maintaining harmonious working relationships and bringing them to an appropriate closure. Importantly this includes multidisciplinary teamwork, cross boundary work and work with wider community networks.
>
> The focus with service users and their families and carers is on the development of partnership working. It is essential that the people who use our services are viewed as partners in care rather than passive recipients of services. In order to achieve this aim, practitioners will often be required to be assertive in their engagement with and follow up of service users, particularly those with more complex problems.

(Department of Health, 2004)

Learners are first asked to consider whether service users are seen as active partners in care or passive recipients of care in the organisation in which they work.

In order to work in partnership with carers, learners need to acknowledge the positive part that families, friends and carers can play in the service user's support network and be able to engage them as partners in care in a way in which both carers and service users are comfortable. Learners are asked to reflect on what carers are saying: "Carers want to be involved, want to be valued and want to secure the best care as early as possible for the person they care for" (Rethink, 2003).

Respecting Diversity (ESC 2)

> If partnership working is to be a reality then education and training programmes will need
> to provide a learning environment, where existing beliefs about age, race, culture, disability,
> gender, spirituality and sexuality can be examined and challenged. Any therapeutic interven-
> tions need to be set within a framework that acknowledges and respects diversity. Although
> all of the areas within this capability are important, it has been acknowledged that there is
> discrimination in many services, and issues of race and culture require particular attention.

(Department of Health, 2004)

To begin to explore this capability further, learners need to understand and acknowledge
diversity relating to age, gender, race, culture, disability, spirituality and sexuality.

It is widely acknowledged that Black people have had particularly poor response from
mental health services in the past.

Box 9.3   Black people and the mental health system

A summary of research highlights:

- An over-representation of Black people in the psychiatric system
- Increased likelihood of Black people coming into the system through a compulsory
  route
- Lack of preventative and after-care mental health services which are appropriate
  for Black and ethnic minority communities
- Over-use of drugs and physical treatments with Black service users rather than
  talking therapies
- Increased diagnosis of psychosis for Black people, particularly schizophrenia
- Increased likelihood of being racially stereotyped by professionals in decisions
  about "dangerousness"

Source: Ferns, P. (2005). Finding a Way Forward: A Black Perspective on Social
Approaches to Mental Health. In J. Tew (ed), *Social Perspectives in Mental Health*.
London: Jessica Kingsley.

Learners are asked to explore what is happening in their local services to ensure that Black
and other minority ethnic people get a better deal in the future. Understanding the impact
of discrimination and prejudice on mental health and mental health services is also an
important part of this ESC. Learners are asked to learn from examples of discrimination
experienced by a service user and to identify what was done or could have been done better
to address the situation.

Practising ethically (ESC 3)

> There is a concern that many mental health professionals understand neither the legal
> rights of service users under their care nor their own legal and professional obligations
> to service users. This capability concerns adherence to professional codes of practice that
> address issues such as informed consent, effective communication, safety, de-escalation of
> aggression and control and restraint.

(Department of Health, 2004)

To begin to explore this capability further and in order to practise ethically learners need to demonstrate the ability to respond to the needs of the people they serve in an ethical, honest, non-judgemental manner. Learners are asked to give an example of how they have done this in their recent work. In addition, they also develop guidelines for their own practice to ensure their approach is ethical, honest and non-judgemental. They are asked to discuss these with a colleague or their supervisor.

It is important to know about policies, practices and procedures concerning the local implementation of mental health and related legislation. Learners rate themselves on awareness and are given a task to find out more in areas where their knowledge is lacking.

Challenging Inequality (ESC 4)

It is particularly important to understand the nature and consequences of stigma and discrimination. Social inequality and exclusion have a potentially devastating effect on the recovery process and will make it difficult for service users to achieve their potential or take their rightful place in society.

(Department of Health, 2004)

To begin to explore this capability further and to be able to challenge inequality, it is crucial to understand the effects of exclusion and discrimination.

The Social Exclusion Unit, in their report "Mental Health and Social Exclusion" (2004) present the problem as:

1. Adults with long-term mental health problems are one of the most excluded groups in society. Fewer than 25 % of adults with long-term mental health problems are employed.
2. Mental health problems cost the country over $ 77 billion a year.
3. Social isolation is an important risk factor for deteriorating mental health and suicide.
4. Severe mental health problems affect one in 200 adults a year.
5. More common mental health problems affect one in six people, with the highest rates in deprived neighbourhoods. GPs spend a third of their time on mental health issues. Costs for anti-depressants have risen and there are variations in access to talking therapies.
6. Over 900,000 adults in England claim sickness and disability benefits for mental health conditions.
7. Mental health problems can have a strong impact on families – both financially and emotionally.
8. Creating sustainable, inclusive communities is about everyone having a stake. Being in work and having social contacts is strongly associated with improved health and well-being. People with mental health problems have much to offer. If they can fulfil their potential, the impact of mental health problems can be significantly reduced.

To be able to challenge inequality, learners also need to understand the role that services have to play in fighting inequality and discrimination.

"Women's Mental Health: Into the Mainstream" (Department of Health, 2002) This report looked at the current state of mental health care for women. Some key messages were:

• Most mental health care for women is provided in mixed-sex environments.
• There is significant variation across the country in the provision of women-only sessions/services.

- There has been serious criticism of mixed-sex in-patient care in relation to women's safety from violence and abuse.
- Women who have used women-only services speak highly of them.
- Women express an overwhelming sense of "not being listened to".

The report also gave guidance on developing gender sensitive services. Some key messages are:

- Gender is a key issue that influences an individual's experience of the world and therefore gender issues should be incorporated into research, service planning, delivery and evaluation.
- To turn these aspirations into action, organisational and individual values and behaviours need to be addressed and challenged.
- It is also important to continue to recognise the uniqueness of the individual.
- To ensure that service planning and delivery are sensitive to gender, there is a need to provide single-sex services in some instances.
- Involving and listening to women should be fundamental to all service planning, delivery and evaluation.
- Leadership in organisations should make a clear commitment to address gender issues.
- An aware and informed workforce is essential.
- The importance of the voluntary sector in provision of mental health care for women should be reflected in robust commissioning arrangements that ensure the financial sustainability of voluntary sector services.
- Access to women staff, women-only interventions and an acknowledgement of women's caring responsibilities, need to be addressed in all settings providing mental health care.
- Individual assessment and care plans should address gender difference and include the following: experience of violence and abuse, caring responsibilities, social and economic situation, physical health care, ethnicity and culture, dual diagnosis with substance misuse, risk assessment and management.

Learners are asked how local mental health services set about providing gender sensitive services including any future plans for improving what is offered. This can be done through contacting someone in their service that takes the lead in improving mental health services for women.

It is one thing to know about inequality but another thing altogether to be able to challenge inequality. Learners are also asked to reflect on a situation where they have been able to challenge inequality and discrimination within their role. They then consider what key strengths they drew on to act in this way.

Promoting Recovery (ESC 5)

> Promoting recovery is the capability that defines the process that service users and providers engage in to enable self-empowerment and self-determination. Recovery is about recovering what was lost: rights, roles, responsibilities, decision making capacity, potential and mental well-being. Recovery is what people experience themselves as they become empowered to achieve a meaningful life and a positive sense of belonging in the community.

(Department of Health, 2004)

To begin to explore this capability further and to be able to promote recovery, learners need to:

- Understand that recovery is a process that is unique to each person.
- Understand the essential role of hope in the recovery process.
- Accept that recovery is not about the elimination of symptoms or the notion of cure.
- Understand that the key element to the recovery process is that the service user is both the driver and co-ordinator of services.

Learners are asked to give their immediate reactions to the quotation below:

> In the mental health services we are used to thinking about people's experience in terms of the supports and interventions that mental health workers provide. We think in terms of in-patient facilities, outreach services, medication, occupational therapy, art therapy, and "psychosocial interventions". We think of symptom reduction and discharge as indices of success. This is the wrong place to start. Everyone who experiences mental health problems faces the challenge of recovery, i.e. rebuilding a meaningful and valued life. Whether a person's problems are time-limited or ongoing, whether or not their symptoms can be eliminated, they face the task of living with, and growing beyond, what has happened to them. The help offered by mental health workers needs to be considered in terms of the extent to which they facilitate, or hinder, this process of recovery.

(Repper and Perkins, 2003)

They are also asked to write their own definition for "recovery" and to consider a service user with whom they are currently working. They can then make a list of things they might do to work with this person in a recovery-oriented way.

Identifying People's Needs and Strengths (ESC 6)

> The focus of this capability is on helping the service user and those involved with them to describe their experiences in such a way as to identify their strengths and formulate their needs. In order for this to be meaningful this must take a whole systems approach and take account of every aspect of the person's life.

(Department of Health, 2004)

To begin to explore this capability further learners need to be able to:

- Carry out (or contribute to) a systematic, whole systems assessment that has, as its focus, the strengths and needs of the service user and those family and friends who support them.
- Work in a way that acknowledges the personal, social, cultural and spiritual strengths and needs of the individual.
- Work in partnership with the individual's support network to collect information to assist understanding of the person and their strengths and needs.

This capability should be at the heart of the Care Programme Approach. Learners are firstly asked to identify their own strengths and talents and list the ones that they are most proud of.

Following from this, they think of a person who uses the mental health services with whom they are associated and write a short positive description of them. They then list this person's needs in a descriptive and positive rather than prescriptive way including their strengths – considering all the person's abilities, interests and talents.

Providing Service User Centred Care (ESC 7)

> This capability is concerned with helping the service user to set goals that are realistic, achievable and meaningful, so that the service user and others involved in the persons care will be able to recognise when a particular goal has been achieved.

(Dept of Health, 2004)

To be capable in this respect learners need to be able to:

- Work alongside the service user to help them to describe their goals as precisely as possible in a way that is meaningful to them.
- Help the service user to identify and use their strengths to achieve their goals and aspirations.
- Identify the strengths and resources within the person's wider network which have a role to play in helping them achieve their goals.

Once again starting from a personal approach, learners are asked to think about and record anything or anybody that they have found helpful at times in their own lives when they have been distressed. What or who helps them deal with the emotional stresses of life and promotes their mental wellbeing?

The "Strategies for Living" team at the Mental Health Foundation asked a similar question to service users to find out people's strategies for living with mental distress (Faulkner & Layzell, 2000). Learners compare their list with the table below that gives an overall picture of the different strategies and supports that people found to be the "most helpful" to them.

Box 9.4   "Most helpful" Strategies and Supports

Relationships with others
- Friends, partners, family
- Other service users/people with similar problems
- Mental health professionals
- Counsellors/therapists
- People encountered in day centres, drop-ins, voluntary sector projects

Personal strategies
- Peace of mind
- Thinking positively, taking control

Medication
Physical exercise
Religious and spiritual beliefs
Money

Other activities
- Hobbies and interests
- Information
- Home
- Creative expression

Source: Faulkner, A. & Layzell, S. (2000). *Strategies for Living*. London: Mental Health Foundation.

Making a difference (ESC 8)

This capability is concerned with ensuring that people have access to interventions and services that have proven efficacy in addressing specific needs. It is essential that people are able to utilise services that value them and those that support them and that will help to make a positive difference.

(Department of Health, 2004)

To develop this capability further and in order to make a difference, learners need to be able to understand the concepts of evidence-based and values–based "best practice" as enshrined in NICE guidance and Psychosocial Interventions training, etc.

NICE (the National Institute for Clinical Excellence) is commissioned by the Department of Health to provide clinical guidance to support the National Service Framework for Mental Health. NICE has produced two types of guidance relevant to mental health services: technology appraisals and clinical guidelines.

Technology Appraisals consider the evidence that a particular treatment is effective or cost-effective for a specific condition.

Clinical Guidelines consider all treatments and services that could be used for a condition or group of conditions.

Learners are asked to read one of the NICE clinical guidelines and then consider how this might effect their work.

Also looking briefly at outcomes for people with severe mental illness, learners reflect on the "clinician's illusion" (British Psychological Society, 2000):

"The course and outcome of psychotic experiences are highly unpredictable. Some people recover completely after only one episode, some people suffer from multiple episodes separated by periods of complete or partial recovery, and some remain continuously affected. Long-term follow-up studies indicate that as many as a third of all people who have psychotic experiences completely recover, and that less than a quarter remain permanently affected. Most people might reasonably hope to recover either completely or partially after a psychotic episode. Many mental health workers, who by definition only come into contact with people who continue to need their help (or for those who need help only occasionally, at times when they need it) fall into the trap known as the "clinician's illusion". They assume that recovery is rare and that most service users are likely to be dependent on services for the rest of their lives. Likewise, although there are thousands of former service users who either no longer have psychotic experiences, or have found effective ways to cope with them and no longer need help from services, current service users rarely have the opportunity to meet them. Because of this both staff and service users are in danger of developing over-pessimistic views about the future." In considering the "clinician's illusion", learners reflect briefly on how much contact they have with people who have completely recovered after a psychotic episode. If they have very little contact, they think of somebody they could talk with who does have contact and can help them improve their knowledge of the person's experience of recovery.

Promoting safety and positive risk taking (ESC 9)

This capability focuses on the issues of risk to the individual and society and how this can best be addressed in a manner that values all those concerned.

(Department of Health, 2004)

Promoting safety and positive risk taking lies at the heart of all mental health work. Services will have risk assessment and risk management strategies, which will link closely to their policy and practice in relation to the Care Programme Approach. Getting the risk/safety balance right is central to this work.

Risk should be considered broadly. Categories of harmful risk for service users may involve:

- A risk of harm to self.
- A risk to harm to others.
- A risk of being harmed by services/treatments.
- A risk of being harmed by others (through exploitation/discrimination).

There is often a tension between promoting safety and positive risk taking. It is through taking positive risks that people develop and grow.

Learners focus on safety and risk in relation to service users with whom it is hard for services to engage. In doing this, the materials do not suggest that these are the only service users to whom this capability applies.

To begin to explore this capability further and in order to practice in a way, which promotes safety and positive risk taking, learners should be able to:

- Demonstrate the ability to develop harmonious working relationships with service users and carers particularly with people who may wish not to engage with mental health services.

The Sainsbury Centre for Mental Health published "Keys to Engagement – review of care for people with severe mental illness who are hard to engage with services" in 1998. They looked at the personal characteristics of staff who are most successful in working with service users who are hard to engage.

The characteristics were:

- Ability to use a needs-led approach and allow the service user's priorities to set the agenda.
- Ability to use the right style for the service users – it may help if they come from a similar ethnic group or have had experience of using mental health services.
- Ability to show "low expressed emotion" in their work – being broadly positive in their outlook and not overly critical when things go wrong.
- Ability to have realistic expectations about the scope for improvement and be committed to long-term therapeutic relationships.

These "hard to engage" service users are often the ones that are felt to pose the greatest risk either to themselves or to others. The aim of modern mental health services is to reach out to them through "Assertive Outreach Teams". Learners are asked to find out more about their local Assertive Outreach Team and also explore the risk assessment and management policy across their local services.

Personal development and learning (ESC 10)

This capability focuses on the need for the practitioner to take an active role in their own personal and professional development. In the same way that service users should be viewed as active partners in their care, not passive recipients, practitioners should be active participants in their own development.

(Department of Health, 2004)

This capability is clearly inherent in the learning materials. Learners are encouraged to explore this capability further and promote their personal development and learning through:

- Access to education and training based on the best available evidence.
- A personal/professional development plan that takes account of your hopes and aspirations and that is reviewed annually.
- Understanding the responsibilities of the service in supporting you in meeting the goals set in the development plan.
- Understanding your personal responsibility to achieve the goals set in your development plan.
- The ability to set personal/professional goals that are realistic and achievable.
- Recognising the importance of supervision and reflective practice and integrate both into everyday practice.
- Being proactive in seeking opportunities for personal supervision, personal development and learning.

These have all been extracts for module 2 of the learning materials. This module introduces the ESCs. Other modules look at them in relation to service user and carer involvement, values-based practice, race equality and cultural capability, and social inclusion.

EVALUATION OF THE LEARNING MATERIALS AND FUTURE DIRECTIONS

The materials were piloted across a wide variety of sites in 2005 and subject to an evaluative process that resulted in a report (Brabban & Brooker, 2006).

The main points from the evaluation report were:

- Overall the evaluation was highly positive.
- Learners and facilitators/mentors rated nearly all aspects of the programme highly, including the clarity of the materials, the style of delivery, the extent to which the programme met their learning objectives, the level of the materials, the learning and organisational support and their enjoyment in participating.
- Individual modules were successful in meeting their aims.

Recommendations from the report included:

Delivery of the 10 ESC Training Programme

- Very careful consideration should be given to any mode of delivery (either CD ROM or workbook-based) whereby learners undertake the programme alone without access to a mentor.

- Service users and carers have a greater contribution to make to the programme as facilitators rather than as participants. This should be made clear.
- A number of learners who used the materials suggested that it would be helpful to have module five (race equality and cultural capability) facilitated by someone from a minority group background.
- The value of the programme, as designed, is debatable for those, such as administrative staff, who are not in direct face-to-face contact with service users.
- It would be beneficial to add further notes and teaching aids for training facilitators.

The Length and Content of the Programme

- The programme clearly takes longer to complete than was originally signposted. Estimates of the time needed to carry out the programme need to be revised significantly.
- The examples within the programme could be re-examined as they emphasise work with service users in adult secondary services. Other examples that might be included are: primary care, older people and children and adolescents.
- There is a need to address some of the more technical wording of the programme (such as "low expressed emotion").

Armed with this useful evaluative feedback, gleaned from a total of 579 returned questionnaires from learners and 75 from facilitators, NIMHE will refine the materials so that they can be used across all mental health services as part of a wide-ranging agenda to imbed the Ten Essential Shared Capabilities as the cornerstone for mental health work in the 21st Century.

REFERENCES

Basset, T., Lindley, P. & Barton, R. (eds) (2005). *The Ten Essential Shared Capabilities – learning pack for mental health practice*. London: NHSU, NIMHE, Sainsbury Centre for Mental Health.

Brabban, A. & Brooker, C. (2006). The Ten Essential Shared Capabilities – An evaluation of the pilot materials. Sheffield: Sheffield University

British Psychological Society (2000). Understanding Mental Illness – recent advances in understanding mental illness and psychotic experiences. Leicester: British Psychological Society.

Brooker, C., Gournay, K., O'Halloran, P., & Saul, C. (2002). Mapping training to support the implementation of the National Service Framework for Mental Health, *Journal of Mental Health, 11*(1), 103–116.

Clarke, S. (2004). *Acute Inpatient Mental Health Care: Education, Training and Continuing Professional Development for All*. Leeds: NIMHE.

Department of Health (1998a). *Modernising Social Services: Promoting Independence, Improving Protection, Raising Standards*. London: Stationary Office.

Department of Health (1998b). *Modernising Mental Health Services: Safe, Sound & Supportive*. London: Department of Health.

Department of Health (1999a). *National Service Framework for Mental Health: Modern Standards and Service Models*. London: Department of Health.

Department of Health (1999b). *Report by the Standing Nursing & Midwifery Advisory Committee (SNMAC). Mental Health Nursing: Addressing Acute Concerns*. London: Department of Health.

Department of Health (2000). *The NHS Plan*. London: Department of Health.

Department of Health (2001a). *Primary Care Key Group Report, in/Final Report by the Workforce Action Team – Mental Health National Service Framework, Workforce Planning, Education and Training*. London: Department of Health.

Department of Health (2001b). *Workforce Action Team – Key Area H: Mapping of Education and Training*. London: Department of Health.

Department of Health (2001c). *A Sign of the Times: Modernising Mental Health Services for People who are Deaf*. London: Department of Health.

Department of Health (2002a). *Mental Health Policy Implementation Guide: Adult Acute Inpatient Care Provision*. London: Department of Health.

Department of Health (2002b). *Mental Health Policy Implementation Guide: Dual Diagnosis Good Practice Guide*. London: Department of Health.

Department of Health (2002c). *Mental Health Policy Implementation Guide: Community Mental Health Teams*. London: Department of Health.

Department of Health (2002d). *Mental Health Policy Implementation Guide: Community Development Workers for Black and Minority Ethnic Communities Interim Guidance*. London: Department of Health.

Department of Health (2002e). *Mental Health Policy Implementation Guide: Developing Positive Practice to Support the Safe and Therapeutic Management of Aggression and Violence in Mental Health Inpatient Settings*. London: Department of Health.

Department of Health (2002f). *Women's Mental Health: Into the Mainstream – strategic development of mental health care for women*. London: Department of Health.

Department of Health (2003a). *Fast-Forwarding Primary Care Mental Health: Graduate Primary Care Mental Health Workers Best Practice Guide*. London: Department of Health.

Department of Health (2003b). *Mental Health Policy Implementation Guide: Support, Time and Recovery (STR) Workers*. London: Department of Health.

Department of Health (2003c). *Breaking the Cycle of Rejection: The Personality Disorder Capabilities Framework*. Leeds: NIMHE.

Department of Health (2003d). *Mainstreaming Gender and Women's Mental Health*. London: Department of Health.

Department of Health (2004). The Ten Essential Shared Capabilities – A Framework for the Whole of the Mental Health Workforce. London: Department of Health/NHSU/Sainsbury Centre/NIMHE).

Faulkner, A. & Layzell, S. (2000). *Strategies for Living*. London: Mental Health Foundation.

Ferguson, K., Owen, S. & Baguley, I. (2003). *The Clinical Activity of Mental Health Lecturers in Higher Education Institutions. Report prepared for the Mental Health Care Group Workforce Team*, Trent Workforce Development Confederation.

Ferns, P. (2005). Finding a Way Forward; A Black Perspective on Social approaches to Mental Health. In J. Tew (ed), *Social Perspectives in Mental Health*. London: Jessica Kingsley.

Gournay, K. (1998). Training the Workforce. In Brooker, C. & Repper, J. (eds), *Serious Mental Health Problems in the Community: Policy, Practice and Research*. London: Bailliere Tindall.

Holmshaw J. et al. (1999). Fitness to practice in community mental health, *Nursing Times*, *95*(34): 52–53.

Repper J. & Perkins, R. (2003). *Social Inclusion and Recovery*. London: Bailliere Tindall.

Rethink (2003). *Who Cares? – The experiences of mental health carers accessing services and information*. London: Rethink.

Sainsbury Centre for Mental Health (1997). *Pulling Together: The Future Roles and Training of Mental Health Staff*. London: Sainsbury Centre for Mental Health.

Sainsbury Centre for Mental Health (1998). *Keys to Engagement – review of care for people with severe mental illness who are hard to engage with services*. London: Sainsbury Centre for Mental Health.

Sainsbury Centre for Mental Health (2001). *The Capable Practitioner*. London: Sainsbury Centre for Mental Health.

The Social Exclusion Unit (2004). *Mental Health and Social Exclusion*. London: Office of the Deputy Prime Minister.

CHAPTER 10

Educators Learning Together: Linking Communities of Practice

Jill Anderson and Hilary Burgess

INTRODUCTION

Mental health educators, engaged in shaping tomorrow's professionals, are faced with seismic change – both in mental health policy and practice and in the landscape of higher education. In teaching, as in practice, there are drives towards integrative thinking and interprofessional working, with a move to engage service users/survivors and carers as active partners. Most professional programmes are, however, delivered through academic and professional programmes that are uni-professional, in which institutional and attitudinal barriers to inclusive education may be significant. Moreover, many educators work in a climate where research is prioritised over teaching, and where opportunities to debate teaching, update practice and policy, or plan curricula in conjunction with others may be limited.

In this chapter we analyse this challenging context for educators and, drawing on the work of the Mental Health in Higher Education project (*mhhe*), explore how learning and teaching about mental health can be enhanced through increased networking and the sharing of perspectives and ideas. The challenge for educators in this context is to allow themselves to become learners, working with colleagues from within their own discipline or profession, from other professions and disciplines, with practice colleagues and students, as well as alongside users of services/survivors and carers. The notion of linking and building communities of practice (Wenger, 1998) provides a conceptual basis for such development and transformation.

THE CHALLENGE OF CHANGE FOR EDUCATORS

Educators engaged in teaching and learning about mental health in higher education must respond to multiple challenges of change. There are changing understandings about what constitutes mental ill-health, and how best to promote recovery. There is a growing awareness of the importance of understanding positive mental health, public mental health and health

Teaching Mental Health. Edited by Theo Stickley and Thurstine Basset.

promotion. In policy, there is a growing emphasis on the development of the mental health workforce and lastly there is the changing nature of higher education itself; its mission, customers and modus operandi.

Conceptions of mental ill-health and mental well-being have altered dramatically over recent years. Slowly but surely, understanding of the possible causes of mental ill–health has broadened and diversified, with new alliances being formed within and across stakeholder groups. Interventions to support those with mental health problems have begun to reflect not only uni-disciplinary but multi-disciplinary approaches, where scientific, genetic, biological, psychological, cultural, social and spiritual perspectives may all play a role. The views and knowledge base of people with lived experience of mental health problems, service users/survivors and carers, have begun to be recognised as key to the development of understanding. At the same time, a growing interest in notions of positive mental well-being has been accompanied by an acknowledgement of the need for conceptual clarity. Mental health, as opposed to the mental health problems for which the term is often used as a (nonsensical!) synonym, is an issue of relevance, not only to those whose problems have been "diagnosed", but to us all.

This changing emphasis has been reflected in a plethora of policy initiatives foregrounding mental health promotion and the prevention of mental ill-health (DoH, 1999; DoH, 2001; Scottish Public Mental Health Alliance, 2001; Welsh Assembly Government, 2002; WHO, 2005); and understanding of the need for socially inclusive practice is developing (e.g. Social Exclusion Unit, 2004). Set against this, there are however moves to introduce more restrictive legislation, and a corresponding fear that holistic perspectives may be undermined. Despite the drive towards "integrative perspectives" (McCulloch et al., 2005) and the inclusion of service users and carers, concerns about risk and dangerousness still reverberate; thus policy appears to be facing in "two opposed directions at once" (Beresford, 2005).

In terms of practice, interprofessional working has been promoted by the creation of mental health trusts (in England), a range of new crisis management and assertive outreach teams, and by practice and training frameworks such as the *National Service Framework for Mental Health* (DoH, 1999) and *Ten Essential Shared Capabilities for the Whole of the Mental Health Workforce* (DoH, 2004). Recent promotion of "talking therapies" is another indication of the direction of travel (Layard, 2004).

Meanwhile, in higher education, enormous changes have also been taking place, with academics perceived to be "dancing on a moving carpet" (Young & Burgess, 2005). Once again potentially contradictory policies prevail, with the drive towards attaining higher research profiles (and thus increased income) potentially undermining simultaneous moves towards enhancing the quality of teaching (Dearing, 1997). Higher administrative loads, lower staff-student ratios and a diminished per capita spend on students, have been accompanied by increased demands for accountability and quality assurance in teaching. At the same time, there has been acceleration in the growth of knowledge. The ways in which higher education is delivered are being transformed (through the expansion of part-time study, open learning, e-learning and work-based learning routes). There is growing emphasis on approaches that support active learning and reflective learning, and on transferable skills (Young & Burgess, 2005, pp. 2–7).

In a growing number of programmes in which mental health is taught, employers now play a part as active stakeholders, either as commissioners or as partners in programme planning. More recently, service users and carers may also be involved as partners and (partially) funded to contribute to student recruitment and the planning, delivery, assessment and evaluation of programmes. Indeed, such participation is a requirement for accreditation of the social work degree (DoH, 2002). Whilst welcomed by most academics, the engagement of multiple stakeholders makes the task of programme planning and provision highly complex (Burgess, 2004), and significant barriers to involvement still remain (Basset al., 2006).

The student population has increased dramatically and, where tuition fees have been introduced, students have moved into a different relationship with universities, as their "customers". The drive towards "widening participation" in higher education has brought in students with diverse experience in terms of, class, ethnicity, dis(ability), educational background and age. This has required Higher Education Institutions to re-think how they support students, fuelled by drivers and performance criteria based upon "retention". In this respect, awareness of the mental health of students has been raised (e.g. Stanley and Manthorpe, 2002; RCP, 2003), though so too have concerns about the capacity of Higher Education Institutions to meet this challenge (Baker et al., 2006). The proportion of students and staff who disclose mental health problems is likely to increase, in line with a growing emphasis on social inclusion, the need to increase recruitment (Ferguson et al., 2005), a duty upon higher education institutions to make "reasonable adjustments" for people with disabilities under the Disability Discrimination Act and the development of substantive roles for service users in education and training fields.

As higher education broadens and diversifies, it becomes increasingly difficult to generalise about the nature of universities and the experience they offer to students, with diversity in terms of the physical environment, the student body, the sense of mission, who is employed to teach and how they are supported. There are well-recognised differences in the respective emphasis placed within different institutions on teaching and research, with teaching often afforded lower status (Young, 2006). In one university, lecturers and students may feel fearful of talking about their own experience of mental health problems; in another, service users may be employed as lecturers. Astonishingly, those two phenomena may co-exist within a single institution.

Between the disciplines most closely involved in mental health teaching too there are well recognised differences, with well established disciplines such as medicine holding much higher status than, for example, relative newcomers to the academy such as social work and nursing (Green, 2006). Differences too can be seen in the degree to which academics remain in touch with practice (Ferguson et al., 2003). Greenbank (2006) argues that "service" should be seen as a third element to be balanced alongside teaching and research – an issue with which professional disciplines have grappled since their inception.

When these worlds – of mental health policy and practice, and of higher education – come together, in learning and teaching about mental health within universities, it is perhaps not surprising that those involved may feel overwhelmed.

TEACHING IN ISOLATION

Of particular relevance here is the isolation experienced by many academics. Brawn and Trahar (2003) describe new lecturers as "isolated in their department, isolated in the university, and isolated by their perceived lack of opportunity to engage in fruitful discussions with colleagues about their teaching" (p. 249). Whilst academic work might appear to take place in contexts which involve cooperation and social contact, "much of that cooperation and contact is tinged with the competition of professional institutional life. There is discussion, and there are meetings, but one of the core functions of the academic – to write for publication – takes place in the lonely privacy of the office and the study" (Evans, 2004, p. 129).

In a teaching context too there may be few opportunities for collaborative practice. It is not uncommon, in some disciplines, for the mental health teaching to be done by a single academic, sometimes in a context where the priorities and interests of colleagues lie in other areas. The relative segregation of different departments or faculties within which mental health is taught (such as Medicine, Psychology, Nursing and Social Work) reflects not only the differing, and at times competing, disciplinary cultures (in evidence in practice too), but also the endemic academic "tribes and territories" analysed by Becher (1989). This isolation may be felt most strongly by those coming from more collaborative backgrounds in mental health practice, and by service user educators who successfully acquire an academic post.

The isolation of teachers has also been a theme for those outside the universities, with evidence adduced that educators are out of touch with professional practice (Ferguson et al., 2003), and that their own training needs are not currently addressed (Brooker et al., 2002). This may be most acute in those disciplines where rigid funding streams and inflexibility conspire to deny opportunities for combining clinical practice with teaching and research. Furthermore, educators are often forgotten in the policy and practice development world. It is rare to see the education and training implications clearly drawn out in national policy documents, or the perspective of educators pro-actively sought in consultations. Educators may be omitted from the descriptions of those for whom conferences, discussion forums or policy documents are seen to be of relevance and feel (rightly or wrongly) that these will not speak to them.

Thus, teaching mental health may be an activity that is both isolated or marginalised within universities, whilst in professional disciplines educators may be on the periphery of mental health developments. rather than at the centre, contributing actively to debate and discussion about how both education and service provision can progress.

If the pedagogical and institutional functions of educators completely displace their ability to manifest their identities as participants in their communities of practice, they lose their most powerful teaching asset... teachers need to "represent" their communities of practice in educational settings. This type of lived authenticity brings into the subject matter the concerns, sense of purpose, identification, and emotion of participation (Wenger, 1998, p. 276).

A CONCEPTUAL FRAMEWORK – COMMUNITIES OF PRACTICE

Wenger argues that, by dint of being human, we are continually engaged in the shared pursuit of all kinds of activity, whether seeking to ensure that our physical needs are met or seeking to make sense – as in debates about mental health – of the world around us. It is, through this collaborative activity, through engagement both with the world and with each other, that we learn. He goes on to note that: "Over time, this collective learning results in practices that reflect both the pursuit of our enterprises and the attendant social relations. These practices are thus the property of a kind of community created over time by the sustained pursuit of a shared enterprise. It makes sense, therefore, to call these kinds of communities,

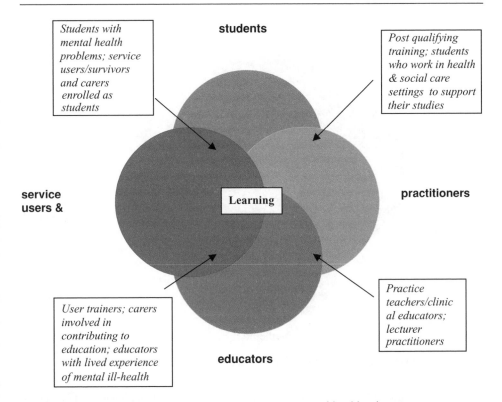

Students with mental health problems; service users/survivors and carers enrolled as students

students

Post qualifying training; students who work in health & social care settings to support their studies

service users &

Learning

practitioners

User trainers; carers involved in contributing to education; educators with lived experience of mental ill-health

educators

Practice teachers/clinical educators; lecturer practitioners

Figure 10.1 Intersecting communities: participants in mental health education

communities of practice" (Wenger, 1998 p. 45). This notion of "communities of practice" provides us with a conceptual framework, to help us both to map and to transform the world of education about mental health.

Traditionally, disciplinary and academic communities can be seen to be cohesive, inward facing, boundaried groups, drawing strength from their differentiation from others and strong roots in the past. There may be diversity within their bounds, but between them can stretch a kind of "no-man's land". It is still, as we have seen, the case that professional bodies, faculties and departments can exist in relative isolation but, as debate opens up we can perhaps see a shift from the notion of no-man's land to one of common ground.

This implies not absolute consensus, nor the loss of one's own identity, but the notion of a safe space in which people can move into closer contact. As interactions between the multiple stakeholders on the common ground increase, as they engage in intersecting communities of practice and, through contact with diverse others, draw increasingly on not just one but on all aspects of their selves – we may move to a position where the isolating forces highlighted above are mitigated. Those employed in higher education and those involved in workforce development may then no longer view each other from opposing trenches. Service users may be or become practitioners or teachers; the prior experience of learners may be fully recognised; opportunities for educators to engage in practice will increase; and all will be linked by our identity as learners (see Figure 10.1).

Furthermore, practice and learning will increasingly span the disciplines and professions, as, for example, social work educators and students start to recognise the importance of

Social work

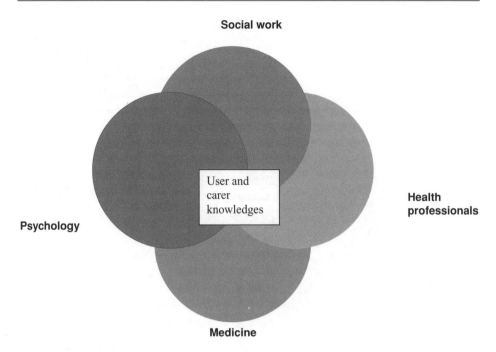

Psychology

User and carer knowledges

Health professionals

Medicine

Figure 10.2   Intersecting communities: knowledge in mental health education

general health and well-being as a prerequisite to preventing or alleviating mental distress or ill-health, and as medical educators and students recognise the links between social inclusion and mental ill-health (see Figure 10.2). Theories and intervention strategies may no longer be "owned" by one discipline or profession.

So, how do we create such an arena, within which new communities of practice can be fostered and engaged? In entering, and starting to cultivate, the common ground – moving, eventually to an "interprofessional place of being" (anon in Colyer et al. p. 61) – the task for all of us may be both to understand and to recognise our own language, values, identity and history, whilst not holding on to unnecessary notions of exclusive practice or differentiation. Potential allies in this task can be those who sit at, or move into, the intersections of the overlapping circles: practitioners who have (re)-assumed identities as students; service users and carers who take on the role of teachers; the psychology undergraduate who undertakes an MA in social work; the course director who experiences a period of depression; the medical educator devising an optional module on medicine and art. In valuing the diversity of perspectives we encounter, and valuing the different aspects of ourselves, we can transform the way in which we learn, and in which we learn together. A central task for all educators may be to facilitate this process (Newell Jones, 2005).

ENGAGING WITH EDUCATORS: PHASE ONE

Recent years have seen the gradual transformation of the no-man's land within mental health education into common ground. In the UK, the Mental Health in Higher Education project has had a small but significant role to play in that. Here we describe its genesis.

The Learning and Teaching Support Network (LTSN), an initiative to enhance the quality of teaching and learning in universities, was launched in 2000 from seeds sown in the Dearing report (1997). The LTSN comprised 24 discipline-based subject centres, hosted by UK universities, and a Generic Centre, based in York. In 2005, this became part of the Higher Education Academy, whose aim is "to help institutions, discipline groups and all staff to provide the best possible learning experience for their students". Whilst quality enhancement has been the aim of the Higher Education Academy, much of this has been achieved through the creation of networks and communities of practice.

In recognising the need for inter-disciplinary dialogue about mental health, representatives of four subject centres of the former LTSN (Health Sciences and Practice, Psychology, Medicine Dentistry and Veterinary Medicine, and Social Policy and Social Work) met together in 2002 to debate how the learning and teaching agenda in mental health might be taken forward together.

A lively two-day workshop for educators from a range of professions and disciplines highlighted the need to make links at local, regional and national levels. For some participants it was their first opportunity to debate mental health education and practice in an interdisciplinary group – an early incursion into "no-man's land". Both similarities and differences of approach were highlighted, as people began to explore the common ground. There was strong support for the continuation of dialogue once this had been established. The Mental Health in Higher Education (*mhhe*) project came into being in January 2003 with the aim of enhancing learning and teaching about mental health through increasing networking and the sharing of approaches across the disciplines in UK higher education.

An initial survey (Anderson, 2003) aimed to get a sense of what people were teaching, the extent of their links with other educators and what they saw as key challenges in learning and teaching about mental health.

- Firstly, it revealed that it was not uncommon for educators to lack connection with others involved in teaching within their own discipline (regionally and nationally), let alone those from other disciplines. Co-location in a single institution (or on the same corridor!) was no guarantee that people would be in touch with one another.
- Secondly, and notwithstanding some investigation of teaching in this area (SCMH, 1997), little has been written that sheds light on how, in detail, others approach the challenge of developing students' understanding about mental health.
- Thirdly, the pace of change in mental health policy and practice, had left some educators reeling. Dilemmas associated with an awareness of the difference between education (in its broadest sense) and training (equally necessary, but different) were highlighted.
- Fourthly, educators across the disciplines drew attention to the impact on learning and teaching about mental health of the issues raised at the beginning of this chapter, including widening participation agendas, research pressures, increasing student numbers and new modes of learning.
- Finally, the role of lived experience in learning about mental health was stressed, that of service users and carers contributing to teaching sessions as well as students' and lecturers' experiences of wellbeing and ill-health.

The first phase of the *mhhe* project allowed for the exploration of these themes and their connections. The lack of an existing national database meant that time had to be spent in beginning to locate those involved in mental health teaching across range of disparate departments and institutions. The issue of identity was key to this. Whilst in some disciplines, such as social work, those teaching a module on mental health would happily identify as a "mental health educator"; in others, such as medicine, those inputting to teaching in the area of mental health might define themselves as clinicians first and foremost. It was important for the project to reach those involved in teaching in areas such as child protection, the care of older people or physical health, where understanding mental well-being and ill-health is essential.

The database, established with the help of participating subject centres in the project's early days, is (in early 2006) approaching its 1,000th entry – still far from comprehensive, but an achievement nonetheless. With the constituency mapped out, the project embarked on developing lines of communication: a news section on the website; a regular e-bulletin; and – to aid speed and currency – an electronic discussion list. In combination, these increase access for educators to information about policy, practice, educational initiatives, sources of funding, training opportunities and publications. An *mhhe* website http://www.mhhe.heacademy.ac.uk/ provides a focal point for these and other aspects of the project's work: collections of resources, work on good practice, news about events and a feedback form.

The principle of service users/survivor and carer involvement in the project was incorporated at an early stage, though accompanied at times by imperfect attempts to translate this into action. The project owes much to those individuals and groups who bore with us in the early stages. *mhhe*'s first national conference focused on service user and carer involvement in mental health education, and in turn led to a good practice guide "Learning from Experience" (Tew et al., 2004) outlining strategies for engaging with users and carers in teaching and learning about mental health across the disciplines. This was co-written by an academic, service user and carer, and jointly published by *mhhe* with the West Midlands development centre of NIMHE and Trent Workforce Development Confederation. Over 2,000 copies were distributed across the UK and the guide is available on-line from the *mhhe* website.

Strategies for introducing students to the diversity and range of ways of understanding about mental health were highlighted in the second major conference, which offered teaching exemplars of many kinds. The need for holistic approaches to teaching, linking mental ill-health with broader notions of mental health and well-being was highlighted. Problem-based learning, models for building skills in communication, a mental health promotion diary, the use of lived experience, and *co-operative inquiry into the involvement of service users in clinical decisions were all demonstrated.*

The third event had a focus on interprofessional education (IPE) about mental health. There has, until recently (Steinert, 2005) been an almost total absence of attention paid to the need for educators to come together as a precursor to such work. This event highlighted the potential benefits of students "learning together to work together" (Barr, 2002) and shared helpful work on defining what we mean by interprofessional education. It provided cautions too about development of a group of IPE experts "in the know" and others – grappling creatively with the dilemmas who, for want of the "right" language and terminology, may be dismissed or undervalued. In this area, above all, there is a need to ensure that we go the extra mile in understanding one another's differing perspectives and ways of articulating them.

Formal aspects of *mhhe*'s work were complemented by conversations with individual educators, who sought support with teaching. For example:

- Hari, a lecturer in mental health nursing, wanted to establish a service user and carer involvement development worker post, and was looking for exemplars.
- Lara, already in such a role and working with the undergraduate medicine programme team to develop a module on self-harm, sought teaching materials to draw upon.
- Tony, a new lecturer, had been asked to take on the "abnormal psychology" module on an undergraduate psychology degree programme. Keen to abandon the medically orientated textbook used to date, he sought dialogue on teaching mental health from psychological perspectives.
- Chris, a social work educator, in the absence of colleagues with an interest in this area, sought help in working out how mental health might be woven throughout the generic social work degree curriculum.
- Selina, leading development of standards for post-qualifying training, sought university-based educators to contribute to a steering group.
- Darcus, heading up a mental health nursing programme, sought others to contribute to validation of a new post-qualifying programme.

CHALLENGES AND RECOMMENDATIONS FROM PHASE ONE

Issues raised and themes identified in the first phase were encapsulated in recommendations made in a report of the first year of *mhhe* in 2004, as follows.

The implications of overlapping roles – user, carer, teacher, student, practitioner - need to be considered at all times, and in relation to each of the following recommendations. An emphasis on beginning to involve service users and carers in learning and teaching, or on initiating interprofessional education initiatives, can obscure the multiple and overlapping roles, and diverse experience, already present in the group.

Opportunities should be increased for educators to debate their teaching openly, on the understanding that this is a mutual process in which all are prepared to learn. This requires the creation of a safe learning environment, informed by: an understanding of and respect for key differences in disciplinary cultures; a recognition of individual difference and similarities; and the role that input from those with lived experience of mental health problems has to play in facilitating students' learning. Whilst this is easy to write, it is not always easy to practice in the face of deeply held beliefs and differentials in power and status.

Interdisciplinary initiatives need to be accompanied by ongoing opportunities for intra-disciplinary debate. Effective collaboration results where each partner has a sense of their own identity and "community of practice" and is clear about their strengths and what they may have to gain. *mhhe*, in conjunction with the individual subject centres, has had a role in raising the profile of mental health and supporting debate within as well as across individual disciplines.

Support needs to be provided for educators to keep in touch with rapidly changing policy agendas, and to inform developments in policy and practice. Opportunities need to be maximised for the active involvement of educators in teasing out and debating the implications for learning and teaching of mental health policy developments. This will have resource (time and funding) implications.

Continuation funding for a systematic network of mental health educators within higher education would facilitate regional and national networking and the dissemination of positive approaches to learning and teaching about mental health. For continuation of *mhhe*'s work, linking and building communities of practice, additional funding was required. It was envisaged that the evolving networks, whilst linking to the agendas of workforce development agencies, would remain independent of government agendas, inter-disciplinary and inclusive.

Further thought needs to be given to support for user and carer involvement in learning and teaching about mental health. It became clear that service user/survivor and carer trainers themselves form an emerging community of practice – part of a wider constituency of survivor workers identified by Snow (2002). Support and capacity building are required, not only for independent trainers and groups, but also for those directly employed (often in quite isolated roles within higher education institutions) to engage and support them.

Higher education needs to be provided in a way that promotes the mental well-being of both lecturers and students. The university as an institution has a role to play in promoting mental well-being, preventing mental ill-health and meeting the needs of students and staff who are experiencing mental distress. Implications need to be drawn out for curriculum delivery in subjects within which mental health is taught. Throughout the project we were reminded of the need for mental health educators to reflect on the links between these levels – the Health Promoting Universities initiative (Dooris, 1999) providing one potential paradigm.

Mental health should be seen not simply as a health and social care issue, but as a fundamental concern of all human beings throughout their lives. An understanding of the concepts of health, well-being and recovery, and the ways in which these are culturally and individually defined, needs to underpin students' learning. Further work could be undertaken to specify mental health learning outcomes for students on generic as well as specialist mental health programmes – in areas such as mental health promotion and the prevention of mental-ill health across the life-cycle – and on the development of teaching materials to support such learning.

Students need to be helped to grapple with complexity and to understand the range of complementary and conflicting perspectives on mental well-being and ill-health. Learning and teaching about mental health brings challenges at many levels. Preparing students to be effective practitioners requires that they are confronted not only with a range of differing and sometimes conflicting explanations, models and perspectives, but that they learn to negotiate the realities of practice within services in flux. Within all curricula there is a need, for a focus on diversity and social inclusion, following concern expressed (in relation to cultural diversity) that "other people's philosophies or world views are not understood or even acknowledged" by mental health staff (SCMH, 2002).

Learning and teaching about mental health needs to be informed by evidence-based practice, the outcomes of research in general and user-led research in particular. Space needs to be created for mental health educators to reflect on the links between their own teaching and research, and to debate the relevance of research findings across the range of disciplines. To date, there has, been only limited research (e.g. Barnes et al., 2000, Carpenter et al., 2003, Carpenter et al., 2006) into the outcomes of different approaches to learning and teaching about mental health, such as interprofessional education or the involvement of service users/survivors as educators. It is important to understand the impact of teaching on students' learning about mental health and, crucially, on the experience of service users. Service user and carer involvement in research has been growing (Turner & Beresford, 2005) and they have a role to play as researchers of teaching and learning.

There is a need for more exploration and the sharing of approaches to interprofessional education about mental health, particularly at pre-registration levels. In recent years considerable effort has gone into promoting interprofessional education, but the learning from this work has not yet widely disseminated. What are the best conditions for promoting interprofessional learning and practice and does it change the outcomes for service users and carers? Further debate is needed about the role of those with lived experience of mental health problems in "interprofessional" education initiatives; an interest of the newly established *Centre of Excellence in Interdisciplinary Mental Health* at the University of Birmingham.

PHASE TWO DEVELOPMENTS

With additional funds from the collaborating subject centres and the Department of Health, *mhhe* entered into its second phase in 2004. Three strands of work were significant, building on the phase one recommendations: regional meetings, intra-disciplinary work and support for service user/survivor and carer trainers.

Whilst national conferences had enabled educators to meet from a broad range of settings and higher education institutions, it became clear that it was not uncommon for academics engaged in mental health teaching within one region, or indeed a single university, never to have met. Moreover, the need to link in with workforce developments locally was underlined by the continuing stream of policy initiatives; new directions within the UK nations, and in England, a growing role for the regional development centres of the National Institute for Mental Health (NIMHE). As new forms of collaborative provision of education and training were emerging, the communities of practice of the workforce and academia were brought together. Thus *mhhe* set out to establish a series of regionally-run meetings, where educators from higher education institutions could meet with service user/survivor trainers, carers, practitioners and workforce leaders to discuss policy developments and exchange ideas and information about teaching. The commonality of task was underlined by the publication in England of the Ten Essential Shared Capabilities for the Whole of the Mental Health Workforce (DoH, 2004), providing an initial focus for debate.

To date, regional networks have been developed in five regions, with work planned on engaging others. Parallel developments in Scotland, Northern Ireland and Wales have been inhibited by lack of resources and capacity. In the most successful meetings, educators have been able to forge new relationships locally and regionally, and there has been a positive cross-fertilisation of ideas and practice. Participants have expressed a desire to continue to meet, rotating the venue within a region to enhance accessibility and ownership. There have also been challenges. At times the interacting communities of practice have brought with them clashes in approach, values, language and objectives. Furthermore, it is not easy to build a sustainable network in the face of heavy demands on everybody's time.

The intra-disciplinary work in phase two has been particularly exciting. Stimulated by collaboration between *mhhe* and the subject centres, a number of initiatives have furthered debate within the different professions and disciplines. This has linked to the "New Ways of Working" initiative from NIMHE as, in turn, the role of different professions has been reviewed. In nursing and the Allied Health Professions energy and enthusiasm for networking is high, with an interest in exploring further the links between physical and mental health and their integration into teaching. In psychology, activity has focused around scoping how mental health is taught within undergraduate programmes and counteracting the tendency, in teaching, for educators to "jump ship" to psychiatry, with a focus on medical rather than psychological models and diagnostic categories (Harper et al., forthcoming). In medicine, a review of undergraduate psychiatry teaching has been taking place under the auspices of the Association of University Teachers of Psychiatry. Service users and carers views have been sought on this, paralleling the increased emphasis recently put on user involvement in medical training (Fadden et al., 2005, Hasman et al., 2006). In social work, a recent discussion paper (NIMHE/CSIP, 2006), on the role of the mental health social worker, has reinvigorated debate and – with the development of the Social Perspectives Network – the time is ripe for an increased emphasis on mental health within generic social work education (Tew & Anderson, 2004). Thus the respective communities of practice have turned inwards to identify the challenges they face, and the nature of dialogue within the profession, in order to turn outwards and engage more effectively with those from other communities of practice.

Finally, *mhhe* has acted as broker for the development of a new community of practice – one for workers employed in universities as Developers of User and Carer Involvement in Education (DUCIE). This has provided a means by which those in such roles, often isolated and complex, can meet, support each other, evolve new practice and where necessary campaign for change. Inevitably, within this group there are also differences to contain and address: those who would call themselves survivors of the mental health system, or those who have no personal experience but coordinate the contribution of others who do; those who work on user involvement strategies only in relation to learning and teaching about mental health, or those whose work relates to other service user groups and issues; those who want to meet primarily for support or those who wish to get involved in campaigning. Embryonic networks, such as the Service User Survivor Trainers Network (SUSTN) and Professional Education Public Involvement Network (PEPIN) will, increasingly, enable individual differences in support and information needs to be addressed.

PHASE THREE OF THE PROJECT AND EMERGENT THEMES

At the time of writing, the *mhhe* project is entering its third phase, linked to the two newly designated Centres of Excellence in Learning and Teaching (CETL) about mental health (at the University of Birmingham and Middlesex University), with additional funds from the Higher Education Academy. The link to the CETLs provides an opportunity for yet another kind of partnership to address some broader questions that are now emerging.

Firstly, how can teaching and learning about mental health be integrated across the curricula of professional courses, rather than remaining confined to a designated "mental health" module or branch programme? Secondly, how can teaching and learning about mental health can be introduced into, or highlighted within, other professional programmes such as teaching, law and the expressive arts? Thirdly, how might concerns to promote student and staff mental health and well-being link to teaching about mental health? Fourthly, how can higher education initiatives in this area (such as *mhhe*) best link with those in other areas (such as training initiatives within Trusts, the voluntary or independent sectors); and professional education and training link with that concerned with workers in new roles? Finally, how might the communities of practice and interest in the UK concerned with mental health education link with others internationally (Deakin Human Services, 1999; McVicar et al., 2005)?

CONCLUSION

In this chapter we have attempted to illustrate some of the complexities and challenges of teaching and learning about mental health in a higher education context. An understanding of these is of relevance, beyond the bounds of higher education, to the myriad communities of interest and practice that have a role to play in transforming education about mental health – through building on uni-disciplinary systems and approaches developed for different purposes and in different times, as well as on a developing history of interprofessional collaboration.

Progress in this transformation will be difficult, and fraught with challenges and ambiguity – as communities of interest, or groups within them, compete for power, or re-engage with former battles for influence. Yet, as Wenger notes, "The need for coordinating perspectives is a source of new meanings as much as it is a source of obstacles. From this perspective, ambiguity is not simply an obstacle to overcome; it is an inherent condition to be put to work" (1998, p. 84).

The Mental Health in Higher Education has been one of a range of initiatives, supporting change in education and training about mental health. Some, like the Mental Health Training Forum, and its associated national mental health education conference, have had a primary focus on training in other contexts and the development of non-professional roles; others, such as Mental Health Nurse Academics UK or the Association of University Teachers of Psychiatry, provide opportunities for educators within a single discipline to meet and develop practice. As the onward drive towards "interprofessional practice and learning" continues, it could be argued that our joint experience in the field of mental health education has much to offer to other areas of education and fields of practice.

In learning together about teaching mental health, educators (of all types), have articulated a set of common goals: to contribute to educating professionals able to provide the high quality services that people experiencing mental health difficulties and their families say they want; to help to promote mental well-being within the communities (including the educational community) in which they work; and to accommodate change and integrative thinking, whilst still being clear about the particular value of their own practice and perspective. The common ground is opening up, and the challenge is, together, to put ambiguity to work.

REFERENCES

Anderson, J. (2003). Keeping in Touch, *Mental Health Today*, September, 24–46. (This article is also available online: http://www.mhhe.ltsn.ac.uk/docs/external/keepingintouch.pdf

Baker, S., Brown, B.J. & Fazey, J.A. (2006). Mental Health in Higher Education: mapping field, consciousness and legitimation. *Critical Social Policy*, *26*(1), 31–56.

Barnes, D., Carpenter, J. & Bailey, D. (2000). Partnerships with service users in interprofessional education for community mental health: a case study. *Journal of Interprofessional Care*, *14*, 191–202.

Barr, H. (2002). *Interprofessional education: Today, Yesterday and Tomorrow*, London: Centre for Health Sciences and Practice.

Basset, T., Campbell, P. & Anderson, J. (2006). Service user/survivor involvement in education and training – overcoming the barriers, *Social Work Education*, *25*(4), 393–402.

Becher, T. (1989). Academic tribes and territories: Intellectual enquiry and the culture of disciplines. Buckingham: The Society for Research into Higher Education and Open University Press.

Beresford, P. (2005). Social approaches to madness and distress: user perspectives and user knowledges, ch 2 in Tew, J. (ed) *Social Perspectives in Mental Health*, London: JKP.

Brawn, R. & Trahar, S. (2003). Supporting the Learner Teacher in Changing Higher Education. In Sutherland, R. Claxton, G. & Pollard, A. (eds) *Learning and Teaching Where World Views Meet*, Stoke on Trent: Trentham Books.

Brooker, C., Gournay, K., O'Halloran, P., Bailey, D. & Saul, C. (2002). Mapping training to support the implementation of the National Service Framework for mental health, *Journal of Mental Health*. *11*(1), 103–116.

Burgess, H. (2004). Redesigning the curriculum for social work education: complexity, conformity, chaos, creativity, collaboration? *Social Work Education*. *23*(2) 163–183.

Carpenter, J. Barnes, D. & Dickenson, C. (2003). *Making a modern care force: evaluation of the Birmingham University Programme in Community Mental Health*. Durham: Centre for Applied Social Research www.dur.ac.uk/sass/casr.

Carpenter, J., Barnes, D., Dickinson, C. & Wooff, D. (2006). Outcomes of interprofessional education for Community Mental Health Services in England: The longitudinal evaluation of a postgraduate programme, *Journal of Interprofessional Care*, *20*(2), 145–161.

Colyer, H., Helme, M. & Jones, I. (eds) (2005). *The Theory-Practice Relationship in Interprofesional Education*. London: Higher Education Academy, Health Sciences and Practice Network.

Deakin Human Services Australia (1999). *Learning together: education and training partnerships in mental health*. Canberra: Commonwealth Department of Health and Aged Care.

Dearing (1997). *Higher Education in the Learning Society*, Report of the National Committee of Inquiry into Higher Education, Department for Education and Employment.

DoH (1999). *National Service Framework for Mental Health: Modern Standards and Service Models*. London: Department of Health [online] http://www.publications.doh.gov.uk/nsf/mentalhealth.htm.

DoH (2001). *Making it happen: a guide to delivering mental health promotion*. London: Department of Health.

DoH (2002). *Requirements for Social Work Training*. London: Department of Health.

DoH (2004). *The Ten Essential Shared Capabilities: a framework for the whole of the mental health workforce*, 40339, London: Department of Health.

Dooris, M. (1999). The "Health Promoting University" as a framework for promoting positive mental well-being: a discourse on theory and practice, *International Journal of Mental Health Promotion*, *1*(4), October.

Evans, M. (2004). *Killing thinking – the death of the universities*. London: Continuum.

Fadden G., Shooter M. & Holsgrove, G. (2005). Involving carers and service users in the training of psychiatrists. *Psychiatric Bulletin*, *29*, 270–274.

Ferguson, K., Owen, S., Beswick, S. & Baguley, I. (2005). *Time to Act. Choosing to Work in Mental Health: The Recruitment of Health and Social Care Professionals*. Lincoln: Centre for Clinical and Academic Workforce Innovation.

Ferguson, K., Owen, S. & Baguley, I. (2003). *The Clinical Activity of Mental Health Lecturers in Higher Education Institutions*. London: Department of Health.

Green, L.C. (2006). Pariah Profession, Debased Discipline? An analysis of social work's low academic status and the possibilities for change, *Social Work Education. 25*(3), 245–264.

Greenbank, P. (2006). *The academic's role: the need for a re-evaluation, Teaching in Higher Education. 11*(1), 107–112.

GSCC (2002). *Requirements for Social Work Training*. London: General Social Care Council.

Harper, D., Cromby, J., Reavey, P., Cooke, A. & Anderson, J. (Forthcoming). Don't jump ship! New approaches in teaching mental health to undergraduates, *The Psychologist*.

Hasman, A., Coulter, A. & Askham, J. (2006). Education for partnership: Developments in Medical Education. Oxford: Picker Institute Europe [accessed on-line December 2006 http://www.pickereurope.org/Filestore/Downloads/E4P_report_19-5-06-_with_cover.pdf]

Layard, R. (2004). *Mental Health: Britain's Greatest Social Problem*. London: Strategy Unit.

Levin, E. (2004). *Involving service users and carers in social work education*. London: Social Care Institute for Excellence.

McCulloch, A., Ryrie, I., St John, T. & Williamson, T. (2005). Has the Medical Model a Future?, *The Mental Health Review*, March.

McVicar J., Deacon D., Curran, V. & Cornish P. (2005). *Interprofessional education initiatives in collaborative mental health care. Report prepared for the Canadian Collaborative Mental Health Initiative*, Mississauga, Ontario, Canada. Available at: www.ccmhi.ca.

Newell Jones, K. (2005). Whose reality counts? Lessons from Participatory Rural Appraisal (PRA) for facilitators of Interprofessional Learning in H. Colyer, M. Helme & I. Jones (eds) *The Theory-Practice Relationship in Interprofesional Education*. London: Higher Education Academy, Health Sciences and Practice Network.

NIMHE (2004). *National Mental Health Workforce Strategy*. London: Department of Health.

NIMHE/CSIP (2006). *The social work contribution to mental health services – The future direction*, London: NIMHE/CSIP http://www.spn.org.uk/index.php?id=836.

Royal College of Psychiatrists (2003). *The Mental Health of Students in Higher Education*, London: RCP [online] http://www.rcpsych.ac.uk/publications/cr/cr112.htm.

SCMH (2002). *Breaking the Circles of Fear: A review of the relationship between mental health services and African and Caribbean communities*. London: Sainsbury Centre for Mental Health.

SCMH (1997). *Pulling Together: the future roles and training of mental health staff*. London: Sainsbury Centre for Mental Health.

Scottish Executive (2002). *Mental Health (Scotland) Bill*. Edinburgh: Scottish Executive.

Scottish Office Department of Health (1997). *A Framework for Mental Health Services in Scotland*. Edinburgh: Scottish Office.

Scottish Public Mental Health Alliance (2001). *With Health in Mind: Improving Mental Health and Wellbeing in Scotland*. Edinburgh: Scottish Council Foundation.

Snow, R. (2002). *Stronger than ever: the report of the first national conference of survivor workers*. Cheadle Heath: Asylum.

Social Exclusion Unit (2004). *Mental Health and Social Exclusion*. London: Office of the Deputy Prime Minister.

Stanley, N. & Manthorpe, J. (2002). *Students' Mental Health Needs: Problems and Responses*. London: Jessica Kingsley.

Steinert, Y. (2005). Learning together to teach together: Interprofessional education and faculty development, *Journal of Interprofessional Care*, Supplement I, 60–75

Tew, J. & Anderson, J. (2004). The mental health dimension of the new degree in social work: starting a debate. *Social Work Education, 23*(2), 231–240.

Tew, J., Gell, C. & Foster, S. (2004). *Learning from Experience, Involving service users and carers in mental health education and training* Higher Education Academy/NIMHE/Trent Workforce Development Confederation. Also available online at http://www.mhhe.ltsn.ac.uk/guides/guide1.asp.

Turner, M. & Beresford, P. (2005). Uxbridge: Shaping Our Lives and the Centre for Citizen Participation, Brunel University.

UKCC (1999). *Fitness for practice*. London: United Kingdom Central Council for Nursing, Midwifery
and Health Visiting.

Welsh Assembly Government (2002). *Well being in Wales*. Cardiff: Welsh Assembly Government.

Wenger, E. (1998). *Communities of Practice: learning, meaning and identity*. Cambridge: Cambridge
University Press.

WHO (2005). *Mental Health Action Plan for Europe: Facing the Challenges, Building Solutions*.
http://www.euro.who.int/document/mnh/edoc07.pdf.

Young, P. (2006). Out of balance: lecturers' perceptions of differential status and rewards in relation
to teaching and research. *Teaching in Higher Education*, *11*(2), 191–202.

Young, P. & Burgess, H. (2005). Dancing on a moving carpet: the changing context, Ch 1 in
H. Burgess & I. Taylor (eds), *Effective Learning and Teaching in Social Policy and Social Work*.
London: Routledge Falmer.

CHAPTER 11

Interprofessional Action Research: Loosening Bricks in the Modernist's Walls

William Spence

INTRODUCTION

The UK government has made it clear that, "There is a national imperative to demonstrate interprofessional teaching and shared learning in all programmes of preparation for health and social care practitioners" (Department of Health, 2001) despite the lack of clarity around the precise nature and benefits of this. This political imperative certainly applies to the major mental health care professions. The preparation for these professions and aspirant professions is largely conducted separately and this reinforces their controlling hierarchical relationships which, rooted in a masculine and patriarchal value system, seldom are considered to be empowering for service users. This chapter discusses the rationale for interprofessional working and some of the precursors and drivers for this in mental health care from a post-modern ethical perspective and report on some action research initiatives that have: involved mental health consumers and carers as partners in student evaluation, brought community nurses and GP registrars together for shared learning, and have increased consumer input to community nursing programmes by the establishment of systematic procedures to enable this.

PART ONE – INTERPROFESSIONAL EDUCATION

Interprofessional education (IPE) is defined as taking place:

> When two or more professions learn with, from and about each other to improve collaboration and the quality of care. (Barr et al., 2005, p. 2)

IPE is a subset of multi-professional education where members of professions learn alongside one another for "whatever reason" (CAIPE, 1997). The push to increase the amount of IPE that is available in health care seems to be driven by a number of factors. The superiority of teams to individuals on work requiring many skills, judgment and experience

Teaching Mental Health. Edited by Theo Stickley and Thurstine Basset.
Copyright © 2007 John Wiley & Sons, Ltd.

seems an important variable (Mohrman et al., 1995). Synergy is assumed to result from well managed team effort where the collective output is greater than the sum of individual efforts (Robbins, 2001). More pragmatically the development in IPE has been attributed in part to the need to deploy staff flexibly (Schofield, 1995). Engels (2002) takes this further and recognises the role of affordability in health care, the changing roles of professions involved and the demographic realities of a Europe where young people are better educated and have more choices available to them than ever before. More skeptically, Walker (1998) has implicated cost containment and a drive for improved efficiency in a UK where the tight central government control over public services developed by the right of centre politics of the 1980's and early 1990's has been retained by the centrist left politics of the present government. A range of IPE drivers relevant to mental health is presented in Table 11.1.

The hope of improved team working as a result of IPE is prevalent in the literature although the effectiveness of team working in mental health care is far from universally accepted. Community Mental Health Teams (CMHTs) are seen as the "mainstay" of the mental health system in the UK however (DoH, 2002) if their multidisciplinary status indicates only the parallel and managed nature of their constituent professionals' efforts (Petrie, 1976). This falls short of an interprofessional approach where planning, implementation, monitoring and review would be expected to be done jointly and where needs assessment may form the basis of another professional's intervention and assessments may be evaluated by other professional members (Barr, 1998). Similarly the claim by psychiatrists to be the natural leaders of multidisciplinary teams (Black & John, 1986) will be familiar to those who have worked in them if this is neither true to the spirit of interprofessional working nor widely agreed. Fundamental flaws in the multidisciplinary community team concept have been identified (Galvin & McCarthy, 1994) and the most glaring of these relate to the disparities between consultant psychiatrists and other members, e.g. those relating to pay and conditions and continuing professional development opportunities.

However the community mental health team has been shown to offer very modest advantages over non team approaches and in particular it may reduce deaths by suicide and where circumstances are suspicious (OR 0.32, CI 0.09–1.12), and reduces the number of people who are dissatisfied with their care (OR 0.34, CI 0.2–0.59) (Tyrer et al., 2002). The abbreviated and perhaps expedient view of interprofessional working offered by the Government includes only its requirement for teamwork, partnership and collaboration, and skill mix and flexible working (Secretary of State for Health, 2000).

The mixed rationale for IPE has not prevented its flourishing however and many established aspects of it are entirely in keeping with modern mental health service aspirations and productive team working. Barr (2002) has outlined a set of conditions for successful IPE and amongst other things; the centrality of service users will be most welcome in modern mental health services. He advocates that competing objectives are reconciled and that interprofessional objectives are compatible with the other elements of the respective programmes.

IPE EVIDENCE BASE

In 2000 Zwarenstein et al., attempted to conduct a review of the effects of IPE on professional practice and health care outcomes for the Cochrane Library. They located 1,042 relevant papers and considered only 89 of these concluding that none met the methodologically

Table 11.1 Suggested benefits and drivers for IPE relevant to mental health care

Drivers for IPE development and implementation
Cost reduction (Walker, 1998)
Promotes collaboration. (Barr, 1994)
Oppose "elitism, rivalry and inflexibility". (Carrier & Kendall 1995)
Reduction in the occurrence of communications breakdowns.
Increase in morale and efficiency.
Avoidance of "unhelpful protectionism". (Freeth et al., 1998)
Enhances personal and professional confidence.
Promotes mutual understanding between professions.
Facilitates intra- and inter-professional communication.
Encourages reflective practice. (Barr et al., 2000)
Cost effectiveness (but difficult to demonstrate). (Koppel, 1998)
Inter-professional education can lead to the development of the necessary skills to operate effectively in multi-disciplinary teams.
For individual staff members:
Exposure to new ideas.
Opportunity to work with different people.
Increased cultural sensitivity.
Enhanced flexibility in working with students.
Better sense of co-operation and networking between departments.
Impetus to discover more community resources.
Engenders a respect for, and understanding of, the role of other associated professions. (McCroskey & Robertson, 1999)
Better prepare students for encountering the complexities of real-life inter-professional problems in the work environment. (O'Neill et al., 2000)
Challenges stereotypes, but allows students to strengthen their own professional identities. (O'Neill et al., 2000; McCroskey and Robertson 1999)
IPE potential benefits:
Enhances motivation to collaborate.
Changes attitudes and perceptions.
Cultivates interpersonal, group and organisational relations.
Establishes common value and knowledge bases. (Barr et al., 2000)
Enhanced communication skills.
(Barr et al., 2000; Finch, 2000; Zwarenstein & Bryant, 2002)
Cultivating interpersonal, group, and organisational relations and developing mutual understanding and respect.
Establishing common values, knowledge, and understanding of differing roles, theoretical perspectives and terminology.
Changing attitudes and perceptions and reducing negative stereotypes through interprofessional awareness and empathy.
Potential to substitute roles and facilitate flexible career routes.
Enhancing collaboration in practice.
Reinforcing clinical competencies. (Priest et al., 1995)

rigorous inclusion criteria. A systematic review of IPE evaluations conducted by Freeth at al. (2002) considered reported outcomes under six categories and the percentage of the higher quality studies demonstrating positive outcomes in that review is indicated in brackets: reactions of learners (51 %), attitude or perception change (27 %), knowledge or skill change (45 %), delivery or organisation of care changes (40 %), changes in behaviour (23 %), and client or patient benefit (17 %). Learner experiences were self rated positively and included the positive evaluation of facilitator input and interprofessional interaction. Knowledge or skill improvements included those related to: the nature of interprofessional teamwork, understanding of the roles and responsibilities of other health care professionals, and the development of interprofessional communication skills. The review largely included studies of post registration health care medical and nursing students undergoing IPE in the workplace or in the training facilities of the employer and more interpretive and critical, prospective, and comprehensively evaluative, studies were called for by the review authors.

MODERNISM

The origins of modernity can be traced back to the European Enlightenment period of the late 17th to the late 18th Century when developments in science and its application displaced prevailing superstitions, and ignorance gave way to reason and order. Prior to this time the Christian church and its clergy dominated social life in Europe and the individual's role in society was less important to that of the collective. Techniques and skills in production were poorly developed in the pre-modern era where the natural and supernatural worlds had sizeable influences on social life and thinking of the time. Social status was fixed at birth and feudalism, based on a landed property ownership, prevailed in this pre-modern age of faith. Italy's renaissance period has been identified by Russell (1988) as a precursor to the Enlightenment or age of reason, and the modern period, where the humanist values of self development, personal autonomy and individualism flourished. The development of trade across Europe gave birth to a mercantile class and, together with developments in science and its industrial application, this drove Capitalism similar to that of modern Western democracies. Almost paradoxically, Kant's (Reiss, 1971) claim that the Enlightenment represented an emergence from the inability of people to use their own understanding came at a time when states were developing their sovereignty through political processes that centred around the use of power in controlling the populous. Liberation from dogma became the Enlightenment's meta-narrative and innovation, and Utopian ambition came to mark the modern period.

POST MODERNISM

The beginning of the post-modern period has been traced to several seminal 20th Century events ranging from the discontent caused by the role of technology in World War One genocide to the 1970's disengagement from grand theories such as Marxism which failed to explain people's lived realities of the time. For Callinicos (1989), interest in post-modernism represented a convergence of several cultural trends. The latter decades of the 20th Century witnessed an increasing appreciation of heterogeneity in the arts and opposition to the international style in architecture. Also the French post-structuralists emphasised similarly heterogeneity in their understanding of reality together with its fragmentary and plural character. Lastly he implicates changes in the social world over this period where the emerging post industrial society was where mass production was replaced by theoretical research as the driver for economic growth. The importance of knowledge generation focused attention on science and the challenges it faced in modelling such a plural environment. Science did not attempt to generate new models of reality but simply sought to generate further scientific "truths" and post modernists repudiated such modern traditions. The modernist's ambition is to discover one grand narrative within which all forms of knowledge may be incorporated, and incredulity towards this position is a defining characteristic of the post-modern perspective (Lyotard, 1984). The lack of consensus on its meaning, however, has caused confusion.

POST-MODERNITY AND IPE IN MENTAL HEALTH CARE EDUCATION

Mental health care education (MHCE) today is characterised by a similar "colonization of minds" found by Butler and Walter (1991) to be experienced by African Americans in Eurocentric schooling in the USA. In MHCE the dominant positivist biomedical culture imposes its control through the dissemination of its research evidence based practice that it largely controls the generation of. It follows that learners will be enthusiastic to be told "how it is" via the transmission of "factual" information. It often comes as some disappointment to many learners to hear that: knowledge is constructed in the minds of people, their expectations of understanding an independent "reality" are artefacts of the late modernity context of their lives, and that their ontological assumptions of realism may be challenged by post-modern nominalism. It follows from this instrumentalist view of knowledge that it will be of equal worth whether constructed by the learner, teacher or researcher and knowledge then becomes a plurality of local narratives that are highly contextualised and not reducible. The local nature of these narratives also precludes their summation in any attempt to form a grand narrative.

In a mental health care arena that has become dominated by the requirement for a quantitative research evidence base, this poses some challenge where the quantitative and empirical evidence base has become, in Foucault's (1980) terms, our current major discourse that most have accepted as our "regime of truth". If accepted, this analysis points us to "the status of those who are charged with saying what counts as true" (Foucault, 1980 p. 131) and, not surprisingly, we can see an apparent correlation in the approach characterised by positivist epistemologies, deterministic views of human nature, realist ontologies, nomothetic methodologies and the traditional mental health professional hierarchy. The post-modern enthusiasm for local narrative is consistent with IPE and any rejection of grand narrative in IPE has the potential to challenge order in mental health services although this has yet to be established. A challenge to the dominant empirical narrative has potential to see the consumers' voice afforded increased status. The dualism evident in traditional psychiatric interpretation of speech acts – where speech is thought to indicate or point to something (Murphy, 1989), and in this case it is psychopathology – is rejected in post-modernism where the patient's language is afforded the status of that which can shape reality. This supports IPE where the social reality is to be found at the junctions of human networks established to promote interpretation. The post-modern community mental health team would be well placed to perform such a role and its members increase in social sensitivity skills has the potential to illuminate the linguistic basis of human behaviour. The current acknowledgement of the significance of even "psychotic" speech acts offers some optimism that such sensitivity may form a larger part of professionals' skills repertoire in the future.

Post-modernism is pessimistic about the potential of the individual to influence society and this pessimism seems apposite in mental health care where service consumer involvement in service delivery in the UK has only had limited impact. The rise of disorganised Capitalism (Lash & Urry, 1987) is marked by reduced state regulation, decline of manufacturing in the West, service class growth that reduces the relevance of class politics, and a more fragmented and pluralistic cultural life and these factors may have contributed to the limited success of the consumer movement in mental health.

Of course this pessimism in relation to personal autonomy is relevant to education in a post-modern society where education may be seen as a method for perpetuating modernity's grand narratives. The status of purportedly evidence based courses in mental health care is one example of this. Educationalists through their interpretation of legislative discourses are required to fix the boundaries of the learner's knowledge to prepare the, "'rational' man to live in a rational society" (Usher & Edwards, 1994, p. 126). In this way, Usher and Edwards (1994) contend, education is used to eliminate "otherness" and reduce "difference, contingency" and "provisionally". It should be apparent that IPE has potential in challenging these assumptions where perspective sharing and high participation are expected. The constructivist approach of IPE is in line with the post-modern approach to education where knowledge is seen as a conceptual means rather than a representation and where these concepts are generated by ourselves and we assume responsibility for this (von Glaserfield, in Davis et al., 1991). The discovery learning of Bruner (1960 & 1964) and meaningful learning of Ausubel et al., (1978) are consistent with IPE which would be required to adopt a cognitive underpinning where the development of learners' understanding of their own learning is a goal. The plurality of post-modern IPE will demand more diverse goals and a cynicism towards higher education's preoccupation with the systems approach and adopt a radical ethic marked by a celebration of diversity and dialogue and minimally structured lesson plans. The reduction in learning environment structure conducive to the facilitation of this construction has ht potential to dissolve boundaries between knowledge and emotional development and this will support the exploration and development of personal value systems which is important to IPE in MHCE.

EVALUATIVE FEEDBACK ON INTERPROFESSIONAL LEARNING SESSIONS

In 2002 the community nursing teaching team at Oxford Brookes and the course leader of the University of Oxford's fast track medical degree course established a forum to discuss IPE possibilities. The group explored opportunities for shared learning between post qualifying but undergraduate specialist community nursing practitioner (SCNP) students – community mental health nurses (CMHN), school nurses (SN), community nurses in the home (CNH), public health nurses (PHN), learning disability nurses (LDN), community children's nurses (CCN), and general practice nurses (GPN) – and undergraduate medical students who were graduates in other disciplines but several organisational factors militated against this. The group explored a number of other IPE opportunities and the first SCNP student and general practitioner registrar (GPR) study event organised by this group took place in May 2003 and this has been developed over the intervening years as an annual event involving subsequent cohorts.

An action research (Hart and Bond, 1995) mode was employed in this study, where the author was the leader of one of the pathways included. Action research has been recognised as an appropriate methodology, which resonates with the aims of education (Glen & Hight, 1992) and was used here to inform the ongoing development of educational practice. It may be seen as a way of generating understanding of a social system in attempting to change it (Lewin, 1946) via its cyclical process involving planning, acting, observing and reflecting (Mayer, 1993). Over the three years the participating cohort sizes for SCNP and GPR students were respectively, 45, 28, 23 and 12, 15, and 24. All three sessions began with an introduction including the outlining of learning outcomes and an ice breaking exercise which comprised the identification and debunking of stereotypes relevant to the professions and specialises involved. The sessions all involved role play shaped by a complex care situation and a "goldfish bowl" method was used where participants each assumed the role: of a member of the other professional group or of supporter/consultant to the student playing the supporter's professional role or of observer. The 2005 session focussed largely on mental health issues and included discussion around a video session produced by the teaching team. This was recorded in a local primary care setting and involved the teaching team, practitioners and a professional actress playing the roles of a complex primary health care scenario where health need related to the care of an individual with a schizophrenia diagnosis and depression in an unpaid carer. Four copies of the video enabled micro group discussion facilitated by general practitioner trainers and nurse lecturers.

Each year all participants were invited to complete the same 15 item, five point Likert style evaluation questionnaire with three additional items seeking qualitative data on respondents' views on the "most" and "least" helpful aspects of the participation of the other professional group with regard to respondents' learning in addition to their "other comments". Four Likert items were reverse scored to reduce response set and these items have been corrected here. Response rates to all distributions of both groups were no less than 92 %.

The fairly high levels of agreement with the positive statements across the first and second years can be seen in figure one where these reached 63 % for nurses in 2004. Much reduced agreement was evident in 2005 where only 25 % & 33 % of nurses and GPRs respectively similarly agreed. The groups' less positive evaluation of 2005 was evident in the high levels of disagreement with the positive statements that reached 55 % for nurses (Figure 11.1). The 52 % GPR disagreement in 2005 was more than double the percentage of disagreement evidenced by either group in previous years.

The evaluation of the three sessions and for both groups is presented in Figures 11.2 and 11.3 where disagreement with the 15 positive statements concerning the session and IPE is presented. The checked bars of figures two and three indicate the higher levels of disagreement with positive statements in 2005 comparison to previous years and the teaching team concluded that this reflected the very different nature of the cohorts. Disappointingly given the aims of IPE, in all sessions no less than 45 % of nurses disagreed that they had learned a lot about the role of the GPR (Figure 11.2) and 81 % of GPRs believed they had not learned a lot about the nurses' role in 2005 (Figure 11.3). General acceptance of the potential to learn from the other discipline was evident in responses to question four although the 2005 GPR disagreement was over double that of the nurses at 71 %. Question five responses indicated the generally stimulating experience of session participants although for the last two years the nurses seem to have found the session to be rather simplistic where the

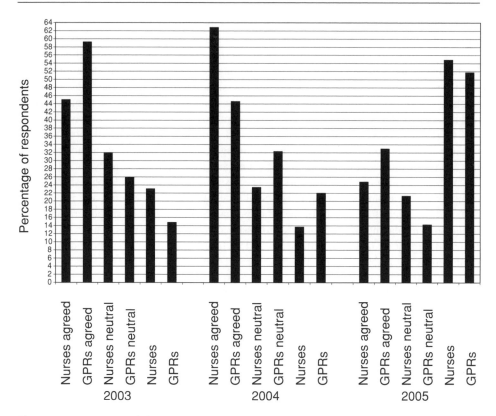

Figure 11.1   Nurses and GPRs' responses to positive statements over 2003, 2004 & 2005

percentage of GPRs disagreeing on this item reached almost seven times that of nurses in 2005. Generally positive attitudes to the other disciplines' role are evident in responses to question 11 and the 77 % of nurses indicating otherwise in 2005 was exceptional.

Qualitative data were collated from the final three open-ended questions of the questionnaire. These were read and typed and formed the basis of post session discussion with the teaching team. Qualitative data were coded and emerging categories were identified and stored on an electronic data filing system, developed for ease of retrieval, and analysed. Manifest content analysis (Fox, 1982) resulted in the identification of several major categories and relevant written evidence of these was noted accordingly. Verbatim quotations were chosen to represent these major themes (Fetterman, 1989) and also included is the year of the session to which the comments relate.

STRUCTURE OF THE SESSION

Not surprisingly the role play exercise was met with a mixed response from both nurses and doctors. The tension often found when this teaching technique is used was evident.

> I know role-play is considered to be useful but I don't find it helpful. I find it nerve racking and disorienting, as I have no acting skills! (GPR, 2004)

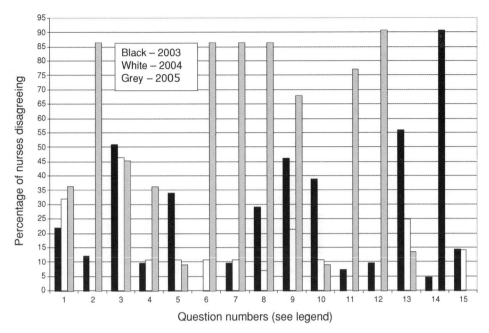

Figure 11.2 Percentage of nurse respondents disagreeing (sum of "disagree" option % and "strongly disagree" option %) with positive statements over 2003 (n = 41), 2004 (n = 28) and 2005 (n = 22).

1. There was little difference between the approaches taken to the scenarios by nurses and GP registrars.
2. This session indicated the benefits of shared education with community nurses/GP registrars.
3. I learned a lot about the role of community nurses/GP registrars GP registrars.
4. I have much to learn from community nurses/GP registrars.
5. The session did not stimulate me.*
6. Nurse/GP registrar participants of the session were at a similar academic level to that of GP registrars/nurse participants.
7. I found the community nurses/GP registrars to be interested in my role.
8. I found the session enjoyable.
9. The input of community nurses/GP registrars today will inform my practice.
10. The session was pitched at an overly simplistic level.*
11. I believe that the community nurses/GP registrars demonstrated a positive attitude towards my role.
12. I found the community nurses/GP registrars to be interested in GP registrars'/nurses' contributions to the discussion.
13. I did not learn a lot from this session.*
14. I am interested in further shared learning opportunities with community nurses/GP registrars.
15. The community nurses'/GP registrars' approach to the scenarios was overly social / psychological / biological in orientation.*

NB A separate questionnaire was used for each group and each prompted the respondents' view of the other professional group.
* Reverse scored item corrected for graphical presentation.

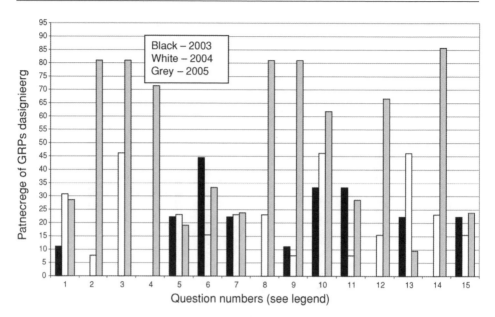

Figure 11.3 Percentage of GPR respondents disagreeing (sum of "disagree" option % and "strongly disagree" option %) with positive statements over 2003 (n = 9), 2004 (n = 13) and 2005 (n = 21).

Several commented that discussion would have been preferable to role play but the rationale for this may not have been related to the achievement of learning outcomes.

> Would have preferred discussion of roles – role play not that good. (CHN, 2003)

Around seven respondents offered suggestions for the use of teaching techniques other than role play.

> Did not find role playing the scenarios a useful exercise but shared learning with GPR would be extremely useful if approached in a different way e.g. exploring a case study from their perspective, discussing & challenging each other's roles. (GPN, 2003)

Preference for role play over skills rehearsal was around equally matched by the reverse.

> I liked the PM slot when people "swapped jobs" – my team members felt a lot more sympathetic to the GP afterward! (GPR, 2005)

> The difficulty of choosing the right scenario – experiment with playing other/own roles. (GPR, 2003)

> Get into smaller groups & discuss in more detail difficult cases & input of various disciplines (not role play). (CMHN, 2003)

> I enjoyed spending the day with other health workers but did not find pretending to play another role helpful. Could we not stick to our own roles but share out skills? (GPR, 2004)

The "goldfish bowl" role of supporter was not well utilised across the microgroups and this may have caused some discomfiture and frustration where participants were unable to operate explicitly in their professional role.

> Perhaps 1 session in different roles than our usual would be enough but with more struc-tured feedback in that area – e.g. if a GPR is playing the part of a GP the GP can

reinforce how they would really approach the problem in the discussion & vice versa. (GPR, 2003)

Minimal opportunity to discuss their perception of our role & our perception of their role. (SN, 2003)

Due to role-play not much time was spent explaining what they CAN offer. (GPR, 2004)

LEARNING ABOUT OF EACH OTHER'S ROLES

The discussion of respective roles was secondary only to the care scenario itself. Whether this was explicit enough is not clear and many participants felt that discipline roles had not been sufficiently discussed. Across all sessions, participants were encouraged to engage members of the "other" professional group in conversation over the refreshments and lunch provided.

I didn't feel that the GP registrars discussed their role. (GPN, 2004)

Not aware enough of the role we were playing and things to offer to make it realistic enough so role-play in role to get more out of it. (GPR, 2004)

More encouragingly, more commented positively than did not on their experiences of learning with and about the other discipline's role.

Learn from each other. New ideas and perspectives. (GPR, 2004)

It provided a greater understanding of their role and approach and increased multi/interprofessional development. (CMHN, 2004)

Reminds me that there are many different ways to approach any problem and that each contribution adds useful info to the "puzzle". (GPR, 2003)

I feel they have much to offer especially if a more holistic approach to learning is taken. It appears that many of them would like to take that approach so this was beneficial. (PHN, 2004)

Very enjoyable. I feel it enables greater working relationships, improves knowledge/understanding and increases the value of respective professional roles. (CMHN, 2004)

I realised they were normal!?! They discussed their roles well, and were appreciative of ours, which is very encouraging. (PHN, 2004)

PERCEPTION OF THREAT

Many participants expressed their experience of feeling threatened and five of the 2005 GPRs commented on their perception of "doctor bashing".

Essentially this is a "doctor bashing" exercise! Despite protests to the contrary, nurses clearly feel that GPs are an evil force and act accordingly towards us! They think we do too little and are paid too much. (GPR, 2005)

Quite doctor bashing! Especially at beginning with post-it notes. Didn't seem to understand our role despite us trying to understand theirs. (GPR, 2005)

This came as a surprise to the teaching team as the stereotypes identified for general practitioners seemed no more negative than that identified for the nursing specialisms. It may be that medical practitioners are unaccustomed to the elucidation of lay stereotypes of their role although these are explored at the beginning of the SCNP programmes when the expectations of the specialist practitioner role are examined. The SCNP students exhibited similar sensitivity in their experience of other parts of the session.

> Came to session feeling positive, but now feel despondent – I think that the attitude expressed by the medical facilitator in groups 3 & 4 demonstrated ignorance about the community nurses role e.g. code of conduct, confidentiality & record keeping which is worrying as this gets modelled to students. (PHN, 2003)

> Felt my role was attacked slightly as I had no medical insight into scenarios & was looking at them from PHN role. (PHN, 2003)

On reflection teaching team members felt that increased detail in the guidelines relating to stereotype coverage might have clarified whether the stereotypes generated by participants were reflective of their understanding of lay stereotypes, those typical of members of their professional group or personal stereotypes and this might have obviated some straightforward concerns here.

> Disappointed that stereotypes (especially nurses of doctors – ? mainly due to numbers) not addressed – felt "taboos" sustained rather than broken down. (GPR, 2003)

> I didn't feel that we gained a lot from the GP registrars as apart from [student's name] they didn't really share their role or ideas. (GPN, 2004)

> I believe they learnt more from us community professionals. (Nurse, specialism unknown, 2004)

BARRIERS TO IMPROVED MUTUAL UNDERSTANDING AND LEARNING

Generally the quantitative data (question 15, Figures 11.2 and 11.3) revealed only limited consideration that the other discipline's approach to the care scenario was overly biological or social/psychological and this was reiterated in the qualitative data.

> Made me less daunted by GPR/Nurse shared learning because everyone had an important role & appeared to respect those roles. (GPN, 2003)

The perception of limited or inaccurate understanding was evident in 10 % of all responses.

> Reinforced lack of understanding of our role – highlighted that GPs are still expecting to be knowledgeable in all areas rather than accessing others who are experts in their field. (PHN, 2003)

> I enjoyed meeting the community nurses, however, the stereotypes regarding GPs still remain. Perhaps explicit descriptions of the roles of each of the participants at the beginning of the day would be helpful. (GPR, 2004)

> Hopefully will help to break down barriers – feels though it is chipping away at the surface. (CNH, 2003)

> Different perspectives when looking at the scenarios. Do GPs know of other's roles? (CNH, 2004)

> Beginning to bridge gaps. (PHN, 2003)

> To understand each other's role a little more. Helps breakdown so called power issues. (PHN, 2004)

> They seemed to have a false perspective of my role as a GP Registrar and no interest in modifying this perspective. (GPR, 2004)

CONCLUSIONS AND RECOMMENDATIONS

The sensitivity of both groups to perceived undervaluing and criticism regarding their roles was higher than expected and further steps might profitably and simply have been taken to obviate this barrier to session IPE. This raises the importance of personal and professional self esteem. A more explicit consideration of this prior to the sessions might have increased participants' meta-cognition and impacted fruitfully on session discussion. Given the hostility experienced by GPRs it may also have proved useful to explore the wider contextual issues of community nurse employment and contrast with that of medical practitioners where this might have been expected to contribute to interprofessional tension, e.g. pay and conditions, philosophy of disorder and care (Purser et al., 1985), professional power levels, continuing professional development opportunities etc. Interestingly there was little evidence of the frequently found assumption of pre-eminence over other health care professional by medical practitioners (Horsburgh et al., 2001).

Feedback from earlier years was used to inform subsequent years' sessions but the variability in the cohorts limited the incremental development gained here. The patient care scenario formed the basis of the session work as recommended by Barr (2002) but no health care consumers were involved in the sessions or their preparation. The involvement of consumers and carers in session planning is desirable and with little extra work this would have been feasible. Despite the tensions evident the teaching team is committed to pursuing this format for IPE with these two groups and aim to develop this further.

PART TWO – CONSUMER INVOLVEMENT IN INTERVIEWING AND STUDENT ASSESSMENT

The School of Health and Social Care has developed increasing consumer involvement in its education provision over recent years and this culminated in the development of policy in 2002 which indicated its intention to ensure that consumers were involved in the planning, delivery, and evaluation of the School's courses.

> The School of Health and Social Care is committed to the involvement of health and social care service users and carers' groups in the planning, delivery and evaluation of programmes, as identified in the School Philosophy. It is appreciated that the level of involvement of service users and careers may vary depending on the module/programme and therefore this needs to be agreed by the programme team and underpinned with appropriate rationale. (Davis, 2002)

The exhortation for community involvement in service development, implementation and evaluation can be traced back as far as the Alma-Ata declaration of 1978 (WHO, 1978). The increased expectations of consumers (Hudson, 1990) may partly underpin the trend which has resulted in the increased salience for the UK Government of the consumers' perspective on and experience of health care (Secretary of State for Health, 2000, DoH, 2001b & c) in the development and delivery of services. The call for increased consumer involvement in the education of health care professionals came from the UK Government and nursing's professional body as long ago as 1996 (DoH, 1996, ENB, 1996) and the benefits of consumer involvement in health care professional education have been well documented if these claims enjoy only limited empirical support (Box 11.1).

Box 11.1. Drivers for Increased Consumer Involvement

Alma-Ata (WHO, 1978) recommended involving community in development, implementation and evaluation of services.

Value for money in 1970's and 1980's (Thompson, 1988).

Consumerism (Hudson, 1990).

Professional body guidelines for consumer involvement in education (ENB, 1996).

"Helpful to include users and carers" in training (DoH, 1996).

Care planning and delivery involvement (DoH, 1999).

National UK surveys of user experience (DoH, 1997).

Service users in planning and delivery (DoH, 2000, DoH, 2001c).

The School's SCNP programme teaching team contributed to the development of consumer involvement in the School and it is from this perspective and experience that this author writes and whose progress is discussed here (Box 11.2). The terminology in the area of consumer involvement often causes confusion and its potential to offend, often-disadvantaged groups, seems high. The team viewed health care consumers as those who

---

Box 11.2   Development of Community Teaching Team's Involvement of Health Care Consumers

March 2001	First "consumer involvement" meeting.
April 2001	Study on student practice assessment.
May 2001	Consumer representative joins group.
July 2001	Survey of consumer involvement in community courses.
July 2001	Terms of reference developed.
July 2002	School policy developed on consumer involvement.
June 2003	School wide survey audit on consumer involvement undertaken.
July 2003	Written consumer evaluation of students piloted.
May 2004	Student practice assessment study published (Spence and El Ansari, 2004)
May 2004	Consumer panel for community field programmes meets for first time.
April 2004	Funding proposal for school wide consumer involvement developed.
August 2004	Small scale student survey (n = 4) of views on consumer evaluation of students.
September 2004	Conference presentation on consumer evaluation work. Consumer evaluation of students' work implemented across community programmes.
April 2005	Internal proposal for consumer involvement in student selection (turned down).
September 2005	Small scale student survey (n = 25) of views on consumer evaluation of students.

Table 11.2 Benefits of consumer involvement in education and several restraining factors

Benefits of consumer involvement

Authors	Benefit
Cook et al., 1995	More positive attitude towards consumers.
	Less stigmatising attitudes in learners.
	More receptive orientation towards consumers.
Wood and Wilson-Barnett, 1999	Increased learner empathy with consumers.
Happell and Roper, 2003	Learners more likely to reflect on impact of practice.
Wykurz and Kelly, 2002	Increases respect for consumers.
	Deepens learners' understanding.

Restraining factors (Hickey & Kipping, 1998 classification)

Issue type	Restraining factor
User issues	Impact of mental health problem on decision making ability.
	Some users do not want to take part.
	Relinquish decision making to health care professionals.
Organisational culture	Lack of organisational commitment (esp. resources).
	Can disempowered staff empower?
	Strategic and equitable distribution of resources.
Professional culture	Illness treated only by professionals (cultural iatrogenesis).
	Psychiatric imperialism – more problems requiring psychiatry.
	Assume that patients cannot hold opinions.
	Willingness of staff to deal with criticism.
	Representativeness of users (Felton & Stickley, 2004).
Wider society	Negative stereotypes.
	Fear of mental illness.

currently use or have recently used the health services that SCNP students will most likely be involved in delivering.

The benefits of consumer involvement are well recognized and some of these are listed in Table 11.2.

The 2001 survey of community programmes at Oxford Brookes University revealed only limited involvement of consumers in programmes (Figure 11.4).

The involvement of mental health consumers in the assessment of post registration community mental health nursing students was developed from an earlier study (Spence and El-Ansari, 2004) of practice teacher experiences that demonstrated the existence of consumer involvement in the assessment of post registration community nursing students. The mechanism for collecting consumer feedback on student performance was informed by a group of relevant practice teachers and the present author who was programme leader. This was set against a backdrop of rather limited consumer involvement in service evaluation by the main employing NHS Mental Health Trust and the group adopted a fairly cautious approach to this development. A questionnaire was developed to tap the consumer's experience of the student's intervention following the end of the student's health care intervention (Table 11.3).

Key implementation actions	Present in programmes
Provide service users and carers with clearly written information about the programmed/modules e.g. course aims; learning outcomes.	Absent from all
Ensure students have information about service users and carers' groups.	Present in all
Gathering service users and careers views, e.g. the course content, their contact with students by: Accessing existing surveys/audits conducted by stakeholders.	Absent from all
Using questionnaires or interviews administered by the programmed team or students as part of learning.	Present in all
Obtaining feedback from service users and careers on their interactions with students, e.g. via questionnaire, assessment of students.	Present in three programmes
Obtaining feedback from students on their own experiences with service users and careers.	Present in four programmes
Consulting actively with service users and careers about curriculum planning, delivery and evaluation through a range of activities: Accessing existing support groups, public meetings, and service user panels.	Present in one programme
Accessing stakeholder groups.	Present in one programme
Holding workshops, open days.	Absent in all programmes
Working with service users and careers on the development of new and existing programmers: Being part of programmed planning teams.	Absent in all programmes
Being involved in staff recruitment.	Absent in all programmes
Being involved in decisions about environment, access, and new facilities.	Absent in all programmes
Service users directly involved in and responsible for aspects of curriculum delivery, for example: As consultants for development of programmers and the work of the School.	Absent in all programmes
Taking responsibility for the management and delivery of some aspects of the curriculum.	Absent in all programmes

Figure 11.4   2003 survey of seven SCNP programmes

The questionnaires items included both a prompt for quantitative and qualitative data and an example of the layout is shown in diagram one. Patient consent was not sought initially but the later develop included a detailed consent form that student were required to use to secure consent prior to questionnaire distribution. The completed questionnaire was required to be returned to the student's practice teacher who would not be able to identify the patient form the questionnaire. Practice teachers used the returned questionnaires to provide feedback to students that would enable their development. The practice assessment

Table 11.3   Questionnaire items for consumer evaluation of student over 2003/2004

I felt that the student listened well to what I had to say.
I felt that the student was able to understand my viewpoint well.
I found the help offered by the student to be effective.
I agreed with the student's assessment of my situation.
I found advice offered by the student to be most helpful.
I felt that the student involved me as much as possible in the care offered.
I felt that the student involved my family and/or friends as much as possible in care offered.
The student inspired confidence in me.
I feel that the student's help resulted in an improvement in my health (or the patients' health,
    where you are a carer) over the period that she/he was involved in my care (or the care of
    the patient, where you are a carer).
The student was able to engage me in meaningful dialogue relating to my difficulties.
I felt that the student developed a good understanding of my local community.
The student had a good knowledge of life.
The student had a caring approach to me.
I found the student to be very approachable.
Overall, I was satisfied with the help provided by the student.

portfolio contained prompts for students and practice teachers to estimate the percentage contribution of various sources of evidence to the assessment of practice and this included the patient and carers' contribution.

Despite these prompts the extent to which patients contributed to the students' final portfolio evidence in the small 2004 cohort of community mental health nurses was very limited (Figure 11.6).

Following the 2004 implementation of the consumer and carer feedback procedure students were given a questionnaire to evaluate their experience of this although responses were too few to warrant any thematic analysis. The format of this questionnaire is presented in Figure 11.7 together with one response.

Levin (2004) has recently called for consumer involvement in education at all levels including: student selection, course design, teaching and learning provision, preparation for practice learning, provision of placements, learning agreements, student assessment and quality assurance. The value of consumer involvement in student selection to "significantly enhance an assessment of how a potential recruit relates to other people" has been recognised by Tew et al., (2004, p. 24) in their good practice guide to consumer involvement in education. They go on to highlight the potential of consumer involvement in interviewing in:

I felt that the student listened well to what I had to say.

Very strongly agree	Strongly agree	Agree	Neither agree nor disagree	Disagree	Strongly disagree	Very strongly disagree

Please comment further on the strengths and weaknesses of the student's listening abilities:

Figure 11.5   Questionnaire layout example

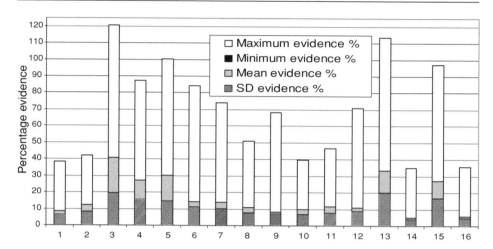

Figure 11.6 2004 CMHN student (n = 4) reported % evidence source across 29 learning outcomes.
1 = Notes of meetings, 2 = Action plans, 3 = A piece of formal reflection, 4 = Review of patientís needs and care, 5 = Citation of literature, 6 = Extracts from a reflective diary, 7 = Short written reports, 8 = Case study, 9 = Critical incident technique, 10 = Observations and witness statements, 11 = Records of discussions with supervisor, 12 = Examples of data collection, e.g. caseload/community profile

demonstrating how the experience of service users is valued, advertising the programme's value base, and in shaping the attitudes and expectations of future students. The proposal to effect this as a next step did not enjoy the support of senior managers. Levin (2004) has highlighted the challenges faced by higher education institutions in implementing consumer involvement in interviewing for places on social work degree courses in 2003 and these – availability of service users and carers, consumer preparation along with other members of the panel, substantial time demands that direct involvement places on consumers, issue of consistency and equity in the process for students, resource implications, including fee payment – should be considered by those for whom this would be a desirable development.

The patient/carer questionnaire feedback raised no matters that I did not anticipate.

Very strongly agree	Strongly agree	Agree	Neither agree nor disagree	Disagree	Strongly disagree	Very strongly disagree

Please indicate the matters that were raised and rate the extent to which they were anticipated by you (from 0 = not anticipated to 7 = highly anticipated).

"All matters were anticipated."

Figure 11.7 Item from student questionnaire

LESSONS LEARNED

The consumer involvement group first met before the appointment of the consumer representatives. This potentially disempowering action set the wrong tone for the group although this was largely retrieved by the recruitment of a very able and politically aware mental health consumer representative whose contribution was sizeable. In financially straitened times in higher education the high prioritisation of consumer involvement cannot be assumed by education managers facing many competing priorities. The virtual hegemony of general health care practitioners in higher education departments offering mental health education may contribute to the de-prioritisation of this issue. The power sharing anticipated by consumer involvement will require a planned and incremental approach to change management where lecturing staff may not be expected to give control of their work particularly where this may already be seen to be overly limited in the tightly controlled workloads of staff commonly found in post 1992 universities.

REFERENCES

Ausubel, D.P., Novak, J.S. & Hanesian, H. (1978). *Educational psychology: a cognitive view*. New York: Holt Rinehart and Winston.

Barr, H. (1994). *Perspectives on shared learning*. London: CAIPE.

Barr, H. (1998). Competent to collaborate: towards a competency based model for interprofessional education. *Journal of Interprofessional Care 12*(2), 181–188.

Barr, H. (2002). *Interprofessional education, today, yesterday and tomorrow: A review*. London: UK centre for the advancement of interprofessional education.

Barr, H., Freeth, D., Hammick, M., Koppel, I. & Reeves, S. (2000). *Evaluations of interprofessional education, a UK review for health and social care*. London: The UK centre for the advancement of interprofessional education.

Barr, H., Koppel, I., Reeves, S., Hammick, M. & Freeth. D. (2005). *Effective Interprofessional Education: Argument, Assumption and Evidence*. Oxford: Blackwell.

Black, E. & John, W.G. (1986). Leadership of the multi-disciplinary team in psychiatry – a nursing perspective. *Nursing Practice, 1*, 177–192.

Bruner, J.S. (1960). *The process of education*. Cambridge, MA: Harvard University Press.

Bruner, J.S. (1964). The course of cognitive growth, *American Psychologist, 19*, 1–15.

Butler, J.E. & Walter, J.C. (eds) (1991). *Transforming the Curriculum: Ethnic Studies and Women's Studies*. Albany, NY: State University of New York.

CAIPE (1997). Interprofessional Education A* Definition. CAIPE Bulletin No. 13.

Callinicos, A. (1989). *Against postmodernism: A Marxist critique*. Cambridge: Polity Press.

Carrier, J. & Kendall, I. (1995). Professionalism and interprofessionalism in health and community care: some theoretical issues. In: P. Owens, J. Carrier & J. Horder. *Interprofessional issues in community and primary health care*. Basingstock: Macmillan.

Cook, J. A., Jonikas, J. A. & Razzano, L. (1995). A randomised evaluation of consumer versus non-consumer training of state mental health service providers. *Community Mental Health Journal, 31*(3), 229–238.

Davis, S. (2002). *Involvement of service users and carers in the curriculum: School of health and social care strategy*. Oxford: Oxford Brookes University.

Department of Health (1996). *Building Bridges. A guide to arrangements for inter-agency working for the care and protection of severely mentally ill people*. London: Department of Health.

Department of Health (1997). The new NHS, modern and dependable, London: The Stationery Office Ltd.

Department of Health (1999). National service framework for mental health, London: Department of Health.

Department of Health (2001a). *Working together, Learning together: A framework for lifelong learning in the NHS*. London: Stationary Office. URL: www/doh.gov.uk/lifelonglearning. Accessed: 22. March 2003.

Department of Health (2000). The NHS Plan, A Plan for investment, A plan for reform, London: HMSO.

DoH (2001b). *The expert patient: A new approach to chronic disease management for the 21st Century*. London: DoH.

Department of Health (2001c). *Involving patients and the public*. London: HMSO.

Department of Health (2002). Mental Health Policy Implementation Guide: Community Mental Health Teams, London: DoH.

Engel, C.E. (2002). *Towards a European approach to an enhanced education of the health professions in the 21st century: Report of the European extraprofessional consultation*. London: CAIPE.

English National Board for Nursing, Midwifery, and Health Visiting (1996). *Learning from each other*. London: English National Board.

Felton, A. & Stickley, T. (2004). Pedagogy, power and service user involvement. *Journal of Psychiatric and Mental Health Nursing*, 11, 89–98.

Fetterman, D.M. (1989). *Ethnography: step by step, Applied Social Research Methods Series, 17*. Newbury Park, CA: Sage.

Finch, J. (2000). Interprofessional education and teamworking: a view from the education providers, *British Medical Journal, 321*, 1138–1140.

Foucault M. (1980). *Power/knowledge: Selected interviews and other writings 1972–77*, (ed) C. Gordon. New York: Pantheon.

Fox, D.T. (1982). *Fundamentals of Research in Nursing*. Connecticut: Appleton Century Crofts.

Freeth, D., Meyer, J., Reeves, S. & Spilsbury, K. (1998). *Of drops in the ocean and stalactites: interprofessional education within healthcare settings*, BERA, Queen's University, Belfast. 27–30 August.

Freeth, D., Hammick, M., Koppel, I., Reeves, S. & Barr, H. (2002). *A Critical Review of Evaluations of Interprofessional Education*, London: Learning and Teaching Support Network for Health Sciences and Practice. URL: www.healthheacademy.ac.uk. Retrieved: 21 March 2003.

Galvin, S.W. & McCarthy, S. (1994). Multi-disciplinary community teams: Clinging to the wreckage, *Journal of Mental Health, 3*, 157–166.

Glen, S. & Hight, N. (1992). Portfolios: An "affective" assessment strategy? *Nurse Education Today, 12*, 416–423.

Happell, B. & Roper, C. (2003). The role of a mental health consumer in the education of postgraduate psychiatric nursing students: the students' evaluation. *Journal of Psychiatric and Mental Health Nursing, 10*, 343–350.

Hart, E. & Bond, M. (1995). *Action research for health and social care: A guide to practice*. Buckingham: Open University Press.

Horsburgh, M., Lamdin, R. & Williamson, E. (2001). Multiprofessional learning: the attitudes of medical, nursing and pharmacy students to shared learning, *Medical Education, 35*, 876–883.

Hudson, B. (1990). Free speech, not lip service. *Health Service Journal*, June, 918–919.

Koppel, I. (1998). *Evaluation of interprofessional education: State of art: The IPE JET study*, BERA, Queen's University, Belfast. 27–30 August.

Lash, S. & Urry, J. (1987). *The End of Organised Capitalism*. Cambridge: Polity Press.

Levin, E. (2004). *Involving service users and carers in social work education*. London: Social Care Institute for Excellence.

Lewin, K. (1946). Action research and minority problems. In: G. W. Lewin (ed.)*Resolving social conflicts: Selected papers on group dynamics*, Kurt Lewin, 1948. New York: Harper and brothers.

Lyotard, J. (1984, original 1979). *The Postmodern Condition*. Manchester: Manchester University Press.

Mayer, M. (1993). Action research, history and images of science, *Educational Action Research, 1*, (2), 317–319.

McCroskey, J. & Robertson, P.J. (1999). Challenges and Benefits of Interprofessional Education: Evaluation of the Inter-Professional Initiative at the University of Southern California. *Teacher Education Quarterly*, Fall, 69–87.

Mohrman, S.A., Cohen, S.G. & Mohrman, A.M. (1995). *Designing team based organisations.* San Francisco: Josey Bass.

Murphy, J.W. (1989). Clinical intervention in the postmodern world, *International Journal of Adolescence and Youth, 2,* 61–69.

O'Neill, B., Wyness, A., McKinnon, S. & Granger, P. (2000). *Partnership, Collaboration and Course Design: An emerging model of interprofessional education.* URL: www.cstudies.ubc.ca/facdev/services/registry/pcacdaemoie.htm. Retrieved on 23 September 2005.

Petrie, H.G. (1976). Do you see what I see? The epistemology of interdisciplinary inquiry, *Journal of Aesthetic Education, 10,* 29–43.

Priest, H, Sawyer A., Roberts P. & Rhodes S (1995). A survey of interprofessional education in communication skills in health care programmes in the UK. *Journal of Interprofessional Care, 19*(3), 236–250.

Purser, H., Fagin, L., Eades, M., & Brunning, H. (1985). Interdisciplinary Working. In: Echlin, R. (1988), *Community Mental Health Centres/Teams Information Pack,* Surrey, Good Practices in Mental Health, Interdisciplinary Association of Mental Health Workers.

Reiss, H. (Ed.) (1971). Kant's Political Writings, Cambridge: Cambridge University Press.

Robbins, S.P. (2001). *Organizational behavior.* New Jersey: Prentice Hall.

Russel, B. (1988). A History of Western Philosophy, London: Unwin.

Schofield, M. (1995). *The future health care workforce: The steering group report,* Manchester, Health Services Management Unit, University of Manchester.

Secretary of State for Health (2000). *The NHS Plan: A Plan for Investment, A Plan for Reform.* London: Stationery Office.

Spence, W. & El-Ansari, W. (2004). Portfolio assessment: practice teachers' early experience, *Nurse Education Today, 24,* 388–401.

Tew, J., Gell. & Foster, S. (2004). *Learning from experience Involving service users and carers in mental health education and training: a good practice guide,* Higher Education Academy/NIMHE/Trent Workforce Development Confederation, Nottingham.

Thompson, A. (1988). The practical implications of patient satisfaction research, Health Services Management Research, 1(2), 112–119.

Tyrer, P. Coid, J., Simmonds, S., Joseph, P. & Marriott, S. (2002). Community mental health teams (CMHTs) for people with severe mental illnesses and disordered personality (Cochrane Review). In: *The Cochrane Library,* Issue 4. Oxford: Update Software.

Usher, R. & Edwards, R. (1994). *Postmodernism and Education.* London: Routledge.

von Glaserfield, E. (1991). An exposition of Constructivism: Why some like it radical, in R.B. Davis., C.A. Maher and N. Noddings, (eds), *Constructivist Views of the Teaching and Learning of Mathematics.* Washington, D.C.: National Council of Teachers of Mathematics.

Walker, D. (1998). The Third Way: Tony's ology for sceptics. *The Guardian,* September 2.

Wood, J. & Wilson-Barnett, J. (1999). The influence of user involvement on the learning of mental health nursing students. *Nursing Times Research, 4,* 257–270.

World Health Organization (1978). The Alma-Ata conference on primary health care, *WHO Chronicle,* 32.

Wykurz, G. & Kelly, D. (2002). Developing the role of the patients as teachers: literature review, British Medical Journal, 325, 818–821.

Zwarenstein, M. & Bryant, W. (2002). Interventions to promote collaboration between nurses and doctors. Cochrane Database of Systematic Reviews, 4.

Zwarenstein, M., Reeves, S., Barr, H., Hammick, M., Koppel, I., Atkins, J. Interprofessional education: effects on professional practice and health care outcomes (Cochrane Review). *The Cochrane Database of Systematic Reviews 2000,* Issue 3, Art. No.: CD002213. DOI:10.1002/14651858.CD002213.

Key Topics in Mental Health Education

CHAPTER 12

Values-based Practice in Teaching and Learning

Bill Fulford and Kim Woodbridge

INTRODUCTION

With so much on the mental health agenda why start with values-based practice? You cannot touch, smell or see values, and it is unlikely that you can truly measure them. "Values" is an abstract concept that we struggle to explain and define. Most of the time, like the air we breathe, values, although influencing everything we do, are more or less invisible!

But we do have sufficient reason to believe that a shared concept known as "values" exists between those receiving and delivering mental health services, also that these values play a significant part in the individual's wellbeing in both cases. At the level of organisations, the importance of values is reflected in such areas as ethical codes, governance and standards – the National Service Framework for Mental Health (Department of Health 1999) for example, incorporates as key values, user-centred practice and multidisciplinary teamwork. Similarly, at the level of day-to-day practice, it is the values of individual stakeholders, both users of services and practitioners that are important. And all these values, both at an individual and organisational level, are likely to be competing, complex and conflicting.

To illustrate the significance of values see Pete's account below.

> My name is Pete. I'm 44 and I live in a room in a house that I share with 4 other people who have mental problems. I live in one of the rooms on the top floor. My friend Colin lives in the other one. I should have a key to lock my room but the key's broken. The light bulb's gone on the stairs so it's very dark in the hall. Elsie is on duty today.
>
> I shake a lot and sometimes dribble. I try to wipe my mouth before I dribble but I'm not always quick enough. I wish I didn't dribble, it's embarrassing when I talk to people. My right arm is hot and swollen. I've seen the GP, he says there's nothing he can do about it. I wonder if it's the chemicals I use that causes it.
>
> My brother visited today. He was really upset when he saw me. He'd come to take me and Colin out for lunch. I had some one else's trousers on and I had to hold them up as they were too big for me. I told my brother I didn't wear underpants, I do but I didn't have any and he was already upset. All my clothes go into the laundry and get lost. I just have to wear what I can find.
>
> My brother, me and Colin went to Tesco, we bought some new clothes, then we went for lunch. I can't chew so I had the soup. I think it's my tablets that make it difficult for me to chew. I take my tablets, Procycladine and Olanzepine.

Teaching Mental Health. Edited by Theo Stickley and Thurstine Basset.
Copyright © 2007 John Wiley & Sons, Ltd.

> On the way back in the car I was teasing my brother, he has satellite navigation. Colin was teasing him as well, I don't think he minds, we all laughed. I like photography, I go to a course at college and develop my own pictures. I want to take landscape photographs. I showed my brother my photos, he wants to frame them they're so good.
>
> It's my birthday tomorrow, my brother left me some presents, some tobacco and a bottle of larger. Colin told him we can't have alcohol in the house. I know my brother cry's sometimes after he visits me.

This account reveals that although by many service standards Pete "has it all" – accommodation, meaningful activity, friends, contact with a relative and income, and he is both taking medication and is not a risk to himself or others – there is something fundamentally lacking from his lived experience. One way of understanding this is through values.

Because values are so important, widespread and complicated it is essential to consciously address them, not in a static way but as a dynamic process. This is where values-based practice comes in. Values-based practice is a new approach to working with values in health and social care that is being actively rolled out through a wide range of policy and training initiatives in such areas as recovery, social inclusion and delivering race equality. (See "Resources for Further Reading" at the close of this chapter for some examples.)

WHICH OF THE FOLLOWING IS VALUES-BASED PRACTICE?

The term "values-based practice" may already be a familiar one or suggest a particular meaning. However this can also lead to confusion. When referring to values-based practice the authors of this chapter have a particular approach in mind. To illustrate this consider the following: which of the statements below would you say was values-based practice?

(a) It is practice that is based on a statement of identified values that it aspires to adhere to.
(b) It is practice that starts from a strong and explicit moral values base.
(c) It is practice that is guided by a previously determined and authorised ethical framework.
(d) It is a way of working in health and social care that starts from respect for individual differences of values and provides a clear process for coming to balanced decisions where values are in conflict.

You may have said all of the above. However, within this chapter when we refer to values-based practice we mean the last of these possible meanings (d). A more detailed definition of values-based practice is that it is the theory and skills-base for decision making where legitimately different, and therefore potentially conflicting, values are in play.

In this chapter we start with a brief outline of the 10 key principles, which are the pointers that make up the "process" of values-based practice and describe the National Framework of Values adopted by the National Institute for Mental Health England (NIMHE) to support the development of values-based practice approaches nationally. We then give some worked examples of values-based practice first for an individual and then for a team. Finally, we outline how values-based practice can be used in training and practice development and summarise some of the key "success factors" and influences for working with this approach. At the close of this chapter, we describe some resources for further reading and study.

THE 10 PRINCIPLES OF VALUES-BASED PRACTICE

The 10 principles that guide the process of values-based practice are outlined briefly below.

1. **Awareness.** To raise awareness of the values present in each situation.
2. **Reasoning.** There are many powerful ways of reasoning about values, including revealing the values present in our own reasoning.
3. **Knowledge.** It is important to get as much information about what is know about values in any situation. This includes evidence-based knowledge.
4. **Communication.** Because there has to be a sharing of the values and the process of coming to a decision, communication is central to all the principles of values-based practice.
5. **Service user centred.** The first source for information on values in each situation is the perspective of the service user concerned.
6. **Multi-perspective.** Conflicts of values are resolved not by applying a "pre-prescribed rule" but by working towards a balance of different perspectives.
7. **Facts and values.** *All* decisions are based on facts *and* values.
8. However values are only noticed when there is conflict, dis-census rather than consensus.
9. Increasing scientific knowledge is leading to an increasing role for values in decision-making.
10. **Partnership.** Decisions are made through people working together and in partnership.

These principles are applied within the following NIMHE Values Framework, please see below:

THE NATIONAL FRAMEWORK OF VALUES FOR MENTAL HEALTH (NIMHE 2005)

The work of NIMHE on values in mental health care is guided by three principles of values-based practice:

1. **Recognition** – NIMHE recognises the role of values alongside evidence in all areas of mental health policy and practice.
2. **Raising awareness** – NIMHE is committed to raising awareness of the values involved in different contexts, the role/s they play and their impact on practice in mental health.
3. **Respect** – NIMHE respects diversity of values and will support ways of working with such diversity that makes the principle of service-user centrality a unifying focus for practice. This means that the values of each individual service user/client and their communities must be the starting point and key determinant for all actions by professionals.

Respect for diversity of values encompasses a number of specific policies and principles concerned with equality of citizenship. In particular, it is anti-discriminatory because discrimination in all its forms is intolerant of diversity. Thus respect for diversity of values has the consequence that it is unacceptable (and unlawful in some instances) to discriminate on grounds such as gender, sexual orientation, class, age, abilities, religion, race, culture or language.

Respect for diversity within mental health is also:

- **user-centred** – it puts respect for the values of individual users at the centre of policy and practice.
- **recovery orientated** – it recognises that through building on the personal strengths and resiliencies of people and on their cultural and racial characteristics, there are many diverse routes to recovery.
- **multidisciplinary** – it requires that respect be reciprocal, at a personal level (between service users, their family members, friends, communities and providers), between different provider disciplines (such as nursing, psychology, psychiatry, medicine, social work), and between different organisations (including health, social care, local authority housing, voluntary organisations, community groups, faith communities and other social support services).
- **dynamic** – it is open and responsive to change;
- **reflective** – it combines self monitoring and self management with positive self regard.
- **balanced** – it emphasises positive as well as negative values.
- **relational** – it puts positive working relationships supported by good communication skills at the heart of practice.

NIMHE will encourage educational and research initiatives aimed at developing the capabilities (the knowledge and skills) needed to deliver mental health services that will give effect to the principles of values-based practice.

So to sum up, in the context of this chapter, values-based practice is:

- a framework drawn from the theoretical principles developed by Bill Fulford and their practical application and evaluation by Kim Woodbridge.
- a process for working explicitly *with* values. This differs from other approaches, which focus on "getting the right values".
- working with personal values such as preferences, aesthetic values, such as what is beautiful, moral values, value messages and value statements.
- based on the belief that that today's health and social care is complex and raises problems, which cannot be addressed by one standardised answer. The values present are multilayered and often conflicting.

The aim of values-based practice is to start with respect for differences and to use the 10 principles to achieve a balance of values in any given situation. The intention is not essentially to achieve a consensus but to develop an understanding and to acknowledge and give space to the different perspectives.

Finally, values-based practice is not something that is done once in the past during training or something that can be done alone, or unilaterally within a team. It is an ongoing process that everyone who is involved in a particular situation, decision, or action is consciously and explicitly engaged in.

CAPTURING THE VBP PROCESS IN PRACTICE

Before teaching and learning values-based practice it is essential to have an understanding of what this can look like in practice. There are several levels and ways to capture the process of VBP. The following are just two examples; one is at the individual level the other is at the team level.

The example at the individual level is within the context of complex decision-making where the individual has been identified as having learning disabilities. The situation was very stressful for the family and there were concerns by the social worker involved that as a result they would be vulnerable to mental health problems in the future. In the case of this example the VBP process has been supported by the use of a process form.

VALUES-BASED PRACTICE PROCESS FORM: A COMPLETED EXAMPLE

This example shows how the VBP process can help with decision-making in a complex situation.

Box 12.1

1. Give a brief description of the decision that is to be made.
    Julie lives at home with her Mum and Dad (Mrs and Mr. Davis). She is an adult and since she was born she has had difficulties with learning and has needed to live with someone to help her cope with every-day life. She also has several physical problems, including difficulty with walking. She doesn't usually walk very far and gets about at home by holding onto things. She has a walking frame and wheelchair for when she goes out.
    Julie's Mum and Dad are getting older and are not very well. Julie's Mum finds it very hard to cope and would like a rest. She also knows that it will soon be time when they will not be able to look after Julie and Julie will not be able to live with them at home. Because of this Julie was given an overnight stay at a residential and day centre. Staying at the centre gave Julie an opportunity to meet her friends and get involved in activities outside her home, such as IT. It was also intended that an assessment of Julie's physical needs would be completed while she was staying. There were more stays planned, about one a month, but Julie stayed once and now does not want to stay again. The decision now is about "what should happen next'. Written by Jane, Julie's Social Worker.

What does this mean to Julie, what does he/she think should happen and what are the reasons for his/her decision?

VBP Principles

1. **Awareness.** To raise awareness of the values present in each situation.
2. **Reasoning.** Revealing the values present in our reasoning.
3. **Service user centred.** The first source for information on values in each situation is the perspective of the service user concerned

I don't think I should go to the day centre again for a stay. I like staying at home because I can watch Mrs Bouquet on TV and be with my cat. I worry that my dad isn't looking after my cat properly when I'm not here (home). It's also easier to get things when I want them, I don't have to walk so far. It was nice to see Mandy, my friend, but the centre was boring. I also missed my own bed and Mum and Dad.

What does this mean to others involved, what do they think should happen and what are their reasons?

VBP principles

1. **Awareness.** To raise awareness of the values present in each situation.
2. **Reasoning.** Revealing the values present in our own reasoning.
3. **Multi-perspective.** Conflicts of values are resolved not by applying a "pre-prescribed rule" but by working towards a balance of different perspectives

Mum:

I think Julie should go to the centre and stay overnight, I need the break and I think it will be good for her. But she doesn't want to go so I don't know what else we can do. She gets very upset if we say she has to go. So I suppose we should leave her be and carry on while we can.

Dad:

I don't know what we should do. She doesn't like going and she gets very upset. I don't know what else we can do. Just leave her alone and carry on.

Jane (Julie's Social Worker):

No one has asked Julie about what she thinks could be done about giving her Mum and Dad a break or what she wants to do when they can't look after her in the future. So I think the next thing I have to do is ask Julie these questions. I need to give her time and space to think about this so may suggest we go out for a coffee.

Emma (staff member from the Centre):

I would like Julie to stay again and I think we should try to encourage her to stay again. Try to make it that she wants to come. Because although she said she doesn't want to come again she seemed to really enjoy it when she was here. She was talking all evening with her friend Mandy, and joined in well with all the others. I noticed that although she didn't seem confident in doing things when she first got here by the next day she was really looking after herself well and I think that must be good for her. Especially because her Mum and Dad will not be able to look after for much longer. It would be really good if she could gradually spend more time here and get more confident and able to look after herself.

Facts and values that would be useful to know when making this decision.

VBP principles

3. **Knowledge.** It is important to get as much information about what is known about values in any given situation.
7. **Facts and values.** All decisions are based on facts and values. What do we know from evidence-based practice that is relevant to this situation?

We don't know much about the values or the research in this area. Jane thought there was some evidence of the impact that loss has on people, which would be useful to know. Also about how people in a similar situation to Julie and her Mum and Dad usually cope.

Decision and next steps: What has been decided and what are the reasons for the decision. Who is going to do what and when

VBP principles

4. **Communication.** Because there has to be a sharing of the values and the process of coming to a decision, communication is central to all the principles of values-based practice.
10. **Partnership.** Decisions are made through people working together and in partnership.

It seems that what is most important to Julie at the moment is the care of her cat, the company of her Mum and Dad and the comfort she has at home. From what Mum and Dad say although it would be good to have a break but they do not want Julie upset. Jane (Julie social worker) and Emma (from the centre) are worried about Julie's wellbeing in the future and think it is good for Julie to become more able to take care of herself away from home. They also want to respect Julie's choice and do not want to upset her.

Jane and Julie will spend time together next Thursday to find out if Julie has any ideas about what else she could do to give mum and Dad and break. Also to find out what Julie thinks would be good to happen for her in the future when Mum and Dad, because of their physical health, are no longer able to take care of her at home.

Then on the following Tuesday Emma and Julie will talk about what would make it more enjoyable for Julie to come to the Centre, if there is anything that would make her want to come.

Jane will try to find the information about how people cope in a similar situation and also about coping with change and loss.

We agreed to meet again on Monday 24 May to catch up on what has happened and then make the next decision about what should happen.

Date: Monday 10 May.

Signed: Julie, Mrs Davis Mr Davis Jane Emma.

VALUES-BASED PRACTICE AT THE TEAM LEVEL: A STUDY

The second example of capturing VBP in practice is taken from studying a home treatment team. Values-based practice is about raising awareness of values, respect for differences and encourages the inclusion of multi-perspectives in decision making. Below are some results from a study of an East London Home Treatment Team. The first graph below shows an observation of the perspectives present at the care review meetings.

The next graph shows the frequency of subjects discussed at the meetings. There are several interesting observations that can be made. For example, this team believed it practiced holistically however this is not evident from the subjects discussed with medication and symptoms at the top of the list. Also the family was often discussed but the carer's perspective is seldom present in the discussion. Finally discharge was discussed frequently yet social networks were rarely mentioned.

HOW VBP CAN BE USED IN TRAINING AND PRACTICE DEVELOPMENT

One of the most successful ways for enabling the taking on of VBP has been through the facilitation of workshops.

The challenge of teaching and learning values-based practice is its abstract nature and facilitating the "working with values" rather than the "working to get to the right values" process. If as a facilitator these challenges can be successfully met then the workshops are a powerful forum for meaningful work. Values-based practice can be used as a way to:

- incorporate a range of diverse perspectives in relation to any given situation.
- provide a structure for balanced decision making when there are complex, conflicting and competing values.
- problem solve complex problems.

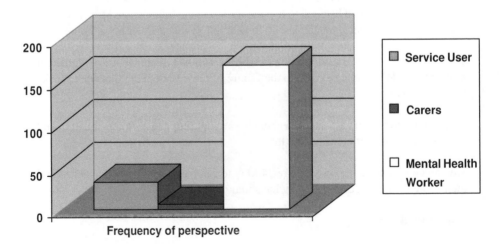

Figure 12.1 Frequency of perspective presented.

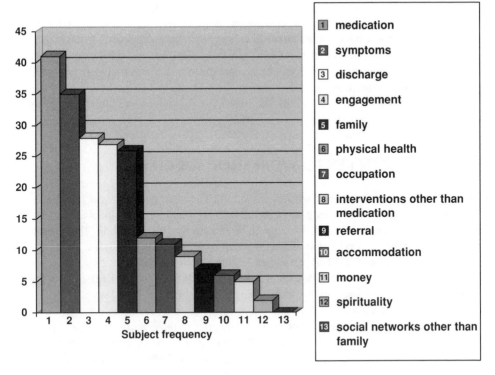

Figure 12.2 Frequency of subject present.

- reflect in depth, at the level of values relating to beliefs and attitudes.
- analyse language within clinical and managerial documentation.
- generate change and innovation in systems, services, roles and relationships.
- underpin, in partnership with evidence-based practice, the essential capabilities for mental health practice.
- provide a foundation for the curriculum of a postgraduate programme in mental health practice.

and VBP workshops have been used to:

- raise awareness of values and value messages present in a given situation.
- facilitate team building.
- consider issues of diversity particularly in relation to black, minority and ethnic groups, within practice.
- develop a team operational policy.
- provide a foundation from different stakeholder perspectives for building a new service provision i.e. the introduction of a crisis team.
- provide managers with an opportunity to reflect on the values within the organisation and service development plans and process.
- provide an opportunity for an NHS Trust Board to consider the Trust's values and aspirations.

- train others to run introductory values based practice workshops.
- crystallise the values underpinning a particular approach and then to develop action plans for change within services based on those values.
- generate new information that will clarify the issues and present solutions to complex questions about delivering care from a human perspective as an alternative to institutional and role defined thinking.
- develop VBP knowledge and skills for practice as a module within a postgraduate programme.

WHAT HAS BEEN KEY TO WORKSHOP SUCCESS?

The style of the workshops has been very important. There has been an explicit recognition that this is a collaborative venture between the facilitator and the participants. There is not a previously identified body of knowledge to be imparted at the workshop. The workshop itself is an adventure, expedition and inquiry, an experiment and study of values-based practice with both facilitator and participant learning from the process.

Very little workshop time has been spent on teaching values-based practice because people struggle to relate the abstract theory to the doing of anything in their real word. If too much time is spent on the theoretical description and explanation of values-based practice there is at best a "that's interesting" response. To really engage those participating and make it meaningful they have to directly engage in the process. For example the question "where you ever made to eat something you didn't like as a child?" which gets the participant to experience the impact of values as a personal preference will get a thriving discussion going no matter what the individual's background.

Also the best discussions have occurred when there has been a very mixed group participating, including clinical, managerial staff, people who have used mental health services, voluntary organisations and relatives of those who have used services matched by a mix in co-facilitators. Most workshops have been co-facilitated from a range of perspectives including service user, chief executive, professor, clinician and relative of a person using services.

Time is extremely important commodity within the workshops and keeping the activities simple. It is far better to have one activity per session where the individuals have time to discuss and respond thoughtfully than to get through several different activities. The activities also need to build in a logical sequence, with a balance of drawing information from the participants and sharing information already prepared.

The ability of the facilitator to stand outside the discussions and to have no prior values agenda has been essential to encourage open exploration of values within the group and for the group members to come to their own discoveries.

We have used a range of methods to evaluate the impact of the workshops: focus groups, questionnaires and anecdotal learning record forms. We have also learnt a considerable amount from keeping our own field notes when delivering workshops. But the work of getting a robust, meaningful and useful process continues, as does the learning from the evaluations we have received. However, a constant observation of all these workshops is that this approach allows each person to equally enter the discussion, as it is not based on any excluding technical language or knowledge. All participants enter the discussion from the human perspective.

OTHER KEY INFLUENCES ON THE WORKSHOPS DESIGN AND DELIVERY

When designing the workshop considerable thought has been given to the following factors:

- The nature and characteristics of adult learners.
- The transferability of learning from the workshops to real world situations.
- The congruence between the principles of values-based practice and the design, delivery and experience of the workshops (to practice what is preached).
- Giving conscious and explicit attention to the dynamic between espoused and acted values.
- The promotion of learning by doing and structured reflection.

CONCLUSION

Addressing values in mental health is a key foundation and first step to a range of circumstances and situations. If this step is overlooked, a sense of getting lost or stuck and frustration is likely to occur. Using the values-based practice framework as described here has proved to be an inspirational and human approach to complex and sensitive situations. There is much further work to complete in developing values-based practice and it is likely to be an ongoing, challenging but important journey.

RESOURCES FOR FURTHER READING

In this section we give a range of publications and of a web-based resources for further reading and study on values-based practice.

Training Resources

(1) Woodbridge, K. & Fulford, K.W.M. (2004). *Whose Values? A workbook for values-based practice in mental health care*. London: Sainsbury Centre for Mental Health.

This training manual, which was developed in a partnership between the Sainsbury Centre for Mental Health (SCMH) and the Department of Philosophy and the Medical School at Warwick University, introduces the principles of Values-Based Practice and includes detailed training materials (suitable for self study or small group work) in each of the four skills areas of Values-Based Practice (awareness, reasoning skills, knowledge and communication skills). "Whose Values?" was launched by the Minister of State in the Department of Health, Rosie Winterton, at a joint SCMH/Warwick Medical School conference in London in 2004 and is the basis of a number of national policy and training initiatives in the UK.

(2) Woodbridge, K. & Fulford, K.W.M. (2005). Values-Based Practice.
Module 4 in Basset, T. & Lindley, L. (eds) *The Ten Essential Shared Capabilities Learning Pack for Mental Health Practice*. For The National Health Service University (NHSU) and the National Institute for Mental Health in England (NIMHE).

This module on values-based practice gives a brief introduction with worked examples. The Ten Essential Shared Capabilities are all built on the twin resources of evidence-based and values-based practice.

(3) Fulford, K.W.M., Williamson, T. & Woodbridge, K. (2002). Values-Added Practice (a Values-Awareness Workshop), *Mental Health Today*, October, 25–27.

This paper describes the first of the series of training workshops that Kim Woodbridge, Toby Williamson and Bill Fulford developed and on which this workbook is based.

(4) Woodbridge, K. & Fulford, K.W.M. (2003). Good Practice? Values-based practice in mental health, *Mental Health Practice*, 7(2), 30–34.

This paper covers similar material but in the form of an interactive workshop suitable for self-study.

(5) Fulford, K.W.M., Thornton, T. & Graham, G. (2006). *The Oxford Textbook of Philosophy and Psychiatry*. Oxford: Oxford University Press.

Although a textbook, the materials in this book are organised around readings and other self-training exercises. The topics include a number of areas of importance in health and social care: concepts of disorder, the history of ideas behind psychiatric diagnostic concepts, the philosophy of science, and the relationship between personal meanings and scientific causal explanations (as a key topic in the philosophy of mind). Part IV, on Values, Ethics and Mental Health, gives detailed introductions to ethics and ethical reasoning, medical law, and Values-Based Practice. This book includes self-test questions, key learning points, and detailed guides to further reading.

(6) West Midlands Mental Health Partnership (February 2003). *Values in Action: Developing a Values Based Practice in Mental Health*. (Unpublished)

This manual was developed by the West Midlands Mental Health Partnership to support training in values for mental health and to provide an informal audit tool to monitor their implementation.

(7) Fulford, K.W.M. (2002). Human Values in Health care Ethics. Introduction. Many Voices: Human Values in Health care Ethics. In Fulford, K.W.M., Dickenson, D. & Murray, T.H. (eds) *Healthcare Ethics and Human Values: An Introductory Text with Readings and Case Studies*. Malden, USA, and Oxford, UK: Blackwell Publishers.

This is an edited collection of classic papers of newly commissioned articles, literature and patient narrative, illustrating the diversity of human values in all areas of health care. The introductory chapter, "Many Voices", spells out some of the key differences between values-based practice and traditional ethics.

Theory

(1) Fulford, K.W.M. (1989, reprinted 1995 and 1999; Second edition forthcoming). *Moral Theory and Medical Practice*. Cambridge: Cambridge University Press.

Bill Fulford's monograph on the value structure of medicine and psychiatry uses ideas and methods from Oxford analytic philosophy. It provides the theoretical grounding for the approach to ethical reasoning as a key clinical skill.

(2) Fulford, K.W.M. (2004). Ten Principles of Values-Based Medicine. In Radden, J. (ed) *The Philosophy of Psychiatry: A Companion*. New York: Oxford University Press.

This chapter spells out the principles of values-based practice as they apply to mental health. The paper includes a case history done as a series of "boxes", each of which is an episode in the story of a particular person, illustrating how the ten principles work out in practice.

Values-Based Practice and Related Areas of Health and Social Care

(1) *User-centred practice*
Wallcraft, J. (2003). Values in Mental Health – the Role of Experts by Experience.

This is a detailed discussion paper exploring some of the key issues about values for the Experts by Experience programme, one of the work programmes of the NIMHE. (Available at www.connects.org.uk'conferences).

(2) *Recovery*
Allott, P., Loganathan, L. & Fulford, K.W.M. (Bill) (2002). Discovering Hope For Recovery From a British Perspective. In Lurie, S., Mc Cubbin, M., & Dallaire, B. (eds) International innovations in community mental health [special issue], *Canadian Journal of Community Mental Health*, *21*(2), 13–33.

A review article mainly about the "recovery" approach to the management of mental disorder but connecting this with values-based practice.

(3) *Spirituality*
Jackson, M. & Fulford, K.W.M. (1997). Spiritual Experience and Psychopathology. *Philosophy, Psychiatry, & Psychology*, *4*, 41–66. Commentaries by Littlewood, R., Lu, F.G. *et al.*, Sims, A. & Storr, A., and response by authors, 67–90.

A research paper drawing on a number of case histories to illustrate the central place of values in psychiatric diagnosis.

(4) *Multidisciplinary teamwork*
Colombo, A., Bendelow, G., Fulford, K.W.M. & Williams, S. (2003). Evaluating the influence of implicit models of mental disorder on processes of shared decision making within community-based multidisciplinary teams, *Social Science & Medicine*, *56*, 1557–1570.

This paper gives full details of work combining philosophical-analytic and empirical social science methods to elicit implicit models (values and beliefs) of mental disorder. The groups studied were psychiatrists, approved social workers, CPNs, people who use services and informal carers.

Colombo, A., Bendelow, G., Fulford, K.W.M. & Williams, S. (2003). Model behaviour. *Openmind*, *125*, 10–12.

This short paper gives the main findings from the study published in full in this reading. It outlines the six models and describes the importance of this work for user-centred practice. Full details of the six models are given in a table.

(5) *Child and adolescent services*
Fulford, K.W.M. & Williams, R. (2003). Values-based child and adolescent mental health services? *Current Opinion in Psychiatry*, *16*, 369–376.

A review article setting values-based practice in a policy context for the UK and illustrating each of the 10 pointers to good process in values-based practice with examples from child and adolescent mental health.

(6) *Links with management and leadership*
Fulford, K.W.M. & Benington, J. (2005). VBM[2]: A Collaborative Values-Based Model of Health Care Decision Making Combining Medical and Management Perspectives. In Williams, G. (ed) *Medical and Management Perspectives in Child and Adolescent Psychiatry*. Oxford: Oxford University Press.

A book chapter illustrating the resources of VBP for bringing together medical (KWMF) and management (JB) perspectives. The VBM[2] of the title captures the idea that differences of values, which are a "problem" to be solved in traditional quasi-legal ethics, become a positive resource for health care decision-making in VBP.

A Sample of Relevant Policies

(1) *Policy framework for values-based practice*
The National Framework of Values in Mental Health (NIMHE 2005).

A one-page framework for VBP in mental healthcare developed for the National Institute for Mental Health in England. Available on the NIMHE website (www.nimhe.org.uk/ ValuesBasedPractise), the website of the Care Services Improvement Partnership (http://nimhe.csip. org.uk/ValuesBasedPractise), or on a site hosted by the Mental Health Foundation www.connects.org.uk/conferences). In hard copy, the framework is published in a joint publication from NIMHE, The Sainsbury Centre for Mental Health & The NHSU (2005) The Ten Essential Shared Capabilities: a Framework for the Whole of the Mental Health Workforce. London: NIMHE, The Sainsbury Centre for Mental Health & The NHSU.

Department of Health (1999) National Service Framework for Mental Health. London: Department of Health.

(2) *Training and Service Development*
Department of Health (2004). The Ten Essential Shared Capabilities: A Framework for the Whole of the Mental Health Workforce. Developed by the National Institute for Mental Health England and the Sainsbury Centre for Mental Health Joint Workforce Support Unit in conjunction with NHSU. London: Department of Health.

Department of Health (2005). New ways of working for psychiatrists: Enhancing effective, person-centred services through new ways of working in multidisciplinary and multi-agency contexts (Final report "but not the end of the story"). London: Department of Health.

(3) *User and Carer Centred Practice*
Department of Health (2005) Creating a Patient-led NHS: Delivering the NHS Improvement Plan. London: Department of Health. Also available at: http://www.dh.gov.uk/assetRoot/04/ 10/65/07/04106507.pdf.

Department of Health (2002) Developing services for carers and families of people with mental illness. London: Department of Health.

(4) *Equalities Publications*
Department of Health (2002) Women's mental health: Into the Mainstream. London: Department of Health.

Department of Health (2003) Mainstreaming gender and women's mental health: implementation guidance. London: Department of Health.

Department of Health (2003) Delivering Race Equality: A Framework for action, consultation document. London: Department of Health.

Department of Health (2003) Engaging and Changing: Developing effective policy for the care and treatment of Black and minority ethnic detained patients. London: Department of Health.

Department of Health (2003) Inside Outside: Improving Mental Health Services for Black and Minority Ethnic Communities in England. London: Department of Health.

Office of the Deputy Prime Minister Social Exclusion Unit (2004) Final report on Social Exclusion and Mental Health. London: Office of the Deputy Prime Minister.

(5) *Commissioning*
Department of Health (2005) Commissioning a patient-led NSH. London: Department of Health. Also available at http://www.dh.gov.uk/assetRoot/04/11/67/17/04116717.pdf.

Welsh Assembly Government (2005) Healthcare Standards for Wales: Making the Connections Designed for Life. ISBN 0 7504 3808 8. Also available at www.wales.gov.uk.

Journals

The International journal *Philosophy, Psychiatry & Psychology* (PPP), which is edited by Bill Fulford with an American colleague, John Sadler, focuses particularly on mental health and combines case studies with in-depth philosophical analysis. It includes articles on a wide range of topics concerned with the ways in which values come into all areas of clinical practice and scientific research. Articles in PPP are combined with commentaries from different disciplinary perspectives and a response from the authors.

Web-Based Resources

http://www.basw.co.uk/articles.php?articleId=2&page=6 Values and principles of social work.

http://www.connects.org.uk/conferences Information on the National Institute for Mental Health in England's Values Framework. Requires registration to log in to website.

http://www.doh.gov.uk/mentalhealth/implementationguide.htm For the extract on values underpinning the Mental Health National Service Framework.

http://www.nice.org.uk National Institute for Clinical Excellence (NICE). Schizophrenia guidelines and other information.

http://wwwnimhe.org.uk National Institute for Mental Health England. For information regarding implementation guides and mental health policy.

www.**nimhe**.org.uk/ValuesBasedPractise, click on NIMHE, then click on The NIMHE Values Framework, and download Values Framework

http://www.nmc-uk.org Code of professional conduct for nursing and midwifery.

http://www.rcpsych.ac.uk/publications/cr/council/cr83.pdf The duties of a doctor registered with the General Medical Council.

http://www.scmh.org.uk For further useful information in general about practice and policy issues.

http://www.scie.org.uk Social Care Institute for Excellence. For information regarding social models of care and other general social care information.

http://www.skillsforhealth.org.uk The Health Functional Map and other curriculum support tools published by Skills for Health.

http://www.warwick.ac.uk The University of Warwick.

http://www2.warwick.ac.uk/fac/med Warwick Medical School.

CHAPTER 13

Emotional Intelligence in Mental Health Education

Dawn Freshwater and Theo Stickley

INTRODUCTION

In recent years, mental health education in the UK has shifted significantly away from practice and has become, as with all training for healthcare professionals, located within the walls of the academy. Mental health care has been pressured to perform in terms of research and evidence based practice. Respective governments have produced national guidelines based upon the best available evidence for the best treatment of various conditions. Rational theories alone however are inadequate in meeting the emotional and psychological needs of people who use mental health services. The implications of this have been recognised and responded to through the production of the Essential Shared Capabilities and a subsequent focus upon values in mental health education; these are dealt with in other chapters in this book. These initiatives are positive in that they draw attention to the human aspects of mental health care that complement a focus upon the rational. It is our contention that it is necessary to focus more upon the world of the emotions of all concerned in the business of mental health education in order to restore and maintain a proper balance. By this we mean that being human is common to lecturers, students, service users and practitioners; as it is our humanity that unites us, so best mental health education and practice is informed by the sharing of our humanity.

Emotional Intelligence

Very little of our lives is governed by logic alone. It is rather our emotional world that motivates our decisions and actions. In recent years, breakthroughs in neuroscience have deepened the way in which we understand emotions as a body state. Goleman, in his best selling book *Emotional Intelligence* (1995) reminds us that we have two minds, a rational mind that thinks, and an emotional mind that feels. Both however store memories and influence our responses, actions and choices. Emotions hold independent views, have a mind of their own quite separate from that of the rational mind. When we consider the significance of the emotions in everyday life, it is noteworthy how little we refer to them

Teaching Mental Health. Edited by Theo Stickley and Thurstine Basset.
Copyright © 2007 John Wiley & Sons, Ltd.

in the business of our lives. The premise of this chapter is that the rational mind and the emotional mind need to be balanced partners; where this relationship is harmonious, intellectual ability increases.

Whilst the focus of this chapter is on emotional intelligence we are mindful of the dialogue between this and other forms of intelligence. The debate around the nature of intelligence has been dominated by the scientific paradigm and superiority afforded to the notion of IQ. It is not our intention to debate the concept of IQ here, expect to note that it is only one proposed model of intelligence. Gardner (1983) for example refutes the monolithic domination of measuring success through IQ and purports seven varieties of intelligence that we are all born with, these being:

- Verbal and mathematical logical alacrity.
- Spacial capacity (as in art or architecture).
- Kinesthetic fluidity (as in sport).
- Music.
- Personal (as in communication and interpersonal skills).
- Charisma.
- Intrapsychic ability (as in congruence and inner contentment and containment).

Arguably, mental health education should incorporate approaches that appeal to the various forms of intelligence. With its shift toward the academic however, mental health education we believe, has become imbalanced towards the scientific paradigm and away from the emotional. A focus upon emotional intelligence is one way of restoring that balance. For the benefit of this chapter we define emotional intelligence as a core aptitude related to one's ability and capacity to reason with one's emotions, especially in relation to others.

Healthcare policy is replete with calls for service user and carer involvement. This includes curricula design and delivery. We would argue that genuine involvement will inevitably promote emotional intelligence amongst learners. By listening to the voices of those who experience the distress and pain of mental health problems and experiencing the subsequent stigma and discrimination, our hearts are moved by human experience. Additionally where curricula and specific modules are informed by service user experience and wishes, there will inevitably be a focus upon qualities and values that inform good practice.

Some are naturally more attuned to emotional life through metaphor, simile, poetry, song, dreams myths and fable. These are all written, as Whyte (1997) notes, in the heart's language. The emotionally intelligent practitioner is one who can work in harmony with thoughts and feelings. Novelists, artists and psychotherapists may be more adept at emotional intelligence as contact with their emotional world is critical to their work, it is also fundamental to the act of caring, and as such mental health curricula need to create space for the work of the heart.

THE NEED FOR EMOTIONAL INTELLIGENCE IN EDUCATION

Much healthcare education, until recently, has functioned via a mechanical hierarchical system based on a task oriented medical model of care. The shift towards more holistic and humanistic models of care over the past three decades emphasise and value the uniqueness of the individual. This shift has necessitated not only a complete reinterpretation of the past healthcare system, but also a recognition that the present system, being forever open, is constantly being reinterpreted. This, as Chaplin (1998) notes is not always a comfortable task and depends upon our capacity for openness. It could be argued that many healthcare systems and educational institutions have previously operated as "closed" systems (Freshwater, 2000; Liaschenko, 1998; Menzies-Lyth, 1970). This was particularly manifest in nurse education, where in the main nursing care was being taught in relation to a particular bodily system, resulting in the nurse approaching the patient on the ward as a malfunctioning body part. The human body (and mind) has been objectified, viewed as a closed system. The current trend is towards nurses and other allied professionals operating in a more subjective, open system.

Knowledge of the whole patient and the systems within which they are located requires a re-positioning of the practitioner so that the gaze moves from the body as an object of intervention to the body of someone living a life. Thus the move towards a more holistic approach to care, coupled with the drive for professionalism and accountability, has required a paradigm shift in the theoretical framework for healthcare practices.

The two existing views of mental healthcare, the traditional task-oriented, activity-based model and the contemporary, relationship forming, holistic model, require very different methods of knowledge and theory generation and it could be argued require very different skills in order for them to be actualised in caring practice. Moreover, these differing ways of viewing practice require the practitioner to respond from a place that is more deeply connected both with themselves and the patient. Educationalists working in mental health, along with other disciplines concerned with adult education, face the challenge of responding to this shift proactively. Traditionally mental health education, like education in general, has used the classic model of education in which learning is viewed as the transmission of the cultural norms and values. Sociologists from the Marxist and functionalist schools of thought argue that education is primarily aimed at producing a labour force, and in reality this is probably the case in healthcare. However, this can lead to definitions of training that emphasise the production of the standardised professional with importance given to the development of pre-defined skills. In the process of such training all students attain the same skills and there is little room for self-expression. Training, in this regard is therefore is symbolic of a "closed system". The role of the teacher in training is that of "custodian", the aim is to get through the curriculum, meeting the statutory competencies along the way. The teacher employs the role of expert and the motivation of the students is assumed to be extrinsic. The teaching process in training may not be viewed explicitly as a parallel process for the process of patient care, nevertheless, it does model a particular stance towards interpersonal relations.

Contemporary models of mental health training and education have attempted to move away from a product oriented curriculum to a more humanistic, process led curriculum (Freshwater, 2000; Parker, 2002; Wagner, 2002). This approach to education allows the individual to develop and deepen awareness of personal knowledge, skills and attitudes in order to attend to the needs of the client. In addition, humanistic education offers a model of interpersonal relations that respects the uniqueness of the individual, favouring empowerment as opposed to guardianship.

The work of Houle (1980), Mezirow (1990), Schön (1987) and Knowles (1990) in adult education has helped to inform the teaching and learning practices in caring courses. Mezirow's (1990) transformative theory of adult learning describes the reconstruction of meaning. Such reconstruction occurs though reflection on experience, reflection connecting the internally personally constructed reality (private) with the external socially constructed (public) reality. Mezirow (1990) defined learning as a process of making new or revised interpretations of the meaning of an experience. The revised interpretations then guide subsequent understanding and action. This definition of learning requires that multiple modes of teaching and learning be used.

However, theory and practice remains divided and, subjective experiential learning is still seen as inferior. This is evidenced in the assessment schedules which maintain a scientific and objectifying criteria even of the diaries and portfolios. Although, it should be noted that in a recent paper Price (2004) speaks of ways in which assessment processes and curricula need to be adapted to take account of the increasing number of reflective and self assessment assignments. These are often viewed as soft options and rarely at the core of assessment of student development. Furthermore, service user involvement is often espoused in the curriculum and yet true and meaningful involvement is often no more than tokenism. An emotionally intelligent curriculum is not atheoretical nor is it anti-cognitive, indeed as Price (2004) it is in fact meta-cognitive. Price (2004) argues for a repositioning of the curriculum to be more practice focused and he argues to include more involvement from practitioners and mentors in the design of education. However he does not address the issue of how to engage users in this process in a meaningful and creative way.

PROMOTING EMOTIONAL INTELLIGENCE CURRICULUM DEVELOPMENT

Reflection

Reflection offers a way of accessing deeply embedded personal knowledge. Schön (1983) purports that thinking, via reflection, adds theory to the action whilst it is occurring, making theory and practice inseparable. Osbourne (1991) recommended that this form of learning needed to be considered further, arguing that both teacher and learner should take the opportunity to learn and reflect together. It has already become apparent that the focus of experiential learning is very much on praxis, that is reflection on experience. Kolb (1984) proposed a model of experiential learning which described a four stage cyclical process and incorporated reflection as a significant phase.

Reflexivity refers to the human capacity to monitor reactions to situations, actions and inner feelings. Humanistic theory places emphasis on the importance of persons as capable of reflecting on experience. McLeod (1996) comments that:

> The possibility of choice arises from reflexivity, since the person does not respond automatically to events but acts intentionally based on awareness of alternatives (p. 136).

Reflexivity, however, brings with it another dimension aside from choice, that of moral obligation. With the existence of choice comes the necessity to examine beliefs and values which underpin the choices. Intentional human action leads the individual to become aware of moral responsibility, locus of evaluation becomes an external and an internal consideration, in other words, becoming aware of the inner world brings with it a necessary awareness of the outer world and one's responsibility to that, that is the other and society.

Reflection has been predominantly defined in terms of a learning tool. Schön (1983) has done much to surface the role of reflection in professional education. In addition, he has raised issues surrounding the application of theory to practice. Schön (1983) describes the limitations of knowledge derived from technical rationality for practice, that is

> the application of research based knowledge to the solution of instrumental choice that dominates the epistemology of professional practice (p. 13).

Schön (1983) argued that practitioners have difficulty in utilising this type of knowledge as it is generated in situations that are context free, thereby ignoring the context of the actual practice situation. Schön (1983) also drew attention to the fact that practitioners do not as a rule make decisions based on technical rationality, but on experience.

Role Modelling

The most obvious potential for students to learn emotional intelligence is through the example set by the educator. If the teacher/trainer demonstrates emotional competence, the student has an opportunity to not only experience the benefit of that competence in terms of getting their own support and guidance needs met but also in terms of learning for their own practice. What therefore are some of the qualities of emotional intelligence from which students might learn? We highlight a few but acknowledge this is not an exhaustive list. For a more comprehensive discussion of these issues we would direct the reader to the work of Carl Rogers in his seminal work *Freedom to Learn* (Rogers, 1969). Primarily, we would expect the emotionally intelligent teacher/trainer to be genuine in their relationships with their students. Genuineness requires the teacher to acknowledge the potential barriers created by the power of their role and to meet the student with respect and achieve a common language. The boundaries and limitations of the student/teacher relationship will need to be appropriate and clear. The teacher will need to make a commitment to the student within the context of their role. This respect and commitment to the student will inevitably engender a sense of acceptance and worthiness. This sense of acceptance Rogers refers to as unconditional positive regard. This cannot be taught in a propositional way, nevertheless, it can be modelled through the teacher/student relationships. There is much evidence to support the efficacy of empathy in therapeutic relationships. A teacher/trainer who can demonstrate empathic understanding to his/her students may well be modelling the most important quality required for mental health practice. Educators are notoriously busy in their work and it is easy for individual tutorial time to be eroded by administration and other commitments. However, we are not necessarily referring to quantity, rather quality of the human encounter.

CRITICAL THINKING, INCLUSIVENESS AND CURRICULUM DEVELOPMENT

Health care education has often been viewed as an essentialist education with the emphasis on producing an individual that is fit for practice. Essentialist education by its very nature tends to make everyone the same. In this sense, one could argue for example that nurse education with its statutory competencies to meet is a training rather than an education. Prior to project 2000 courses in the UK, nurse education was largely an apprenticeship model of training, akin to the pre-technocratic model described by Bines and Watson (1992). This model comprises the acquisition of skills through on the job training with theoretical components taught block or day release. The goal of traditional nurse education then has been to teach specific skills and knowledge in order that students can reach a certain standard of behaviour, attitude and work as defined by the educational establishment and in the case of nursing the United Kingdom Central Council for Nurses, Midwives and Health Visitors (1992) (more recently the Nursing Midwifery Council). However, we would argue that there is no such thing as the "typical" nurse, nor for that matter the "typical student", propositional knowledge does not allow for difference or diversity, an issue that causes not only the students in the learning environment some discomfort, but also has implications for the standardisation of "patients" and their care. Furthermore it could be argued that traditional approaches to nurse education attempts to narrow the consciousness of the student nurse as opposed to expanding it (Newman, 1994).

An emotionally intelligent approach to teaching and learning embodies aspects of the transformational learning model (Askew & Carnell, 1998). The function of transformatory education is to support the individual's growth through self-reflection and analysis of individual experiences. Hence the self and the learner are seen as an "open" system. From an epistemological standpoint this type of knowing is in the domain of experiential knowledge, that is knowledge gained through direct personal encounter with a person or subject, it is knowledge gained through and in relationship, something that is central to the work of the mental health professional. In relation to Carper's (1978) framework it is the domain of personal knowledge, what Polanyi (1967) termed "tacit knowledge" and what critical theorists refer to as critical or emancipatory knowledge (Fay, 1987; Habermas, 1972). In this sense it is closely aligned with that Rolfe et al. (2001) term "critical reflection" and what Freshwater (2006) describes as "thinking about how you are thinking" in order to think more critically and in context. Mezirow (1981) in his definitive work on levels of reflection viewed this level of awareness as encapsulating both the affective domain and experiential domains, alongside the theoretical and discriminating resulting in critical consciousness. With the help of critical consciousness mental health professionals are able to identify their thoughts, feelings and actions, and comment critically on the origin of the same, a crucial aspect of maintaining therapeutic boundaries and helping others to find their own edges.

Shotter (1975) argues that critical consciousness leads to responsible actions; that is actions that are intentionally and insightfully chosen from amongst others. Responsible actions are surely an intended aim and outcome of health care education? They are expected in clinical practice and as such mental health practitioners are expected to be critically aware of their intentions in order to make deliberate and therefore responsible choices. The extent to which individuals become aware of their intentions through traditionally delivered curricula is debateable. However a study by Freshwater (2000) demonstrated that transformation that occurred through engaging with a reflective curricula, clearly impacted on degree of emotional engagement with the users/carers. Mental health care is difficult work, both technically and emotionally, and leads to disengagement with both self and others. We argue that learning that takes place purely within a propositional framework can perpetuate this disengagement, whereas creative curricula, that encompass emotionally intelligent content and modes of being may facilitate a deeper engagement with self and lead to therapeutic practices.

CREATIVITY

Earlier we discussed the notion of different types of intelligence. It is generally thought that western education is limited in the forms of intelligence it appeals to with greater emphasis upon rational learning. One way of developing emotional intelligence is through creative approaches to education. One chapter in this book illustrates this well with the use of drama in mental health education, although it is acknowledged that not all teacher/trainers will have the confidence or skill to facilitate drama in the classroom. It is not inconceivable to invite a drama student into the classroom in order to act the part of a person who is depressed or in distress, rather than relying upon role-play. Even without an actor the potential for role-play should not be underestimated. It is our experience that students have a love/hate relationship with role-play; whilst they might hate the thought of it, it nearly always evaluates well as a learning method. The potential for drama for education is enormous. Another chapter in this book (Chapter 13) gives an account of the development of a video for use within the classroom. The video is made by a person who has (reluctantly) used mental health services. The showing of this video to a classroom full of students is a perfect way to focus the students, minds on the perspective of the service user, without having to invite into the room a guest speaker. The video serves as a useful tool for stimulating discussion. If the class size is too big for discussion, smaller groups can be formed with a list of critical questions, e.g. *how did the person's values conflict with the values of services? How might the person have felt when she was admitted to the ward? How might the person's race and culture impacted upon her experiences of services?* Watching a professionally produced video from the service user's perspective will help students to develop empathic understanding.

Another way to encourage this deep thinking is through service user artworks. There is a growing body of service user art available. One exercise might be to distribute copies of service user art and ask each student to study the picture. A sheet of prompts can be given out with questions such as: *What feelings are expressed in the work? How would you describe the colours? What depth or texture can you see in the picture? What do you think the picture represents? Etc.* Once the students have answered all of the questions they are asked to take their own words and turn them into a piece of prose or poetry. Consequently they finish with a creative externalisation of their own response to the work. The students become engaged with the expression and meaning of the service user's artwork.

As well as art, there is a growing literature published by service users illustrating their experiences of mental health problems and subsequent use of services. One of the benefits of accessing this literature is that people are not being expected to repeatedly tell their stories in front of students. Some of these accounts are listed here for reference:

- *Raising Our Voices* by Adam James. Handsell, UK 2001.
- *From the Ashes of Experience.* Edited by Phil Barker, Peter Campbell and Ben Davidson. London: Whurr 1999.
- Chipmunka Publishing have published approximately twenty books written by service users. Their list can be located at: http://www.chipmunkapublishing.com/.

Additionally, students can be directed to service user led research reports such as:

- Faulkner, A. (1997) *Knowing Our Own Minds.* London: Mental Health Foundation.
- Mental Health Foundation (2000) *Strategies for Living: The Research Report.* London: MHF

- Rose, D. et al. (1998) *In Our Experience: User-Focused Monitoring of Mental Health Services in Kensington and Chelsea and Westminster.* London: The Sainsbury Centre for Mental Health.

SUSTAINABILITY

Mental health practice is emotionally laborious. There has been much written regarding the notion of emotional labour in the healthcare arena. In an environment where practitioners are expected to give constantly of themselves, emotional wear and tear is inevitable. What we would like to consider is how emotional competence can be sustained, both throughout the curriculum and through practice. What needs to be made clear however is that workers are not ground down just because of the emotional demands of the client group but also by the unreasonable demands of a system that is inadequately developed for what it is expected to provide.

Mental health care is a complex business and we question its sustainability whilst located within the system organised around the medical model. It is when we look carefully at the needs of mental health service users that we discover the complexities of the issues in question. Not only does the person experience the effects of mental distress, but we also encounter dire social needs including loneliness, unemployment, poverty and housing, the effects of alcohol and drugs, social stigma and rampant discrimination. Furthermore, people also experience debilitating side-effects of powerful drugs. Existing hospital services designed around a medical model of care are now effectively out of kilter with the demands placed upon the system because of the complex social problems that people endure. The system that is limited by the medical model will inevitably fail. This therefore is the context of emotional labour in mental health care.

Primarily, educators need to be realistic about the real world of practice and support students in their practice journeys. We recommend weekly group supervision sessions for when students are on practice placements. It is during these sessions that students may not only reflect critically upon their practice but also *let off steam* and support one another. Emotional labour can only be sustained if it is supported and the emotions are allowed to be expressed. Through sharing emotions in a safe and supportive environment, students may learn not only increased self-awareness but also the all-important ability to *manage* emotions.

SUMMARY

In developing an emotionally intelligent curriculum there are a number of challenges to be faced, not least how to articulate the philosophical underpinnings of emotional intelligence in such a way to facilitate practical operation. Teachers and trainers in established institutions may feel as though they are swimming against the tide. For others, decreasing resources mean smaller rooms with larger student numbers and any attempt at emotional engagement with the subject of mental health is too demanding to sustain. By helping our students to develop emotional skills, we are giving them more than technical skills training will ever give. It is our contention that emotional development alongside the skills of critical reflection is fundamental to mental health training and education. Emotional engagement of professionals with people who use mental health services is necessary for the sake of humanity. It was Mahatma Gandhi that once said: "The best test of a civilised society is the way in which it treats its most vulnerable and weakest members". Today, the people with whom we work, more often than not are the most vulnerable and weakest, and often with the fewest rights. As mental health professionals and training those to work in the field, we have a duty to help equip our students to be able to meet the task of providing emotional and intellectual understanding in the care they provide in the future.

REFERENCES

Askew, S. & Carnell, E. (1998). *Transformatory learning: Individual and Global change.* London: Cassell.
Bines, H. & Watson, D. (1992). *Developing Professional Education.* Buckingham: Open University Press.
Carper, B.A. (1978). Fundamental Patterns of Knowing in Nursing, *Advances in Nursing Science,* 1(1), 13 –23.
Chaplin, J. (1998). The Rhythm Model. In Bruna-Seu, I. and Colleen- Heenan, M. (1998) (Eds) *Feminism and Psychotherapy.* London: Sage, Chapter 8
Fay, B. (1987). *Critical Social Science.* Cambridge: Polity Press.
Freshwater, D. (2000). *Transformatory Learning in Nurse Education.* PhD thesis: University of Nottingham.
Freshwater, D. (2006). Teaching and Learning Reflective Practice. (In this volume).
Gardner, H. (1983). *Frames of Mind.* New York: Basic Books Inc.
Goleman, D. (1995). *Emotional intelligence.* New York: Bantam.
Habermas, J. (1972). *Knowledge and Human Interest.* London: Heinnemann.
Habermas, J. (1972). *Knowledge and Human Interests.* Heinemann: London.
Houle, C.O. (1980). *Continuing Learning in the Professions.* San Francisco: Jossey Bass.
Knowles, M.S. (1990). *The Adult Learner, A Neglected Species.* 4th Edn, USA: Gulf.
Kolb, D. (1984). *Experiential Learning as the Science of Learning and Development.* Englewood Cliffs, Prentice Hall: New York.
Liaschenko, J. (1998). The shift from the closed body to the open body – ramifications for nursing testimony. In Edwards, S. (ed) *Philosophical Issues in Nursing.* London: Macmillan
McLeod, J. (1996). The Humanistic paradigm. In Woolfe, R. & Dryden, W. (1996) (eds) *Handbook of counselling psychology.* London: Sage, Chapter 3
Menzies Lyth, I.E.P. (1970). *The functioning of social systems as a defence against.* London: Tavistock.
Mezirow J. (1990). How critical reflection triggers transformative learning. In Mezirow et al., (eds) *Fostering Critical Reflection in Adulthood.* San Francisco: Jossey Bass, 1–20.
Mezirow, J. (1981). A critical theory of adult learning and education. *Adult Education, 32,* 3–24.
Newman, M. (1994). Health as expanding consciousness. 2nd Ed National league for Nursing Press: New York.
Osbourne, P. (1991). Research in Nurse Education. In Cormack, D. (1991) (ed) *The Research Process in Nursing.* Oxford: Blackwell Science, Chapter 33.
Parker, M.E. (2002). Aesthetic Ways in Day-to-day Nursing. IN Freshwater D. (ed) *Therapeutic Nursing,* (pp. 100–120). London: Sage.
Polanyi, N. (1967). *The tacit dimension.* New York: Doubleday.
Price, B. (2004). Learning from patients. *Nursing Standard, 18*(26), 18–26.
Rogers, C.R. (1969). The Necessary and Sufficient Conditions of Therapeutic Personality Change, *The Journal of Consulting Psychology, 21,* 95–103.
Rolfe, G. Freshwater, D. & Jasper, M. (2001). *Critical reflection for nurses and the caring professions: A users guide.* Basingstoke: Palgrave.

Schön, D.A. (1983).*The Reflective Practitioner: How Practitioners Think in Action*. New York, Basic Books.

Schön, D.A. (1987). *Educating the Reflective Practitioner.* London: Jossey-Bass.

Shotter, J. (1975). *Images of man in psychological research*. London: Methuen.

UKCC (1992). *Code of Professional Conduct*. London: UKCC.

Wagner, L. (2002). Nursing Students' Development of caring Self Through Creative Reflective Practice. In Freshwater D (ed) *Therapeutic Nursing*, (pp. 121–144). London: Sage.

Whyte, D. (1997). *The heart aroused: Poetry and the preservation of the soul at work*. London: The Industrial Society.

CHAPTER 14

Teaching Recovery to the Support Time and Recovery Workers

Esther Cook

Bridges need to be built between what some consider airy fairy approaches to solid helpful practice, the only way to do this in training is to interact and value existing opinions of those in disagreement, learn from them rather than allow them to feel opposed! Everyone's opinion is valid.

(Workers' feedback, via anonymous questionnaire)

INTRODUCTION

This chapter could equally be titled "Recovering about teaching and learning". This is because the profound nature of recovery, that is how human beings overcome life difficulties to change and grow, touches us all. As it puts emphasis on our own experience and expertise we are called to examine the traditional roles of teacher and learner.

In other words who "owns" the idea of recovery from mental health problems? Who is the expert? The person using the service or the person providing the service, or the trainer with the flipchart pen standing at the front of the training group? In terms of service provision, the idea of recovery has tipped the old model of professionals who "know best" tending to the needs of "mental patients" on its head in favour of the idea of "experts by experience". People who experience mental distress are not just "service users" or "patients"; they are also people with a wealth of life knowledge and expertise in surviving mental health problems and the trauma of going through mental health services. In this sense, the person who is recovering is the expert. In this chapter I consider how this translates to teaching and learning about recovery. As recovery trainers, we need to find ways of drawing upon our unique experiences to bear on the task of improving the support of others in recovery.

We have all recovered from various problems: mental or physical health problems, relationship breakdowns, loss and bereavement. It is this process of personal recovery that helps to inform our teaching of recovery. Perhaps even the process of adjusting our thinking to contemplate the notion of "expert by experience" is a form of recovery.

Over the last few years, East Suffolk Mind in the UK has been involved in a variety of different recovery training courses. My involvement in these has been in differing roles, as trainer, tutor, development programme manager and therefore as learner. Here I explore these experiences, and look at the lessons learnt.

THE SUPPORT TIME RECOVERY PROGRAMME

In late 2003 East Suffolk Mind first got involved as a first wave pilot site in the National Health Service (NHS) nationwide Support Time and Recovery (STR) to implement a new role for mental health support. We formed a project team comprising service users, workers, managers and partnership agencies. We hoped that by embracing the idea of recovery we would improve our service by naming what it is workers do to support people to move on effectively. Thus we would be offering a service that clearly "does what it says on the tin". Training would be the main part of this process.

In order to take stock of how we supported people in their recovery, we sought feedback via service user designed and led research. Informal yet in-depth interviews conducted by Cathy Walsh of the Suffolk User Forum offered clear and insightful feedback. We were pleased to hear that service users said that they found support beneficial in keeping themselves well, that they felt listened to, were shown respect, given good advice and supported in a non-judgemental and culturally sensitive way.

Not all of the support sounded conducive to recovery; as the study told us "Some workers newly introduced to service users were quite presumptive and gave unsolicited advice". There were also issues around boundaries and confidentiality that needed clarifying, e.g. "A service user was introduced to a friend of an STR worker with the words 'This is a client' ". In addition, there were found to be differences between individual workers: "Some service users found that the STR did "therapeutic talking" and did not offer practical help as much as would have been liked". Some means of ensuring everyone offered similar kinds of support, albeit stamped with a personal style, was important to guarantee that support was flexible to each individual's recovery journey. This kind of critical yet constructive feedback would give us something to measure our progress against later.

Our training plan was as follows:

- To devise our own training for existing staff incorporating the service user research and feedback from managers and workers.
- To pilot different models of recovery training in order to build a training route for STR workers.
- To "Fast track" six "experts by experience", people who have used or currently use services, to be ready for STR work via a combination of Certificate in Mental Health Work Level 2 and work placements.

Drawing on the idea of being a "recovering service" supporting "recovering workers' we aimed to model recovery values through the support offered during training. We summarised the support that we expected STR workers to offer the people using the service as follows:

STR workers encourage you to think about what recovery means to you personally and to explore who you really are, your hopes for the future, what is important to you, how you can take control and responsibility of your life and make time to enjoy yourself. Your STR worker will arrange to spend time with you on a one-to-one basis. They will work with you to think about where you are right now and together you will draw up an action plan outlining the next steps for your recovery.

We questioned whether these values could equally be applied to the support offered by a tutor or trainer to each learner.

RECOVERY, WHAT RECOVERY?

In early 2004, we realised that we had no shared working definition of recovery. Amongst workers there were some questionable definitions of what recovery meant floating about, for instance that certain service users can recover and others can't or that the worker had to "make" people recover. The implementation guide offered by the NHS didn't offer a detailed breakdown of the attitude and approach needed to support people in recovery. Most workers' response to STR job descriptions detailing tasks such as "listening" was understandably "But I already do this stuff!". We wanted to train workers to provide a recovery service, but we didn't feel confident in defining what it was workers needed to do to support people effectively in their recovery until we had engaged with the people who would come to us for training. Then we felt as though we were in a Catch 22 situation. It seems that we were not alone in our lack of definition. Suffolk Users' Forum reported in their research that service users did not find the term "recovery" helpful as some felt that they were managing a chronic condition. The project team had first hand experience of this at a meeting where a service user reacted strongly to the idea of recovery, expressing anger and disbelief that after years of being told that they were ill, we should be suggesting that they could recover. It was unsurprising then that some care co-ordinators were reported to be concerned about the possibility that focussing on recovery would mean neglecting a "duty of care". Such confusion further suggested that it was useful to approach the training programme itself as support for a "recovering organisation" needing to regain our own sense of expertise.

CONTENT AND STYLE OF TRAINING

Traineeships for "experts by experience" for those with personal experience of mental health problems were set up in partnership with local colleges and training organisations. The traineeships focused upon a qualification, the City and Guilds Certificate in Mental Health Work Level 2. The course included both taught times and work placements. The Certificate level 2 was made up of five days teaching plus tutor time examining: principles of mental health work, the experience of mental distress, effective communication, the working environment and developing as a mental health worker. Five practice-based assessments were set, linking to work placements of six months duration. Practice placements were supported by supervision and mentoring. The method of training was a mixture of lecturing and experiential group work with a strong focus on work practice. The style attempted to follow recovery values of being supportive and inclusive and highlighting the strengths and expertise of participants whilst encouraging debate and new perspectives.

WORKING TOWARD RECOVERY: A 3-DAY PERSONAL DEVELOPMENT COURSE FOR STR WORKERS

Based on "360 degree" feedback from people using the service, workers and managers, the aims we agreed with trainer Helen McClean were to consolidate participants' present working practice, promote further understanding of their role in the healing process and optimise personal and team resources for the work satisfaction of staff as well as the benefit of the clients. Helen, a qualified Gestalt therapist has an engaging and lively training style, aiming to increase participants' skill-base through individual reflection, practise and shared experience, this again upholding recovery values within the training of staff. The training drew on each participant's own experience of recovery, for instance from bereavement, or some other loss, in order to foster a profound and personal definition of what recovery is. The training took place over three days, with sessions on: forming the working alliance, testing the STR Working Alliance and consolidating and finishing.

LONDON DEVELOPMENT CENTRE FOR MENTAL HEALTH "STR RECOVERY INDUCTION TRAINING" PILOT

London Development Centre (LDC) STR Programme manager Marks Tebbs co-ordinated "Recovery Model" training as a result of feedback from initial national pilots of the NHS Recovery training. The original materials were given out as a reference guide for participants, and a new session design drafted by trainers with further handouts in discussion with LDC. The learning outcomes of the original pilot were refined and elements introduced such as "recovery in the light of the STR role", "strategies to promote recovery", "re-framing and problem solving" and "models of change". In addition, a list of "Do's and Don'ts" about training style such as "don't use jargon" was agreed by the trainers as a guide to facilitating the course. The training methods placed much more emphasis on using personal experience and group work and less on presentation work; where presentations were done, these were made accessible and interactive.

WHAT WORKED?

A Training Method and Style Which Engages with Personal Feelings and Experiences

Training styles supporting self-awareness, reflection and getting in touch with feelings were valued as was the trainer sharing experiences and thus enabling participants to do the same. For instance, following the ESM training one participant commented, ". . . everything Helen [the trainer] says is so relevant makes you feel comfortable to put your feelings across and is easy to understand. Sharing experiences makes you understand other people's feelings and makes you more aware of your own and also where other people are coming from. This makes you listen to other people more and let them talk". The effectiveness of this experiential approach was bourne out in the LDC pilot with participants commenting that applying personal experiences to recovery was helpful. For some this was a new way of learning.

Practical Content

Participants valued content which could be applied directly to their work practice. In the ESM pilot, exploration of flexible boundaries was found to be useful, as in the idea of the "Friendly Professional". In the LDC pilot the idea of the Wellness Recovery Action Plan captured the imagination of many in the group.

"Experts by Experience" Traineeship

Trainees found the Certificate in Mental Health Work Level 2 to be a helpful qualification. One said "The teaching part of the certificate course was good as it provided support for the study and provided opportunities for positive debate and ideas sharing". Another that it was "A good opportunity, with good tutor support, very thought provoking and educative". Trainees also appreciated a clear induction pack provided by their work placement and the accessibility of support from both the project and course tutor. Having a workplace mentor was found to be very useful to be able to check things out and formal supervision from the line manager was also valued.

From a tutor's point of view, it was remarkable to teach a group with a wealth of personal knowledge. Experiential and discussion-based exercises always bore great fruit, with high levels of empathy and understanding of the range of subjects from listening skills to benefits; the lived expertise of trainees gave them a natural edge. The differing points of view in the group provided a great way of putting this personal experience into a learning framework, a process underpinned and evidenced by the assignment work. Managers who supported trainees in their placements felt the scheme worked well for them, one commenting that their trainee was a good choice and showed enthusiasm for the role.

WHAT PEOPLE GOT FROM THE TRAINING

Traineeships

Trainees fed back that they were able to fit their own experiences in to a framework and shift from the position of "patient" or "service user" to "expert by experience" and that this has helped with personal recovery. For instance one person said; "The opportunity to be involved has been a good experience and the concept to use life experience and build on this to help other people is a good one". Asked what they had gained from the experience, comments were as follows; "Self-confidence, focus and direction". "Has given me a life", "Highlighted strengths I didn't know I had", "Rewarding and therapeutic" and that it was "very positive to have a qualification". Some also felt that they had gained an ongoing improvement in communication skills and confidence from the learning experience as well as time management skills. What was gained from the experience in terms of personal motivation is demonstrated movingly in a poem written by one trainee:

Start Something

A new something
A true something
Just get the hell up
And do something
Maybe prove something
To someone your thing
Is something worth
The time they bring

Your crusade
A cause
Something worth applause
Forget about your flaws
And get out there
Go get yours

I know what you mean
It ain't all gonna shine
The rain comes at time
And everything I thought was mine
Gets washed away
Gets torn down
Gets thrown around and
Broken like me

But it can be fixed
It's just a chip
Build on it again
Make it strong
And the more you build
and get pulled down
The quicker you learn to build
For the next time around
You get used to getting it right
To putting up a fight
With your last ounce of might
and soul

When I start something in me
Other people can see
Other people can know
And watch me glow
and realise
There's a fire burning inside
A handful of pride
And a heart full of contentment

WORKING TOWARDS RECOVERY

Existing East Suffolk Mind workers taking part in the ESM recovery training gained in terms of their own practice. One worker wrote:

This course has helped us understand and look at new ways of dealing or doing things better and feel more comfortable and confident about doing them.

When asked to summarise the key learning points for themselves, participants listed the following:

- What recovery is.
- How to listen.
- Client-led practice.
- What you can and can't do in practice – e.g. respecting confidentiality.
- Reflective practice: being honest with client and self.
- How to ask different questions and find out what really matters to the client.
- Understanding the recovery journey of yourself and your client.
- Safe, flexible boundary – not rigid, but working with the "in-between".
- The relationship between client and worker.

Asked what they would do differently as a result of the training participants answered as follows:

- Talk about recovery with client and check out what it means to them.
- Understand that everyone can recover depending on what this means to them.
- Look at how to manage symptoms rather than "treat" them.
- Look beyond symptoms to the whole person.
- Try new things such as music group.
- Be more honest with clients and working more in partnership.
- Recognise "whose problem" it is and not looking to cure.
- Recognise own prejudices.

All in all, quite an impressive shift was achieved, with much evidence of self-reflection.

LONDON DEVELOPMENT CENTRE

Participants' feed back was very positive, with one participant saying that it was the best training they'd had since starting the job several years ago, as a result of the training, they would try out the Wellness Recovery Action Plan and models of working with change with the people they support. In terms of doing things differently, comments included spending more time with the people they support, applying the tools for recovery to themselves, and finding out more about people's experiences, echoing the experience of the ESM pilot.

WHAT HAPPENED AS A RESULT OF THE TRAINING: TRAINEESHIP

By the end of the traineeship, one person was employed by East Suffolk Mind as an STR worker, one found employment with another mental health organisation, one gained employment outside of mental health, one moved into higher education, and two, whilst finding the experience to be useful, decided to take up mental health work at this point.

As an organisation we have gained tremendously from employing an "expert by experience" and would like to extend the scheme. The one trainee now employed by East Suffolk Mind demonstrates the special kind of expertise gained through using services;

> I understand how frustrating it can be to be judged and told what other people think is best for you. I am also aware of how insensitive some professionals can be in thinking they are right and in some instances one has to question whether some really are in the right area of work and not on some kind of power trip.

In the same vein, this ex-trainee demonstrates how her own experiences of recovery give her a wealth of knowledge to draw on in supporting others in their recovery.

> ...I like to get to know people for myself, accepting the person as they are and where they are in the hope of supporting them to get to where they should be. I have also learnt how important it is to feel valued and for people to have confidence in you. Therefore I try to make a point of reflecting back peoples' achievements and positive qualities in addition to their potential and ability.

One colleague noted:

> As a project the traineeship has proved to be a very valuable scheme, it has enabled us to recruit a very promising worker who would not have had the opportunity without the experience the traineeship scheme gave her.

The impact on people using the service is still being measured, though anecdotally there are promising signs of an improved recovery focus, for instance more take up of learning and employment opportunities by our service users. In addition, one tenant of a Support Time Recovery Housing project summed up the changes to the service as follows:

> I often missed appointments with my support worker and found the time with him was restricted. Now there is a new set-up...if I want to try new things I can rely on staff to support me...I know I will have help to do the things I need to do to make a real difference to my life.

CONCLUSION: RECOVERING LEARNERS, RECOVERING TEACHERS

In teaching and learning about recovery, the approach that is adopted is vital to its success. If we imagine participants in recovery training to be recovering learners, it follows that they should be properly supported and involved with a conscious reference to recovery values and they should be helped to acknowledge and use their own personal expertise. When this is taken on board, the results can be transformative, as was demonstrated by learning and changes in practice as a result of the ESM and LDC training pilots and by the journey undertaken by the expert by experience trainees. The more formal and academic kinds of teaching, as with the NHS pilot workers, were less successful.

Recovery is not a dry subject, so as trainers we should be willing to personally engage with the subject drawing on experiences of recovery within our own lives. Not just recovery from mental health problems but also from physical illness, loss and bereavement, relationship breakdown, work problems. We need to be ready to facilitate training based on personal experience rather than "chalk and talk" learning, which can be alienating. It makes sense that trainers who are experts by the experience of their own recovery from mental distress are ideally placed to do this work. This personal expertise, as with practitioners and educators, should be underpinned with sound training skills and personal awareness enabling trainers to safely enable people to examine their own experiences.

Recovery is not just about those that have used services. Anybody engaging in mental health education should be encouraged to identify their own expertise by engaging with their own personal experiences of recovery both within work roles and as human beings. In this sense the idea of recovering organisations, recovering workers and "recovering recovery trainers" is a useful one.

To paraphrase our earlier sketch of an STR worker, our experience suggests that rather than taking on the traditional "expert" teacher role, an effective recovery trainer should enable learners to engage with their own lived expertise by encouraging learners to think about what recovery means to them personally and to explore who they really are. The trainer should take pains to help learners think about goals and aspirations in their work, how they can take control and responsibility of their work role and make time to enjoy themselves within this role. Recovery trainers should take time to get to know their learners and help them think about where they are right now in terms of practice as well as supporting them to draw up a development plan outlining the next steps for their journey as a worker.

CHAPTER 15

Towards Social Inclusion

Peter Bates

INTRODUCTION

The launch of the UK Government's Social Exclusion Unit's report *Mental Health and Social Exclusion* in June 2004 represented both a completion and starting point. It was the culmination of a lengthy process of gathering evidence and building alliances that successfully moved the issue up the political agenda. It was also the start of a new process of implementing the report's recommendations that includes work on staff training. This chapter is a personal account of the early months of that training from the perspective of one trainer.

BECOMING A SOCIAL INCLUSION TRAINER

In 1986, I attended a training course on the principle of normalisation in mental health services (Wolfensberger, 1972). The facilitator, David Brandon, invited participants to cascade the training to others and I took the opportunity to run a further eight or nine courses. This led to a search for people who shared a similar perspective, which was accelerated when the local educational psychology service invited Jack Pearpoint and Marsha Forest over from Toronto to talk about including children with severe disabilities in ordinary classrooms. I was able to examine more of the relevant literature during a period of study at the Tizard Centre, University of Kent and the practical implications were explored with the mental health service where I worked.

In 1998 Liz Sayce commissioned the Mind inquiry into social exclusion (Dunn, 1999) and I was invited to contribute evidence to the panel. A job move allowed me to start work with a group of kindred spirits at the National Development Team (NDT) in 1999 from where I provided induction training for the Mainstream team at Imagine in Liverpool. Subsequent work with the Sainsbury Centre for Mental Health, the National Institute for Mental Health in England and the Government's Social Exclusion Unit provided further opportunities to examine the theme, and invitations to deliver social inclusion training to mental health services around the country offered a test bed for emerging insights. By early 2004 I had developed an 8-day training programme and contributed a chapter to the core curriculum for all mental health staff (Bates, 2005).

Teaching Mental Health. Edited by Theo Stickley and Thurstine Basset.
Copyright © 2007 John Wiley & Sons, Ltd.

Box 15.1   A Social Inclusion Syllabus

Theme 1 – Goals and Values

- Introduction to inclusion
- Announcing person-centred approaches
- User involvement and empowerment
- Learning about evaluation

Theme 2 – Working with individuals

- Community mapping
- Strategies for supporting individuals to make connections
- Matching people and community opportunities
- Growing friendships

Theme 3 – Working with community agencies

- Building social capital
- Building capacity in community organisations
- Delivering inclusion training to community organisations
- Employment
- Supported volunteering

Theme 4 – Is your organisation on board?

- Modernising day services
- Helping your organisation promote inclusion

Theme 5 – Is it working?

- Reviewing inclusive projects
- Assessment of inclusion

THE COURSE

The 8-day training programme is summarised in Box 15.1. It is designed as a menu of stand-alone modules, allowing customers to select one or more items from the programme and then spend as much time as the audience needs on each module. The training has been adapted and delivered to mental health, drug and alcohol, learning disability and physical impairment services; to service users, staff and students, and to groups ranging from cooks and care assistants to commissioners and senior managers.

SOME THOUGHTS ON CONTENT: THE POWER AND DANGER OF SIMPLE IMAGES

With such a diverse group of course participants, it has seemed important to discover simple, memorable and potent images. As a travelling speaker, I often meet people who attended something I did months or years ago, and they sometimes tell me about the things they have remembered from my sessions. Usually it is the "inclusion traffic lights", although "fantasy birthday" and "inclusion beads" often get a mention too. Such potent images have their drawbacks, as some individuals are beginning to misunderstand and misuse them. One solution has been to offer guidance on some of these misunderstandings (e.g. Bates, 2005), but the bigger challenge is to consider how trainers can help people to become more mentally agile – to adopt good ideas until they cease to help and then discard them in favour of better ones.

A further way to maximise the potency of images is to weave them into lively presentations. For example, in explaining a choice, I might stand in one place to describe the first option and then physically move to take up the second position before explaining the alternative stance. This low-key attempt to dramatise the message helps kinaesthetic as well as auditory learners.

SIMPLICITY OR COMPLEXITY

A few course participants have complained that the inclusion agenda is too simple and obvious to justify the time allocated to training. This illustrates the point that David Morris (2005) makes when he sums up social inclusion as "simple in principle but complex in application". Indeed, the task of delivering training to groups with such a varied level of academic experience demands that materials are comprehensible at a basic level while offering further challenges to those who wish to probe further.

This remains a serious challenge, especially when an audience includes people with learning disabilities and others with postgraduate qualifications. Attempts are made to adjust the pace of teaching on each day to the particular audience and differentiate the materials to individual participants through the use of extension materials, repetition of key points and storytelling, but some modules resist these attempts at clarity without oversimplification. Powerpoint slides are designed to be uncrowded, contain few words and make active use of colour and pictures – an approach which a few have condemned as "patronising".

THE POWER OF STORY

Whilst I find that personal testimony from people who have used services helps my own understanding, I have not yet found a way routinely to include people who have used services in the delivery of my training. Clients rarely wish to pay a double fee when a single trainer will suffice, and full-time travelling across the whole country takes me out of my home-based networks that might provide first-hand stories. Joint training with another person demands a rare quality of relationship, trust, responsiveness to each other, familiarity with the training materials and shared sensitivities to the audience. Furthermore, I feel that there is often a tension between biography and parable – between holding true to the life story of the person giving their account, and the message that is needed at this point in the syllabus. As a second best, I have gathered many snippets of stories that I tell myself during training.

Some trainers in the inclusion field, such as John O'Brien and David Pitonyak, enhance their storytelling by showing photos and giving detailed accounts of the lives of their disabled friends. Listening to these presentations often makes me feel that I am impoverished in my personal network as I do not have such vibrant, personal friendships with people who use services. I have sometimes felt that there is a suggestion of criticism in the air (but not from John or David), that my training somehow lacks authenticity if I do not spend occasional weekends camping with a disabled friend, or providing informal crisis support to a neighbour with mental health issues. No one has ever said anything, and I resist the temptation to massage my authenticity rating by seeking out certain friendships or talking about them in public.

I prefer a stance in which failure is illustrated from my own life, and success is revealed in the lives of others. I remain nervous about my own ability to remain true to the story of the individual concerned while helping them to think carefully about appropriate confidentiality, but without parading the intimate details of another person's life for my training pleasure. I have similar concerns about the disclosures of many media celebrities!

The full training programme does involve a site visit to an ordinary community location and an hour with guests who are interviewed by small groups of course members. These sessions often bring a tangible increase in engagement with the issues as staff add their current personal experience to the process.

JUST MENTAL HEALTH?

The (NDT) works across both mental health and learning disability services and has been involved in the social inclusion agenda in both fields. Indeed, the social inclusion course was developed as a joint response to the day service modernisation programme in both services. In addition, the launch of the Client Services Improvement Partnership within the Department of Health in 2004 heralded a welcome broadening of perspective from "silo" thinking within individual client groups to one that acknowledged areas of similarity and common experience.

The result is that I have delivered the training programme to a variety of audiences, and frequently illustrate its messages by the use of stories from either field. This is consistent with the inclusion agenda that celebrates shared humanity rather than artificial categories of need, encourages participants to build connections with inclusion workers in other fields, equips people to respond to service users who might carry multiple labels, and promotes creative thinking rather than the rigid application of solutions stolen from other people's lives. Despite explaining the reasons why I use information and examples from other parts of society, a few participants report that this is difficult for them or even suggest that the stories are somehow irrelevant to their work area.

PRACTICAL CONSIDERATIONS: INTELLECTUAL PROPERTY AND ADMINISTRATIVE SUPPORT

It is a point of principle for me to acknowledge sources wherever possible and offer training participants full references. As a result I have developed a personal library of quotations and a fairly extensive reference list (800 items on social inclusion) that can be e-mailed to anyone who asks for it. A proportion of my original work is submitted for publication (around 55 items have been accepted to date) but the dilemma remains about what to do with unpublished original work. My current practice is usually to offer training participants a transcript of the content of Powerpoint slides rather than the slides themselves. Such training resources are often the fruit of substantial labours and form a key aspect of the product that the NDT sells to generate income for organisational survival, so it seems fair to provide customers with the intellectual material but reduce the ease by which these could be passed to competitors.

I remain ill at ease with this arrangement and do not apply it consistently. The alternative viewpoint has much more appeal – that good ideas belong to people who use services, so should be widely shared, that customers buy the explanations and embellishment rather than just the Powerpoint slides and that a generous spirit brings economic as well as spiritual rewards.

Sending out these follow-up materials all takes time, along with booking trains and hotels, checking venue locations and sending out confirmation details, and I often find this happens after 9pm at night or at weekends. Work/life balance is a continuous tension and it is hard to see how a trainer who had less enthusiasm for the subject would survive for very long.

FEEDBACK AND EVALUATION

I find that traditional evaluation forms are of little help to me. Scores are invariably fairly good, while isolated comments indicate that one person has not got on well with one exercise, while another valued the same activity highly. Comments about the room temperature, catering or uncomfortable chairs are directed at the person arranging these things, rather than the travelling trainer. Although the training department may use the general scores to draw inferences about one trainer over another, they do not tell me much. Participants sometimes like to have a place that they can lodge some remarks, and occasionally practical advice comes in, such as the person who used a feedback form to advise me how to use a function key on the computer!

This all means I have to find other means of collecting useful feedback. Coffee and lunch breaks are valuable times for asking participants how they are getting on and whether anything can be different. I have sometimes admitted to individuals (afterwards) that a particular exercise has just been used for the first time, in an attempt to obtain candid feedback on whether it was an effective piece of communication. End of session post-it exercises often pin down the commitments that staff wish to make as a result of training and can give people a chance to write brief messages to the trainer.

THE NEED FOR FLEXIBILITY

My personal style is to prepare an outline programme, but keep a loose rein on how much time each element takes. My own creative process is energised by the live training situation, and I often spontaneously generate new ideas that extend an established exercise and can be tried out straight away. This has demanded that I keep all my training materials to hand – for example, Powerpoint slides are individually indexed and can be used at a few moments' notice. It also requires that a careful record is kept of what has been used where and what has worked, or the most effective ways to engage people can be lost.

Some participants find the somewhat free-flowing nature of this training difficult to handle and would prefer to begin each day with a pack of materials that will definitely be used and a precise timetable of what will be covered in each segment of the day. I partly address this need by sticking rigidly to break times and by providing electronic copies of slides and handouts within days of the end of the event.

DIVERSE TEACHING STYLES

As the learning styles of participants can be expected to be quite diverse, I have tried to match this with a variety of teaching styles. Each day is planned in two columns – content and format. Pairs work, group-work and team feedback are varied with marketplace exercises (where people interview one another informally), poster-writing and poster-reading, and low-key role play. The challenge is to find a style that enables participation while creating enough space for anxious or self-conscious participants to feel at ease.

One approach that I use quite frequently is to invite people to work in small groups and give an account to their colleagues of one of the people that they support. Training messages are then woven into this story by the trainer. However, this is not always easy – particularly when some staff have no real experience of doing inclusion work. Other participants cannot see how the social inclusion agenda can work with "their" client who has such a serious disability or displays so little enthusiasm. This moves the focus of training from information to emotions such as hope and creativity.

THE FUNDAMENTALS: FACTS OR HOPE?

Whilst inclusion training aims to impart a body of information, it is also a matter of the heart. Participants need to feel what it is like to be excluded, to have their hope stirred and energised, to remember why they came into the work and apply creative energy to the task of increasing people's life chances. Occasionally, feedback at the end of a course shows that a delegate has made this journey. How should the trainer support this journey? I would hesitate to claim any winning formula.

How the trainer meets participants for the first time is critical. Many people feel that they operate in a blame culture where overwork is encouraged and staff are constantly subject to criticism for not doing enough. Within this setting, the visiting trainer is bringing another frown, another criticism of custom and practice and another bundle of new jobs to add to the pile of things that have to be done. Some staff cope by developing their "reframing" skills by which existing activities are given new titles so that they simultaneously meet a range of targets. In many cases this is legitimate, but can be destructive when it means that every real change to work patterns or priorities is resisted. Arriving in the context, the trainer can perhaps make progress by listening first. Indeed, most of us find it hard to listen until we have been listened to.

Furthermore, a blame culture can mean that successes are ignored, while gaps or failures are pored over in a mistaken effort to impose learning by crushing workers. The vast majority of people are only too ready to review their own work critically, and need nothing so much as some recognition and encouragement for their efforts – even from a visiting trainer. Combining the need to listen with space for people to celebrate successes leads to an introduction format that might include an opportunity for participants to tell everyone about one thing that is going well and another than is causing some concern. Participants reveal a great deal about themselves and their organisations through the amount of time and the degree of animation that goes into their answers.

Perhaps part of the job of raising levels of hope is done when people feel that their disappointments and discouragements have been genuinely heard. Another part may be to do with daring to talk about attitudes, hope and how to maintain a quiet optimism in the face of occasional disappointments. I have been told that the demeanour of the trainer matters too – that a pessimistic and discouraged trainer tends to impart a similar mood to trainees. I feel that this area needs further consideration, particularly as hope is crucial to recovery, yet mental health staff often suppress it (Social Exclusion Unit, 2004).

SKILLS OR WORLDVIEW?

For some participants, inclusion training serves to provide an alternative language for things that they have believed in and practised for as long as they can remember, and perhaps some additional skills to turn those values into action. But for others, the training becomes a battleground between worldviews. One person resigned when the group decided to involve service users at Board level, another person began by claiming that community does not exist, and a third explained that the outside world was so hostile that it is best to keep people safe inside mental health services until the storm of hate crime and discrimination blows over.

There seems to be no easy way to challenge negative, pessimistic or stereotypical world-views. Perhaps they need to be named, so that people can recognise that their position is an option amongst several. People seem to invest heavily in their worldview, and rarely re-spond to criticism or evidence about "a better way". If the person's worldview is restricting opportunities for service users (and I think that our deeply held beliefs always leak out to others), then the task properly belongs to the person's line manager or mentor, rather than a visiting trainer. In addition, job descriptions, person specifications and written statements describing the purpose of each service need to make clear what is expected of people, especially at a time when services are in transition.

At a more subtle level, social inclusion thinking is a challenge to the dominant worldview of mental health services. A glance at the budget sheet or the checklist of inspection bodies will reveal that the focus is on symptom management rather than exclusion prevention, on managing services rather than building community, on reducing risk rather than creating opportunity. Some traditional power holders may adopt the language of inclusion, but only to reinforce their own power base and disable opposing viewpoints. At times, inclusion trainers and their allies are no more than a few faint voices crying against a pervasive and dominant system, so it makes sense to accept that the journey will be long, arduous and sometimes lonely.

BLENDING THE PERSONAL AND THE PROFESSIONAL

The recent appointment of a man previously convicted of people smuggling to the post of Head of Social Inclusion (Newcastle Evening Standard, 2005) generates questions about immigration law, the rehabilitation of offenders and the personal experience and character needed for a role in championing inclusion. I find social inclusion coherent with my personal belief system (I am a practising Christian) and so it is more than a job or a bare espousal of the principle of equal rights.

An inclusion perspective also challenges traditional views on the maintenance of "professional distance" by asserting the common humanity shared by staff, service users and other citizens who live together in shared communities.

This means that training invites people to draw on their experiences as human beings by talking about the feeling of exclusion, the nature of friendship, personal communities and what makes us feel that we belong. I have never had anyone attending the course who has expressed a problem with this style of learning, although this may have been eased by encouraging participants to look after themselves by sharing only as much as they feel comfortable disclosing. Indeed, some sessions have been enriched by deeply personal disclosures.

PERSONAL ISSUES: HARNESSING THE INSIGHTS OF EACH TRAINING GROUP

Sometimes I get anxious about my training – perhaps a particular audience seem to be especially well versed in the subject, or they are seeking to apply the materials to a field of work that is unfamiliar to me. Perhaps the latter group thought little of this particular module, or perhaps I am just lacking confidence today. The pressure of this situation can lead to several kinds of distortion.

Firstly, anxiety can lead me to abandon any attempt to introduce all the people in the room to one another, preferring instead to get on with delivering the training. Some people know all the other delegates already and want to hear from the trainer, while others feel that introductions are an essential courtesy. If the group is larger than perhaps 15 people, meaningful introductions can take an hour and few participants can remember all that disparate information. However, it does provide raw material for break-time discussions, illustrations for many of the issues that come up later, and helps people to feel that their prior experiences are valued, rather than the trainer implying that they are somehow incompetent.

Secondly, anxiety can mean I spend more time on delivering information and less on encouraging participants to think. The day becomes dominated by a lecture format, so experiential learners are left behind. I pepper the information with quotations and references to create the illusion of weight, and this can leave non-academics behind. I give less time to exploring dilemmas and begin to suggest that there are simple fixes, answers that rely on obedience to a set of rules rather than creativity. Worst of all, this anxiety can encourage the trainer to lay aside proper humility and adopt an arrogant attitude – naively thinking that one always has something worthwhile to say.

Thirdly, anxiety can push the trainer into expecting audiences to spend more time listening and less time speaking. The work of the inclusion trainer is to help people reflect on their own values and practice, and the most successful mix seems to be a few well-chosen facts and thinking tools combined with lots of time to explore. People who sit silently and seemingly compliant during lectures will vigorously engage in group work, wrestling with the issues and sometimes with one another in an attempt to make sense of the inclusion perspective. Sometimes one or more group members wish to explore their ideas by challenging (and sometimes verbally attacking) the trainer. I enjoy this kind of energetic discussion, especially when other group members take up a variety of positions and join in with the debate, but if the group as a whole seem hostile or if one member dominates any discussion, it is tempting to retreat into lecture-giving.

An approach that draws out the ideas and experiences of participants has other advantages too. Whilst some training sessions need to be a simple repetition of what has been delivered elsewhere, other exercises can form part of a growing body of knowledge in which the trainer draws out the insights of the group, collates them with the work of previous groups and feeds the result back to participants.

For example, several groups started with a blank sheet of paper and created a checklist for mapping arts venues; subsequent groups then sorted and grouped the work of their predecessors and others voted on the usefulness of the points made. The result is that each group covered similar ground – they explored similar concepts and thought about similar issues, but new resources were gradually created, refined and disseminated. This has the added advantage of modelling participative resource development, but does not fit too well into a standardised assessment framework that demands an identical experience for all cohorts.

PERSONAL DEVELOPMENT

As a small agency in a competitive market, there are few opportunities for attending training events run by others, and always work to do: marketing, scanning the policy environment, maintaining a reasonable knowledge of the evidence base and so on. In addition, I like to write for publication, and this activity is only rarely funded.

Colleagues in the NDT also spend a great deal of time travelling, so it is difficult to find time to pool resources, work together on new materials or receive the friendly criticism of a colleague who watches me at work. This means that quality assurance and personal development relies on internal rather than external factors.

Some training packages aim to deliver quality standards by aligning the work to established qualifications. This is just too hard. There are many possible awards frameworks that include a wide range of potential qualifications and the accreditation process is expensive and too complex to learn without investing a great deal of time and effort. Some trainers have enhanced their marketing brochures by indicating that the course provides material that is relevant to a specific module of a specific qualification. Some universities offer this service for a fee, but it is difficult for the non-academic to find adequate definitions of competencies and some audiences would not particularly value a certificate. Furthermore, this route demands adherence to a strict syllabus rather than the degree of flexibility that allows me to be responsive to each audience and workplace.

TRAINING OR ORGANISATIONAL DEVELOPMENT?

While some clients simply invite me to adopt the role of trainer, others seek a broader relationship where the focus is cultural and organisational development, and training is just one part of this process. Whilst the NDT is heavily involved in consultation, service review and support for organisational development, the training role is simpler.

However, training usually takes place in a turbulent organisational environment, where budgets are shrinking and change is a constant companion. Day services staff have been shielded from much of the change agenda that has swept the wider health and social care environment in recent years, and so their acute distress in the face of current change is sometimes met with a degree of incredulity by more senior managers; however, it is no less real. One result is that participants in training events occasionally need to ventilate feelings about management style, the pace of organisational change, consultation processes, salaries or workload pressures. Students attending full-time courses may be pleasantly free of these "distractions", but they risk missing out on the gritty reality that practising staff know all too well.

For frontline staff to adopt socially inclusive practice certain organisational conditions need to be met, such as empowerment and creativity, distributed leadership, positive risk-taking and person-centred service design. This means that training might reach out to challenge individual practice, all parts of the mental health service and the wider community. The trainer's task is to encourage people to acknowledge the part that they can play in re-focusing their own practice and the behaviour and attitudes of others, whilst helping people to avoid undue self-blame or condemnation of others.

The training is also practical enough to yield precise recommendations about individual and team behaviours, so some of the most fruitful sessions occur when all the relevant decision-makers are present and my role can slip from trainer to facilitating a staff meeting where staff plan timetabled action. This demands sensitivity that acknowledges rather than usurps the role of established decision-making forums.

CONCLUSION

All trainers attempt to provide material that is relevant to their audience in content, pitch and pace, as well as individualised to each trainee's learning style. Travelling trainers must address their own professional development, quality assurance and the challenge of embedding their work into the organisations they serve. Inclusion trainers face similar dilemmas to those training in empowerment or recovery as these topics share a potent mix of the personal, political and professional. Finally, training in an emerging topic such as social inclusion demands creativity, effort to keep up with the fast-moving "edge" of what is known about the subject and humility as one increasingly falls behind.

REFERENCES

Bates, P. (2005a). Developing socially inclusive practice module 6 in Basset T., Lindley P. & Barton R. (2005) *The ten essential shared capabilities: Learning pack for mental health practice* London: NHS University. Available at http://www.lincoln.ac.uk/ccawi/esc/default.htm

Bates, P. (2005b). *Accidents at the inclusion traffic lights: mistakes and misunderstandings in supporting people to achieve social inclusion* Ipswich: National Development Team. Available at www.ndt.org.uk.

Dunn, S. (1999). *Creating accepting communities: report of the Mind Inquiry into social exclusion.* London: Mind.

David Morris is the Care Services Improvement Partnership lead for social inclusion. Personal communication.

Newcastle Evening Chronicle, *I've nothing to hide* 14 July 2005.

Social Exclusion Unit (2004). *Mental Health and Social Exclusion.* London: Office of the Deputy Prime Minister

Wolfensberger, W. (1972). *The Principle of Normalisation in Human Services* Toronto: National Institute of Mental Retardation.

CHAPTER 16

Race Equality and Cultural Capability

Peter Ferns

The term "Black" is used in this chapter as a political term of solidarity between people who are vulnerable to "White" racism as a result of their skin colour and physical appearance – that is their "race" where this term is used as a social concept with no credible scientific basis. Capital letters are used to emphasise the political nature of the terms "Black" and "White". "Minority Ethnic" refers to *any* ethnic group ("Black" or "White") who are in a minority compared to a dominant ethnic group and who are also vulnerable to society-wide oppression and discrimination based on their ethnicity, culture or religious beliefs. The acronym "BME" thus stands for Black and Minority Ethnic.

This chapter explores the implementation of a training and education initiative in relation to Race Equality and Cultural Capability (RECC). RECC training materials were produced as part of the RECC training strategy of NIMHE (The National Institute for Mental Health in England) and the national strategy 'Delivering Race Equality'.

David "Rocky" Bennett was a young African Caribbean man who died in 1998 while being restrained in a psychiatric clinic following an incident involving racial abuse. An inquiry into his death came up with the following key recommendations:

> "All who work in mental health services should receive training in cultural awareness and sensitivity . . .
> . . . All managers and clinical staff, however senior or junior, should receive mandatory training in all aspects of cultural competency, awareness and sensitivity. This should include training to tackle overt and covert racism and institutional racism.
> . . . All medical staff in mental health services should have training in the assessment of people from the black and minority ethnic communities with special reference to the effects of racism upon their mental well being."

(Norfolk, Suffolk and Cambridgeshire Strategic Health Authority, 2004)

One of the biggest challenges facing modern mental health services in the UK is the need to provide culturally appropriate and non-discriminatory services to BME communities in a rapidly changing and increasingly complex society. There is a great deal at stake for us as a society if we do not meet this challenge as countless numbers of people and their families will be exposed to unnecessary mental distress with the attendant incidence of

Teaching Mental Health. Edited by Theo Stickley and Thurstine Basset.
Copyright © 2007 John Wiley & Sons, Ltd.

individual tragedies, damage to the fabric of communities and significant economic losses. We cannot afford to carry on ignoring this challenge and allowing the problem of racism in mental health services to grow and become even more entrenched resulting in serious long-term harm being caused to our BME communities who hold so much of this country''s capability, energy and enthusiasm to contribute to the well-being, cultural richness and prosperity of society as a whole. It would not only be a tragic waste of human potential for these communities but also for everyone committed to building a strong, diverse and inclusive culture in this country.

The term "Race Equality and Cultural Capability" was adopted as a result of an initiative by the Sainsbury Centre for Mental Health to review training around race equality in mental health services nationally in 2005. A panel of people involved in race equality training was created to look at a working title for the proposed training commissioned by NIMHE to train the mental health workforce on "cultural capability". It is important to understand why these terms have been adopted as the title for this training initiative reflects an approach to a complex issue which has never been clearly defined or yielded any consensus and continues to be very hard to pin down due to rapidly changing social and political factors. An attempt will be made to summarise these complexities prior to describing the RECC materials as this discussion provides a vital context for the materials as a whole. In summarising these issues, use will be made of two fundamental and over-arching "models" of the key concepts involved; these models have informed the main principles, values and design of the RECC materials.

DEFINING RACE EQUALITY

Concepts around "race" and "culture" have waxed and waned over the years and we have seen the emergence and demise of terms such as "race awareness training", "anti-racism training", "multiculturalism". Other terms are changing or falling out of favour such as "cultural awareness", "diversity training", "equalities training" and "cultural competence" (Bennett, 2006; Ferns, 2006). The concept of race equality proposed in the RECC materials flows directly from a thorough analysis of institutional racism in mental health services. The model presented here is used in the RECC materials to enable practitioners to reflect on their services and explore ways of improving them for BME people. Six "themes of institutional discrimination" emerged from analysis of research studies, BME service user-led surveys and audits of service quality conducted by the author''s training consultancy. We have developed approaches to counteract these patterns or "themes of institutional discrimination" and found the resulting "themes of race equality" to be extremely valuable in taking a critical look at improving any mental health service. The following is an extract from the RECC materials summarising these themes.

The six **"themes of institutional discrimination"** can be summarised as follows.

Theme 1 – Assimilation

Assimilation means that people from a different cultural group to the dominant group are put under some degree of pressure to "fit in" with the dominant culture. This may seem like a good way of reducing tensions between different ethnic groups but there are some real difficulties with this approach. Culture is very difficult to define – so who decides if someone is "fitting in"? Is this desirable anyway? Culture can be a very important part of a person"s sense of identity – so does it make sense to effectively say to people that they should forget about their culture and join in with the dominant culture? At the heart of the problem with this approach is that it is essentially just a form of cultural arrogance in assuming that we have nothing to learn from other cultures and that "our culture" is better. This position does not reflect the reality of how all cultures have developed in the past with a process of constant interaction and mixing.

Assimilation shows itself in service settings in lots of hidden ways through the environment, decor, the assumptions of staff even down to their body language, facilities and activities available but most powerfully in the values and beliefs embedded in the way the service has been set up overall. All of this results in people from a different cultural background not feeling comfortable in a setting or organisation as an employee. For example, lesbian and gay culture in the workplace may be subtly but powerfully devalued by colleagues who assume that everyone is in a heterosexual relationship. This may result in a gay or lesbian person feeling that colleagues think of them as "odd" or "different" and may even lead to people feeling that they must "hide" their sexuality for fear of discrimination increasing their levels of stress and anxiety at work.

Theme 2 – Under-reaction or Over-reaction

The issue of under-reaction and over-reaction to BME people in mental distress is a long-standing problem, originally a term coined by a Black psychiatrist called Aggrey Burke in the 1980's. Several inquiries into cases involving BME service users (usually Black men) have illustrated the impact of this discriminatory approach, from Randolph Ince in the 1980's, to Orville Blackwood and Christopher Clunis in the 1990's, and more recently, David "Rocky" Bennett in 2004. "Under-reaction" refers to when services fail to respond to a significant and growing problem resulting in an avoidable crisis occurring. Whereas "over-reaction" refers to when services intervene in a punitive and controlling way where there are BME people (or other groups vulnerable to oppression) resulting in coercive action that jeopardises the basic human rights of the person involved. In both cases there is an inappropriate level of response to a mental health situation which increases the likelihood of discriminatory practice and poor outcomes.

Theme 3 – Disempowerment and Stereotyping

BME people and other people vulnerable to oppression are often subjected to stereotyping and institutional discrimination. The effect on the individual is to treat the person as a member of an "out-group" in society and thereby take away their individuality and sense of being in control of their own future. It becomes difficult for people to know when they are being discriminated against or whether there is genuinely another reason for the way they are being treated by others, particularly those with authority and power in society. The skills and talents of the individual are effectively ignored and service organisations engage in "block" treatment of human beings as if they are "all the same" or worse still as "commodities" to be traded by service organisations in some unpalatable market of human misery. The overall impact upon the person serves to create a powerful feeling of being out of control of desting destiny, making the person feel less powerful than they actually are. These processes of disempowerment along with the factors of prejudice, stereotyping and institutional discrimination can then fuel a longer-lasting and more serious problem of "internalised oppression" for the individual concerned.

Stereotyping also happens in services in hidden ways through the language being used about service users, the appearance of buildings where services are provided (bars on windows denoting dangerousness, etc . . .) and the labels which are put onto people. Stereotyping means that assumptions are made about an individual's personal qualities, skills and even personality because they happen to belong to a particular social group. Essentially stereotyping takes away a person's individuality and results in people being treated in a "block" way, as members of a devalued group.

Theme 4 – Service-led Approaches

Service-led approaches are damaging for all service users because services tend to view organisational priorities as being of equal and sometimes greater importance than the individual's needs. BME people are often seen as being more "difficult" and "complex" in terms of meeting individual needs and so are particularly prone to this type of approach from services.

The service ends up:

- slotting BME people into existing services rather than creating new and more appropriate services;
- carrying out assessments which focus narrowly on determining whether people are eligible to use services rather than helping people to identify their needs;
- providing services that are based on stereotypical professional views of what people's need are rather than their real needs;
- creating "block" services that are not very well designed for the individuals using them;
- having a focus on filling existing inappropriate services rather than identifying the gaps where services need to be developed for BME communities;
- blaming individuals as being "the problem" rather than questioning the appropriateness of their service provision when needs are not adequately met.

Theme 5 – Poor Access to Services

Barriers to access for BME people include:

- difficult bureaucratic procedures in getting referred to existing services in the first place;
- information about services not being in languages and formats that are useful for local BME population bearing in the mind the changing natures of many communities, for example with refugee and asylum seeker communities;
- suitable services being located in the wrong areas for BME people, requiring long journeys or hazardous trips into areas which may feel hostile for some ethnic groups;
- a lack of representation of BME staff within the workforce as this gives BME communities more confidence that the service is anti-discriminatory and may possess the capability to deliver a culturally appropriate service.

Theme 6 – Erosion of Rights

A strong feature of mental health services for BME communities is the fear that services will not uphold the basic human rights of people in the "system". This is partly due to media coverage but is also because of some high profile and very poor examples of practice resulting in people being over-medicated, denied competent and sensitive treatment, being exposed to racist abuse and in extreme cases being injured or even killed within the system. There is a fundamental lack of trust in many BME communities that members of their communities will get a good quality mental health service at times when people are at their most vulnerable. Despite examples of good practice in some parts of the country with BME people, it is still not common enough to change perceptions yet for the majority of them.

The six "**themes of race equality**" which can work against and prevent the negative processes outlined above can be summarised as follows.

Theme 1 – Valuing Cultural Diversity

Valuing cultural diversity begins with reinforcing the cultural identity of individual service users and taking the issue of cultural background seriously in practice. Understanding where a person is coming from in terms of their cultural identity involves enabling BME service users to feel comfortable in sharing their cultural beliefs and values with practitioners. It means that the service user and their families and carers should be viewed as the "experts" in their own cultural identities. Hence, BME service user participation is essential for culturally appropriate practice.

On a wider front, services should be made more culturally appropriate for BME individuals and communities. Culturally appropriate services are not just about having the right posters on the wall or having the right kind of food available to service users. The "iceberg" model mentioned earlier in the RECC materials, suggests that the real challenge is to develop mental health services that are inclusive of people's beliefs and values.

Theme 2 – Preventative Approaches

Preventative approaches require services to ensure that their priorities are to provide support and early interventions to everyone who may need mental health services. Under-reaction and over-reaction is not only damaging to people, it also results in long-term and costly problems for services further down the line. Services need to intervene in a timely fashion when problems are detected rather than wait until a crisis occurs, so a responsive service is crucial for a truly preventative approach. Preventative services must also increase opportunities for people to grow and develop and to build "resilience" and "endurance" in relation to mental distress.

Theme 3 – Autonomy and Advocacy

There are bound to be times when people will be unable or unwilling to express their own point of view and interests in services. It would be necessary to provide assistance to people to advocate for themselves at these points. Independent advocacy is required for advocates to be able to truly represent the service user's viewpoint and interests. The ultimate goal of any advocacy should be to enable and empower service users to speak for themselves and take more control of the important decisions being made in their lives. For BME service users it would be best to have someone advocating who understands the experience of racism and surviving the psychiatric system. Ideally BME people should have access to a group of BME service users/survivors so that they can generate a sense of solidarity as well as gain exposure to positive role models leading to greater self-confidence and hope for the future.

Theme 4 – Holistic Approach

A holistic approach requires services to view service users not just as individuals but as members of families and communities and take into account wider social and community factors in assessing individual needs. Assessments have to be balanced with consideration given to the personal strengths and interests of the person and a wider view of their needs, not just a narrow focus on "symptoms" of mental distress or problems in the person's life.

Many mental health services focus on just the basic needs of people for everyday survival but services need to move beyond this goal to really improve the quality of life for service users. Services must help people to identify a desirable personal future and achieve the kind of lifestyle people would want. There are often discriminatory barriers preventing people from achieving their goals for happiness and fulfilment and services must focus on assisting people to remove these barriers.

Theme 5 – Participation and Information

Mental health services have to be more proactive around equality issues and reach out to groups who have been poorly served or excluded in the past. The lack of credibility created by a legacy of poor services in the past will be a serious barrier to progress unless service providers work actively to establish credibility with BME communities. One of the most effective strategies for gaining credibility is to enable the genuine participation of BME service users and their communities in the design and improvement of services. A good first step for services is to provide accessible and accurate information to BME people about what is available in the locality.

Participation has to be meaningful for the people involved and so having a carefully thought out strategy is essential with resources set aside to implement improvements that are needed. There is now an increasing number of examples of BME service user-led audit and service improvement initiatives to draw examples of good practice in participation (Ferns et al., 2003).

Theme 6 – Safeguarding Rights

Mental health services have the potential to infringe people's rights so there must be safeguards to ensure that people are protected from abuse and exploitation. Compulsory admission to hospital and forced medication are all unique to mental health and so robust safeguards are required to protect people's human rights. Policy and procedures to promote equality and diversity have to be implemented and monitored to be of any real value. Systems such as monitoring the quality of services are best undertaken in partnership with BME service users, families and carers to guarantee that judgements about service quality are based on criteria that are important for BME people. Complaints procedures should be fully accessible to BME service users with the necessary supports.

Leaders in service provision must ensure that they model and promote good practice in their decision-making and that they support BME service user participation. Participation is vital for safeguarding rights as it acts as a check and balance against misuse of practitioner power increasing the likelihood of culturally appropriate practice. Finally, practitioners have to start taking individual accountability for promoting race equality in their own practice and within their teams. This includes training where the learning gained must be put into practice if we are to ever really change the culture of mental health services.

Defining Cultural Capability

The term "capability" is preferred in the RECC materials to "knowledge and skills" or "competence" for various reasons related to current definitions of these terms. Knowledge and skills refers to the specific individual and technical attributes of a practitioner that enables them to complete certain tasks related to their job role. "Competence" incorporates knowledge and skills of the person or what is required for practice but also takes in the values and ethical underpinnings to practice. Competence can vary according to the work context, the role of the person and the personal qualities an individual brings to their work. I would argue that "capability" incorporates the other two concepts and goes beyond current competence in job role. Capability consists of a combination of knowledge, skills, values, personal qualities, experience, wisdom or learning from experience, and "conation" or the ability to apply capability in practice. Capability is also not just about current capability in job role but encompasses future capability or potential competence to perform in an untried role. Thus capability is the most complex concept of the three outlined above and is by far the hardest to ascertain or develop.

So, "cultural capability" has to address all of the factors associated with capability but within a diverse cultural context helping to define and inform transcultural practice in mental health. The RECC materials address the issue of capability rather than competence as they attempt to build on people's experience, increase reflective practice and grow wisdom to improve decision-making as well as encourage people to apply their learning in practice. A recent publication sums up cultural capability in this way:

> Cultural competence is one facet of professional competence that could be seen to affect all aspects of practice. Leavitt (2002) defines cultural competence as:
>
> > "a set of behaviours, attitudes and policies that come together in a continuum to enable a health care system, agency or individual practitioners to function effectively in transcultural interactions".
>
> An individual's view of healthcare will be based on their culture and they will interact and respond accordingly. As healthcare professionals, we will have a view of healthcare that is based on our expectations and that of our professional philosophy. Our starting point

is therefore likely to be very different from that of service users. To establish an effective therapeutic relationship we need to understand the client's worldview.

Understanding the "culture" of colleagues and staff is equally important in developing working relationships that are mutually beneficial and that ensure equality of treatment.

(CSP, 2005, p.16)

The publication goes on to define the key elements of "cultural competence" in a very useful way that has informed the RECC materials.

Key elements of cultural competence

- Self-awareness – as part of becoming culturally competent, practitioners need to identify, explore and question their own values and beliefs
- Knowledge – practitioners need to be aware of the similarities and differences between cultures
- Recognition – of the impact that culture has on an individual's perception of the world and therefore of health and illness.
- Ability and commitment – to use this knowledge, self-awareness and recognition to think about their practice and how to deliver it in a way that maximises the involvement of clients and therefore the benefits to them.
- Maintaining competence involves thinking about, and reflecting on, practice and the learning that has taken place. This is a continuous process that includes evaluating assumptions, attitudes and values that underpin professional behaviour."

(CSP, 2005, pp. 18–19)

Ultimately, the effectiveness of any cultural capability training is dependent upon the quality of analysis of the concept of "culture" itself. A superficial analysis of culture can lead to tokenism or cultural stereotyping. The RECC materials emphasise the complexity of culture, offer a multi-layered model of culture and provide a structured approach to working with cultural differences that does not fall into the trap of "cultural stereotyping" of specific ethnic groups. Culture is viewed as a dynamic and fluid social concept where individuals and groups interact with each other and develop within a cultural framework that they actively shape while being influenced by it.

Training about cultural capability without a strategy to address individual and institutional racism based on a thorough analysis of power dynamics and structural inequalities will have a limited impact on discrimination in services. So, cultural capability is necessary but not sufficient in tackling institutional racism. Race equality and cultural capability approaches are integral to good practice – they are not "special" or "different" approaches to practice. In other words a race equality and cultural capability approach improves mental health services for everyone and is an ordinary part of good practice.

RECC TRAINING STRATEGY

The nature of RECC training is different from other forms of mental health training in several ways. RECC training seeks to go beyond the development of individual knowledge and skills of practitioners. The training has to examine the power dynamics between service users and practitioners, challenge the values of practitioners and encourage reflective practice. All these requirements go far beyond straightforward teaching of technical knowledge and skills such as mental health legislation. Due to the political nature of racism, training on this issue is subject to higher levels of scrutiny by organisations and the wider community and especially BME communities. More questions are asked about the use of resources on this type of training by organisations than any other in relation to political pressures and "value for money" concerns and by BME communities who tend to be most concerned about tangible improvements in services for BME people. Demands of this training involving greater accountability to organisations and BME communities mean that greater pressure is transmitted to commissioners and trainers.

Institutional racism is systemic in nature so RECC training must also be systemic in its approach to address it. Practitioner training must, of course, address the behaviours and practice of employees but it also must aim to influence leadership behaviour in the organisation, shape systems and structures to support anti-discriminatory practice and thereby change the whole culture of organisations. The diagram below illustrates how the different elements of "whole systems" service improvement are interlinked and what the RECC training strategy aims to achieve (Figure 16.1).

It is clear that there must be the right kind of work environment for promoting race equality and cultural capability if any training initiative around this subject is going to be effective. We will now examine how this model of service improvement has been reflected in the design of the RECC materials.

RECC TRAINING

ORGANISATIONAL CULTURE

ORGANISATIONAL CULTURE

LEADERSHIP CAPABILITY

DESIGN OF SYSTEMS & STRUCTURES

PRACTITIONER CAPABILITY

ORGANISATIONAL CULTURE

ORGANISATIONAL CULTURE

Figure 16.1 A whole systems approach to RECC training.

THE RECC MATERIALS

The Delivering Race Equality Action Plan recommended that:

> A more active role for BME communities and BME service users in the training of profes-
> sionals, in the development of mental health policy, and in the planning and provision of
> services; and... all who work in mental health services should receive training in cultural
> awareness and sensitivity... all managers and clinical staff, however senior or junior, should
> receive mandatory training in all aspects of cultural competency, awareness and sensitivity.
> This should include training to tackle overt and covert racism and institutional racism...

(Department of Health, 2005)

The RECC materials are an extension of the "Essential Shared Capabilities" learning materials (see Chapter 9) and provide a focused, higher level of training around RECC. The
RECC materials are organised into twelve training sessions of approximately two hours
duration, forming three modules. An outline of the learning objectives for these sessions is
shown in the Appendix.

Design

Individual Learning

Individual learning in the training programme is enhanced with extensive written materials
which are provided to participants as pre-course reading thereby reducing the pressure on
learners to absorb large amounts of theoretical material during the direct training sessions.
This enables trainers to focus on facilitating participants to discuss their views and apply
their learning through a series of practical exercises thereby deepening their understanding
of the theories and concepts being presented. Learner's notes and handouts are available
to participants on each training session to help guide them through the practical exercises
and provide them with notes on any presentations by the trainers. Full references for the
materials and suggestions for further reading along with a list of useful websites and videos
are included in each section of the materials.

Reflective practice is reinforced throughout the materials with questions to elicit individual reflection on important theoretical or practice issues. Participants will also be encouraged to use a Personal Learning Log which will be provided as part of their personal folder
of materials and which can form part of a portfolio of evidence for Continuous Personal
Development or for National Vocational Qualification purposes.

Team Learning

The RECC materials can certainly be used with whole teams and indeed it will be suggested
that this happens as it could potentially be the most effective way of improving practice
with BME service users. There are exercises that have been devised for use within teams to
highlight the importance of valuing cultural differences amongst team members as well as
taking a critical look at team-working and the culture of teams. In practical terms for service
delivery, it may best to have clusters of workers from a small number of teams involved as
this also presents valuable opportunities to improve multi-agency working in a locality. The

biggest challenge of having whole teams in training terms is where there is a strong team culture that is resistant to being challenged by the trainers or the materials.

Leadership Learning

Many of the exercises in the RECC materials can provide invaluable data and evidence of practice with BME service users for leaders in service organisations. The problem of confidentiality is always present, especially in organisations that are sensitive to criticism or negative feedback and respond punitively towards staff who challenge the "status quo". However, trainers may still find ways of feeding data back to leaders in such organisations while preserving confidentiality. Certain exercises in the RECC materials have been designed specifically to give feedback and provide information for leaders about current practice by aggregating anonymised data – these have been called "Practice Checkpoints" in the materials.

The purpose of feeding through such data to leaders is to enable them to make better judgements about policy and procedures and ultimately design better systems and structures to support and deliver anti-discriminatory practice. The "bottom-up" flow of information about current practice begins to demonstrate the value of listening to service users, communities and front-line staff leading to an increased potential for more participatory services. Most importantly, leaders get an invaluable insight into the culture of their services and critical questions are raised about how effectively leaders are driving the right culture within service organisations that make them "fit for purpose" from the viewpoint of service users and staff.

Learning and Practice

Following each session there are suggestions for small workplace projects designed to link learning in that session to practice. It will be suggested that the results of these workplace projects could be recorded in Personal Learning Logs and/or shared with colleagues and line-managers in supervision. It is important for participants to have an opportunity to discuss any aspect of their learning experience on the RECC programme with their supervisor or line-manager – eventually their learning and completion of work projects could feed into a system of appraisal or personal development.

General Design Issues

The RECC materials make extensive use of BME service user quotes drawn from previous work on service user-led audits and surveys. Much of the materials have been developed over a period of eight years with BME service user trainers delivering training through Ferns Associates and the Critical Readers Group for the RECC materials have included experienced BME service user/survivor trainers. It is one of the central design principles to present BME service user perspectives and interests throughout the programme.

The RECC materials provide a solid foundation training programme on race and culture issues in mental health for all practitioners. Each session is comprised of a core set of training materials for any practitioner but an additional set of resource materials is being planned to enable trainers to adapt this core set of materials to different practitioner groups working in settings such as forensic services, housing, children and adolescent services, older people, acute wards and Approved Social Workers. This will increase the flexibility of the materials with different practitioner groups in terms of content.

Eventually, it is planned that the paper materials will be supplemented with a CD-Rom version containing all the materials required including additional reading materials for students who wish to study certain topics in more depth. It has been stated that the materials form a foundation level training on race and culture issues in mental health and it is envisaged that a higher level skills development programme will need to be produced to build on this foundation training.

Delivery

The materials have been divided up into twelve sessions to allow maximum flexibility in training delivery. Sessions can be delivered over a period of months or they can be combined to form one-day workshops or longer block courses. "Practice Checkpoints" or work projects could be set for participants to complete between sessions or training days.

The materials have been designed to be delivered to a multi-disciplinary participant group. The wider the variation within the training group the better the exercises will work and the discussions will be richer. Some of the exercises that touch on professional cultures could be used to highlight the quality of local interagency working.

It is being recommended that the materials are delivered by two trainers, at least one of which should be a BME service user/survivor trainer. This will ensure a strong focus on BME service user issues and a more cogent challenge to professional practice. We have found the quality of teaching and learning to be greatly improved in having skilled BME service user trainers delivering such material in the past.

The requirement to have at least one BME service user trainer co-training with another trainer throws up several challenges and interesting ways of working to deliver the RECC training. The participation of BME service users in training is still in its infancy even though there are several excellent service-user trainers operating in the mental health field. The scale of the RECC project to deliver training to all mental health practitioners is massive and will require a significant increase in the numbers of BME service user/survivor trainers nationally. Furthermore, there are implications for training skills development opportunities targeted at this group of potential service user trainers.

The RECC materials will make demands on the skills of any mental health trainer and people delivering the training will need to have a good grasp of all the course contents as well as the theoretical and value-based underpinnings to the materials. Coupled with the skills necessary for co-training between BME service user trainers and other trainers, the preparation for trainers to deliver the materials to a high standard will have to be thorough and well-planned. It is for this reason that a robust process of training for trainers is being proposed with an accreditation process for every trainer. Eventually, it is anticipated that the RECC training itself as well as the training for trainers will attract a recognised and respected set of qualifications.

Delivering the RECC materials will be challenging as well as personally rewarding and people involved in delivery on a regional basis will require support, coaching and practice development. Ongoing monitoring of quality of training delivery will be important and the establishment of a regional training support group in relation to RECC may provide many of these functions. The potential impact on the dynamics around mental health training in a region through this initiative could be fundamental and it would be fascinating to set up a longer-term evaluative study.

EVALUATION

An independent evaluation of the pilot of RECC materials is being undertaken by the Sainsbury Centre for Mental Health – led by Dr Joanna Bennett and Dr Jayasree Kalathil. It is the first time that such a thorough evaluation process has been undertaken of RECC training in the mental health field and the evaluation framework has been developed from an evidence base built up by the Sainsbury Centre for Mental Health through an extensive evaluative study of race equality training across the country. It is hoped that the framework used in this study will inform the development of some useful and practical tools for managers that will accompany the RECC materials themselves.

We are keen to ensure that every opportunity to strengthen a "whole systems" approach is taken in the implementation of the RECC training and this will be carried forward through the evaluation process as well. It is vital for the success and full effectiveness of the training to have the full commitment and involvement of senior management in the target organisations. Therefore a set of useful and practical evaluation tools is being planned for use by managers interested in measuring the impacts of RECC training and wishing to ensure sustainable improvements in their services. The issue of training for managers in the use of these tools and in relation to RECC itself has been raised and options are currently being explored.

Initial ideas for an evaluation framework are in the box below.

Box 16.1   Initial Ideas for an Evaluation Framework

BASELINE AUDIT MEASURES

- Examination of relevant policies, procedures and systems
- Leadership practice
- Organisational culture
- Professional practice
- Self assessment
- Service user experience

TRAINING DELIVERY MEASURES

- Learner experience
- Impacts on practice
- Line-management supervision

POST-TRAINING AUDIT MEASURES

- Systems and structures audit
- Leadership practice

- – Organisational culture
- – Practice development
- – Sustainability of improvements

LOOKING AHEAD

Organisational cultures and systems in public services are increasingly becoming target-driven and outcomes are being more carefully monitored than at any other time in the past, especially in relation to "value for money". In this context all training in services can be marginalised as it tends to affect long-term trends rather than yield short-term gains in quality of practice and service provision. Given the political dimension of RECC training and sometimes the unwelcome emphasis on tackling institutional racism, this particular type of training tends to be even further marginalised and vulnerable to tokenism and lack of implementation in practice. Consequently, RECC training must be effective and delivered to a high standard when an opportunity to introduce a strategic approach to promote race equality and increase cultural capability does present itself.

It has only recently been understood just how vital good mental health and well-being is to us as a society. The Social Exclusion Unit report (SEU, 2004) has demonstrated the far-reaching consequences of not investing in mental health services in social, economic and most importantly, ethical terms. Fundamentally, mental health services have always been about social justice as much as about treating individuals who are mentally distressed. Mental health services have a crucial role to play in building a strong and inclusive culture in this country as they deal directly with the quality of life for individuals and their communities. Mental health never has been and never will be purely a matter of medical intervention in people's lives. Modern approaches to mental health emphasise the "holistic" and complex nature of mental distress and services must tackle the complexity of social problems if they are to connect and deal with the reality of people's lives.

At the heart of this "holistic" approach is a fundamental respect for and valuing of the uniqueness of human beings and their different cultures. It is in this way, by ensuring mental health services are appropriate and effective for BME people, we will improve services for all. Social injustice weakens us as a democratic society leading to a sense of grievance, alienation, frustration, distress, anger and conflict. If we have learned nothing else from the past decade, with the growth of global terrorism and increasing exploitation of vulnerable groups, we should now be in no doubt about the destructive power of racial and ethnic injustice. Mental health and responses to the mental distress of our most marginalised and vulnerable groups are accurate gauges of how well our society is doing in terms of social justice. The mental health training agenda must meet this challenge and put race equality and cultural capability at the cutting edge of the formulation of a new definition of professionalism in mental health services. BME service users and their communities are no longer willing to be passive recipients of a service led by "experts". People want to be genuine partners in developing culturally appropriate and proactive mental health services, as well as crisis-oriented services. Mental health training can begin to model how such a partnership can work by ensuring that BME service users and their families are involved in the training of all practitioners in the future.

APPENDIX

MODULE 1 – SELF-AWARENESS		
SESSION 1 ⇨ REFLECTING ON CULTURE	SESSION 2 ⇨ REFLECTING ON BELIEFS	SESSION 3 REFLECTING ON DECISION-MAKING
• Introduction to a useful model of culture and an appreciation of the complexity of culture. • Greater clarity about how culture, power, privilege and oppression are inter-related within society. • An understanding of how culture influences and shapes our identity and impacts on our social interactions with others.	• An understanding of how culture influences the process of diagnosis in mental health work. • Participants will be better able to identify their own beliefs and values in mental health work and issues they may need to consider when working with people who may hold different values (both staff and service users). • Recognition of the impact of practitioner beliefs and assumptions on work with service users in the mental health system.	• Knowledge of a model to help analyse how "professional" judgements and decisions are made in mental health work. • Identification of personal, team and organisational styles of decision-making. • Increased ability to recognise the sources of potential bias in making decisions about situations involving institutional discrimination.

MODULE 2 – RACE EQUALITY AND CULTURAL CAPABILITY		
SESSION 4 ⇨ REFLECTING ON COMMUNICATION	SESSION 5 ⇨ WORKING ACROSS DIFFERENT CULTURES	SESSION 6 UNDERSTANDING RACE EQUALITY IN MENTAL HEALTH SERVICES
• Better appreciation of the importance of communication within mental health services generally (staff to staff and staff to service users), and appreciation of how poor communication can contribute to unnecessary misunderstandings and conflicts.	• A better understanding of the complexity and challenges of transcultural practice in mental health work.	• Ability to recognise and analyse of patterns of institutional racism in mental health services and its impact on service users, families, carers and practitioners.

SESSION 4 ⇨ REFLECTING ON COMMUNICATION	SESSION 5 ⇨ WORKING ACROSS DIFFERENT CULTURES	SESSION 6 UNDERSTANDING RACE EQUALITY IN MENTAL HEALTH SERVICES
• Increased recognition of the central importance of relationships between practitioners and service users and how the nature of these relationships has an impact on every aspect of care within services. • Acknowledgement of the importance of power in communication and the choice practitioners have to use their professional and personal power in positive or negative ways.	• Ability to use a model to gain a more structured view of cultural differences and confirmation of the importance of inclusivity. • Consideration of the impact of culture on the experience, expression of and responses to mental distress.	• Better understanding of the way that institutional discrimination impacts on service delivery. • Clarification of the key elements of a race equality approach in mental health services.

SESSION 7 ⇨ WORKING IN AN EMPOWERING WAY	SESSION 8 ⇨ WORKING IN PARTNERSHIP WITH BME FAMILIES & COMMUNITIES	SESSION 9 UNDERSTANDING DISCRIMINATORY SITUATIONS
• A better understanding of BME service user/survivor perspectives. • An analysis of the process of internalised oppression multiple discrimination and how BME people may enter a "spiral of oppression". • Ability to understand and apply a model of empowerment for BME people.	• To gain a better understanding of BME family/carer empowerment. • To identify effective ways of working in partnership with BME families/carers. • To look at ways that mental health practitioners can help to promote the empowerment of BME communities.	• An appreciation of the dangers of superficial analyses and short-term solutions in complex mental health situations. • Ability to use a "whole systems" model of examining discriminatory situations involving BME people. • Identification of effective ways of tackling institutional racism at different levels.

MODULE 3 – BME MENTAL HEALTH PRACTICE		
SESSION 10 ⇨ IDENTIFYING NEEDS IN A HOLISTIC WAY	SESSION 11 ⇨ PROVIDING CULTURALLY APPROPRIATE ASSISTANCE	SESSION 12 ANTI-DISCRIMINATORY RISK WORK
• Clarify the principles of a holistic approach to mental health service delivery. • Practice using a holistic and anti-discriminatory process of assessment. • Identification of the key elements of good practice in conducting transcultural assessment interviews.	• Appreciation of the importance of "cultural appropriateness" in holistic planning. • Ability to judge the cultural appropriateness of therapeutic interventions. • Identification of some useful questions for reviewing a person's package of assistance in a participatory way from different perspectives of the people involved.	• An understanding of how judgements about risk can lead to discriminatory practice. • Formulation of a set of principles for anti-discriminatory risk work. • Examination of some key issues of suicide and self-harm with a focus on transcultural practice.

REFERENCES

Bennett J. (2006). *Achieving race equality through training: a review of approaches in the UK. The Journal of Mental Health Workforce Development*, *1*(1), May 2006. Brighton: Pavilion Publishing.

Chartered Society of Physiotherapy (2005). *Competence and capability resource pack*, London: The Chartered Society, of Physiotherapy.

Department of Health (2005). *Delivering race equality in mental health care – An Action Plan for reform inside and outside services; and the Government's response to the independent inquiry into the death of David Bennett*. London: Department of Health.

Ferns P., Trivedi P. and Walker D. (2003). *Letting Through Light: Ealing Service User's Audit*, available at: http://www.londondevelopmentcentre.org/resource/local/docs/ealingLTL.pdf.

Ferns P. (2006). "*Chinese people don't take milk and love to eat jelly?*" (SPN website article at www.spn.org.uk).

Leavitt R. L. (2002). Developing Cultural Competence in a Multicultural World: part 1. *PT magazine*, *10*(12), 36–48.

Norfolk, Suffolk and Cambridgeshire Strategic Health Authority (2004). *Independent Inquiry into the Death of David Bennett*. London: Department of Health.

Social Exclusion Unit Report (2004). *Mental Health and Social Exclusion*. London: Office of the Deputy Prime Minister.

CHAPTER 17

Psychosocial Interventions: Implementation in Practice

Lorraine Rayner, Norman Young and Madeline O'Carroll

INTRODUCTION

Psychosocial interventions (PSI) for psychosis have a sound empirical base and have been widely recommended for implementation throughout mental health services in the UK (Scottish Intercollegiate Guidelines Network, 1998; National Institute for Clinical Excellence, 2002). PSI are complex and delivered to service users with complex needs by mental health practitioners with the aim of promoting recovery (Repper & Perkins, 2003). The core strategies employed by the practitioner encompass; case management (usually a strengths model see Ryan & Morgan, 2004); individual cognitive behavioural therapy for psychosis (Nelson, 1997), and cognitive behavioural family intervention (Tarrier & Barrowclough, 1997). Education and training for practitioners in PSI for psychosis has been led by a collaborative of educational providers through the Thorn initiative (Gamble, 1997) and over the last five years the core interventions have expanded to meet the widening skills agenda in mental health service provision (O'Carroll et al., 2004).

In our review of Thorn courses (O'Carroll et al., 2004) we noted that the majority of Thorn lecturers' work was centred around the coaching of clinical skills and the teaching of the PSI literature. Thorn course lecturers noted that the focus on teaching was at the expense of research and consultation, additionally, course leaders described continuing poor implementation of PSI into routine practice.

In this chapter we will describe the good practice elements of the Thorn course and address the question of how can academics specialising in PSI facilitate the implementation of PSI? We will propose that academics can influence and improve implementation by working through each of the established academic roles of; educator, researcher, and consultant, and through an appreciation of theoretical frameworks describe the diffusion of innovations in health care services. We will discuss how this may be achieved through the use of three case studies drawing upon a model of implementation developed from a systematic review of the literature on the diffusion of health care innovations (Greenhalgh et al., 2005).

Teaching Mental Health. Edited by Theo Stickley and Thurstine Basset.
Copyright © 2007 John Wiley & Sons, Ltd.

PSYCHOSOCIAL INTERVENTIONS EDUCATION AND TRAINING

The Thorn initiative started at a time when Government policy had made a firm shift to caring for people who experience psychosis in the community. Community mental health practitioners were being asked to act as named workers for people seen by community mental health teams (Department of Health, 1990). They were expected to perform assessments, devise a care plan and review the care plan with the multidisciplinary team. For those with enduring mental health problems the attraction of combining psychosocial interventions, such as family intervention (Leff et al., 1985), with the pharmacological management of symptoms was seen as an increasing aspiration in delivering evidence based interventions.

In 1991 the Sir Jules Thorn Charitable Trust provided £500,000 to set up a specialist mental health nurse training similar to that provided for Macmillan nurses in palliative care (Tarrier et al., 1998). Two sites, based at the Institute of Psychiatry in London and the University of Manchester began running the programme in 1992. The broad aim of the Initiative was to train community psychiatric nurses in problem-centred interventions for people with serious mental illness. The programme of study included case management, family interventions and psychological interventions, with students being assessed both on their theoretical knowledge and their clinical skills. Throughout the course students developed their clinical skills through supervised work with service users. This work was audio-taped and the tapes used as part of the assessment process.

From 1997 onwards a small number of "satellite" courses were set up by course graduates and in the late 1990s there was a rapid growth in sites across the UK. By 2004 there were 13 sites in the UK with an expanded curriculum of evidence-based interventions for psychosis, which attracted professionals such as occupational therapists, nurses, social workers and psychologists. Presently all the courses are hosted by higher education institutions typically at degree level with some at masters level.

Supporting the development and validation of courses is the National Thorn Steering Group (TSG) consisting of programme leaders and experts in the field. Through its quality forum the TSG supports the applicant institutions through the validation process and oversees the re-validation of existing courses. The TSG's second forum, the research sub-group, provides a national meeting through which programme leaders can gain peer support for their research, and collaborate on projects.

The Thorn initiative provides a useful model for the successful diffusion of a specialist evidence based course. The collegiate support that the course leaders obtain through the TSG maintains the emphasis on skills acquisition through experiential learning (Milne et al., 2001), and fidelity to published accounts of effective practice. However, one measure of success for skills based courses in mental health is whether the education and training can be transferred into routine practice and promote recovery amongst service users. Graduates from Thorn courses still voice difficulties in implementation and place particular emphasis on their organisation's ability to support psychosocial interventions. The challenge for Thorn programme leaders is the ability to use their skills in research, development and consultancy in order to transform practice.

THE DIFFUSION OF INNOVATIONS IN HEALTH SERVICE ORGANISATIONS

Psychosocial interventions' poor record of implementation into routine care (Kavanagh et al., 1993; Hughes et al., 1995; Fadden, 1997) has been attributed to a number of factors which include; benign neglect on the part of the organisation to maintain support for initiatives; lack of time for practitioners to complete the intervention; and the large number of competing demands on practitioners. Such problems are not confined to mental health but are recognised across a broad range of evidence based interventions and as a result provoked a number of implementation strategies based on change management theory (Mulhall & Le May, 1999).

The utilisation of theoretical models that explain implementation in complex organisations can assist the academics in both their research, and practice engagement. Such models can be found in the literature on diffusion of innovations. Diffusions research is an extensive area of academic study, so for the purpose of this chapter a recent health service model will be described and used to critique three case studies on PSI implementation, from this critique a discussion follows on best practice for academics working in this area.

Research on the adoption of innovations is dominated by the work of Everitt Rogers (Rogers, 1995) who, in the 1950's, researched the adoption of hybrid corn by Iowa farmers in the United States of America. Everitt Rogers' research, and that which followed, all draw on a number of research traditions, and are set across a wide range of subjects and settings. In 2002, the Service Development Organisation commissioned a review of the literature on the diffusion of innovations in health service organisations. Trisha Greenhalgh led the review and in their published account (Greehalgh et al., 2005) they proposed a working model that provides a basis with which to understand and promote the implementation of complex innovations such as psychosocial interventions. Greenhalgh et al. (2005) provide an extensive account of their model, but for the purpose of this chapter only a brief description is provided. The model sets out four broad elements these are:

- the innovation;
- the outer context;
- the inner context;
- the linkages between components.

An innovation is defined as:

> a set of behaviours, routines and ways of working, along with any associated administrative technologies and systems, which are 1) perceived as new by a proportion of stakeholders; 2) linked to a provision or support of health care; 3) discontinuous with previous practice; 4) directed at improving health outcomes, administrative efficiency, cost effectiveness, or user experience; and 5) implemented by means of planned and coordinated action by individuals, teams or organisations (Greenhalgh et al., 2005, p. 28).

Psychosocial interventions may be considered as an innovation containing many constituent parts, such as cognitive behaviour therapy, and family interventions for psychosis. Psychosocial interventions are therefore a complex innovation and as with any innovation possess many inherent nuances and qualities. A number of these attributes have been found to be important in determining how quickly and widely the innovation spreads through a health service organisation. The standard characteristics identified by Greenhalgh et al. (2005) are: *compatibility:* how compatible the innovation is with the perceived norms of the intended adopters and the organisation; *complexity:* the perceived intricacy of the innovation and the perceived effort required for adoption; *trialability:* the opportunity to test out the innovation before an adoption decision is made; *observability:* how visible the benefits of the innovation are to the adopters; and *reinvention*: what potential is there for the adopter to modify the innovation to suit their needs.

The outer context is defined by the social, political and technological environment within which the organisation exists. The inner context refers to the organisation, the people within it and the systems and processes that influence the breadth and speed of adoption. The inner context is broken down into: the system antecedents; system readiness; the adopters, implementation and routinisation, and consequences.

When an innovation is introduced to an organisation its reception will depend on the structures and slack resources within it. Such system antecedents are complemented by the capacity of the organisation to accommodate new knowledge, and its ability and receptiveness for change. Additionally, the system's readiness to adopt an innovation will be dependent on the organisation's goals, the tension between these goals and the present state, and the support that exists for the innovation in both terms of motivation and resources.

The process of adoption is not passive, it has been shown to be dependent on a series of factors attributable to the adopter, and forms the third component of the inner context. The psychological characteristics of the individual, for example their tolerability for changes in routine, learning style and personality traits, all contribute to the adoption process.

These factors are strongly tied into the individual's personal goals and the goals of the organisation. Hence, adoption is more likely to be implemented and sustained when the meaning attached to the innovation by the intended adopter is congruent with that of the organisation's top management. Furthermore, the degree of freedom granted by the administration, to the individual, in deciding whether to adopt, or not, will affect the pace and spread of adoption. When an authoritative position is taken early adoption is seen. However, when greater autonomy exists there is generally greater, and sustained, spread of innovation to be seen later in the adoption process. Finally, any change to the system will have consequences which may affect the earlier elements of the system and either promote or inhibit the adoption of the innovation.

The last element of the model – linkages between components – describes the characteristics of the assimilation process within the organisation. Adoption and assimilation by the individual and organisation are significantly affected by the transfer of knowledge. Under this heading the importance of opinion leaders and product champions in, reducing uncertainty about decisions, leading change, and facilitating the transfer of knowledge, are explored. Such individuals, or agencies, link the elements of the model and facilitate their action by bringing people and knowledge together.

IMPLEMENTATION IN PRACTICE

The following section will examine the complexities of implementing PSI in practice through the presentation of three case studies. These case studies based on real life examples will identify the challenges that are faced by service providers and academics.

Greenhalgh et al.'s (2005) headings of "the innovation", "the outer context", "the inner context" and "linkage between components" are used to aid the analysis.

Box 17.1 Case Study One

In 2000 a city mental health NHS trust, with their local university built on previous work in relapse prevention for psychosis (Young et al., 1999). The innovation was a service user held booklet that guided the client and their care coordinator to identify early signs of relapse and develop an action plan for the early, middle and late stages of relapse.

In order to maintain adherence to the booklet structure, and reduce the risk of developing inaccurate relapse plans, a two-day training programme was devised. In the first day students were provided with a CD-ROM that provided the knowledge base for relapse prevention work. On the second day students developed their clinical skills in relapse prevention by preparing, rehearsing, enacting and reflecting upon their simulations of relapse preventions sessions.

To facilitate the implementation of this work in routine practice the intervention was integrated into the Care Programme Approach documentation, and the training provided to groups containing 12 practitioners. The training was also incorporated into pre-registration preparation and the Thorn course. In two settings the uptake of the intervention was monitored through a review of case notes before and after training. The results showed poor adoption in one setting (a community team) and modest adoption in another (rehabilitation inpatient ward).

The innovation	The rationale for reducing one element of psychosocial interventions into a small and well-defined intervention was to reduce complexity. The aim of providing supporting materials was to increase adherence and fidelity to a set procedure and avoid potential adverse effects.
	Practitioners reported that the training was beneficial, and that the intervention was highly relevant to their work.
	Whilst the intended outcomes of the innovation were not immediately observable (the prevention of relapse) the production of a relapse plan was.
The outer context	The innovation was implemented during a time of unprecedented policy development for mental health and an emphasis on collaborative ways of working with service users.
The inner context	The implementation of the innovation came at a period of great service development including the introduction of new teams, the care programme approach, a new computerised system, and pay system (agenda for change). Hence there were a number of competing developments for staff's time and attention.
	Despite the development of relapse plans being seen as good practice there was little in the way of tension between this practice and existing practice. Adoption of the practice was expected, but not formally monitored or imposed.
	Staff reported that finding a "suitable client" difficult and some said that they lacked the confidence to start the intervention preferring to work observe and then implement, alongside some in-house supervision and support.

	There was a range of people who adopted the practice and a couple who were enthusiasts.
Linkage between compo- nents	In both the sites that were monitored there was some follow on support from the lecturer practitioner who provided the training, and in the inpatient setting there was senior nurse participation and support. In the CMHT a product champion facilitated much of the linkage between components of the inner system. In other clinical areas where adoption took place there appeared to be an influential clinical leader.

Box 17.2 Case Study Two

This case study focuses on a rehabilitation service for people with serious and enduring mental health problems. The service comprised of a number of community teams, day service and residential teams. Initially three nurses, working in different parts of the service attended the Thorn initiative training. On completion of their training a strategy was devised that would enable PSI to be implemented across the service. This strategy consisted of two main initiatives: first the routine use of standardised, structured assessments used on the Thorn programme and second introductory training on PSI. Also the trust and the local university established a local Thorn programme. All staff accessed the in-house introductory PSI training. All care co-ordinators received training on the use of standardised assessments. A number of staff from different teams in the service completed the Thorn course locally. After a couple of years, despite the service strategy, individual teams' implementation of PSI was inconsistent. Though some teams had some success with the use of standardised assessments, implementation was reliant on the motivation of individuals to integrate PSI into their own individual practice. The use of family work was particularly problematic with few practitioners using the family work model after completion of their training. A merger with acute services further distracted both managers and practitioners from the implementation of PSI.

The innovation	The main approach to implementation of PSI was training of practitioners and the use of standardised assessments. Training was provided at three levels: introductory training for PSI, training to use standardised assessments and the local Thorn programme. Psychosocial interventions were perceived as useful to those practitioners that had undertaken the Thorn programme, less so to those that had just a basic knowledge. For some practitioners PSI was perceived as incompatible with their values and norms, PSI was seen as too prescriptive and inflexible. PSI was seen as complex, in this service it was seen as being more applicable to particular parts of the service, i.e. community teams. The focus on the use of standardised assessment as the main means of using PSI tended to reinforce perceptions of inflexibility. Managers though only having limited knowledge about PSI saw links with the implementation of evidence-based practice.

The outer context	At the time there were a number of policy drivers that positively impacted on the implementation of PSI; the National Service Framework for Mental Health had just been published. However changes in service structures within the Trust had a negative impact.
The inner context	At the initial onset of this development the service had some slack resources; this enabled the three nurses to be seconded for the project. The service was receptive to change, and had ability to absorb new knowledge and innovation. A range of innovative projects has been implemented previously. PSI did fit with the goals and values of the service and there was some tension for the need of change particularly around the need to provide evidence-based interventions. Resources were available to support training. The service had a robust clinical supervision system in place.
	Practitioners who had completed the Thorn programme were motivated and capable in using PSI in their day-to-day work.
	But once training had been completed, the service relied on a more informal, diffusion model, "let it happen", rather than "make it happen".
	Apart from training and the use of standardised assessment the implementation of PSI in the service lacked clear and specific goals. Training needs analysis was limited. Some parts of the service set targets of having one team member trained, others had no targets. There was a lack of specialist supervision for those completing training. There were no practice development forums to discuss issues of integrating PSI into practice.
	The mergers with the acute services caused the focus on PSI to be lost and energies were diverted into looking at new managerial and clinical structures and time to look at development projects was not available.
Linkage between components	The three original nurses acted as PSI "champions" and other nurses following completion of the Thorn programme acted as opinion leaders and change agents in their teams with some success.

Box 17.3 Case Study 3

This case study outlines the different approaches used by an urban Mental Health NHS Trust to implement psychosocial interventions over a ten-year period.

In the mid 1990s the Trust decided to send staff to one of the two Thorn courses that existed at that time. Once the staff completed the course the Trust resolved to set up its own course and approached a local University to be the educational partner. A Thorn course was established with a clear direction from both the Trust and the University.

During the early years there was direct liaison between the Trust and the University and regular meetings to review progress on implementation. The Thorn course continued to recruit staff and have a high rate of completion compared to other Continuing Professional Development courses. Although the students had to produce a strategy for implementing psychosocial interventions on completion of the course, in practice many found it difficult to continue using the skills once the course finished.

However more recently the Trust has established functional teams and a number of Thorn graduates have been recruited to these teams. Anecdotal reports suggest that they are more successful in using their skills in teams whose practice reflects a psychosocial perspective.

Over the years the Trust faced a number of external challenges including an unfavourable report by the Commission for Health Improvement that resulted in much of the training emphasis being shifted to ensure that staff had completed mandatory training. The Trust in line with contemporary recommendations was also shifting its training and research emphasis from community to acute care. This involved a number of team-based training initiatives and short courses as well as modules that included psychosocial approaches in acute settings.

The innovation	A range of training initiatives including: ward based training in the use of assessment tools with follow up supervision. Short courses (3 days) focusing on engagement, assessment and using coping strategies.
The outer context	The case study covers nearly ten years from initial planning to the present and this period coincides with mental health being made a health priority by the government and the subsequent introduction of many new policy initiatives. This includes the introduction of the National Service Framework for Mental Health (Department of Health 1999), the creation of Mental Health NHS Trusts as well as the integration of health and social services. The commissioning of education has also undergone considerable change from consortia to confederations to Strategic Health Authorities.
The inner context	Clearly at Trust level it has been necessary to focus on the integration of the initiatives outlined above. In addition the new enlarged Trust had to audit staff and services in order to develop an education and training strategy as well as identifying service development. The number of Thorn commissions began to reduce as the emphasis shifted to training teams in psychosocial interventions. Although in theory this seemed promising, in practice provision was never made to train whole teams but only those members of the team who were available when the trainers arrived.
Linkage between components	During the early years there was strong linkage between the University and the Trust that enabled modifications to be made to the delivery of the Thorn course in order to improve adoption of the techniques on completion of training. There was also discussion of proposed training initiatives at the development stage. Over time this linkage has gradually reduced.

These case studies, based on real life examples, highlight the challenges of implementation. All three case studies raise important questions and dilemmas, for example about the scope of PSI and what implementation of PSI really means, the different needs of practitioners and managers, as well as national and local priorities. There are common issues seen in the studies that can provide the opportunities for academics to consider their meaningful involvement in implementation. As has been already stated, PSI is not just one specific innovation therefore implementation can be complex. Care study one and two show how a reductionist approach was used, whereby one element of PSI was targeted; relapse prevention in case study one and standardised assessment in case study two. A robust rationale supports this approach, with change management literature suggesting that it is preferable to start with small, realistic goals (Fullan, 1986). It is perhaps too high an expectation that any one service or Trust can attempt to implement all elements of PSI at once.

Changes in mental health policy, like the National Service Framework and the emphasis on service user and carer involvement provided drivers towards the adoption of PSI. However other policy changes, such as the emphasis on clinical governance and inspection caused tensions for Trusts and PSI tended to miss out in the competing priorities.

Training was an integral part of the innovation in all case studies. Case study two and three having a greater emphasis on the use of the local Thorn programme. Again an admirable strategy but evidence shows that training alone is not enough to ensure implementation (Brooker & Brabban, 2004). Case study three identifies the challenges that have to met when team training is attempted. The difficulties of delivering training in clinical areas, where clinical demands take precedent should not be under estimated.

A striking feature seen in all case studies is the impact of changes in the inner context, many arising as a result of policy changes in the outer context. Reorganisation of teams and creation of new services impacted in a negative way in all three examples. Changes in local policy – the CPA policy in Case Study 17.1 and shifting local priorities in Case Studies 17.2 and 17.3 all meant a loss of focus from the implementation of PSI.

Linkage between the different parts of the system is vital (Greenhalgh et al., 2005). Opinion leaders, champions and change agents all play an important role in communicating information about the innovation and bringing about change. Case Study 17.1 shows the potential role for an academic, with a lecturer practitioner fulfilling a linkage role. In Case Study 17.2 nurses on completion of the Thorn programme acted as champions for PSI. In Case Study 17.3 close links between the trust and the university enabled academics some influence.

The Case Studies show some small successes were achieved, but there were gaps where academics could have provided linkage with the innovation and the inner context, in their core roles of educator, researcher and consultant. All had established links between the Trust and the local university and there was potential to build on this. So in Case Study 17.1, there was a greater need for support in trialling the use of the relapse prevention package following training. Practitioners needed more support in adapting it to their work. An academic could have worked with individual teams to tailor the intervention to their own needs. The academic could have provided ongoing support and supervision. Similarly in Case Study 17.2, an academic could have worked with teams to see how they could use and adapt the standardised assessments to their particular service users. In Case Study 17.3 there was the opportunity for an academic to advise on how PSI could be adapted for particular teams and so develop curriculum to meet these needs. In all Case Studies 17.3 was the opportunity for academics to facilitate supervision and a practice development forum for Thorn practitioners, enabling practitioners to adapt PSI to their own area.

In all examples there was a role for the academic to undertake research. Results from process and outcome evaluation research would have enabled changes to be made to the relapse prevention package and the use of standardised assessment. Action research methods seem particularly relevant to this area of implementation (Lewin, 1946; Carr & Kemmis, 1986). This type of research with its emphasis on participation, change and improvement and its focus on processes seems to be a particularly useful approach.

THE WAY FORWARD

An analysis of these Case Studies therefore indicates ways the academic can influence and improve implementation. But it is important to emphasise that it is primarily NHS Trusts' responsibility to look at implementation, universities and academics have a part to play but cannot take the lead. Nursing is relatively new in higher education and roles linking Trusts and other health care providers are just beginning to emerge. In the recent Chief Nursing Officer's review of mental health nursing, it is recommended that relationships between universities and service providers are strengthened (Department of Health, 2006). Certainly for the academic involved in PSI programmes links with the Trust need to be explicit and formalised. Table one summarises the roles and tasks that the academic could undertake at the levels of innovation and the inner context. It provides different ways to be involved in the established roles of educator, researcher and consultant. However it would be naive and unrealistic for us to expect academics to undertake these roles without formal recognition by both universities and local providers. Academics' workloads are high and particularly fulfilling some of the tasks under the consultant role may be difficult, though many of these come under practice development, an essential role for academics in health and social care.

Box 17.4 The Role of the Academic in Implementation of PSI

	Educator	Researcher	Consultant
The innovation	Devise local training packages. Develop curriculum to meet local needs	Process outcome evaluation research	Advise on areas for implementation and implementation strategy. Advise on reinvention of PSI
Inner context	Provide training to teams. Work with individual practitioners	Action research projects. Process evaluation research	Assessment of readiness to change in teams. Facilitate supervision and practice development forum

---

For many universities the pre-registration curriculum is seen as the main priority as it is the main source of funding. This can be seen as a barrier for academics to become more involved in implementation of PSI, as most resources are directed towards pre-registration programmes. However there may be an opportunity to explore PSI in the pre-registration curriculum. There is certainly little published research to indicate what knowledge and skills newly qualified nurses have on PSI. With the mental health nursing review (Department of Health 2006) recommending a review of pre registration training this seems an opportune time to consider the impact of PSI in this area. Until now PSI has been mainly confined to learning after registration.

CONCLUSION

This chapter has summarised the background to PSI, its evidence base and the initiatives in training, undertaken in the past decade, particularly the Thorn programme. Using a series of case studies and a contemporary model of implementation an analysis has been presented that identifies some of the challenges involved in the implementation of PSI. PSI is not one innovation; it is complex and requires an innovative strategy at different levels: at strategic levels such as at NHS Trust board level, team/service level and at a practitioner/service user level.

There is a role for the academic in implementation beyond the basic level of providing teaching, though the importance of providing high quality training programmes should not be under estimated. This can be summarised under the key headings of educator, researcher and consultant and consists of a range of tasks that will support the implementation of PSI. However these roles must be formalised with Trusts and given their deserved recognition by both universities and health providers.

REFERENCES

Brooker, C. & Brabban, A. (2004). Measured Success: A scoping review of evaluated psychosocial interventions training for work with people series mental health problems. NIMHE/ Trent WDC.

Carr, W. & Kemmis, S. (1986). *Becoming critical: Education, knowledge and action research.* London: Falmer Press.

Department of Health (1990). *The Care Programme Approach for People with a Mental Illness.* London: HMSO.

Department of Health (1999). *The National Service Framework for Mental Health.* London: HMSO.

Department of Health (2006). *From values to action: The chief nursing officer's review of mental health nursing.* London: HMSO.

Fadden, G. (1997). Implementation of family interventions in routine clinical practice following staff training programs: a major cause for concern. *Journal of Mental Health, 6*(6), 599–612.

Fullan, M. (1986). *The management of change.* Chapter 5, pp. 73–86, The meaning of educational change. New York: Teachers College Press.

Gamble, C. (1997). Education. The Thorn programme: it's past, present and future. *Mental Health Care, 1*(3), 95–97.

Greenhalgh, T., Robert, G., Bate, P., Kyriakidou, O. & Macfarlane, F. (2005). *Diffusion of innovations in health service organisations: a systematic literature review.* Oxford: Blackwell Publishing.

Hughes I., & Abbati-Yeoman, J. (1995). *A S.T.E.P. forward: a guide for people working with schizophrenia sufferers and their families.* Cardiff: Shaddowfax.

Kavanagh, D.J., Piatkowska, O., Clarke, D., O'Holloran, Manicavasagar, V.P., Rosen, A. & Tennant, C. (1993). Application of cognitive behavioural family intervention for Schizophrenia in multi-disciplinary teams: what can the matter be? *Australian Psychologist, 28*, 181–188.

Leff, J., Kuipers, L., Berkowitz, R. & Sturgen, D. (1985). A controlled trial of social intervention in the families of schizophrenia: two year follow up. *British Journal of Psychiatry, 146*, 594–600.

Lewin, K. (1946). Action research and minority problems. *Journal of Social Issues, 2*, 34–46.

Milne, D., Claydon, T., Blackburn, I., James, I. & Sheikh, A. (2001). Rationale for a new measure of competence in therapy. *Behavioural and Cognitive Psychotherapy, 29*, 21–33.

Mulhall, A. & Le May, A. (1999). *Nursing Research: Dissemination and Implementation.* London: Churchill Livingstone.

National Institute for Clinical Excellence. (2002). *Schizophrenia: core interventions in the treatment and management of schizophrenia in primary and secondary care. Clinical guideline 1.* London: NICE.

Nelson, H. (1997). *Cognitive Behavioural Therapy with Schizophrenia: A practice manual.* Cheltenham: Nelson Thornes.

O'Carroll, M., Rayner, L. & Young, N. (2004). Education and training in psychosocial interventions: a survey of Thorn initiative course leaders. *Journal of Psychiatric and Mental Health Nursing, 11,* 602–607.

Repper, J. & Perkins, R. (2003). *Social Inclusion and Recovery.* London: Bailliere Tindall.

Rogers, E.M. (1985). *Diffusion of Innovations*, 4th edn. New York: The Free Press.

Ryan, P., & Morgan, S. (2004). *Assertive Outreach: A Strengths Approach to Policy and Practice.* London: Churchill Livingstone.

Scottish Intercollegiate Guidelines Network (1998). *SIGN 30: Psychosocial Interventions in the Management of Schizophrenia.* Edinburgh: SIGN.

Tarrier, N. & Barrowclough, C. (1997). *Families of Schizophrenic Patients: Cognitive Behavioural Intervention.* Cheltenham: Nelson Thornes.

Tarrier, N., Haddock, G. & Barrowclough, C. (1998). Training and dissemination: research to practice in innovative psychosocial treatments of schizophrenia. In:*Outcome and Innovation in Psychological Treatment of Schizophrenia* (eds Wykes, T., Tarrier, N. & Lewis, S.), Chapter 12, pp. 215–236. Chichester: John Wiley & Sons, Ltd.

Young, N., Hopkins, A., & French, G. (1999). Developing tools to help in series enduring mental illness. *Mental Health Nursing, 19*(3), 9–12.

CHAPTER 18

Exploring Practitioners' Relationships with the Pharmaceutical Industry

Neil Carver and Russell Ashmore

INTRODUCTION

This chapter is not an attack on the use of drugs in psychiatry per se but examines how students may be introduced to issues arising from their contact with the pharmaceutical industry. Anecdotal and research evidence suggests qualified mental health nurses (MHNs) have regular encounters with the pharmaceutical industry, largely through its promotional activities. In a survey of 347 mental health nursing students (Ashmore et al., 2007), 80 % estimated that over a one year period qualified MHNs had had more than one contact with pharmaceutical representatives (PRs). It is also evident that the relationship between MHNs and the industry is complex and not confined to the supply and receipt of medication or product information. Consider the following:

- A unit manager suggested ward staff should not order "post-its" but "get them from a rep." instead.
- A mental health nurse expressed concern that there would be no training for their team without "drug company money".
- At a recent mental health nursing conference an employee of a pharmaceutical company commented that the only reason companies give out gifts to nurses was because they asked for them.

These examples may not seem particularly dramatic but they do illustrate some of the complex dynamics in the relationship between MHNs and the industry. To some people the relationship is unproblematic; the pharmaceutical industry is considered to be a benevolent force for good and an inexhaustible source of funding and resources. Another version of this relationship may see nursing reduced to a state of dependency on the industry, with individual nurses "exploiting" their benefactor and then being seen as the guilty and greedy party. However, regardless of the value of the pharmaceutical industry (to the economy and health care) and an apparently ever-increasing appetite for "partnership" working in the

Teaching Mental Health. Edited by Theo Stickley and Thurstine Basset.
Copyright © 2007 John Wiley & Sons, Ltd.

NHS (e.g. DoH, 2004) there is increasing concern about the impact of the industry on clinical practice. In addition the industry's promotional activities and attempts to win influence have been described as "relentless and pervasive" (House of Commons Health Select Committee (HCHSC), 2005, para. 271).

Not surprisingly the bulk of this concern has been generated from within medicine and has increasingly addressed the industry's influence on the education of doctors. The extent of this concern is apparent from the following quotation:

> Both the ethical arguments and the limited available empirical evidence lead to the conclusion that the best policy is for medical students to have no contact with drug companies. The onus is on advocates of any other policy to show they can achieve better outcomes.

> (Rogers et al., 2004, p. 413).

The authors do not feel that there is sufficient evidence to simply substitute "nursing" for "medical" in the above quotation at present, however, it is argued here that:

(a) the ethical arguments and evidence alluded to above have significance to the practice of mental health nursing; and
(b) at minimum, nursing students should be enabled to explore the dynamics of drug company influence so that they can make informed choices about engaging with the industry.

CONCERNS ABOUT THE PHARMACEUTICAL INDUSTRY AND NURSING STUDENTS

There are a variety of concerns regarding the activities of the pharmaceutical industry. Firstly, it has been argued that the industry has been able to exert undue influence on the "impartial" academic press, despite the existence of peer review mechanisms. Smith (2003, 2005) has outlined some of the many ways in which the industry can exert influence over published research. Carver and Ashmore (2004) have recently expressed concern over the lack of requirement in many nursing journals to supply even the simplest of declarations of competing interests. Secondly, it has been suggested that promotional activity (including advertisements in journals (Mansfield, 2004) may in part lead to non-rational prescribing of medication. For example, the HCHSC report (2005) describes the over-prescription of benzodiazepines as the "legacy of a bad campaign" (HCHSC, 2005, para. 234). Moncrieff (2004) has also argued that drugs "so dominate psychiatric practice that it is not easy to develop alternative forms of treatment" (p. 10) despite research suggesting that they might be valuable. Furthermore, it has been suggested that "the nature and theory of psychiatry are being shaped by the interests of the industry" (Moncrieff et al., 2005, p. 85) particularly in reinforcing over-simplistic biological explanations about mental disorders. Concern has also been voiced that medical organisations have become too dependent on the industry for funding (Kerridge et al., 2005). The Royal College of Psychiatrists has recently said it now aims to keep its income from commercial sponsorship to around 5 % (Shooter, 2005). In contrast, the Royal College of Nursing obtains 30 % of its sponsorship from the industry (HCHSC, 2005).

Little is known about service users or the general public's attitudes to nurses' relationships with the industry. However Beresford (2005) has suggested there needs to be: "...honesty about the way the whole mental health system is based on a collusive relationship with the drugs industry" (p. 86). Certainly some service user organisations accept funding from the industry (Herxeimer, 2003) although it is an issue that provokes fierce debate (Campbell, 2005). In addition, there is some research in medicine suggesting service users may disapprove of health care professionals accepting gifts, particularly when thought to influence prescribing (Gibbons et al., 1998).

In one study (Ashmore et al., 2007) 98 % (n = 324) of students reported that promotional items from pharmaceutical companies were present in clinical areas and used in interactions with service users. If this constitutes advertising then there is a danger that nurses are perceived as endorsing products or companies.

With the bulk of both empirical evidence and opinion articles focused on qualified medical staff there is a need to establish why nurses and more specifically nursing students should address this field. To begin, it should be acknowledged that at least some of these issues are recognised in the field of nurse prescribing. There are currently 35,500 nurse prescribers in the UK (HCHSC, 2005). The HCHSC (2005, para. 144) stated that the extended/supplementary prescribing programme includes: "... sections designed to equip nurses with the knowledge to assess evidence that may be provided by drug company representatives". Unfortunately there is no published evidence on whether these " sections" are effective. However, it does seem that nurses attending such programmes consider the issues important. In a co-authored article (Davies & Hemmingway, 2005), Davies commented that as a programme leader for such a course that the role of the pharmaceutical industry is a matter of some debate among students.

There are two problems with limiting the teaching of these issues to prescribing courses (or any other post-qualifying course on medication management). Firstly, any student or qualified nurse is a potential prescriber, a fact that is recognised by the industry (PharmaMarket Letter, 1995). Research has shown that qualified nurses may already have been exposed to industry influence for several years (Ashmore et al., 2007) before any formal teaching input on these issues. As noted earlier, within medicine there is increasing recognition of the need to explore students' relationships with the industry (Rogers et al., 2004). These authors argued that medical students are socialised into accepting the status quo and either accumulate "debt" through accepting industry gifts or come to accept that it is acceptable to expect something for nothing. As they go on to say this is problematic since: "Normalising something –for –nothing relationships risks a decreased sensitivity to the moral implications of unequal relationships" (Rogers et al., 2004, p. 412).

The second problem is that all nurses (regardless of their intention to prescribe or not) may pass on information to clients about medication. Jordan et al. (1999) has highlighted concerns regarding the extent to which the continuing professional education of community mental health nurse was organised by representatives of pharmaceutical companies. It is worth noting that some respondents in this study were worried about bias but felt "unable to pinpoint specific inaccuracies" (p. 1077). This could be read as a specific acknowledgement that, at present, mental health nurses are ill equipped to evaluate both promotional activities and materials; a state of affairs equally recognised in medicine (Ziegler et al., 1995; HCHSC, 2005).

EXISTING EDUCATIONAL INITIATIVES

Published accounts of educational initiatives in this field appear limited to medicine. As part of a thematic review of studies examining interactions between PRs and doctors in training, Zipkin and Steinman (2005) reviewed evidence surrounding educational and policy initiatives. The evidence from the nine educational interventions reviewed suggested that such interventions: "... can be effective at raising trainee awareness of influence and increasing their scepticism towards information presented to the industry" (p. 784). Nevertheless they recognised that there are limitations to the data and concluded it was insufficient to recommend the inclusion of any *particular* intervention. While some interventions involved conventional teaching methods such as lectures, perhaps the most innovative and contentious example involved pharmacists role-playing PRs and giving a presentation to students (Wilkes & Hoffman, 2001). The presentation was based closely on real industry materials and students were unaware of the pretence until after they discussed the merits of the talk.

The authors have piloted a one-day workshop delivered in the third year of an Advanced Diploma in Nursing studies course. The aims of this workshop are that students will:

- explore mental health nurses' relationship with the pharmaceutical industry;
- identify potential advantages and disadvantages of this relationship;
- identify attitudes towards this relationship;
- understand the purpose of "gifts" given by the pharmaceutical industry.

The workshop is a mix of didactic lecture presentation and small group discussion centred on "typical" scenarios. Core areas focused on include: " gifts", value of educational seminars and advertising in journals. The following recommendations are based on our experiences, informal evaluations of the above workshop and a review of the literature.

CURRICULA AND POLICY ISSUES

The issue of pharmaceutical company influence may be viewed by lecturers as peripheral or even irrelevant to a nursing course. Morrison-Griffiths et al. (2002) noted that some lecturers already feel that the curriculum is too full to even include more basic pharmacology. Nevertheless, we believe the evidence cited throughout this chapter is sufficient to warrant the inclusion of these issues into curricula.

In addition, we suggest that mental health nursing departments maintain an open register of lecturers' competing interests. Interests could also be declared to students at the beginning of teaching sessions. In medicine it has already been recognised that it is important to encourage role modelling in this area by faculty staff (Zipkin & Steinman, 2005). Furthermore the HCHSC (2005) suggested registers of interests be maintained by the professional bodies in health care detailing all substantial gifts, hospitality and honoraria received by clinicians. The Government (DoH, 2005) agreed with this in principle but suggested the best way of monitoring dealings between NHS staff and business was by NHS employers utilising existing NHS guidance (DoH, 1993, 2000). This guidance describes when NHS employees should declare business or financial interests and advises a register of casual gifts and hospitality be kept which can be audited and *be available on request to the public*. It is clear that if the HCHSC (2005) recommendations had been accepted then lecturers who are nurses would be required to declare interests. As it stands this group is not required to do so. This oversight is strange given nurse lecturers have considerable potential to influence students.

We also believe that health care lecturers should consider that the educational environment is free of promotional merchandise from pharmaceutical and other commercial companies. Without this any debate regarding the presence of promotional material in clinical environments is likely to founder. Given the extent to which industry promotional activity has become normalised it may also be necessary to win the "hearts and minds" of other lecturers, who may have existing involvement with the industry. Finally, the involvement of students, service users and qualified nurses should be considered in developing any policies in this area.

APPROACHES TO TEACHING

As previously mentioned, research has shown that students are almost certain to encounter promotional activity in clinical areas (Ashmore et al., 2007). The endorsement of these activities by staff may result in confusion from students particularly if lecturers decide to challenge them. It may be important to remember that what *is* the case is not necessary what *ought* to be the case and students should be encouraged to reflect on both their own and their colleagues practices in this area.

A further point is that; in our experience individuals who feel the need to defend their behaviour or beliefs can dominate sessions. The situation is worsened when students who have accepted gifts are introduced to arguments suggesting that they perhaps should not have done so. Our informal evaluations with students revealed they wished that they had been made aware of the arguments *before* commencing clinical practice. In response to this we suggest a minimum of three sessions take place throughout the curriculum. The first could introduce the arguments, the second could examine practices that they have observed and the third would develop the arguments in the context of their approaching role as a qualified practitioner. In addition, we suggest that any teaching initiative takes a good humoured and non-judgemental approach to these issues. Certainly students are more forthcoming if they do not feel defensive. Some defensiveness also seems to arise because individuals may be reluctant to accept that they are susceptible to promotional activity. Research has now firmly demonstrated the existence of the "third-person effect" (TPE). TPE has been described as: "... the tendency for people to perceive the media as more influence on others than on themselves" (Douglas & Sutton, 2004, p. 585). The current evidence suggests that people will have a tendency to underestimate the extent to which their attitudes are changed as a result of drug promotion.

It may also be useful for lecturers to use non-threatening analogies to explore the influence of promotional activity. One such analogy may be the apparent indifference of adolescents to health promotion messages about smoking. This may also be explained by the TPE, which has been described as an "invulnerability bias" and: "... people's tendency to wrongly imagine that they are not personally at risk from environmental or health hazards" (Douglas & Sutton, 2004). Student nurses may well be able to recognise this phenomenon in themselves when they were younger. If they are able to accept this dynamic they may be more open to the idea that their indifference to advertising is in fact a self-serving bias and potentially illusory.

We also believe that lecturers should avoid the use of emotional terminology during sessions. Discussion of the industry inevitably invokes strong emotions. For example Ashmore et al. (2007) showed students used terms such as "brainwashing" and in sessions refer to "bribes" to describe the promotional activities of the pharmaceutical industry. The use of such terms illustrate the strength of feeling among individuals but their use leads to arguments that can be incomplete (Brody, 2005), superficial and inaccurate. For example, drug reps. are often characterised as "liars", however there is little evidence that this is the case. A heated debate focussing on this accusation simply diverts attention from the fact that there are many subtle methods of manipulating data for persuasive purposes, particularly in verbal presentations (Ziegler et al., 1995).

Lecturers must also be prepared to help students link apparently innocuous behaviours such as accepting a pen from a "drug rep". with the general impact of promotional activities as a whole. Students often state that small gifts are "nothing" or consider them to be "free". Our experience is that students are very conscious of the immediate benefits to them as individuals of accepting a pen (for example) but fail to recognise any negative consequences of such behaviour since they appear very remote from them.

It is important to be very clear about the specific issue concerning the industry under discussion. There is a tendency for people to over generalise in this field. For example, an argument against a specific marketing technique may be characterised as an all out assault on the use of drugs in psychiatry. Such over generalisation clouds the issues and provides a distraction from the original argument.

Occasionally when students recognise the scale of industry activity and the fact that many of the issues are highly politicised they simply "turn off". Should this occur, it may be useful to remember that inaction is to collude with the status quo. In addition, students can be helped to explore the ways in which their voice might be heard. For example, they may be directed to professional organisations such as the RCN or encouraged to use discussion groups such as that run by NIMHE (http://kc.nimhe.org.uk).

Attention should also be drawn to actual subjective experience of drugs as well as their objective characteristics. The curriculum should also include critiques of pharmacological treatments, e.g. Breggin (1993) and the value of alternatives to them, e.g. Bracken (2001). While the benefits of pharmacological treatments are widely publicised curricula should also draw attention to perhaps less well known problems such as the fact that adverse drugs reaction account for 5 % of all hospital admissions (HCHSC, 2005).

Generally students in the western world live in a culture in which advertising and promotion is endemic and recognised by many as an accepted part of the fabric of society. Students may therefore feel advertising is acceptable in health care. Teaching should always recognise students' previous experience, but they should be encouraged to differentiate between personal and professional beliefs and behaviours at minimum. Students should be introduced to codes regulating qualified practitioners' conduct in this area. In the UK these are:

(a) Standards of Business Conduct for NHS Staff (DoH, 1993);
(b) Commercial Sponsorship-Ethical Standards for the NHS (DoH, 2000); and
(c) NMC Code of Professional Conduct (NMC, 2002).

We also suggest that students engage critically with these codes of practice and learn to appreciate they are not "fixed in stone". For example, the above codes give the impression that accepting small gifts is unproblematic; yet fail to give any good reason for any practitioner to accept gifts from commercial companies. This is unsatisfactory.

A further problem is that conventional academic literature searching in this field is time consuming and may require accessing publications from a wide variety of sources such as media studies. There are two web-based organisations that collate up-to-date information on relationships with the industry and have many links to other relevant sites in this area. The first, called Healthy Skepticism, may be found at http://www.healthyskepticism. org/. The other, No Free Lunch, can be found at http://www.nofreelunch.org/ and http://www.nofreelunch-uk.org/.

Finally, teaching in the UK should also draw attention to The Association of the British Pharmaceutical Industry (ABPI) Code of Practice (2003). The ABPI is the trade association representing manufacturers of prescription medicines. In 1993 it established the Prescription Medicines Code of Practice Authority (PMCA) to operate its code of practice addressing the promotion of medicines to members of the health professions. The Code is voluntary and according to the ABPI (2003) is accepted by virtually all pharmaceutical companies operating in the UK.

SESSION CONTENT

There is a need to draw attention to balanced and available sources of information on drugs or other products. Based on ABPI information the HCHSC (2005) stated the industry spends $1.65 billion per year on "marketing and promotional efforts" while the government spends 0.3 % of that sum ($ 4.5 million) on independent medicines information to prescribers. The HCHSC (2005) suggested that there is a lack of consistent and reliable independent advice for prescribers. The Government however did not accept this and highlighted several sources of information for practitioners. These included: The British National Formulary (BNF); Drugs and Therapeutics Bulletins which is distributed to all doctors in the UK (HCHSC, 2005); information from the National Institute for Clinical Excellence and the National Prescribing Centre the Cochrane Collaboration and the James Lind Library.

In our experience students often describe pharmaceutical company advertisements in nursing journals as being good sources of information. No official sources cite advertisements as a source of information for practitioners and of course although advertising does give information its purpose is to persuade rather than to inform (Mansfield et al., 2005). Students should be made more aware of the extent of pharmaceutical company influence in academic journals. As mentioned above, issues include the significance of declarations of interests (Carver & Ashmore, 2004) and advertising (Ashmore & Carver, 2001; Scott et al., 2005). Furthermore, students should be given a basic understanding of the role of the Medicines and Healthcare products Regulatory Agency (MRHA).

Mental health education needs to recognise ways in which drug companies may attack or even co-opt those who may be thought to be independent of drug company influence. For example, MHNs have an increased interest in working with or listening to service user groups and voluntary sector organisations. It is often imagined these groups articulate or give voice to the disenfranchised. However, as noted earlier concern has been raised that patient groups do not always declare substantial sources of funding which may be from the pharmaceutical companies (Herxeimer, 2003).

Furthermore, students need to be orientated to the roles of personnel employed by the industry. According to the ABPI the term "'representative' means a representative calling on members of the health professionals and administration staff in relation to the promotion of medicines" (ABPI, 2003, p. 6). It is also worth noting that the pharmaceutical industry is able to invent roles for some of its employees, for instances "Nurse Advisors" (Ryan, 2002) or "Healthcare Development Managers" (NIMHE, 2005).

Finally, teaching should highlight that despite the scale of promotional activity it is still potentially possible for both qualified and unqualified nursing staff to take action should they wish. For example, consideration could be given to the idea of creating clinical environments free from promotional materials.

CONCLUSION

It is unlikely that the profile of the pharmaceutical industry in psychiatry will decrease and it is almost inevitable that individual nurses and nursing organisations will increasingly have to confront the many issues arising from the industry's attempts to gain influence, even if that influence is argued to be benign. The process of educating practitioners about this influence has begun in basic medical education. Although it may be supported by greater evidence than exists in nursing the authors here suggest it should be no less a priority in the education of mental health nurses.

DECLARATION OF INTERESTS

At the time of writing, the first author is a trustee with Sheffield Mind. MIND has a policy of not accepting funding from the pharmaceutical industry. Both authors have received travel expenses from service user and health care professional groups to give talks on the pharmaceutical industry. They have also presented papers on relationships with the pharmaceutical industry at a number of national and international conferences. Both of their names appear on the No Free Lunch UK website.

REFERENCES

ABPI (2003). Code of Practice for the Pharmaceutical Industry. London: ABPI.

Ashmore, R. & Carver, N. (2001). The pharmaceutical industry and mental health nursing, *British Journal of Nursing*, *10*(21), 1396–1402.

Ashmore, R., Carver, N. & Banks, D. (2007). *Mental health nursing students' relationship with the pharmaceutical industry, Nurse Education Today* (In Press).

Beresford, P. (2005). Where would we be without the pharmaceutical industry? A service user's view. *Psychiatric Bulletin, 29*, 86–87.

Bracken, P.J. (2001). The radical possibilities of home treatment: postpsychiatry in action. In: Brimblecombe, N. Acute Mental Health Care in the Community: Intensive Home Treatment. London: Whurr Publishers.

Breggin, P. (1993). *Toxic Psychiatry Drugs and Electroconvulsive Therapy: The truth and the Better Alternatives*. London: Harper Collins.

Brody, H. (2005). The Company we Keep: Why physicians should refuse to see pharmaceutical representatives, *Annals of Family Medicine, 3*(1), 82–85.

Campbell, P. (2005). On Taking Money from Drug Companies. The Advocate, October, 7–8.

Carver, N. & Ashmore, R. (2004). Anything to Declare? Competing interests in mental health nursing journals. *Journal of Psychiatric and Mental Health Nursing, 11*, 620–622.

Davies, J. & Hemmingway, S. (2005). *Pharmaceutical Influences – Nurse prescribers: eyes wide open. Nurse Prescriber* 30 Dec 2004; *1*(12). Available at: http://www.nurse-prescriber.co.uk. Accessed on 20th April 2005.

Department of Health (1993). Standards of Business Conduct for N.H.S. Staff. London: Department of Health.

Department of Health (2000). *Commercial Sponsorship – Ethical Standards for the NHS. London: Department of Health.*

Department of Health (2004). *Choosing Health. Norwich: The Stationary Office.*

Department of Health (2005). Government Response to the Health Committee's Report on the Influence of the Pharmaceutical Industry. Norwich: The Stationary Office.

Douglas, K.M. & Sutton, R. M. (2004). Right about others, wrong about ourselves? Actual and perceived self-other differences in resistance to persuasion. *British Journal of Social Psychology, 43*, 585–603.

Gibbons, R.V, Landry, F.J., Blouch, D.L., Jones, D.L., Williams, F.K., Lucey, C.R. & Kroenke, K. (1998). A Comparison of Physicians' and Patients' Attitudes Toward Pharmaceutical Industry Gifts. *Journal of General Internal Medicine, 13*, 151–154.

House of Commons Health Select Committee (2005). The Influence of the Pharmaceutical Industry Volume I. London: The Stationary Office Limited.

Herxeimer, A. (2003). Relationships between the pharmaceutical industry and patients' organisations. *British Medical Journal, 326*, 1208–1210.

Jordan, S., Hardy, B. & Coleman, M. (1999). Medication Management: an exploratory study into the role of community mental health nurses. *Journal of Advanced Nursing, 29*(5), 1068–1081.

Kerridge, I., Maguire, J., Newby, D., McNeill, P.M., Henry, D., Hill, S., Day, R., MacDonald, G., Stokes, B. & Henderson, K. (2005). Cooperative partnerships or conflict-of-interest ? A national survey of interaction between the pharmaceutical industry and medical organizations. *Internal Medicine Journal, 35*, 206–210.

Mansfield, P. (2004). Commentary: Accepting what we can learn from advertising's mirror of desire, *British Medical Journal, 329*, 1487–1588.

Mansfield, P.R., Mintzes, B., Richards, D. & Toop L. (2005). *Direct to Consumer Advertising, British Medical Journal, 330*, 5–6.

Moncrieff, J. (2004). Is Psychiatry For Sale ? Healthy Skepticism International News January to March 2004, Vol. 22, No. 1–3. Available at: http://www.healthyskepticism.org/news/2004/1to3.htm. Accessed on 23rd September 2004.

Moncrieff, J., Hopker, S. & Thomas, P. (2005). Psychiatry and the pharmaceutical industry: who pays the piper? *Psychiatric Bulletin, 28*, 84–85.

Morrison-Griffiths, S., Snowden, M.A. & Pirmohamed, M. (2002). Pre-registration nurse education in pharmacology: is it adequate for the roles that nurses are expected to fulfil? *Nurse Education Today, 22*, 447–456.

NIMHE (2005). Why should NIMHE have a Partnership Group with the Pharmaceutical Industry? Available at: http://kc.nimhe.org.uk/upload/natpharmastatement.pdf. Accessed on 29th November, 2005.

NMC (2002). Code of Professional Conduct. London: Nursing and Midwifery Council.

Pharma Marketletter (1995). Nurses' evolving role: new communications, challenges and opportunities for pharmaceutical companies. *Pharma Marketletter 22*(25).

Rogers, W., Mansfield, R., Braunack-Mayer, A. & Jureidini, J. (2004). The ethics of pharmaceutical industry relationships with medical students. *Medical Journal of Australia, 180*, 19 April, 411–414.

Ryan, K. (2002). Nurses in the pharmaceutical industry: Part 1: Unravelling the role of the Nurse Adviser. *Pharmaceutical Field*, April, 32–33.

Scott, T., Stanford, N. & Thompson, D.R. (2005). Killing me softly: myth in pharmaceutical advertising. *British Medical Journal, 329*, 1484–1487.

Shooter, M. (2005). Dancing with the Devil? A personal view of psychiatry's relationship with the pharmaceutical industry. *Psychiatric Bulletin, 29*, 81–83.

Smith, R. (2003). Medical journals and pharmaceutical companies: uneasy bedfellows, *British Medical Journal, 326*, 1202–1205.

Smith, R. (2005). Medical Journals Are an Extension of the Marketing Arm of Pharmaceutical Companies. Public Library of Science Medicine. www.plosmedicine.org. May 2, 5, 364–366.

Wilkes, M. S. & Hoffman, J.R. (2001). An innovative approach to educating medical students about pharmaceutical promotion. *Academic Medicine, 276*(12), 1271–1277.

Ziegler, M.G., Lew, P. & Singer, B.C. (1995). The accuracy of drug information from pharmaceutical sales representatives. *Journal of the American Medical Association (JAMA) 273*(16), 1296–1298.

Zipkin, D. & Steinman, M. (2005). Interactions Between Pharmaceutical Representatives and Doctors in Training A Thematic Review. *Journal of General Internal Medicine, 20,* 777–786.

PART III

A Variety of Approaches

CHAPTER 19

Revisiting Psychosis: A Two-Day Workshop

Mark Hayward, Alison Blank, Philip Houghton and Becky Shaw

INTRODUCTION

"Challenging attitudes towards psychosis has been one of the greatest achievements of the British Psychological Society over the past 10 years" (Ann Cooke, personal communication). Central to this achievement has been an innovative report that challenges the dominance of a narrow view of psychotic experiences as primarily a symptom of an illness that is treated by medication. *Understanding mental illness: recent advances in understanding mental illness and psychotic experiences* (BPS, 2000) encourages understandings of psychosis and psychotic experiences that are informed by social and psychological factors, and by the views of those who experience psychosis. Yet any report is only as influential as the process through which its message is disseminated. Mindful of this fact, the authors of the report recognised a "need for a national programme of training for mental health workers to enable them to make use of the ideas and information in the report" (Cooke, 2000, p. 7). This hope became a reality in 2001 when the UK Department of Health funded the development of a number of learning materials, one of which was a training manual for a two-day workshop, "Psychosis Revisited" (Bassett et al., 2003). This chapter explores the uplifting experience of delivering this workshop over the past few years, with particular emphasis on the value of the relationships formed with service user colleagues.

THE WORKSHOP

A trainers' manual was drafted in April 2002. The manual was originally written for two trainers working together to run the workshop for a team of approximately 20 workers on two consecutive days. The manual stated that one of the trainers should be a psychologist. Service user involvement was suggested but not required.

The programme for the workshop was as follows:

Teaching Mental Health. Edited by Theo Stickley and Thurstine Basset.
Copyright © 2007 John Wiley & Sons, Ltd.

Aim

For participants to take a fresh look at psychosis and examine ways in which the team can work with people who have psychotic experiences.

Day 1: Frameworks for Understanding

This day allows participants to take a step back and consider psychosis with an open mind, and to consider understandings that offer an alternative to the biomedical approach.

- Introduction and the contested nature of mental health – this first section sets the scene for considering other ways of understanding psychosis and psychotic experiences, and places an emphasis on the personal understandings of the individual experiencing psychosis.
- Public/professional/team perspectives – this section helps participants begin to identify the similarities and differences between some understandings of psychosis with which they may be familiar. For example, their own understandings as mental health workers and those of the general public; it also includes an art exercise to encourage participants to go beyond words when thinking about psychosis.
- Service user perspectives – this is the central session of the workshop, and an opportunity for participants to hear first-hand accounts of individuals' experiences, not only of psychosis, but also of receiving services. There is an opportunity, within a safe environment, to ask questions of people who have personal experience of psychosis and service use.
- Understandings, causes, cultural context, formulations – this part of the workshop begins to locate psychosis within a biopsychosocial framework that is sensitive to cultural influences. It also introduces the participants to the concept of formulation – a process by which past events in an individual's life are linked with current psychotic experiences to enhance context and meaning.
- Shifting paradigms and raising hope – in this final part of Day 1 participants are encouraged to focus on the importance of hope, not just for their clients but also for themselves and their colleagues.

Day 2: Approaches and Interventions

Whereas Day 1 focuses largely upon understandings and raising questions and awareness for participants, Day 2 explores interventions and approaches and culminates in a team or individual action plan.

- Introduction and reflections – time is set aside at the beginning of Day 2 to reflect on learning from Day 1. It is also a chance to debrief on some of the issues and emotions that are inevitably aroused by the session on service user perspectives.
- Hope, recovery and fighting discrimination – this section looks in more detail at the need for a hopeful, recovery led approach, and considers barriers to this way of working, including an examination of stigma and discrimination. The session requires participants to evaluate their own service for evidence of stigmatising attitudes and discriminatory practices.

- Psychological interventions – this session focuses on the value of talking to people about their psychotic experiences. A cognitive behavioural framework is introduced as a process by which these conversations can be developed and orientated towards the development of meaning and possible change.
- Other approaches – medication, self-management and self-help, complementary, work, ordinary support – this pragmatic session asks participants to consider their own needs for support and interventions when in a crisis. It places an emphasis on the ordinariness of some support, and suggests that service users very often have support systems or ways of looking after themselves in place that may not be so different from those used more widely.
- Action plan – strategies for putting the action plan into practice. This is most useful if done as a team but individuals or groups who work together still have something to gain from reflecting on what they have learned and identifying changes they wish to make to their own practice.

THE JOURNEY BEGINS

Following the development of the draft training manual, the next step was to pilot it. This is where our (first and second authors') journey began. Eager to influence the views and practice of others in relation to psychosis, we volunteered to facilitate the first workshop. At this stage we had no relationships with service user colleagues other than the users of the services in which we worked, so user involvement was organised through the CAPITAL Project Trust[1] who took responsibility for the session on "service user perspectives". The workshop was delivered to a community mental health/ assertive outreach team over two consecutive days. Contrary to the original intention to offer the workshop only to teams, a second workshop was received over two consecutive days by a group of 15 practitioners, predominantly unqualified, from a variety of mental health settings. This workshop was facilitated by a nurse and a social worker, both of whom had been participants in the first workshop. Service user input was provided by service users known to the facilitators.

With respect to both the trainers and the participants the pilots were an early example of the ability of the workshop to act as a catalyst for interprofessional exploration. The most striking aspects of this exploration through the pilots were:

The impact of user involvement – Our service user colleagues spoke of their experiences of psychosis and service use through a process of interview followed by a question and answer session (see Hayward et al., 2005 for a full account of the process by which the safety of service users and participants was ensured during this session). These interviews were watched in respectful silence as the participants collectively acknowledged that they were witnessing something out-of-the-ordinary. There was a sense of us all being caught in the power of a process that acknowledged the ability of individuals to overcome considerable adversity, and subsequently opt to endure further anxiety as they spoke publicly about their experiences in order to positively influence the care received by others. Yet, this power was not attributable solely to the very raw, traumatic and shocking experiences that were recounted by one of the service users. Humour played an important part in the session and the more positive experiences of the other service user provided a necessary balance. A

---

[1] The CAPITAL Project Trust is a user organisation that has influence with regard to service development, research and training throughout West Sussex, for further information please see Chapter 3.

focus upon recovery was also important in engendering hope as each service user spoke of building lives that were of a better quality, despite setbacks, than the lives that had preceded the onset of their psychotic experiences.

Prior to the workshop we anticipated that we might need to play a part in somehow protecting the service users from hostility that may have been aroused within participants as a consequence of a perceived attack upon their practice. In reality this could not have been more different. Not only did the service users demonstrate that they were well versed in looking after each other, the hostility was expressed as a sense of indignation and outrage, and directed towards the services that had "cared" for one of the service users in such an abusive manner.

The challenge of working with a team – Training whole teams presents an exciting opportunity as participants will have a mandate to carry out actions agreed at the workshop. However, facilitating whole team training poses many challenges. Firstly, there is the need to secure the attendance of those individuals who are the most powerful and influential members, which is not always easy when the training potentially questions the culture of a team. Within the first pilot workshop this challenge was met to the extent that the Consultant Psychiatrist and Consultant Psychologist each attended for one of the two days. Second comes the challenge of facilitating the involvement of these individuals without allowing them to railroad an evolving team process.

A further challenge concerned the containment of team hopelessness, cynicism and internal team politics, necessary in preventing the workshop from becoming unfocused and assuming the air of an away day. The airing of such negative emotions was a natural consequence of asking a team to consider how it understood and attempted to support service users with complex needs – individuals who may have been on the teams' caseload for many years and who may have been perceived as "difficult to engage". Consequently, containment involved a balance of facilitating the expression of frustration, problem solving and reconnecting the discussions to understandings and interventions associated with psychosis; this drew extensively upon many of the skills and experiences of ourselves as facilitators.

The receptiveness of workers without a professional training – In contrast to the challenges that were presented by working with a team, it became apparent during the second pilot workshop that individuals without professional training had a great desire for knowledge and expressed openness towards new understandings of psychosis and ways of working with individuals with complex needs. The participants seemed to be more intuitively attuned to the needs of service users, in a manner that enabled them to be more available to the development of relationships that were collaborative and had a genuine sense of reciprocity. This did not seem to be a chosen ideological position as many participants entered the workshop desiring a "professional" knowledge base of the kind which seemed to be valued by many of their more powerful and influential colleagues within mental health services. Yet their availability to service users and their everyday, ordinary approach to understanding distress and recovery were consistent with some of the major tenets of the workshop, and in this respect their position was validated and encouraged throughout the two days.

Following the pilot workshops the draft training manual was revised in a number of ways to reflect some of these themes prior to its publication in 2003. Most significantly, revisions stated that the involvement of service user contributors was essential and that the training should be offered to both teams and groups of individual practitioners. The requirement that one trainer needed to be a psychologist was modified to include any mental health worker who had current experience of using psychological interventions in their day-to-day work. The published manual also suggests that the workshop could be run over two non-consecutive days, or even as four half days if this format were more suitable to trainers and participants.

STARTING SMALL...

Having experienced the benefits of creating a space within which psychosis and psychotic experiences could be reflected upon, we were keen to continue facilitating and learning within Psychosis Revisited workshops. However, we faced a quandary: should we offer the training to teams, potentially the most effective agents of change, albeit amidst the challenges outlined above; or should we work with the hunger and openness of those practitioners without a professional training? Whilst we acknowledged that this latter group of workers may have a limited ability to influence the practice of teams and organisations, this was traded against their closer proximity and greater availability to service users. There was also some concern expressed about creating difficulties for unqualified staff by challenging traditional understandings of psychosis (largely biomedical) and rendering them frustrated within a system over which they had little, if any, control or power. However we are not aware of this having happened in practice.

We decided to start small by offering workshops as part of the in-house training pro-gramme for workers without a professional training. Initially these workshops were run in accordance with the manual, mixing didactic teaching with small group work and reflection on clinical practice. However it soon became apparent through feedback that many partic-ipants had limited experience of learning about mental health in such traditional formats, thus requiring the introduction of more varied and interactive methods of learning. The introduction of mime, role-play and visual demonstrations each created the opportunity for participants to connect with and understand psychosis in a number of ways. This began a process of learning about the flexibility of the manual, and its suitability as a framework for leaning that could be adapted to the needs of a local context.

One particular change that was introduced in response to feedback concerned the Day 2 session on "Psychological interventions". The manual focuses this session upon the con-ceptualisation and treatment of psychotic experiences within a cognitive behavioural frame-work. Participants were responsive to this, acknowledging the value of talking to people about their psychotic experiences. However it soon became clear that there was a need for more direction in how to begin these conversations. Consequently, we developed a brief role-play involving the parts of "worker" and "service user". Performed by the two trainers, the role-play demonstrates a number of methods of communication that can be utilised by the worker to maximise the likelihood of the conversations evolving into meaningful explorations. For example, the need for empathy, using the service user's language to de-scribe unusual experiences, expressing a genuine desire to learn and suspending disbelief. Such conversations can assist in the development of a collaborative relationship, which can facilitate future in-depth discussions that may draw extensively on a theoretical orientation such as cognitive theory.

We have also developed, in conjunction with other colleagues, a one day follow-up training session which focuses purely on talking to people about their psychotic experiences. It is a practical, skills-based day, which involves three trainers, one of whom is a service user, across the whole day. It has been well received and serves as a useful supplement to the two-day workshop.

Despite changes to the workshop content, the centrality of the contributions of our service user colleagues has remained unaffected. These lived experiences continue to be the pivot around which the workshops revolve; they provide anecdotal evidence to which much of the workshop material can be connected, and identify recovery in its idiosyncratic forms. The open acknowledgement of vulnerability can set a tone for the remainder of the workshop by encouraging a healthy level of personal disclosure. In addition to first-hand accounts of psychosis and of receiving services heard within the workshop itself, much of the learning material that accompanies the manual, as well as material brought in by trainers, is based upon accounts of service use and psychotic experiences. Such stories are a powerful means to bring alive the learning taking place, making the workshop more meaningful still.

Within many workshops this process continues to take the form of service user colleagues "telling their stories" within the session on service user perspectives. However, scope for more extensive involvement has been embraced within the one-day follow-up workshop and our colleagues in Nottingham have run a series of two-day workshops with a facilitating team that included two user trainers (Houghton et al., 2006). One of the issues we are currently seeking to address is the development of a 'ladder of involvement' (Goss & Miller, 1995) where user colleagues can contribute as much or as little as they wish, with ultimately the training team being made up of one worker and one service user trainer.

Having started small by deciding to focus on the learning needs of workers without a professional training, we have been enormously encouraged by the apparent desire of care teams to expose a critical mass of their members to this training process. Participants have returned to their work bases after the training and actively encouraged attendance to the extent that a majority of colleagues from a number of establishments have often attended the workshop over the annual in-house cycle of three to four workshops.

...AND THINKING BIG

Whilst initially targeting the needs of workers without a professional training, our vision extended across disciplinary and geographical boundaries. Consequently, the training manual has received considerable exposure outside of the Trust in which we work. Assured of its appeal and relevance, and comfortable in our role as co-trainers we embarked on a crusade to bring this resource to the attention of other professions. This has been achieved in a number of ways, but chiefly through the presentation of papers and/or workshops at national conferences. Over the last two years the workshop has been presented in a variety of necessarily customised forms to nursing, psychology, occupational therapy, medical, educational and managerial audiences. We have also written about it in the psychology, medical, occupational therapy and nursing press.

Mindful that the training process should not become dependent on our energies alone, we have also been attempting to embed Psychosis Revisited within established programmes of professional training. To date this has necessitated creativity as we have delivered modified versions of the workshop to clinical psychology trainees and students on an occupational therapy programme. Ideally, these workshops will lead to opportunities to train the trainers of these programmes to deliver the workshop as part of their curricula.

Networking at conferences has brought us into contact with other workers keen to utilise the manual, or who have already done so. One relationship formed in this way has given rise to a collaborative project to evaluate the efficacy of the training. Initially invited to present a modified half-day version of the workshop to possible future trainers in Nottingham, we subsequently collaborated on a cross-site evaluation of six workshops (Houghton et al., 2006).

THE NOTTINGHAM EXPERIENCE

Soon after the training manual was published a small number of us (including the third and fourth authors) met to think about running a series of workshops in Nottingham. The workshop appealed to us as it seemed to offer something different. To begin with, the fact that user involvement was integral to the workshop made it stand out from other training packages, and its emphasis on non-medical ways of understanding and working with psychosis also added to its appeal. After hearing more about the training from those in West Sussex we decided to run a pilot of three workshops within Nottingham. We also wanted to build on and extend the degree of service user involvement in the workshops. Rather than service users solely being involved in the session on "service user perspectives", we made a decision very early on that the planning, organisation and running of the workshops should be a collaborative project involving both professional workers and service users.

The approach of including service users across all levels of the training, we feel, has been incredibly rewarding. However there is also a need to remember that not all service users feel able to, or want to take part in the entire process. Creating a culture where service users feel supported throughout the training process and able to take part in as much or as little as they wish to, is something that needs to be constantly worked at and reflected upon. Within the initial pilot workshops we found that one key ingredient was enabling the training teams to spend a good deal of time together, not only to make sure everyone felt comfortable with the training, but also with each other. This is especially important when different members of the team have different levels of confidence and experience in delivering training events.

Since the initial pilot, we have received funding to run a further nine workshops within the Trust, and we are currently half way through this initiative. This of course brings its own opportunities and challenges. On the positive side, new trainers, (both service users and professional workers) have been able to work alongside people who have delivered the workshops before, allowing them to build up their confidence in a more protected environment. To further encourage this, we have set up regular meetings for trainers who have experience of using services to provide a supportive forum where ideas and experiences can be shared, and to allow potential trainers to find out about the initiative in a safe environment.

Naturally, there are challenges involved in running a larger training initiative. To begin with there is a need for a more structured communication, decision-making and administrative structure to support the additional numbers of training teams and workshops. It is also important to try and ensure that the new trainers coming in share the value base which is at the heart of the training (see themes below), and we have been reminded of the importance of new training teams spending enough time together prior to the workshop to ensure people feel as comfortable as possible when delivering the training. Overall though, notwithstanding the increased challenge of rolling out the training on a larger scale, the fact that the workshops continue to be on the whole received very positively gives us reassurance that the values and approaches captured by Psychosis Revisited are vitally important in improving the input provided to people experiencing psychosis.

THEMES FROM THE WORKSHOPS[2]

Described below are some themes that arose from the evaluation of six workshops within West Sussex and Nottingham. They represent themes that resulted from an analysis of qualitative data as well as those that were generated informally in discussion.

From the Analysis of Qualitative Data

- *Validation of my own practice*
  Many respondents found aspects of the workshops validated their own practice or gave them cause to reflect critically on their own practice, an approach they appeared to welcome rather than feel threatened by. For example, one respondent said, "little things can have a big impact. I've always suspected this – nice to hear it said".
- *A three dimensional approach to psychosis*
  The three-dimensional understanding reflected a deeper understanding of psychosis and its impact on individuals, families, workers and services. One respondent said they had learnt about "seeing psychosis in a different light", whilst another described "Its [psychosis] various complex ways and effects [on each] individual".
- *Hearing service users' stories*
  The value of hearing service users' stories was important for many of the participants. One said, "[I have learned that] the service users stories still touch me". A number of respondents commented more extensively on service user involvement, e.g. "service users are having a stronger voice and [more] input" and the positive impact this had in areas such as "breaking down barriers".
- *Hope and Recovery*
  The importance of hope and the possibility of recovery were considered important in many responses. For example, one respondent spoke of ". . . Nurturing the spark of hope. . . most important", whilst another commented on "how negative you become without realising and [I learned] how to be more hopeful".
- *Respect and relationships*
  Respect (for service users but also for colleagues) and the importance of good relationships with service users were considered by a large group of respondents to be one of the three most important things they had learned, e.g. "To treat each client as the individual they are".
- *Communication and Listening*
  Communication, with particular emphasis on listening was seen as an important theme. Mainly this referred to listening to service users but also the importance of good communication with colleagues and other agencies was highlighted. For example, one person said they had learned "to listen more and talk less".

From Discussions

- *Being Human.* Participants discussed how easy it could be to forget about the importance of everyday human qualities such as warmth, being friendly, listening,

---

[2] The themes first appeared in Houghton, P., Shaw, B. Hayward, M. & West, S. (2006). Psychosis Revisited: taking a collaborative look at psychosis. *Mental Health Practice, 9,* 40–43. Reproduced by permission of RCN Publishing Company.

developing relationships and showing concern, but how central they are in helping people recover.

- *The importance of "small talk"*. The positive impact of having everyday conversations with service users using everyday language was seen as being incredibly therapeutic, and often overlooked in busy environments.
- *Shrinking the gap between "us and them"*. This theme was linked to "being human" and stresses the need for workers to avoid distancing themselves from service users and the importance of working collaboratively rather than from an expert position.
- *The importance of activities*. Creating opportunities for service users to participate in meaningful activities was highlighted as a central role for workers. Such activities can lead to the valued social roles that are central to processes of recovery.
- *Combating discrimination*. The workshops focused in part on the discrimination within society towards people who experience mental health difficulties. As well as combating such discrimination on a wider scale, the importance of addressing discrimination in our own work and services was highlighted.
- *The meaning of "psychotic" experiences*. Experiences, which can be superficially viewed as "mad", were reframed as valuable sources of information about the client's difficulties, both past and present. This perspective served as an encouragement to workers to talk with clients about their unusual and sometimes bizarre experiences.

GROWING RELATIONSHIPS

> ... The concept of relational being reduces the debilitating gap between self and other, the sense of oneself as alone and the other as alien and untrustworthy. Whatever we are, from the present standpoint, is either directly or indirectly with others. . . . We are made up of each other. . . we are mutually constituting.
>
> Gergen, 1999, pp. 137–138

The concept of relationships is central to the workshop: the collaborative and reciprocal relationships we develop with the users of the services we provide; the relationships that can develop between participants as a result of an increasing intimacy that comes from working together over two days; and the close relationships that have been nurtured between members of the training team.

The process of developing the training manual and delivering the training has been (and still is) an evolving, bottom-up approach, dependent on some of these relationships and fuelled by the passion of the people involved. This passion is for influencing the practice of others towards a more eclectic, pragmatic and humane approach to people who experience psychosis. The journey has been an intensely personal one, with many challenges along the way. Working closely with service user colleagues has required us to closely examine our own vulnerabilities, our attitudes to psychosis, and to look for evidence of discriminatory attitudes within our own practice. Relationships evolve over time, and as groups of trainers we have become increasingly comfortable with one another, confronting the barriers of worker/service user, challenging traditional mental health work boundaries around ways of being with users of services, boundaries between being colleagues and being friends. Within each training group we have also learned about each other's strengths and weaknesses, and defined roles for each other and ourselves within the two-day workshop. As the training groups expand we plan to set aside further time for getting to know each other as we meet for both work and play. Throughout the process we have all sought to establish open and non-hierarchical relationships to enable shared decision making, develop effective working partnerships, and to achieve mutual empowerment.

REFLECTIONS

From the Workshop Participants[3]

- Well informed.
- I need to adopt a more hopeful approach to recovery.
- I will listen to and hear patients better, will be more open-minded.
- Wetted my appetite for more courses.
- Liked the interactive nature of the training style.
- A lot of doubts about some of my philosophies and work practice were dispelled.
- I feel I can build on what I have learned today.
- Very inspiring and challenging in a safe environment.
- I will put ideas into actions, don't always presume we know what's best for them.
- This course was at a good level for me to learn new things, I will take back a lot of new ideas to share with my colleagues.
- A very good structured course, this course has helped me to find new approaches to helping people.
- Thank you, brilliant.

From One of the Service User Contributors (West Sussex)

I wanted to get a little bit of confidence back and challenge myself. I felt I had a little bit of power to influence how the future of mental health services might be.

It has really helped me grab hold of my problems and deal with them. Each time I have presented it has become easier. It's even become enjoyable. I didn't think I'd ever say that.

I've had some lovely feedback. People coming up to me and saying "Can I hug you?" and "Can I shake your hand?" One girl wrote a note saying "you're wonderful for what you've been through and the quality of life you've got now – keep going". It was really good for me to get that.

From One of the Service User Facilitators (Nottingham)[4]

As a service user I was involved in the training package delivery on all three of the training events. Service user involvement was done a bit differently than from the psychosis revisited

---

[3] The reflections from the workshop participants and service user facilitator (West Sussex) first appeared in Hayward, M., Blank, A. & Cooke, A. (2005). A fresh approach to psychosis . . . revisited. *Clinical Psychology Forum, 152*, 17–19.

[4] The reflection from the service user facilitator (Nottingham) first appeared in Houghton, P., Shaw, B., Hayward, M. & West, S. (2006) Psychosis Revisited: taking a collaborative look at psychosis. *Mental Health Practice, 9*, 40–43. Reproduced by permission of RCN Publishing Company.

manual. The manual suggests that service users just deliver one session. I did not want to be wheeled in just for one session. We were involved not only in delivering throughout the whole of the two days but also in all the decision making, design and evaluation of psychosis revisited. I felt fully involved as an equal in all aspects and I think our input and teamwork made the training more successful by this. By having service user involvement throughout the workshops meant the training was balanced, real and more valuable to the participants. Although being involved throughout was valuable it was quite hard especially when some of the staff who came had treated me in hospital. This became a role reversal for the staff and myself and although quite a balancing act at first, with some adjustment it did become useful and insightful for the participants. On reflection I think the training went very well which was reflected in the evaluations.

I felt that the staff did seem to come with low morale and a feeling that things wouldn't change no matter how much they wanted things to. The action plans produced and the themes that arose out of the training I hope will be carried forward by management as the staff's motivation for change would be a shame to lose and a lot of good things could come from this. If psychosis revisited is to continue, service user involvement should remain at the heart and although some elements might be changed I think service user involvement should be flexible enough to allow service users to input in the way they feel most comfortable.

The one thing that I will remember from the training is what one trainee said to me:

> "it has lifted me and rekindled all those reasons why I wanted to do nursing in the first place which I had lost. I now know that just sitting and being human with a patient or making them a cup of tea is just as important or perhaps more important than the medication or note taking. Thank you."

This is the reason I think service user involvement is important to me as it means I can help staff to realise that it's not miracle science to help someone. All you need to do is show you care about the person you are helping, listen to what they need and help them with this in the way they want to do it. I am glad the participants gained so much from the training and hope many more will gain in the future.

From the Professional Trainers

Relationships developed with service user colleagues and workshop participants have added immeasurably to the depth and breadth of the validation we require to continue challenging the dominance of the biomedical model. Psychosis Revisited has played a vital part in strengthening our belief in the ability of mental health workers to connect with a pragmatic training process that has the potential to significantly influence practice.

SUMMARY

Psychotic experiences are connected meaningfully to a person's life history and an understanding of these connections will facilitate future recovery. Our experience highlights the value of creating an environment within which mental health workers can begin or continue to examine their practice in relation to these possibilities.

Psychosis Revisited creates a space over two days where understandings of some complex and often baffling examples of human experience can be explored. Within this space the training manual offers a flexible framework that can guide exploration and respond to evolving discussions. Suitable for modification to meet the learning needs of teams or groups of individuals with varying levels of training and experience, the workshop is not an end in itself, but merely a catalyst for creativity and reflection. Further opportunities to hone these abilities and review changing practice are a vital part of any process of learning and it is suggested that the workshop be run as part of a broad training and development strategy across mental health services.

REFERENCES

British Psychological Society (2000). *Understanding mental illness: Recent advances in understanding mental illness and psychotic experiences* – the report is available from: Mind Publications for £15 – publications@mind.org.uk. The BPS website for no charge – www.understandingpsychosis.com.

Basset, T., Cooke, A. & Reid, J. (2003). *Psychosis Revisited: a workshop for mental health workers* – order from Pavilion Publishing phone: 01273 623222, www.pavpub.com

Cooke, A. (2000). Pressing home the truth, *Open Mind, 107*, Sept./Oct.

Gergen, K.J. (1999). *An invitation to social construction*. London: Sage.

Goss. S. & Miller, C. (1995). *From margin to mainstream: Developing user and carer centred community care*. York: Joseph Rowntree Foundation.

Hayward, M., West, S., Green, M. & Blank, A. (2005). Service innovations: service user involvement in training. *Psychiatric Bulletin, 29*, 428–430.

Houghton, P., Shaw, B., Hayward, M. & West, S. (2006). Psychosis Revisited: Taking a collaborative look at psychosis. *Mental Health Practice, 9*, 40–43.

CHAPTER 20

Developing Problem-based Learning for a Pre-registration Mental Health Nursing Programme

Carol Cooper and Sue Gunstone

INTRODUCTION

In this chapter the philosophy underpinning problem-based learning (PBL) and its suitability for pre-registration mental health nurse education is examined. There seem to be many similarities between these two phenomena, which is explored briefly. Following this, the reader is guided through the development of our PBL curriculum by exploring issues from the initial idea through to implementation. This was a major change for the department where it was developed and we acknowledge that change can be a difficult process, consequently the strategies for managing this are discussed. An essential starting point for any curriculum change is the philosophy, which is where we will commence our discussion.

PHILOSOPHY

PBL has been in use in health education for many years, starting in medical education at McMaster University, Canada in the early 60s (Neufeld & Barrows, 1974). Their philosophy focussed on specific capabilities and characteristics that they wanted to develop in students, as opposed to a specific knowledge base. Life long learning was an important element of this as they highlighted the need for doctors to have these skills. They assumed that students were responsible, motivated adults, a fact that was highlighted in the research carried out by Norman and Schmidt (1992). Miligan (1999) also identifies these links to andragogy and states that the bulk of literature is optimistic about its potential in relation to nurse education. The consensus in the literature is that PBL is a useful tool of epistemological reform in higher education (Maudsley, 1999), as well as an appropriate pedagogical technique for educating adults for professional practice (Biley & Smith, 1998). However recently, Haigh

Teaching Mental Health. Edited by Theo Stickley and Thurstine Basset.

(2005) has raised concerns about implementation of PBL into nursing curricula without critical appraisal of its suitability.

The educational philosophy of PBL hinges on the premise that students should be actively involved in the process of learning, acquiring knowledge within the appropriate context (Barrows & Tamblyn, 1980). Wood (2005) in his research on PBL and mental health nursing concurs with this. He found that mental health students became "more self-motivated, autonomous and reflective as learners" (p. 195).

There are clear identifiable links in this approach to findings of cognitive psychology, as it is recognised that learners who have to take charge of their own learning needs coupled with finding answers to supplement their knowledge will be more likely to retain this (Schmidt & Moust, 2000). Schmidt and Moust (2000) further explain that PBL is a form of constructivist learning, as students are engaged in constructing theories about their world represented by the problems presented. Constructivism as a philosophical position views knowledge as something the learner creates for themselves. This also reflects our viewpoint that learners need to explore widely and not be constrained by our worldview.

As we noted earlier in our discussion PBL has been used in health education for many years it is only recently that mental health nurse education has explored its use in programmes. Nurse education is continually evolving to meet the needs of a diverse and ever challenging society. PBL, we believe, is one approach which will enable us to respond in a timely manner to this ever changing healthcare scene.

MENTAL HEALTH NURSE EDUCATION

The introduction of PBL was one of the recommendations made as an appropriate teaching method to enable nurses to adapt, and meet, new and changing health care needs (United Kingdom Central Council, (UKCC), 1999). This recommendation has been supported by subsequent policy initiatives such as, The Capable Practitioner (Sainsbury Centre for Mental Health, 2001), The Knowledge and Skills Framework (Department of Health (DOH), 2004a) and The Ten Essential Shared Capabilities (DOH, 2004b). These in turn have contributed to the mental health nursing review (DOH, 2005) which identifies that the profession needs to develop new roles and skills to care for those affected by mental health problems in the future.

Examples of skills developed by PBL are:

- communication;
- interpersonal relationships;
- lifelong learning;
- team working;
- leadership;
- working in groups;
- utilising research to enhance practice.

These same skills are equally valuable to today's mental health nurse and identified in the literature above. Likewise they are required for the mental health workforce of the future. Although this chapter focuses on mental health nursing, PBL is equally a pertinent approach for our multidisciplinary colleagues to implement as illustrated in the policy initiatives above.

Having had the chance to explore some of the philosophical aspects of PBL we will now guide the reader through the process of implementation.

PROCESS

In our department the process commenced with general discussions of our mental health pre-registration course provision at a staff "away day" forum. There appeared to be an inherent dissatisfaction amongst lecturers with the present delivery mode based on traditional teaching methods and in particular to this group of postgraduate students. The main concerns expressed were that there was a perceived lack of student-centred learning and prior knowledge and skills were not taken into consideration in course delivery.

The student population was an important consideration in the decision to develop a problem based learning course. Our pre-registration postgraduate students had certain characteristics, which we believed were conducive to this type of course. They were mature students who had a cognate degree, evidence of recent study and previous experience in a caring role. There would be a maximum number of 25 students in a cohort and this course would last for 2 years. These features, we believed were conducive to implementing a PBL approach. Following the initial discussions and the identification that the pre-registration post-graduate course was due for review a development team was identified.

UNDERSTANDING PBL

One of the initial tasks for the development team was to begin to understand some of the terminology used in PBL. A working definition was needed and Alavi (1995) describes PBL succinctly as an approach, which places the student at the centre of the learning process and is aimed at integrating learning with practice. Barrows and Tamblyn (1980) clarify this further by defining it as "the learning, which results from the process of working towards the understanding of, or resolution of, a problem". (p. 1). These two definitions gave us our reference point.

The PBL process begins with a trigger. These are materials used to stimulate discussion (Wilkie & Burns, 2003) and the learning process. They can take various forms such as case studies, medication cards, songs, videos or photographs. Fixed resources are used to support the topic being analysed in the trigger. They can be lectures, workshops, and clinical skills sessions, some of which can be delivered by service users, carers and lecturers.

The roles within the PBL groups are also important to understand. The facilitator is someone who promotes, enhances, encourages and eases the way for the team during PBL (Wilkie & Burns, 2003). In our department this is a member of the teaching team who has an understanding of the processes involved. It has been suggested that senior students or clinicians could also fulfil this role (Wilkie & Burns, 2003). The students also nominate two group members, who rotate, for the specific roles of scribe and chairperson. The scribe is charged with noting the discussion and capturing issues raised. Whereas the chairperson's main role is to manage the discussion and tactfully engage all group members, ensuring the work is completed within the given time (Wilkie & Burns, 2003).

There are different ways of working through the trigger to identify learning outcomes, we utilise a modified form of the Maastricht Seven Steps which colleagues in our Midwifery and Children's Department found to work well in nurse education.

> **Box 20.1   The Maastricht Seven Steps**
>
> 1. Clarify – to what extent do you understand what the situation is about.
> 2. Define – any unfamiliar vocabulary/terms/concepts.
> 3. Analyse – "brainstorm" any possible explanations. What are the possibilities?
> 4. Sift and Sort – decide what is probable and what can be found out. Begin to group similar ideas together.
> 5. Identify Learning Outcomes – formulate learning issues for self-directed learning.
> 6. Investigate and Learn – fill gaps in your knowledge through self-study.
> 7. Report Back – share your findings with your group and try to integrate the knowledge acquired.
>
> Adapted from Schmidt, H. G. & Moust, J. H. C. (2000). Factors affecting small group tutorial learning: a review of research. In D. H. Evensen & C.E. Hmelo (eds), Problem based learning: a research perspective on learning interactions. Mahwah, NJ: Lawrence Erlbaum.

DEVISING A CURRICULUM – WHICH MODEL?

Savin-Baden (2004) suggests that there are at least 50 ways of getting involved in a PBL curriculum and goes on to outline eight different models. Our chosen model is closest to the integrated approach that is based on the principle that PBL is not merely a strategy but a curriculum philosophy. It is based on the McMaster model where students working in small teams are facilitated by a tutor to tackle one problem at a time. The curriculum exists in an integrated approach where problems are sequential although assessment is not necessarily linked to a PBL approach. This is where we differ slightly as we felt the assessment strategy should reflect the teaching methodology.

MAKING IT HAPPEN

A lead developer was identified who gathered key people from the department to form the initial core review group. This group met to brainstorm the possibilities and requirements from different stakeholders' perspectives. These stakeholders included: service users and carers, service side staff, students and lecturers. Another strategy employed was to keep all staff members informed of proposals and to gauge interest and support for this radical change. This was done by ensuring notes of meetings highlighting discussion points were circulated to all staff coupled with regular updates presented at Department meetings. In terms of change management this would be Hersey and Blanchard's (1982) selling strategy.

The literature indicates that key areas for support needed are: a critical mass of people interested within the department, the Head of Department or budget holder especially with regard to resource implications and the support of other stakeholders (Boud & Feletti, 1991). Having established that there was support and motivation to make this change we moved to the next stage that was characterised by wider consultation, further refinement and checking out of our proposals. One interesting discovery was that the new developments encouraged us to review and enhance our skills; at the same time this generated a renewed enthusiasm for educational debate, a point illustrated by Roberts and Ousey (2004). At the same time our current students also seemed to see the benefits and value of this new approach.

At this point a reference group was formed to increase the number of people involved in debating the proposed development. The membership comprised representatives from the workforce confederation, clinicians, service users, carers, library staff, students, lecturers from the initial review group, course leaders from other post graduate mental health nursing courses, department head, placements officer and course secretary. This group were charged with the responsibility of refining and guiding the proposed new course, ensuring its feasibility from their individual perspectives.

This also entailed a degree of education for some of our colleagues who were less familiar with the PBL approach and therefore struggled with some of the concepts when translated to practice. Within these discussions there were several important issues raised such as students learning styles (Honey & Mumford, 1995), resource implications, and the evidence base. The crux of many of these debates appeared to be differences in interpretations of PBL and differing philosophical viewpoints. For example the issue of whether the students needed a reading list or not highlighted these debates. There was a continuum of thought ranging from a minimalist approach of no reading list through to a more traditional approach that students should be given a comprehensive reading list. The compromise was a list of five key texts covering Nursing studies, Psychology, Sociology, Users and Carers perspectives and a basic book on PBL.

Another consideration was maximum group size, which was set at 12 as proposed by Wilkie and Burns (2003). The role of facilitator was another area for much debate. Once again the continuum previously discussed was in evidence. On a pragmatic level facilitators were identified who were enthusiastic and recognised the need for further education and training. It was apparent that as experienced mental health lecturers we already had many skills in this arena that just needed fine-tuning and agreement on parameters. The issue of how many facilitators were involved in each unit was considered and a pragmatic decision taken that there would be a small core of facilitators who would change groups each trigger. This was encouraged due to the difficulty in lecturers being able to commit to the whole unit, in addition this enabled other facilitators to become involved and consequently further develop their own skills.

Other strategies employed were visits to other departments within the School of Nursing and Midwifery, external Schools of Nursing already utilising PBL approaches and workshops facilitated by experts within the school. This was to discuss issues and to observe PBL sessions. Attendance at PBL conferences also increased our knowledge base, which was supplemented by library colleagues who helpfully developed a staff resource list.

Although there were quarterly Reference Group meetings some members were unable to come and others could be seen as laggards (Rogers, 1962). However people were kept involved by the distribution of appropriate information and requests to feedback any issues and views. Service users were one group who were unable to attend so were consulted by the lead developer at their chosen venue(s). Although this process has been presented here in a linear format this is not entirely accurate as these issues and the development and validation of the course were running concurrently.

After internal and external validation the challenge was to make the course work. The reference group evolved into the course implementation group, which was a departmental team, focusing on delivery of the course. In the language of organisational change the innovators and early adopters were joined by the early and late majority (Rogers, 1962).

The lead developer became the course leader and mainly members of the original core team became the four unit leaders. Each supported by a deputy, these people came from the early adopters (Rogers, 1962). This team collaborated with the stakeholders identified earlier.

The implementation group were charged with addressing the following issues:

- course management;
- translating learning outcomes into content;
- developing the timetable;
- devising course, facilitator and unit handbooks;
- trigger development;
- facilitating input from service users, carers and clinical staff;
- evaluation;
- development of assessment methods;
- identifying library resources;
- placement preparation including support for practice staff;
- addressing the role of administration staff;
- reviewing recruitment information;
- preparation of new students;
- preparation of external examiner;
- staff support.

This list of issues reminds us of the learning objectives students identify when using the Maastricht Seven Steps with their trigger material.

As previously mentioned many of the above learning outcomes were dealt with concurrently as they were all interlinked and no one issue took priority. The initial challenges were to translate the learning outcomes into meaningful course content. This commenced with Unit 1, the co-ordinator and deputy in conjunction with the Implementation Group devised templates for the timetable plus unit and facilitator handbooks. This team also created the triggers; one of the difficulties here was the meaningful involvement of service users, carers and clinical staff. Though these groups were involved in the reference group, other commitments prevented them from continuing on a long-term basis. As we were unable to develop trigger material with representatives present, this was shared with them on an individual basis, clearly this is not true collaborative working (Breeze et al., 2005) and at present our department is working on a strategy to improve the situation.

An evaluation strategy was thought to be very important as this is a new development and there is dearth of literature on PBL in mental health nursing curricula. There were three strands to the evaluation: the standard University requirement for feedback on quality of teaching and learning as well as clinical placements. Secondly the innate need to evaluate PBL by all those participating and thirdly a research project to contribute to the slowly developing body of knowledge on PBL and mental health nursing. All these threads were integral to the development of the course and have been designed to feedback into the process.

Assessment methods were designed to compliment PBL and assess the depth of learning. A variety of methods were chosen including patchwork text (Scoggins & Winter, 1999), case presentation, audio taped interview, poster and supporting papers. These are not only academic pieces of work but reflect some of the skills required in mental health practice and we find the involvement of clinicians in their development essential.

We were very conscious of the need to make the course explicit to everybody concerned therefore development of course, facilitator and unit handbooks were crucial to the success of the course. There are a variety of resources, which are needed to support the course including library facilities, placement mentors/assessors, administration staff and IT support. Education and support for the people involved was vital. For our clinical colleagues, who are taking on the roles of mentor/assessor, this involved us taking the information out to them initially with follow up support available.

Preparation and support of students took a number of forms; this process began with recruitment. As part of this change we have had to update our marketing and publicity materials to reflect the new PBL approach. Interview and selection procedures have not changed apart from ensuring that the students have an understanding of PBL at the point of interview. They get their first chance to experience the PBL approach on their pre-course study day, when we guide them through a small trigger. This engagement with the PBL approach is developed throughout the course culminating in the students organising and facilitating their own conference. There is ongoing support, academically, clinically and personally throughout the course. At the commencement of the course the students were allocated to their PBL group, part of this process involved considering gender mix and the location of their future clinical placements.

Another aspect for consideration is the choice and preparation of our external examiner. In this case the external examiner already had some experience in PBL and so our main task was to share our ideas and plans with them so they were fully informed and they could offer constructive comments for improvement.

Throughout this process regular meetings and support, combined with the distribution of notes to colleagues unable to attend has enabled all those involved to keep up to date, be part of the change and be supported in their respective roles. Interestingly those directly involved in course delivery have mainly attended the meetings, which are open to all interested parties. This support will continue to be a regular feature throughout the course and is especially important for new people engaging in the PBL process.

CONCLUSION

Poikela and Poikela (2005) have warned that the change to PBL needs to be carefully considered. On reflection we addressed and developed strategies for the following: the mechanical application of PBL by teachers, the curriculum, assessments that complement this, and finally evaluation. Other essential aspects to be dealt with are the need to actively manage change including preparation and support for all involved.

There is much debate in the literature regarding issues for facilitators (Wilkie, 2004), selection of students (Al-Nasir & Robertson, 2001) and how gender may affect suitability for using PBL (Reynolds, 2003) we have identified some areas that we are beginning to address for the future. The course structure is an issue for debate; ideas already aired include reducing the amount of time students spend in University and utilising practice areas as the venue for trigger development and delivery. Hopefully this will help us reduce the theory-practice gap further (Price, 2003). We have already highlighted our dissatisfaction with our attempts at collaborative working and are looking at ways of involving users and carers as assessors alongside academics and practitioners. The issue of peer assessment is also discussed in the literature (Alavi & Cooke, 1995) in relation to students assessing their colleagues and we see this as a natural progression.

We believe that the next formal review of the course will be an opportunity to be more radical. There are clear areas where the course has been positive. Staff enjoyed teaching on this programme and there is an enthusiasm for using PBL. Initial analysis of student data from the evaluation strategy has been mainly positive, some of the benefits they have identified are an improvement in their problem solving skills and team working. The course also seems to have worked well in practice and students have successfully completed their clinical proficiency statements. Our ultimate aim at the conclusion of this course is that we have mental health nurses who will be fit for practice and purpose coupled with a positive view of mental health nursing (Happell & Rushworth, 2000).

REFERENCES

Alavi, C. (ed) (1995) in introduction, *Problem-based Learning in a Health Sciences Curriculum*. London: Routledge.

Alavi, C. & Cooke, M. (1995). Chapter 11 in Alavi, C. (ed) *Problem-based Learning in a Health Sciences Curriculum*. London: Routledge.

Al-Nasir, F.A. & Robertson, A.S. (2001). Can selection assessments predict students' achievements in the premedical year?: a study at Arabian gulf University. *Education for Health*, *14*(2), 277–286.

Barrows, H. & Tamblyn, R. (1980). *Problem-based learning an approach to medical education*. New York: Springer Publishing Company.

Biley, F.C. & Smith, K.L. (1998). The buck stops here: accepting responsibility for learning and actions after graduation from a problem-based learning nursing education curriculum. *Journal of Advanced Nursing*, *27*(5), 1021–1029.

Boud, D. & Feletti, G. (eds) (1991). *The Challenge of Problem-based Learning*. London: Kogan Page.

Breeze, J., Bryant H., Bryant, L., Davidson, B. & King, S. (2005). Power shift promotes partnership. *Mental Health Nursing*, *25*(3), 4–7.

Department of Health (2004a). *The Knowledge and Skills Framework and the Development Review Process*. London: DOH Publications.

Department of Health (2004b). *The Ten Essential Shared Capabilities: a framework for the whole of the mental health workforce*. London: DOH Publications.

Department of Health (2005). *The Chief Nursing Officer's Review of Mental health Nursing in England*. London: DOH Publications.

Haigh, C. (2005). PBL, Viral spread and the role of nurse education. *Nurse Education Today*, *25*, 1, 1–2.

Happell, B. & Rushworth, L. (2000). Can educational methods influence the popularity of psychiatric nursing? *Nurse Education Today, 20*(4), 318–326.

Hersey, P. & Blanchard, K (1982). *Management of Organizational behaviour: utilizing human resources*, 4th edn., Englewood Cliffs, N.J.: Prentice Hall.

Honey, P. & Mumford, A. (1995). *Using your learning styles*. Berkshire: Pete Honey.

Maudsley, G. (1999). Do we all mean the same thing by "problem-based learning"? A review of the concepts and a formulation of the ground rules. *Academic Medicine*, *74*(2), 178–185.

Miligan, F. (1999). Beyond the rhetoric of problem-based learning: emancipatory limits and links with andragogy, *Nurse Education Today*, *19*(7), 548–555.

Neufeld, V.R. & Barrows, H.S. (1974). The "McMaster philosophy": an approach to medical education. *Journal of Medical Education*, *49*, 140–150.

Norman, G.R. & Schmidt, H.G. (1992). The psychological problem-based learning: a review of the evidence. *Academic Medicine*, *67*(9), 557–565.

Poikela, E. & Poilkela, S. (2005). *PBL in context: bridging work & education*. Tampere: Tampere University Press.

Price, B. (2003). *Studying Nursing Using Problem-Based & Enquiry-Based Learning*. Houndmills: Palgrave Macmillan.

Reynolds, F. (2003). Experiences of inter-professional PBL: a comparison of male and female students views. *Journal of Inter-professional Care, 17*(1), 35–44.

Roberts, D. & Ousey, K. (2004). Problem-based learning: developing the triggers. Experiences from a first wave site. *Nurse Education in Practice, 4*, 154–158.

Rogers, E.M. (1962). *Diffusion of innovations*. New York: Free Press

Sainsbury Centre for Mental Health (2001). *The Capable Practitioner*. London: Sainsbury Centre for Mental Health.

Savin-Baden (2004). *Problem-based Learning: Reason in Madness*? Keynote Speech. Problem-based Learning; A Quality Experience? University of Salford, 16th September 2004.

Schmidt, H.G. & Moust, J.H.C. (2000). Factors affecting small group tutorial learning: a review of research. In D. H. Evensen & C. E. Hmelo (eds) *Problem based learning: a research perspective on learning interactions*. Mahwah, NJ: Lawrence Erlbaum.

Scoggins, J. & Winter, R. (1999). "the patchwork text": a coursework format for education as critical understanding. *Teaching in Higher Education, 4*(4), 485–499.

UKCC (1999). *Fitness for Practice*. London: UKCC.

Wilkie, K. & Burns, I. (2003). *Problem-Based Learning: a handbook for nurses, Houndsmill*. Palgrave Macmillan: Basingstoke.

Wilkie, K. (2004). Becoming facilitative: shifts in lecturer's approaches to facilitating problem based learning. In: Baden, M. S. & Wilkie, K. (eds), *Challenging research in problem based learning*. Maidenhead: Open University Press.

Wood, S. (2005). The experiences of a group of pre-registration mental health nursing students. *Nurse Education Today, 25*, 189–196.

CHAPTER 21

Using Problem-based Learning in Mental Health Nurse Education

**Paul Bickerstaffe, Ben Hannigan, Steve Wood
and Norman Young**

INTRODUCTION

As Carol Cooper and Sue Gunstone observe in their contribution to this book, the use of problem-based learning (PBL) as an educational tool to encourage students to think like mental health nurses in clinical practice is well recognised. Developing the necessary critical thinking skills to make sound clinical decisions is a prerequisite of producing a competent and capable practitioner. The ability to work effectively as part of a team is also seen to be of great importance. The success of PBL in achieving these goals depends on a range of factors.

This chapter will focus on the following issues:

- the development, refinement and use of **PBL trigger** materials;
- approaches to **working with students**;
- **the student experience;**
- the incorporation of PBL into **assessment strategies**.

In focusing on these four key issues we draw on our experiences of introducing PBL into a module followed by pre-registration mental health nursing students at the School of Nursing and Midwifery Studies in Cardiff University. This module is taken by students in their third and final year of preparation, and aims to develop skills and knowledge for practice in community mental health care settings. The module runs over a 14-week period, of which the first eight are university-based. In the remaining six weeks students work with mentors located in working age or older adult community mental health teams (CMHTs).

Teaching Mental Health. Edited by Theo Stickley and Thurstine Basset.
Copyright © 2007 John Wiley & Sons, Ltd.

PBL is a major part of our approach to learning and teaching in the first eight weeks of this module. Four PBL "cycles" have been developed, each spanning a two-week period. Trigger material presented to students at the start of each cycle relates to the care of a fictitious new user of community mental services and his family. Cycle one introduces students to "Peter". Every fortnight students receive new information about Peter and his and his family's needs. Over eight weeks Peter's story evolves, with students being exposed to scenarios of growing complexity. For each cycle students work in groups to generate answers to the questions:

- what do we know?
- what do we need to know?
- how will we find out what we need to know?

At the end of each fortnightly cycle students present the fruits of their work together, and are ready to begin the PBL process once more with the presentation of additional trigger information to start the next cycle.

Between triggers the students are given time to research the PBL scenario, and to participate in lectures and skills training associated with the topic exemplified in the trigger material. Some sessions are delivered through computer-assisted learning, in which materials are linked to a central set of web pages, which bring together the module timetable, PBL triggers and PBL guidance.

PBL TRIGGERS

PBL begins with the presentation of stimulus materials to students. Materials are intended to provoke critical and creative thinking, and can come in a variety of forms. They should always, however, appear real to the student, and reflect as closely as possible the types of scenarios encountered in actual nursing practice (Wilkie & Burns, 2003). Careful construction of triggers can also encourage students to consider information from a number of different perspectives. For example, video clips of role-played team discussions or encounters between practitioners and service users, or authentically produced referral and other letters and associated documents, can expose students to the insights of workers from a variety of disciplines and to the experiences of service users and their carers.

Replicating the real world of community mental health practice authentically has been one of the aims of our module. The cycles of constructing, testing and re-engineering our web, our computer aided learning packages and our professionally produced video material to support our PBL activities has been an exhaustive process. The resultant product starts with PBL cycle 1, which comprises a letter from a GP followed by a video clip of this new referral being discussed in the context of a multidisciplinary CMHT meeting. As many community mental health nurses can testify, letters from GPs to CMHT workers can be short, leaving practitioners with a considerable task in terms of information-gathering. Our trigger letter introducing Peter aims to replicate this, as is demonstrated here:

Box 21.1   Trigger Referral Letter

Oak Tree Surgery
Oak Tree Lane
Cardiff
CF1 4AB

Central Cardiff Community Mental Health Team
Beech Drive
Cardiff
CF1

October 31, 2005

Dear Colleagues

Peter Robson d.o.b. 21/09/75
3 Urban Mansions, Cardiff, CF2 4TG

I saw Peter in surgery two weeks ago, and again yesterday. He is under stress having lost his job five months ago. I think he is depressed, and I have started him on fluoxetine 20 mg daily. His wife came with him for his last appointment, and she is worried about her husband. Apparently he has been behaving unusually for some time. Sometimes Mr Robson's behaviour frightens his children.

Please could you arrange to see this gentleman and advise.

Yours sincerely

Dr A.B. Brown MB ChB MRCGP

The information we provide to students at this point is purposefully "ill-structured" (Kanter, 1998). Having read the trigger referral letter reproduced here and digested the role-played team discussion, students' options for action are not predetermined. This, of course, is analogous to the kind of situations community practitioners often find themselves in.

WORKING WITH STUDENTS

PBL is in line with an androgogical approach to student learning. Students are regarded as active participants, rather than passive recipients, in the learning process. As we have found, this can be a challenge, particularly for students used to more traditional approaches to learning. It needs to be acknowledged that students require both support and guidance. As the unfamiliar is often viewed with varying degrees of anxiety and scepticism, before embarking on PBL students need to be clear what PBL is and why it is being used. To this end, we have found it useful prior to the commencement of our PBL cycles to facilitate an orientating session to explain the philosophy behind, and the process of, PBL, and the expectations this style of learning places upon students. One approach we have used here has been to turn "finding out about PBL" itself into a PBL-style problem, and to support students' own explorations of the processes and aims of PBL.

We have also found that, if effective learning relationships are to be established, an early opportunity is needed for students to air their expectations of lecturers. It is crucial at this stage that students are given the space to raise any concerns they may have, and to clarify any immediate issues related to the PBL process. Mutually agreed ground rules can usefully flow from discussions of this type, addressing areas such as punctuality, attendance, commitment and participation, and the respecting of individual views and opinions. However, our experiences also suggest that it is continuous lecturer support throughout the PBL process, which is of critical importance. One-off lecturer input is insufficient; the development and maintenance of effective facilitative relationships over time is crucial.

As Carol Cooper and Sue Gunstone in their chapter state, much of the PBL literature points to the role of the lecturer as that of a *facilitator* in the learning process. However, little has been written about what such a role might actually entail. Without further clarification, "facilitation" has the potential to be interpreted in a variety of ways. The amount of guidance, direction and information provided to students inevitably varies from lecturer to lecturer. Conversely, the demands placed on lecturers can vary widely from group to group. This appears largely dependant on whether or not students have had previous experience of PBL, but also on their preferred learning style. It is therefore imperative from the outset that all lecturers involved in the PBL process come to a general agreement on what the role of the facilitator constitutes. In our module we have also taken practical steps to maximise the chances of effective facilitator/student relationships developing by timetabling agreed "stock take" sessions where groups of students report back on work in progress in the company of a member of the module teaching and facilitation team.

One issue centres on whether or not lecturers should be regarded as content experts (Johnston & Tinning, 2001). Most nursing departments will be home to staff with a broad range of expertise able to illuminate most, if not all, of the themes dealt with in PBL cycles. Utilising the specific knowledge and skills of individuals within a department can assist students to explore issues in greater depth. In our module, for example, as the story of "Peter" and his family unfolds a new issue emerges centred on Peter's use of drugs. Part of our facilitation at this point is directed at encouraging students to make contact with a Consultant Nurse member of our department with specific expertise and responsibilities in the substance misuse area. It is also worth noting that the research suggests lecturers who share their clinical experiences are viewed favourably by students, as this helps them to relate theory to clinical practice (Pang et al., 2002). As nursing practice, and the context in which it takes place, is constantly changing it is important for university-based lecturers to be aware of their own limitations, particularly if they have been out of clinical practice for an extended period. Accessing practising nurses, and other healthcare professionals, who have up-to-date knowledge and experience should be encouraged. Pointing students in the right direction, in order that they can access specialist knowledge, enables them to base their learning within the context of current, local healthcare service provision.

Another key issue we have encountered is the role of teaching staff in managing the dynamics within groups. Part of the philosophy underlying PBL is that students can learn a great deal from the *process* as well as the content. Naturally, the aim is to make this a positive learning experience. Therefore, helping to resolve group relationship issues and problems that arise from group working is an important part of the facilitator role. In our experience, common issues causing conflict within groups are lack of student commitment, poor attendance and 'bossy' individuals. As Wray et al. (2004) observe, difficulties of this type are often part and parcel of the real-life PBL experience. It is thus important that teaching staff are aware of potential difficulties associated with student group dynamics, and can identify when intervention is needed. We have found that, in all groups, there are always likely to be teething problems. If difficulties are persistent and significant, and groups are unable to resolve these internally, then teaching staff may need to appropriately intervene. As a large amount of group work is done without direct observation or supervision, opportunities to identify problems associated with group functioning may be limited. The ability of teaching staff to establish open and trusting relationships with groups, so that students feel confident enough to express their concerns, is thus paramount.

Resolving problems can be both difficult and time-consuming. Nevertheless, if students are to gain a positive experience from the PBL process problems need to be dealt with sensitively and effectively. Minor issues can often be resolved by reiterating the ground rules initially agreed between staff and students prior to commencing PBL. However, issues such as persistent non-attendance pose particular difficulties, and in our experience are usually coupled with a lack of group participation and commitment. It is difficult to deal with these issues face-to-face if individuals are not attending. We have, on occasion, elected to contact students by post reminding them of the importance of attending and participating. It may sometimes be appropriate to engage directly with individual students to both ascertain reasons for non-participation and to negotiate solutions.

Monitoring functioning of groups is a major challenge. Ideally, each PBL group would be facilitated by the same lecturer throughout. In reality, lecturers often facilitate a number of groups simultaneously, and in many cases (as in our module) facilitation is carried out by teams of lecturers. It is therefore imperative that team members communicate regularly to ensure effective monitoring and management of groups. If resources permit, a second lecturer, acting as an observer, can be helpful in monitoring group dynamics. Providing students with accurate and constructive feedback on how they are progressing as a group can improve their experience. Furthermore, hypothesising that their group interactions are a mirror of team processes in clinical practice has been a valuable source of student learning (Hartley, 1997).

THE STUDENT EXPERIENCE

Despite a burgeoning PBL literature relatively little is known about the experience of students (Savin-Baden, 2000). Whilst positive feedback can help support the continued use of PBL, particular attention also needs to be paid to negative student experiences. In Savin-Baden's view, however, reports of negative aspects of PBL are largely missing from the literature. Reactions from students to the PBL experience are likely to reflect personal predilections and preferred learning styles; PBL can never please all students all of the time. However, much can be done in the light of student evaluations to make the experience of PBL a positive and productive one for the majority of students.

Evaluating the student experience has been a key part of our approach to the incorporation of PBL in our community mental health care module. For example, one of the specific evaluation exercises we have used is a card sort technique. Here, students are invited to write down anonymously aspects of the module which they would change, and aspects which they would keep. Single items are written on single sheets of card, with collation of students' responses being followed by an impromptu content analysis of items and a roundtable discussion.

Students we have worked with have given a wide variety of reactions in their card sort evaluations, as have other groups of students whose views have been reported elsewhere (see for example: Wray et al., 2004). These range from PBL as being highly beneficial and useful, through to PBL being a waste of time and an excuse for lecturers not to teach. Our students have sometimes questioned the timing of our introduction of PBL, or have commented on the amount of effort required relative to the effort needed for other types of learning activity. In the light of our and our students' experiences, there does appear to be a case to have PBL running throughout the duration of courses rather than just in specific modules. Many of our final year students have told us that PBL would have been more beneficial had it been introduced at a much earlier stage in their education.

Whenever and wherever PBL is introduced in mental health nursing courses, if it is the first time students have been exposed to this approach apprehension is likely to remain. Often it is only afterwards that students reflect back on their engagement with PBL as a positive learning experience. We recall, for example, a student who had completed her community mental health care module with us giving an account of a real-life practice experience almost exactly mirroring events explored in one of our PBL triggers. Our experience confirms, though, that groups of students who have experienced PBL early in their courses seem more at ease than those exposed to it only in their final year. This is supported by the evaluation comments of many of our students.

Students may feel particularly comfortable with what they are used to: being taught didactically by someone with perceived expert knowledge. The shift to a more active learning role, requiring a different type of intellectual exertion, does not appeal to everyone. Add to this the uncertainty created by presenting complex and ill-defined scenarios and you have, potentially, a recipe for student anxiety and confusion. However, creating feelings of uncertainty and challenging students to formulate responses in conditions characterised by the possession of only partial information and a lack of certainty is part and parcel of the PBL process. Students often seek reassurance that they are on the right track. The role of teaching staff then may be to support students and to draw analogies with the uncertainties inherent in clinical practice. Lecturers might also use these opportunities to emphasise the supportive function of clinical supervision for practitioners. Feedback from students indicates that lecturers who are sensitive to the concerns of their students and offer support and guidance in this way are more highly valued than those whose approach is more *laissez faire*.

In recognition that different students have different learning styles, many modules and courses making use of PBL use this approach alongside other, more traditional, teaching methods. Our module is a hybrid example of this type. Whilst PBL is firmly embedded in our module delivery (and has now been incorporated into the module's assessment strategy), the recurring rhythms of our university-based weeks also include lead lectures to provide students with factual information, skills-based sessions to enhance clinical practice, journal clubs and talks from nurses in practice. Student evaluations suggest that incorporating more familiar teaching styles alongside PBL has been well received, and has provided some reassurance to students trying to remain on the right track in responding to PBL triggers.

Measuring the effectiveness accurately, or otherwise, of PBL from the students' perspective is particularly problematic. Their perception of PBL often changes greatly as they go through the process, and for some, changes only occur once the PBL process is complete. For most students, however, the PBL experience is a predominantly positive one. Even if they express anxieties and concerns at the outset, our experiences are that once they become familiar with the process most students evaluate PBL favourably by the end of their course. There is some anecdotal evidence to suggest that it is only when students go into clinical practice and come face-to-face with complex and ill-structured problems do they fully appreciate the value of PBL. This has been borne out for us during post-practice meetings with students, as exemplified by the student referred to above who spoke of practice scenarios closely mirroring the PBL scenarios she had previously grappled with. It is difficult to determine how long after engaging with PBL the benefits are likely to become apparent, although Wood (2005) suggests that a period of around a year after registration may be necessary to discover whether PBL has had an influence on former students' decision-making. Comprehensive evaluations of PBL, of a type which we have not so far attempted, could usefully collect data from students and former students at different points, both during and after participating in the PBL process. This suggests a need for further, good quality, research into the student experience and the outcomes of engaging in PBL.

ASSESSMENT STRATEGIES

During our early experiences of using PBL in our module, one consistent comment from students was that the effort expended and the learning gained was insufficiently reflected in the module-specific assessment. Taking the opportunity afforded by a curriculum-wide assessment review, we made the decision to construct a new assessment strategy linked to the PBL process. The linking of a traditional/summative assessment to PBL has been a major challenge. Immediate questions raised included, for example: how congruent would it be for a non-traditional teaching and learning approach, like PBL, to be linked to a traditional method of assessment? Two main issues occupied us: creating an assessment that reflected the underlying philosophy of PBL in relation to group working, but which was also able to assess the student as an individual; and encouraging students to be creative in pursuit of their own learning interests but still making sure that the module's learning outcomes were demonstrably met.

The emphasis on group cooperation and group learning is fundamental to the philosophy of PBL. Students are encouraged to share the factual knowledge they acquire, and in so doing develop the interpersonal skills necessary to work effectively as part of a team. Ultimately it is envisaged that these skills will transfer to the practice environment and be useful to students making the transition to full and valued members of the multi-disciplinary team. In the assessment guidelines provided to students we emphasised that an important aspect of the assignment we were asking them to complete was their demonstration of their ability to reflect on the process of PBL, as well as on the content of what they had learned. Students were asked to consider how they had developed personally and professionally from the experience. As a new type of assessment, unlike any previously engaged in during their education, students felt some considerable anxiety. PBL also became not just a learning activity, but an assessed set of tasks which, like all assignments, needed to be passed. We believed, however, that the PBL process would benefit from its linkage to a summative assessment, and would encourage greater participation on the part of less-engaged students. Surprisingly, however, the level of commitment still varied significantly from student to student.

There are a number of possible explanations for non-engagement, even where PBL is linked to formal assessments. Feedback from student evaluations suggested that, as this was the beginning of their final year, students' dissertations took precedence as this part of the whole-year assessment was to have more of an impact on overall degree classifications. Another factor identified by students continues to be the practical difficulty in physically meeting up to progress work due to students living and working in different locations. The availability of technological advances may help to resolve this as an issue in the future. In particular, the use of e-learning platforms may be beneficial, and indeed some members of our department have participated in technologically mediated PBL with other student groups in an attempt to facilitate interactions between geographically distant learners. Over-reliance on technology, however, runs the risk of detracting from the central PBL ingredient of working purposefully together and experiencing face-to-face group dynamics. Surprisingly, many students also still struggle with accessing and using technology; this emphasises the continued need to focus on learning, rather than on technology for technology's sake, in course design (Centre for Studies in Advanced Learning Technology, Lancaster University, 2001).

As the level of commitment shown by students continued to vary, anxiety, and sometimes animosity, emerged within groups where members feared that non-participation could adversely affect the grades awarded to those committed to the PBL process. Our response included attempting to allay these concerns by offering reassurance that the difficulties encountered in groups, and student reflections on these, could be usefully incorporated into summative assessments and be used to generate valuable insights for future use in similar situations.

Our second area of concern in designing a PBL-oriented assessment strategy was to strike the balance between encouraging, and valuing, student creativity and ensuring that module learning outcomes were being met. Students have asked the question, "Am I including the right factual information?" In attempting to achieve this balance our assignment guidelines were made deliberately vague about the actual content expected of students. We clearly hoped that students would be able to use their initiative to explore issues which they felt were relevant. However, a dilemma exists between encouraging students to be self-directed in their learning and seeking out information relevant to their learning needs, and ensuring that they focus on the key issues which will help them to resolve the problems posed by the PBL triggers and achieve prescribed learning outcomes. Students want to know whether or not they are including pertinent information, as they are being summatively assessed.

Guiding students in their assessment preparation and clarifying questions raised has, again, been an issue for us as facilitators to address. As a team we were of the opinion that for students to perceive PBL as a positive experience they needed a significant degree of support with their assignment preparation. We have thus been relatively proactive, with one of us (PB) writing and sharing with students his version of producing a reflective PBL assessment of the type required. The intention here was that this would reassure students that this was a doable assignment, and that, as a new form of assessment, this would clarify expectations for the lecturers marking submitted work. Initial impressions are that it has achieved both of these objectives. Students were reassured that this form of assessment would not disadvantage them, even if their PBL group had experienced difficulties with regard to variable levels of commitment amongst individual members. The marking team also gained a clearer idea on what to expect and how to apply the marking criteria to the assignment.

CONCLUSION

In this chapter we have drawn on our experiences of introducing PBL into a module followed by third year pre-registration mental health nursing students at Cardiff University to address four key issues: the development of PBL triggers; working with students; the student experience; and the incorporation of PBL into assessment strategies. PBL, we have found, can be hard work. For students and lecturers used to more traditional approaches to learning and teaching, the process-based philosophy of PBL can be testing. Using PBL means slipping out of comfortable roles, and embracing considerable uncertainty. Despite the challenges, we remain, though, convinced of the value of problem-based learning in developing creative and context-aware mental health practitioners.

REFERENCES

Centre for Studies in Advanced Learning Technology, Lancaster University (2001). *Networked Learning in Higher Education Project: effective networked learning in higher education. Notes and guidelines*. Lancaster: Lancaster University.

Hartley P. (1997). *Group communication*. London: Routledge.

Kanter S.L. (1998). Fundamental concepts of problem-based learning for the new facilitator, *Bulletin of the Medical Library Association*, *86*(3), 391–395.

Johnston A. & Tinning R. (2001). Meeting the challenge of problem-based learning: developing the facilitators. *Nurse Education Today*, *21*, 161–169.

Pang S.M.C., Wong T.K.S, Dorcas A., Lai C.K.Y., Lee R.L.T., Wai-man L., Mok E.S.B. & Wong F.K.Y. (2002). Evaluating the use of developmental action inquiry in constructing a problem-based learning curriculum for pre-registration nursing education in Hong Kong: a student perspective. *Journal of Advanced Nursing*, *40*(2), 230–241.

Savin-Baden M. (2000). *Problem-based learning in higher education: untold stories*. Buckingham: Open University Press.

Wilkie K. and Burns I. (2003). *Problem-based learning: a handbook for nurses*. Basingstoke: Palgrave.

Wood S. (2005). The experiences of a group of pre-registration mental health nursing students. *Nurse Education Today*, *25*, 189-196.

Wray J., Oliver K., Payne J. & Prince C. (2004). A view from the field: some of the realities of "doing problem based learning". *Nurse Education in practice*, *4*, 151–153.

CHAPTER 22

Teaching and Learning Reflective Practice

Dawn Freshwater

INTRODUCTION

It is over two decades since Donald Schön developed the idea that reflection is a way in which professionals can bridge the theory-practice gap. This was based on the ability of practitioners to uncover knowledge about their practice through reflecting in and on action. Since then reflective practice has become very much a focus of teaching and learning across the health care professions. It is assumed that effective health care research, education, practice and leadership are grounded in the complexity of human relationships and therefore require systematic and careful thinking for successful and therapeutic outcomes. This chapter outlines the methods and processes of reflective practice in training and learning, examining in detail the strategies available to promote deep reflection on action and reflection in action.

REFLECTION, REFLECTIVE PRACTICE AND CRITICAL REFLECTION: DEFINING THE TERMS

One of the major challenges for any professional interested in reflection and reflective practice is that of defining the terms. Early attempts at defining reflection drew upon the work of philosophers, one of the earliest being posited by John Dewey (1933, p. 84). Dewey defined reflection as the "active, persistent and careful consideration of any belief or supposed form of knowledge in the light of the grounds that support it and the further conclusions to which it tends". Subsequently many other writers have followed on with their own definitions; these nearly always linking reflection to learning from experience. Over twenty years ago Boyd and Fales (1983) described reflection as an internal learning process in which an issue of concern is examined. Thus, meaning is created and clarified in terms of self, resulting in a changed conceptual perspective. In this sense the individual may come to see the world differently and as a result of new insights can, in turn, come to act differently. The pivotal part of this definition is that it involves a change in the self; "in other

Teaching Mental Health. Edited by Theo Stickley and Thurstine Basset.
Copyright © 2007 John Wiley & Sons, Ltd.

words it is not just individual behaviour that has changed but also the individual, hinting at the transformational potential of reflective practice" (Freshwater, 1998, 2000, 2002, 2006).

Johns (1995, p. 24) provided a slightly different perspective when over a decade ago he defined reflection as: "the practitioner's ability to access, makes sense of and learn through work experience, to achieve more desirable, effective and satisfying work". For Johns the issue of concern is one that Boyd and Fales (1983) allude to, and comes from the experience of conflict or cognitive dissonance in practice. Interestingly this was also the thrust of the work of Arygris and Schön (1974) who discussed the notion of action theories, positing that all human actions reflect ideas, models or some kind of theoretical notion of purpose and intention and ways in which these purposes and intentions can be executed (Freshwater, 1998; Freshwater, 1999; Freshwater, 2000; Rolfe et al., 2001). Agyris and Schön (1974) also noted that people often say one thing and do another, hence although individuals have a personal theory, when it is operationalised, there is often a contradiction. Agyris and Schön (1974) took their ideas further, developing the concept of espoused theories, (the stated purpose or intention), and theories in use, (the attempt to put stated intentions or purpose into action). Hence, espoused theories are those to which individuals claim allegiance: theories in use are those theories that are present when action is executed. Human action therefore is never atheoretical or accidental, even if the theory involved in the action is implicit or tacit. Thus it could be argued that reflection is a way of redeeming theories in use which may be tacit and that practice, in this sense, is theory generating (Greenwood, 1998; Freshwater & Avis, 2004).

REFLECTION AS A TEACHING AND LEARNING TOOL

Reflection has been, and continues to be, a significant tool for facilitating teaching and learning. Donald Schön (1983) did much to surface the role of reflection in professional education, describing, as he did, the limitations of knowledge derived from technical rationality for practice. He went on to argue that practitioners have difficulty in utilising this type of knowledge as it is generated in situations that are context free, thereby ignoring the context of the actual practice situation, drawing attention to the fact that practitioners do not as a rule make decisions based on technical rationality, but rather on experience.

Schön identified two main aspects of reflective practice, these being reflection on action and reflection in action. Reflection on action is a retrospective process and as such is the thinking that occurs after an incident with the aim of making sense and using process outcomes to influence future practice. Reflection in action relates to the intuitive art of thinking on one's feet. Several writers have adopted and developed some of Schön's earlier ideas linking them to reflexivity, reflection before action and the theory practice gap, however, his work has also been subject to some heavy criticism since its publication, mainly with regard to the concept of reflection in action, which it has been suggested, needs further clarification (Day, 1993; Eraut, 1995). Eraut (1995), for example, made a comprehensive critique of Schön's work, arguing that some of his work was unclear. Whilst Eraut might be justified in pointing out the lack of clarity (and perhaps reflection) in Schön's early works, it should of course be noted that these are Eraut's own reflections, which are also open to further refinement and clarification.

Freshwater (2002) links the practice of reflection to an essential skill for mental health practitioners, that of self-awareness. Referring to the therapeutic relationship she comments that "reflection helps the practitioner to reform their identity through being in relation with themselves, the patients and others in contrast to having an identity that is formed purely by their surroundings".

In 1981 Mezirow's work directly linked levels of reflection to approaches and modes of education. He proposed a continuum of reflective ability that began with consciousness and moved to critical consciousness and eventually towards perspective transformation through teaching and learning experiences. There are many examples of educationalists and theorists who have adopted Mezirow's (1981) work in their own explorations of reflectivity, Paget (2001) for instance in his study of practitioners' views of reflective practice's impact upon clinical outcomes, identified degrees of perspective transformation across a number of practitioners. Other researchers have been interested in the role of deep learning to facilitate perspective transformation.

Greenwood (1998) explored this idea in depth, presenting two types of framework existing in relation to the process of reflection; these being single and double loop learning. Developing the concept of single and double loop learning from the work of Arygris and Schön (1974) she notes that the reflective practitioner may respond to a reflection on a situation in two ways. On the one hand the practitioner may search for an alternative means to achieve the same ends, the actions are changed in order to achieve the same outcomes, Greenwood terms single loop learning. Alternatively, the practitioner may respond not only by exploring alternative means to achieve the intended outcomes, but may also examine the appropriateness of the chosen ends. Thus double loop learning: "involves reflection on values and norms and, by implication, the social structures which were instrumental in their development and which render them meaningful" (Greenwood, 1998' p. 1049).

This could be interpreted to mean that the practitioner is actively engaged in examining themselves and themselves in relation to other, in this instance the social structure within which they operate. This type of reflection requires a great deal of self-monitoring and discipline, but encourages learner autonomy by facilitating in the learner the ability to check their own development.

Elsewhere, (2005) I also note the differing levels of reflection that can be enhanced or inhibited through the teaching and learning processes, distinguishing features of reflection, critical reflection and reflexivity. Simply stated this describes reflection as a focussed way of thinking about practice, whatever that practice is. Practices are subject to a degree of scrutiny and examination with the aim of achieving a deeper awareness and understanding of that practice. Critical reflection differs in that the practitioner is not only thinking about their current practices, they are also subjecting the way they are thinking about practice to a degree of interrogation. In other words, the practitioner is thinking about how they are thinking, whilst simultaneously thinking about their practice. Our ways of thinking have been heavily socialised not only by professional training and academic learning, but also by political, ethical, historical and cultural traditions. As such, our thinking is both constructed by our contextual position, and as we exist in that contextual position, we also contribute to constructing it. Having an awareness of this meta-level of contextual influence on both our thinking and our practices and bringing it to bear through reflective processes is termed reflexivity. (Reflexivity is both a method of collecting data about practice and a research method in its own right). In this sense, Freshwater and Rolfe (2001) differentiate reflexivity as a turning back on itself and a type of meta-reflection, emphasising its critical nature of unsettling previously held assumptions to gain new awareness.

It is not the intention here to describe and perpetuate hierarchies of reflection, for all levels of reflection are dependant on the others, and represent a cyclical and repetitive movement, as opposed to a logical, linear progression through stages. It might seem obvious to point out, but deep learning can only be made known by coming to the surface. Similarly, reflection and critical reflection are precursors to reflexivity and as such are interdependent. It would seem preferable to advocate an approach to reflection that provides a structure within which structures can be deconstructed. One such framework is that of transformational learning based in experiential processes.

EXPERIENTIAL LEARNING

Experiential learning is firmly rooted in the humanistic school of psychology; John Dewey (1933) for example suggested that life experiences were the foundation for the learning process; whilst Rogers (1983) believed that all meaningful learning took place through experience. McLeod (1996) captures this point saying: "rom a humanistic point of view, learning is always experiential in nature and is always a process that occurs in a relational context" (p. 143). Experiential learning can be described as a way of learning as doing (Dowd, 1983). Heron (1982) defines the experiential learning technique as one that involves the whole person and his experience to a greater or lesser degree. Learning experiences are designed to be a process of personal discovery, encouraging the learners to inquire as to how they and others have come to know caring and the caring practices of nurses. However, not all learning involves learning to do. Similarly, Rogers (1977) argued that experiential methods of teaching were particularly meaningful for adults, who may be impatient of learning that is detached from reality. Burnard (1990) identifies three main tenets of experiential learning, personal experience, reflection and transformation of knowledge and meaning. Experiential learning is considered to be an effective means of educating health professionals and there are many examples and advocates of its use. Health care is a practice based discipline and therefore learning by experience is an integral part of learning about that practice. This integration of this approach to teaching and learning has necessitated a radical alteration in the conception of what constitutes education. Much of the learning about what it means to be a practitioner occurs informally when students identify with all the attitudes and practices displayed by tutors and other practitioners. Through experiential learning, the roles of the teacher/facilitator and the student become less differentiated with the learner being actively encouraged to take responsibility for their own learning through the process of reflection.

Nearly 15 years ago Burnard (1992) reported the findings of a research study, highlighting that experiential learning is active rather than passive, involves personal learning and requires reflection. Hence experiential learning is not simply learning by doing, for knowledge at this level remains public. In addition there needs to be interaction both with the material and the inner world (private domain) of the learner through reflection in order to make the learning personal. As Burnard (1992) comments the key issue is to remember to reflect, drawing upon Reyner (1984), he adds that it is easy to let life occur and to not notice what is happening. Reflection calls for a conscious decision to notice what is happening and to study what is happening to you. Knowles (1990) mooted that activity that involves personal learning involves the self. Where there is a change to something personal, the sense of who one is, is also changed. In Burnard's study (1992) two outcomes of experiential learning dominated the findings; these were the development of self-awareness and the development of interpersonal skills. The idea of self-awareness links directly with reflection, any shift in self-awareness necessitates even a small amount of inward reflection. In other words the development of self-awareness is an active and reflective process.

Experiential learning can be felt to be threatening; it has already been noted in this study that experiential learning causes discomfort and challenge. In a further study, it was found that one of the reasons for students finding experiential learning threatening was that it was "personal" as opposed to the more impersonal approaches such as lectures. Exploration of experiences and connected feelings is potentially an anxiety provoking situation and students can sometimes feel awkward and unsure of what is expected of them. Exploration of feelings can also be threatening for the teacher. Students are liable to make discoveries for which the teacher had not planned and high levels of emotion can be expressed. Hence, a certain level of anxiety and discomfort is likely to be felt by both the student and the teacher. Although it could be argued that discomfort is a precursor to growth.

Joyce (1984) poses the question how can the learner be made comfortable and uncomfortable simultaneously. The work of Heron (1982) implies that participating in experiential learning should be voluntary and states that the student should be allowed to withdraw from the situation at any time. However, this is not always an easy opportunity for the learner to afford, students may feel the need to conform to the group norm and as such feel oppressed. For students to feel comfortable enough to make these sorts of uncomfortable choices there needs to be a climate of trust, support and acceptance. Knowles (1990) identifies a learning climate as one in which learners feel physically at ease, psychologically accepted and respected and where there is allowance for freedom of expression without fear of ridicule. Various methods have been used to create this relaxed atmosphere. Exercises such as "warm up" exercises and "icebreakers" are commonly employed, although some students find these "relaxing" exercises threatening in themselves.

Given that much of the literature gives the impression that it is the teaching method that is responsible for success, there is little wonder that methods of teaching and learning are a matter for concern and debate. The role of the teacher in experiential and reflective learning is that of facilitator. It has been stated that all that is needed to facilitate learning is human experience itself. Facilitation, defined here, as making things possible for another through a process which makes it simpler for the individual to achieve their goal makes specific demands upon the facilitator, namely that the facilitator requires a high level of self-awareness gained through ongoing self-exploration and reflective practice. The facilitator is also encouraged to be congruent at all times, implying that the facilitator is expected to match their own words with their actions.

Kagan (1985) points out that unease and anxiety in the facilitator – which may be caused through lack of experience – could possibly lead to an atmosphere of discomfort. Others would argue that unless there is some unease and anxiety in the facilitator then learning will not be maximised (Joyce, 1984). It could be said that whether or not the facilitator is anxious is immaterial, what matters is that the facilitator is aware of and congruent with how they are feeling.

There is a wealth of literature to support the many practical ways of working with experience to facilitate reflective practice – role-play, for example, is felt to give immediate and long term benefits bringing together thinking, feeling and doing; whereas interpersonal process recall provides an opportunity for both reflection on action and reflection in action. Whatever modality is utilised, the facilitator encourages a climate of safety in the group to give support and is seen to be available. They are required to know their own limits in order to maintain an overview of what is learnt. Any number of experiences can be facilitated through such medium as theatre, art, photo language technique, writing, simulated clinical experience and role-play. The experience alone however is not sufficient and reflective practice is encouraged as a way of integrating the new experience with the past. This type of reflection requires a great deal of self-monitoring and discipline, but encourages learner autonomy by facilitating in the learner the ability to check their own development. Other ways of working with experience reflectively include discussion, critical incident analysis and brainstorming.

Reflective learning offers a way of accessing deeply embedded personal knowledge. Schön (1983) observed that thinking, via reflection, adds theory to the action whilst it is occurring, making theory and practice inseparable. In this form of learning both teacher and learner; student and clinician; professional and user can take the opportunity to learn and reflect together. In this way the focus of reflective learning is very much on praxis, whereby theory, practice and research are seen as inextricably linked and interdependent.

Reflective practice is crucial to the development of mental health practice and is a key interpersonal skill for mental health practitioners. The development of interpersonal skills is a strong component of many healthcare curricula, however, it if often taught as *content,* rather than experienced as *process.* Good patient care hinges on the quality of the practitioner-patient communication, where a deeper encounter is seen to lead to better practice of skills and where better practice of skills will lead to a deeper encounter. Interpersonal skills development can be facilitated in a number of ways that emphasise both process and content. Often in interpersonal skills, specifically on therapeutic communication skills training there is extensive use of exercises in trios with an observer and sometimes in where an observer cannot be spared. Emphasis is on the importance of feedback and where an observer is present they provide direct feedback to the listener and the speaker, whilst avoiding being drawn into discussion of the speaker's subject or experience. Feedback should be specific and concrete; describing what is seen and heard. As the observer, it is important to sit close enough to hear and see, but out of eye contact with the other members of the trio. The task of the observer is to concentrate on what is happening between the listener and speaker rather than on the story. The feedback is important to the listener in developing their communication skills. Feedback is also offered with respect and openness and with a degree of reflection on the part of the observer.

Reflection can also be facilitated in groups using frameworks such as action learning (Freshwater et al, 2006) or Socratic dialogue, a process developed in Germany in the 1920's by Nelson (1987), and inspired by Socrates. Socrates proposed that important insights are not learnt from other people, rather he espoused that this type of knowledge is carried within and is experienced in everyday life. Socrates would use dialogue to attempt to awaken his scholars up to their tacit knowledge. Socratic dialogue is suitable as an experiential learning method as it attempts to impart to reasoning a practical form not by reading about issues that one is concerned with, but by reflecting upon them together with others. Boele (1997) suggests that: "Socratic dialogue puts into practice two devices of philosophy: "know thyself" and "dare to use your brain" (p. 49).

Reflective practice can be learnt through the process of keeping a journal, the benefits of which have been much extolled. Generally keeping a journal is seen to be advantageous to learning although not all students respond positively and in some cases procrastination prevails. Some structured models of reflection had been developed by way of providing a structure and format for those learners who find it hard to begin without some way of organising their thoughts (Rolfe et al., 2001). Although I personally believe that learners should be encouraged to use journals to reflect in their own style, whether this be structured or unstructured, other writers assert that the aims of keeping a journal need to be clear so as to clarify the purpose to the learner and for the organisation (Lyte & Thompson, 1990). Some of the aims included:

* facilitating reconciliation of theory-practice issues through exploration of applied theory to practice;
* to assist the development of the learner's personal growth through increasing self awareness in relation to patient and colleague interaction;
* to encourage the effective use of independent learning by stimulating motivation to set own learning objectives;
* to stimulate learning through analysis, discussion and documentation of critical incidents.

Reflective writing has the potential to stimulate both subjectivity and objectivity, enabling individuals to distance themselves from an experience whilst simultaneously reporting a subjective experience. Reflective writing also takes the individual deeper, under their own veneer, and additionally provides a forum for the individual to step forward and speak their voice. Vezeau (1994) confirms this stating: "it [writing] is my most political act" (p. 175).

Furthermore, the writing and narrating of stories is also closely linked to the development of consciousness through the art of reflection (Van Manen, 1990). Writing helps to capture events that may usually be lost in the mists of time. Reflecting on such events, the individual is able to plot their own developmental processes. In this way the journal can be used as both an assessment and evaluation instrument. This self-assessment and evaluation process is congruent with the concept of adult education and experiential learning.

SELF AWARENESS

Development of self-awareness is a vital part of any mental health practice and can be achieved through a variety of fora, some of which have already been mentioned. The mental health practitioner is expected to recognise their own personal values, beliefs and prejudices as well as their own emotional and physical needs. Distractions to being fully *present* with the user can come from the inner world of the practitioner as well as from external sources. They may appear in the form of prejudice, passing judgement, clashes of values or the nurse's own emotional needs. Developing self-awareness involves exploring one's own personal motivations, including the motivation for caring and choice of specialism, i.e. mental health. It is also closely linked to the skill of self-disclosure, which should be in the interests of helping the user/carer or colleague to achieve deeper self-understanding or to assist in self-exploration. Self-awareness enables the practitioner to be selective and appropriate in the use of self-disclosure.

Self-awareness also assists practitioners to monitor their levels of stress and coping, recognising when they are reaching their limits and when they need support. In addition it is a way of monitoring the need for further education and training, in this sense reflection leads to teaching and learning, which in turn leads to further reflection and sets up the dynamic cycle of lifelong learning. Being self-aware encourages the individual to be open to learning from the experience of others and to receiving constructive feedback on their own work in such arenas as clinical supervision.

PRESENCE

Being available or "presencing" is closely linked to the concepts of reflection and is a central tenet of the therapeutic relationship; it is partly developed through increasing and expanding self-awareness. As Buber notes: "In order to be able to go out to the other you must have the starting place, you must have been, you must be with yourself" (1958; p. 72). Presence, like authenticity, is not merely a sentimental attitude towards the patient, rather it "depends firmly and consistently on how the nurse conceives of human beings" (Freshwater 1999: p. 32). It is a way of being, rather than a technique that can be applied. Essentially presence is a gift of both time and self, articulated wonderfully by Kleiman who observes: "To alleviate aloneness, this is a most expensive gift. To give this gift of time, and presence in the patient's space, a person has to value the outcomes of relating" (2001, p. 162). Many authors link the notion of presence with that of reflection in action. Boykin (1998), for example, suggests that intentional and authentic presence involves a way of listening and communication that gives of oneself. She goes on to argue that presence requires practice, can grow through reflection in action, and heightens one's awareness of the moral nature of things.

There are a number of challenges that face the practitioner committed to authenticity, reflective practice and presence. These include organisational challenges (for example issues related to power dynamics and hierarchical structures); historical challenges (linked to the prevailing dominant discourses, in this case the medical model and positivistic science), and political challenges (related to the emerging policy initiatives and rationing of resources). Health care professions are currently facing a crisis of both retention and recruitment of staff, with many qualified professionals leaving their profession, frustrated by the barriers to providing good quality care and disillusioned by lack of resources. Challenges such as staff shortages (alongside other resource issues such as lack of privacy due to cramped conditions) militate against the development of meaningful therapeutic relationships, in which reflective skills can be honed, practised and reciprocated.

SUMMARY

Teaching and learning reflective practice is not simply a matter of outlining and imparting content to the learner. Reflection is a process that needs to be developed over time and in context; hence when teaching and learning the skills of reflection, the facilitator more often finds themselves in the position of teaching the student how to learn, rather then teaching content. The emphasis is on process rather than product, although of course, the skills of reflection and reflective practice produce their own outcomes. One of the functions of reflective practice is that of enabling the practitioner to identify their own professional development needs and translate these into action. This includes the identification of further training and education. Mental health practitioners wishing to learn, for example, counselling skills to complement their practice can embark upon training programmes to help them get started, and those practitioners already using counselling skills may find that they wish to refine and fine-tune their skills, or develop specialist-counselling skills.

Reflective practice provides a way for caring individuals to explore and confront their own caring beliefs and how these are executed in practice. Further, it is about transforming self and thereby caring in practice (Freshwater, 1999). That reflective practice involves a transformation of self means that it may represent a threat to many practitioners, who largely survive (understandably) by the defence of not allowing themselves to reflect too deeply about their own responses to patients. Caring inevitably evokes deep responses and there are times when defences are important, however, it is also helpful to be able to reflect upon the impact of those defences and to use them intentionally and deliberatively.

REFERENCES

Argyris, C. & Schön, D.A. (1974). *Theory in Practice: Increasing Professional Effectiveness.* Washington, DC: Jossey Bass.

Boele, D. (1997). The benefits of a Socratic dialogue or: Which results can we promise? *Inquiry XXVII*(3), 48–70.

Boyd, E. & Fales, A. (1983). Reflective learning: The key to learning from experience. *Journal of Humanistic Psychology, 23*(2), 99–117.

Boykin, A. (1998). Nursing as caring through the reflective lens. In Johns, C. and Freshwater, D. (eds) *Transforming Nursing through Reflective Practice.* Oxford: Blackwell Science.

Burnard, P. (1992). *Counselling: A guide to practice in nursing.* Oxford: Butterworth: Heinemann.

Burnard, P. (1990). *Learning Human Skills. An experiential guide for nurses.* 2nd edn. Oxford: Butterworth Heinemann.

Day, C. (1993). Research and the continuing professional development of teachers. An inaugural lecture. University of Nottingham: School of Education.

Dewey, J. (1933). *How we think: A restatement of the relation of reflective thinking to the education process.* Boston: Heath.

Dowd, C. (1983). Learning through Experience. *Nursing Times, 27,* 50–53.

Eraut, M.E. (1995). Schön shock: A case for reframing reflection-in-action? *Teachers and Teaching, 1,* 9–21.

Freshwater, D. (2005). The Poetics of Space: Researching the concept of spatiality through relationality. *Phychodynamic Practice, 11*(2), 177–188.

Freshwater, D. (2002). *Therapeutic Nursing. Improving patient care through reflective practice.* London: Sage.

Freshwater, D. (2000). *Transformatory learning in nurse education.* Portsmouth: Nursing Praxis International.

Freshwater, D. (1999). Communicating with self through caring: The student nurse's experience of reflective practice. *International Journal of Human Caring, 3*(3), 28–33.

Freshwater, D. (1998). From Acron to Oak Tree: A neoplatonic perspective of reflection. *Australian Journal of Holistic Nursing, 5*(2), 14–19.

Freshwater, D. Avis, M., (2004). Analysing interpretation and reinterpreting analysis. *Nursing Philosophy, 5,* 4–11.

Freshwater, D., Walsh, E. & Esterhuizen, P. (2006). Teaching and Facilitating Clinical Supervision. In Bishop, V. (ed.) *Clinical Supervision.* Basingstoke: Palgrave.

Freshwater, D. & Rolfe, G. (2001). Critical reflexivity: A politically and ethically engaged research method for nursing. *NTResearch, 6*(1), 526–537.

Greenwood, J. (1998). The role of reflection in single and double loop learning. *Journal of Advanced Nursing Practice, 27*(5), 1048–1053.

Heron, J. (1982). *Education of the affect. Human potential research project.* Guildford: University of Surrey.

Johns, C. (1995). Framing learning through reflection within Carper's fundamental ways of knowing in nursing. *Journal of Advanced Nursing, 22,* 226–234.

Joyce, B.R. (1984). Dynamic Disequilibrium: the intelligence of growth. *Theory into Practice, 23*(1), 26–34 Winter.

Kagan, C.M. (1985). *Interpersonal skills in nursing*. London: Croom Helm.

Kleiman, S. (2001). Josephine Paterson and Loretta Zderad's. Humanistic Nursing Theory with Clinical Applications. In Parker, M. (ed) *Nursing Theories and Nursing Practice*. Philadelphia: F. A. Davis, Ch. 12.

Knowles, M.S. (1990). *The adult leaner, a neglected species*. 4th edn. USA: Gulf.

Lyte, V.J. & Thompson, I.G. (1990). The diary as a formative teaching and learning aid incorporating means of evaluation and renegotiation of clinical learning objectives. *Nurse Education Today, 10*, 228–232.

McLeod, J. (1996). The Humanistic paradigm. In Woolfe, R. and Dryden, W. (eds) *Handbook of counselling psychology*. London: Sage, Ch. 3.

Mezirow, J. (1981). A critical theory of adult learning and education. *Adult Education. 32*, 3–24.

Rogers, C. (1983). *Freedom to Learn in the 80's*. Ohio: Charles Merrill.

Rogers, J. (1977). *Adults Learning*. Milton Keynes: Open University.

Rolfe, G. Freshwater, D. and Jasper, M. (2001). *Critical reflection for nurses and the caring professions: A users guide*. Basingstoke: Palgrave.

Schön, D. A. (1983). *The reflective practitioner*. London: Temple Smith.

Van Manen, M. (1990). *Researching lived experience*. New York: State University of New York Press.

Vezeau, T.M. (1994). Narrative inquiry in nursing. In Chinn, P. and Watson, J. (1994) (eds) *Art and Aesthetics in nursing*. New York: National League for Nursing Press.

CHAPTER 23

The Buzzing, Blooming Confusion of Clinical Practice: Preparing Mental Health Nurses to Generate Knowledge Within, From and For Practice

Líam MacGabhann and Chris Stevenson

THE PROBLEM OF EVIDENCE?

The last decade has seen fervent attempts to underpin health care practice through the dissemination of evidence based knowledge. Evidence based practice has become the new mantra of health care disciplines. What constitutes evidence is contested to some extent, but the Randomised Control Trial (RCT) reigns supreme in the evidence hierarchy. The obsession with the RCT, and its characteristics (objectivity, producing generalisable knowledge) permeates into other research approaches. Qualitative inquirers frequently try to justify their methodological stance with reference to the criteria for good quantitative research. In educational curricula, the influence of the evidence hierarchy is seen in the preference for teaching nurses about research based on philosophies of empiricism, positivism and post-positivism, which resonate with modernism or a technical rationality paradigm. The majority of teaching about qualitative research is about "mainstream" qualitative approaches, which incorporate some degree of "realism", that is the view that there is an external reality that can be captured at least in part or approximately. Thus, the influence of modernism exerts itself as these positions share the position that the research enterprise is separate from the subject of the research (Rolfe, 2006) at least to some degree. Research, from these modernist influenced positions, is still on or about practice rather than situated within it. It is still the

Teaching Mental Health. Edited by Theo Stickley and Thurstine Basset.
Copyright © 2007 John Wiley & Sons, Ltd.

researcher's interpretation that is fore grounded.[1] In effect, the research socialisation of nurses, in so far as it is effective at all, encourages nurses to think of research as exterior to their practice, rather than embedded in it; the source of generalisable evidence rather than practical knowledge.

Yet, the translation of modernist informed research knowledge into the practice setting is limited (Funk et al., 1995; Retsas, 2000; Rodgers, 2000; Parahoo, 2001; Pallen & Timmins, 2002) despite a significant investment in strategies to utilise it (Winch, Henderson et al., 2005). Knowledge constructed and developed by outsiders to the practice environment will not necessarily apply *in* practice (Meleis, 1991). Practical nurses recognise this themselves (Stevenson, 1996). Perhaps one of the greatest frustrations for nurses undergoing an educational process, is the mismatch between the knowledge learned and its perceived applicability or relevance to their practice. Rolfe (1996) argues that nursing is a micro practice where much of the generation of knowledge and change is situated between individual nurses and patients. If we accept this argument then it is unlikely that generalisable evidence based practice coming from a technical rationality paradigm will easily translate into nursing practice. If knowledge generation for practice continues to focus on or about nursing (Rolfe, 2006) rather than being embedded *within* practice, barriers to integrating research into practice are not likely to fall.

To summarise, the evidence-practice gap is understandable when research is seen as something "apart" from practice. "Detached researchers tend to produce detached evidence, and do not and cannot capture the 'reality' of nursing practices that are enacted in a context of continuous flux" (Stevenson, 2005, p. 197) – a buzzing, blooming confusion (Beckett 1957). The generation and interpretation of knowledge continues in one environment whilst its application is to occur in a very different environment often with alternate values systems and perceptions. Rorty notes that all "knowledge"[2] relies for its content and point on contexts of application and that when we generalise away from contexts of application in a search for generalities we end up with empty abstractions that do not guide our action at all.

This chapter has three function knowledge:

- to demonstrate that knowledge can be generated from practice and that the knowledge so produced is useful in engaging with the theory-practice gap for mental health nurses;
- to outline a practical inquiry approach that illustrates how the erosion of researcher and researched can be achieved and knowledge from (Shotter 1993) practice be generated in the form of a practical theory;
- to suggest a four pronged educational methodology for preventing the preferencing of any single methodology (approach to knowing) and the privileging of some knowledge over other knowledge.

KNOWLEDGE FROM PRACTICE – "KNOWING OF THE THIRD KIND"

Of course it is not true that because there is so little evidence based knowledge utilised in nursing practice that nursing care is therefore uninformed and useless. The range of

---

[1] There are, of course, some exceptions. See Reed (2003) for nursing research which attempts to present a multivocal analysis of practice.

[2] As knowledge is a contested concept, at least for Rorty, it is placed in inverted commas.

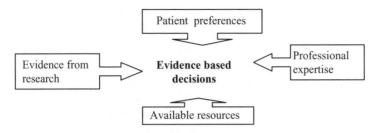

Figure 23.1 *Source*: Cullum, N. (2004). Centre for Evidence Based Nursing. University of York.

understanding incorporated into practice is wide, and evidence based decisions incorporate more than just gold standard research evidence. The practice environment itself plays a significant role in this broader perhaps more effective approach to evidence based practice (see Figure 23.1).

Stevenson (2005) has explored the value of knowing from being in practice, that is the generation of situated knowledge or what Shotter (1993) refers to as knowledge of the third kind. This is knowledge that both comes from and is indispensable to practical functioning (see Figure 23.1).

THE CONTEXT WHERE KNOWLEDGE IS GENERATED AND APPLIED

Since pre-registration and much postgraduate nurse education has moved into higher institutions there has been an unravelling of what was arguably the integration of teaching, learning (knowledge acquisition) and practice within one social system, that of health care provision. One aspect of this move has been the contemporaneous broadening of educational curricula and a clearer focus on learning about evidence based knowledge *about* practice. Situated, inherited or local knowledge has become "second best".

A further aspect was the new systems that nurse teacher/tutors/lecturers found themselves in and the requisite conduct expected. New status was associated with lecturing from the university above that of clinical teachers who chose to remain in the practice areas (Malik, 1993). The practice remit of educators that were delivering most of the emerging curricula was diminishing to nothing more than a liaison or student support role (Murphy, 2000). In essence, the educators were placed in a position similar to that of the detached practice researcher. In recognition of this role deficiency, government policies and professional board requirements began to insist that lecturers should have a more proactive practice role (DoH, 1989; UKCC, 1994). The lecturer practitioner role evolving in the 1980's (Vaughan, 1987) was one that was expected to bring back the integration of knowledge/theory and practice into nurse education (Rhead & Strange, 1996). The route to achieving the desired outcome was not clearly spelt out; for example, whether the lecturer practitioner was to use close practice contact to guide her/him to clinically relevant topics; whether the lecturer practitioner was to be the bridge for knowledge transfer from the academy to the practice area. Unsurprisingly, the initiative has met with limited success. An alternative idea is to re-situate inquiry, knowledge production and learning back into practice contexts.

PRACTICAL INQUIRY AND PRACTICAL KNOWLEDGE

In practical inquiry,[3] (see Figure 23.2) the inquiry process is collective and collaborative. Dewey (1929) noted that we all have an experimental attitude, a desire to know more about our world. We inquire *into* situations (Dewey, 1938), often those where we identify a problem or a need to improve; for example, how a nursing team might improve the involvement of people who use services. Inquiry involves looking at elements of the situation and their relationships in order to develop "thick" description that leads to a practical theory – a term coined by Shotter (1984) and taken up by Cronen (1995, 2001). Cronen (2001) sees practical theories as a set of:

- theoretical principles, for example, psychoanalytic approaches to analysing why nurses avoid dying patients (Menzies Lyth, 1959);
- definitions, for example, what constitutes "support"(Ellis et al., 2005);
- models, for example, Roy's (1971) adaptation model;
- methodologies, for example, ethnography.

The constituents are always "work in progress" and are enriched by ongoing practical inquiry. Practical theories direct us "what to *do* in order to be more intellectually or

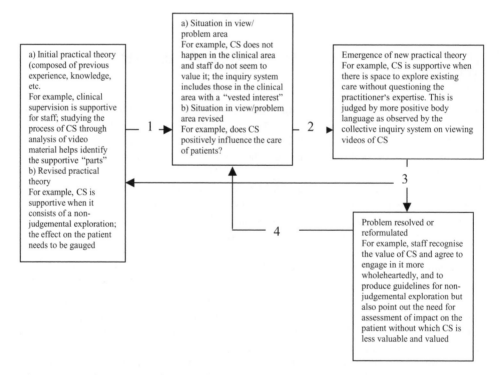

Figure 23.2 The process of practical inquiry (adapted from Stevenson, C. (2005). Practical inquiry, practical theory in nursing. *Journal of Advanced Nursing*, **50**, 196–203.)

---

[3] For a full discussion of practical inquiry in nursing see Stevenson (2005).

emotionally connected to a phenomenon... For example, ... [to] direct us to offer physical and psychological comfort to a patient in distress, to instruct us to imagine being in the other's place, and *through this* we gain an understanding of caring as a phenomenon (Stevenson, 2005, p. 199).

Inquiry involves stakeholders (whether identified as researchers, practitioners, patients/ clients, or lay) conjointly producing meaning that is local rather than capturing some pre-existing reality which has predictive power to other situations. Dewey (1925, 1958) described this as the meaning that arises from synchronized interaction that occurs in an episode of time:

> In practical theory development it is expected that important contributions to theory will come from practitioners in the course of their work and that those who are primarily theorists will engage with practitioners and themselves become involved in applied work. (Cronen 2001, p. 29)

The only difference between stakeholders is their different frameworks of sense making. There are no inherently superior routes or practices towards generating knowledge. Thus, the trained or formal researcher has no privilege over lay attempts at gaining knowledge about the world.

The elision of boundaries in relation to who is responsible for "finding out" is important for a practical discipline which needs practical theory. Put succinctly, our claim is that "human inquiry is a communication process (Cronen & Chetro-Szivos, 2001) constituted of varied conversations (Pearce, 1999)" (Stevenson, 2005, p. 198). The inquiry process involves constructing rather than simply reflecting or reporting on reality. The phenomenon that we inquire into is changed by the act of our inquiring (Cronen, 2001). Practical inquiry and practical theory are self sustaining and self creating, and the process involves inquiry informing theory and theory informing inquiry in an ongoing cycle. The similarities with an action research cycle (Lewin, 1946) are obvious. The cyclical process mirrors also the learning in practice described above and fits more generally for nursing as a practical discipline, because clinical practice is a buzzing, blooming confusion (Beckett, 1957), volatile not stable and therefore not subject to the operation of "normal" science (Kuhn, 1962), which seeks the hidden laws behind the processes, to *understand*.

Practical theories are judged by their consequences rather than with reference to abstract criteria that are used within more traditional research approaches (for example, validity, reliability and generalisability). There is no attempt to judge practical theories by the degree to which they are true or represent the real world. Practical theories use a pragmatic version of truth (James 1904, derived from Dewey & Schiller) that judges theory in relation to how far it allows people to go on with their enterprises, how far the enactment of the theory makes a practical difference (Stevenson & Beech, 2001).

Practical theory is not generalisable in the sense that grand theories, for example, relativity, are generalisable. Practical theory is useful in the way case law is useful in offering a precedent that can itself be tested in relation to new situations (Kennedy, 1979; Kvale, 1996).

> In case law, a specific case generates a new principle of law. It is not then applied to all new cases unreflectively. Rather, its applicability is ascertained by examining evidence and developing arguments for its use. The case law may be affirmed or rejected in the process of examination against each new case. However, it can develop through use towards a richer principle.

(Stevenson 2005, p. 200)

In a nursing context, a "case law" approach would mean learning from a "unique outcome" in nursing. For example, in mental health practice, a conversation with someone hearing multiple voices might reveal a new way to relate to the voices, say by hearing them as a musical fugue.[4] Subsequent encounters with people hearing voices may affirm of reject the fugue principle, or allow extension, for example, by defining how long the voices need to be heard as a fugue. Critically, there is no assumption that the fugue principle can be generalised to any and all cases. It is put up against each new case to see whether or no it fits, can be modified to fit or is too divergent.

The exploration in the sections above on generating knowledge from practice and practical inquiry serves to demonstrate the possibility of different approaches to knowing about the world of nursing practice. The descriptions also demonstrate the divergence from traditional inquiry paradigms to "knowing from" approaches. This presents a challenge in relation to the preparation of nurses who may already be steeped in traditional quantitative and qualitative approaches or who may need to gain comfort with both traditional and non-traditional inquiry in the course of an educational programme. The following section presents an educational methodology that can help with the delivery of information about research through disrupting the taken for granted assumptions and practices of both the teacher and learner.

LIBERALISING DEFINITIONS OF KNOWLEDGE

As we have indicated earlier, there is significant pressure on educationalists (DoH, 1989; UKCC, 1994) to promote evidence based practice. Best evidence is taken to be knowledge based in modernist research approaches and the diligent lecturer teaches the learner to distinguish the knowledge wheat from the knowledge chaff. In this section we highlight four means of disrupting existing patterns in teaching nursing students about research, evidence and knowledge.

(i) Raising the Academy's Awareness of the Difficulties of Taking 'Evidence', Especially Modernist Based Knowledge, into Practice

Assuming research informs much of nursing students' knowledge at least through higher education institutions, then a brief look at some of the barriers to research utilisation in practice should help inform educators about barriers to integrating modernist knowledge *in particular* within practice settings. One of the difficulties in applying knowledge in practice is trying to bring more ingredients into a melee already overstretched. Oft times practice cultures are reluctant or apparently unable to change. (Funk et al., 1995; Retsas, 2000; Rodgers, 2000; Parahoo, 2001; Pallen & Timmins 2002). Practitioners need to be convinced that any research will make a difference, integrate into the "system", apply locally and come with a defined process of implementation. Box 23.1 is a tool adapted from an amalgamation of the above authors' findings, which teachers and learners can work through in order to

---

[4] A polyphonic musical composition.

gain an appreciation of the need to think more creatively about the nature of knowledge and the research that produces it. Identifying barriers in practice environments will give an indication of how to judge successes and/or the need to consider other approaches, e.g. as discussed already.

Box 23.1   Addressing Barriers in Research Utilisation

- **Organisational**
  - How much control over the research and implementation process does the practitioner have? *E.g. no authority over process, service imposed...*
  - What is the level of support from clinical and managerial colleagues?
  - Is there protected time or allocated work hours to implementing the evidence?
  - What is the "nature" of the service in relation to research?

- **Communication of research findings**
  - How are the research findings presented? *E.g. as a set of guidelines to go ahead with, as a possible way forward or one of several options to work with....*
  - How accessible is the relevant evidence to practice?
  - How can practitioners know which evidence is best practice amongst such an array of choice?

- **Characteristics of Adopter**
  - What research evaluation/appraisal skills have the potential adopter/implementer or project champion got?
  - Has the person/people the requisite research education?
  - What is the attitude of the adopter towards research?
  - What service/practice development skills have they?

- **Characteristics of research**
  - To what extent is the research applicable to clients/patients and/or practitioners?
  - What kudos is associated with particular findings from clients/patients, practitioners and service perspectives?
  - How understandable is the research to practitioners and clients/patients?
  - How believable is the research to practitioners?

Box 23.2   Framework to Evaluate Research for Use in Practice

- **Utility**
  Usefulness to need?
- **Quality**
  Source and understandability?
- **Effectiveness**
  Benefits/risks to patient?
  Meeting aims of treatment?
- **Practicality**
  Efficiency, meeting purpose?
- **Effort for staff/group?**
- **Impact on patient care?**

- **Staff**
  Safety, workload?
- **Control**
  With who & over who?
- **Feedback**
  Available from practice, evaluation?
- **Feasibility**
  Likelihood of working?
- **Status quo**
  Fitting with current practice?

French's (2005) evaluation framework is useful also in challenging the idea that evidence based knowledge can be introduced and counted as "successful" in a straightforward way.

(ii) Emancipatory Teaching

The dominance of traditional inquiry paradigms can be likened to the male dominance that has generated feminist critiques in relation to work, education and family life. Feminist critiques, are meant, in part, to increase women's consciousness. Lather (1994) recognises that such critiques can be too abstract and she tries to introduce a performative aspect to teaching about emancipation. Using data gathered during research, Lather constructs four narrative vignettes "to tell four different stories about my data" (Lather, 1994, p. 101). She grounds the four tales roughly in line with Van Maanen's (1988) distinctions of *realist, critical, deconstructivist, reflexive*. These are defined as follows:

1. Realist – stories which assume that there is a solid world that will be accurately reflected through the application of adequate method and theory;
2. Critical – stories which describe the power implicit in texts[5] by probing below the taken for granted ways of making sense and so producing knowledge that challenges dominant meaning systems;
3. Deconstructive – stories which bring to the fore the unsaid in the text, especially incidences that help challenge the position that the text "stands for itself", with a view to creating "stories that disclose their own constructed nature" (Lather 1994, p. 105);
4. Reflexive – stories which repopulate the text[6] by informing the reader of the motives and struggles of the narrator.

Lather uses the vignettes as a pedagogical tool, defining pedagogy as "the transformation of consciousness that takes place in the intersection of the teacher, the learner and the knowledge they produce together" (Lather, 1994, p. 104). In thinking about teaching and learning about non-traditional research approaches, the power of this educational technique lies in its challenge to the underlying assumptions about research, to the existing defined conceptual systems. The persuasiveness rests on being able to present different approaches alongside one another and challenge the predominance of orthodox routes to the production of knowledge by simultaneously inscribing and deconstructing meaning. Research orthodoxy suppresses the creative and innovative and maintains the hegemony of the researcher over the researched. Research orthodoxy involves the self sustenance of metanarratives (Lyotard, 1984), "stories with a legitimising function, that is, stories that define the rules by which other stories can be legitimately told" (Rolfe, 2006, p. 11). It is not the educationalist's task, however, to bludgeon the student into new understandings. The challenge is to put the mechanisms in place through which the student can come to new understandings her/himself. The exercise in Box 23.3 is an educational tool to support a consciousness shift in relation to research, evidence and knowledge:

---

[5] Texts are defined in the context of the chapter as anything that can be read for meaning, including written and spoken words, behaviour, film, art.
[6] A phrase adapted from Billig's (1986) analysis of depopulated texts.

Box 23.3

Staff on Maple Ward have noticed that the people who are patients there spend a long time each day in the smoking room or watching TV in the lounge. There are several theories as to why this is. The Consultant Psychiatrist understands this as a lack of motivation due to the mental illness or side effects from medication which, nevertheless, are better than the illness. The psychologist recognises that there may be some motivational difficulty, but is also aware that people need to work actively in talking therapy to overcome psychological issues, the senior nurse believes that understaffing and the inability to give people time to tell their personal stories is a problem and the occupational therapist is of the view that there needs to be more activities offered on the ward. The patients may also have an opinion about the situation but nobody has thought to ask them. The lack of consistency suggests that the area needs to be researched.

Allocate students to one of four groups and brief them as follows (depending on the group you may have to adapt the language to fit their level of development/understanding):

Group 1. The scientific realists
You are of the view that there is a real world that can be captured through quantitative data collection, statistical analysis, the development of causal laws and theory that generates hypotheses to test in order support or question the theory. For you, the gold standard in research is the randomised control trial (or a meta analysis of these, for example a Cochrane systematic review). You are interested in quasi experimental design as an alternative when RCTs cannot be run.

Group 2. The critical theorists
You are of the view that power is always present in stories, writing, action (texts) around a phenomenon. You are interested in interrogating the texts to describe the implicit power and so challenge dominant meaning systems.

Group 3. The deconstructionists
You are interested in examining texts to unearth the unsaid, to look for ambiguities and contradictions in stories that people have in relation to a phenomenon. You are aware that what you produce is only another story, but you deal with this by identifying the fissures and anomalies and the constructed nature of your production.

Group 4. The reflexive researchers
You are aware that the researcher is inevitably a part of the research process. You are as concerned with how we know as about what can be known. You are willing to expose your own contribution to the production of "knowledge" and this is stated overtly.

Give each group 45 minutes to produce one side of A4 which outlines their approach to researching why people who are patients spend most of their time in the smoking room/lounge.

Have these sheets duplicated so that each person has a set of four. Rotate the groups so that Group 1 becomes Group 2, etc. Then ask the newly formed groups to argue for their new position to their colleagues, using the notes provided.

(iii) Postmodern Irony

The pedagogical tool that Lather uses has resonance with the work of the philosopher Richard Rorty in that both seek to disrupt versions of the world taken as reality. Rorty (1989) describes his position as that of a postmodern ironist. Rolfe (2006) presents this as the position of never being able to "fully justify their judgements to others or to themselves, but nevertheless maintain[ing] them in the belief that they are the best available at the present time" (p. 9). Rorty's work (1979, 1982, 1989, 1991, 1998) consistently embodies a position against modern epistemology.[7] Because of its association with scientific progress, modern epistemology presents a stone wall in relation to forms of thought and claims to knowledge that are distinct from it. Extrapolating from Rorty (1989), the educationalist's aim is to promote social justice (in this case the introduction of practical inquiry with its elision of the power between researcher, lay and researched). This is achieved through the process of re-description rather than argument. Beliefs may be changed through argument, but a change in what we consider to be interesting ways of appreciating our worlds arises from acquiring new vocabularies. In this sense, the presentation of different readings of text offers new vocabularies that nurses can take as interesting without feeling that they have been propelled to them by the arguments of the educator.

(iv) Relocating Learning

The challenge for educational programmes is how to merge the underpinning beliefs, perceptions and practices of people in two very different environments that can enable collective critical reflection (Freire, 1996). This collective reflection may be the key to integrating theory and practice on common ground. Rolfe (1996) and Penny and Warelow (1999) in their critiques of educational programmes argue for theory practice integration through praxis. This involves a clear shift in focus for educational programmes. The teacher can no longer be central to the learning process, nor necessarily the student/practitioner. For if praxis is a means to learning then the patient and other influences also play a part. The practice setting can then become the focus for learning (Chapman, 2004) with the teacher participating in a dialogue (Bakhtin, 1981) that joins people together in a temporary world of experience intent on generating useful knowledge and a consequent transformation in practice.

This learning in practice offers students and practitioners the freedom to locate their learning in the context of everyday practice. It does not negate the need to embrace other worldviews, though it does offer the opportunity to integrate these with the realities of their own environment. Previously identified barriers may no longer apply, mismatches can be renegotiated and the process of knowledge creation and application can possibly be embedded into individual and organisational practices where hitherto barriers were insurmountable.

CONCLUSION

In this chapter we have tried to establish the place of practice generated knowledge as one way of getting over barriers/problems of integration of practice and knowledge. Of course,

---

[7] Defined as the how we come to know about our world.

such an approach is not easy. It requires re-visioning by those who would traditionally do research and those that traditionally would concentrate on service delivery. It requires the ability to embrace change and think differently. We have set out some ideas of how educational practices that serve to cement the status quo might be altered to prevent imposing or privileging any one knowledge system over another.

REFERENCES

Bakhtin, M.M. (1981). *The dialogic imagination: Four essays.* Austin: University of Texas Press.

Beckett, S. (1957). *Murphy.* New York: Grove Press.

Chapman, L. (2004). Practice development: advancing practice through work based learning. *Work Based Learning in Primary Care, 2*, 90–96.

Cronen, V. (1995). Practical theory and the tasks ahead for social approaches to communication. In *Social Approaches to Communication* (Leeds-Hurwitz W. ed.). New York: Guilford, pp. 217–242.

Cronen, V. (2001). Practical theory, practical art, and the pragmatic-systemic account of inquiry. *Communication Theory, 11*, 14–35.

Cronen, V. & Chetro-Szivos, J. (2001). Pragmatism as a way of inquiring with special reference to a theory of communication and the general form of pragmatic social theory. In: D. Perry (ed), *American Pragmatism and Communication Research.* New York: Erlbaum, pp. 27–65.

Cullum, N. (2003). Strategies for achieving evidence based practice. *National Council for Nursing and Midwifery 3rd Annual Conference,* Dublin, 16–17 Nov.

Department of Health (1989). *A Strategy for Nursing – A Report of the Steering Committee.* London: DOH.

Dewey, J. (1925 (original)/1958). *Experience and Nature.* New York: Dover.

Dewey, J. (1929 (original)/1938). *Logic: The Theory of Inquiry.* New York: Henry Holt.

Ellis, D., Jackson, S. & Stevenson, C. (2005). A concept analysis of support. *In*: J. Cutcliffe and H. McKenna (eds) *Essential Concepts in Nursing.* Oxford: Elsevier.

Freire, P. (1996). *Pedagogy of the Oppressed.* London: Penguin Books.

French, B. (2005). Evaluating research for use in practice: what criteria do specialist nurses use. *Journal of Advanced Nursing, 50*(3), 235–243.

Funk, S.G., Champagne, M.T. et al. (1995). Barriers to using research findings in practice: the clinician's perspective. *Appl. Nursing Research, 4*, 90–95.

James, W. (1904). *What is Pragmatism?* from a series of eight lectures dedicated to the memory of John Stuart Mill, *A New Name for Some Old Ways of Thinking*, in December 1904, from William James, Writings 1902–1920, The Library of America.

Kennedy, M. (1979). Generalising from single case studies. *Education Quarterly, 3*, 661–678.

Kuhn, T. (1962). *The Structure of Scientific Revolutions.* Chicago: University of Chicago Press.

Kvale, S. (1996). *Interviews: An Introduction to Qualitative Research Interviewing.* Thousand Oaks: Sage.

Lather, P. (1994). Staying Dumb? Feminist Research and Pedagogy With/in the Postmodern. In: H. Simons and M. Billings (eds), *After Postmodernism.* Thousand Oaks: Sage.

Lewin, K. (1946). Action research and minority problems. *Journal of Social Issues, 2*, 34–46.

Lyotard, J.-F. (1984). *The Postmodern Condition: A Report on Knowledge.* Manchester: University of Manchester Press.

Malik, M. (1993). Theory-to-practice links. *Senior Nurse, 13*(4), 41–46.

Meleis, A.I. (1991). (2nd edn) *Theoretical Nursing: Development & Progress.* Philadelphia: Lippincott.

Menzies Lyth, I. (1959). The functioning of social systems as a defence against anxiety; a report on the study of the nursing service in general hospital. *Human Relations, 13*, 95–121.

Murphy, F.A. (2000). Collaborating with practitioners in teaching and research: a model for developing the role of the nurse lecturer in practice areas. *Journal of Advanced Nursing, 31*(3), 704–714.

Pallen, P. & Timmins, F. (2002). Research Based Practice: myth or reality? A review of the barriers affecting research utilisation in practice. *Nurse Education in Practice, 2*, 99–108.

Parahoo, K. (2001). Research Utilization among medical and surgical nurses: a comparison of their self reports and perceptions of barriers and facilitators. *Journal of Nursing Management, 9*, 21–30.

Pearce, W.B. (1999). *Using CMM: The Co-Ordinated Management of Meaning*. A Pearce Associates Seminar, San Mateo, California, 4 August 1999.

Penney, W. & J. Warelow (1999). Understanding the prattle of praxis. *Nursing Inquiry, 6*, 259–268.

Reed, A. (2003). *Social Network Meetings in Acute Psychiatry*. Unpublished PhD Thesis, University of Northumbria.

Retsas, A. (2000). Barriers to using research evidence in nursing practice. *Journal of Advanced Nursing, 31*, 395–606.

Rhead, M. & Strange, F. (1996). Nursing lecturer/practitioners: can lecturer/practitioners be music to our ears? *Journal of Advanced Nursing, 24*, 1265–1272.

Rodgers, S.E. (2000). A study of the utilization of research in practice and the influence of education. *Nurse Education Today, 20*, 279–287.

Rolfe, G. (1996). *Closing The Theory-Practice Gap: A New Paradigm for Nursing*. Oxford: Butterworth Heinemann.

Rolfe, G. (2006). Judgements without rules: towards a postmodern ironist concept of research validity. *Nursing Inquiry, 13*, 7–15.

Rorty, R. (1979). *Philosophy and the Mirror of Nature*. Princeton, NJ: Princeton University Press.

Rorty, R. (1982). *Consequences of Pragmatism*. Minneapolis: University of Minnesota Press.

Rorty, R. (1989). *Contingency, Solidarity and Irony*. Cambridge: Cambridge University Press.

Rorty, R. (1998). *Truth and Progress: Philosophical Papers, Volume 3*. Cambridge: Cambridge University Press.

Roy, C. (1971). Adaptation: a basis for nursing practice. *Nursing Outlook, 19*(4), 254–257.

Shotter, J. (1993). *Cultural Politics of Everyday Life: Social Constructionism, Rhetoric, and Knowing of the Third Kind*. Milton Keynes: Open University Press.

Shotter, J. (1984). *Social Accountability and Selfhood*. Oxford: Blackwell.

Stevenson, C. & Beech, I. (2001). Paradigms lost, paradigms regained: defending nursing against a single reading of postmodernism. *Nursing Philosophy, 2*, 143–150.

Stevenson, C. (2005). Practical inquiry, practical theory in nursing. *Journal of Advanced Nursing, 50*, 196–203.

Stevenson, C. (1996). Taking the pith out of reality: a reflexive methodology for psychiatric nursing research. *Journal of Psychiatric and Mental Health Nursing, 3*, 103–110.

United Kingdom Central Council for Nursing, Midwifery and Health Visiting (1994). *The Future of Professional Practice – the Councils Standards for Education and Practice Following Registration*. London: UKCC.

Van Maanen, J. (1988). *Tales of the Field: on Writing Ethnography*. Chicago, Ill.: University of Chicago Press.

Vaughan, B. (1987). Bridging the gap. *Senior Nurse, 6*(5), 30–31.

Winch, S., Henderson, A. & Creedy, D. (2005). Read, Think, and Do!: a method for fitting research evidence into practice. *Journal of Advanced Nursing, 50*(1), 20–26.

CHAPTER 24

Enquiry-based Learning and Service User Involvement

Janet H. Barker and Brenda Rush

INTRODUCTION

The current education agenda for mental health professionals in the UK is driven by the need to produce clinicians able to practise effectively within the Government's modernisation agenda for health care (Department of Health, (DH), 2001). Preparing individuals who are fit for practice is a challenge for educationalists who seek to find learning methods that will ensure that the professionals of the future can meet the demands of ever-changing services. This chapter explores the way in which two learning approaches, namely Enquiry Based Learning (EBL) and Mental Health Service User Involvement in the classroom were brought together in an innovative project, which is of relevance to health and social care education both nationally and internationally.

There is within the modernisation agenda an imperative to develop collaborative approaches in all areas impacting on service provision including the development of services and individual care planning and care delivery. A central tenet of the drive towards collaborative or partnership working has been service user involvement and as such has been advocated in various reports relating to professional health and social care education. Collaboration with peers is also viewed as essential, with EBL promoted as a method through which communication and team-working skills can be developed.

The University of Nottingham, School of Nursing supports both EBL methods and service user and carer involvement, both featuring in a number of modules within the pre-registration and post-registration programmes. The two learning approaches however, had not been previously used together. This chapter outlines how we did this. Beginning with a brief overview of the concept of EBL, we then consider service user involvement in nurse education. We describe the piloting of an integration of these two approaches with mental health students on a pre-registration Diploma in Nursing programme. The evaluation of the initiative and learning points are also be discussed.

Teaching Mental Health. Edited by Theo Stickley and Thurstine Basset.
Copyright © 2007 John Wiley & Sons, Ltd.

This chapter is reproduced with permission from Nurse Education in Practice. From Rush, B. 2006. Involving Mental Health Service Users in Nurse Education through Enquiry-based Learning, volume 6, pp. 254–260.
© 2006 Elsevier Ltd.

ENQUIRY-BASED LEARNING

EBL is a broad term used to identify enquiry driven approaches to learning. It is beyond the remit of this chapter to fully explore the philosophical underpinnings of EBL and these have been well rehearsed elsewhere (see for example Grandis et al., 2003). Suffice it to say that the concept of EBL arose from Problem-based Learning (PBL) approaches used in medical education in the USA. Both approaches are intended to facilitate collaborative approaches, critical thinking and deep learning. However what differentiates one from the other is the "problem" aspect of the process. PBL is focussed on identifying solutions to problems whereas EBL is seen as being less concerned with solutions and more focused on encouraging critical reflective thinking though the exploration of issues from different perspectives.

EBL uses practice related scenarios (triggers) to encourage students to explore theoretical and clinical issues by accessing a range of resources. In this way students not only develop a deeper understanding of the nature of nursing but also "learn how to learn" (Price, 2001). Whereas traditional approaches to education focus on teaching and the transmission of knowledge from teacher to student, EBL is intended to encourage students to be active learners rather than passive recipients of knowledge.

Typically the EBL process involves:

- small group student directed activities;
- engagement with opened-ended practice orientated scenarios/triggers;
- identification of current knowledge and learning needs;
- exploration, discussion and presentation of evidence.

Working in small groups enables all students to participate fully in the learning process. The procedure for EBL is often modelled on the Maastricht "seven jump" process (Wood, 2003), which begins with the lecturer providing "trigger" material which is typically a written scenario of a practice situation, video clips or parts of journal or newspaper articles. Unfamiliar terms are clarified, the issues are identified by the students and a "brainstorming" session is held to discuss possible explanations, with the students sharing their knowledge and identifying gaps therein. In PBL, students offer tentative solutions to the identified problems. Learning objectives are formulated and students then take private study time to gather appropriate information. The final step involves the students identifying their learning resources and sharing the results with their peers in the group. Enquiry/problem-based learning approaches follow similar or adapted processes.

The role of the lecturer in EBL is that of facilitator and although the lecturer usually provides the trigger material, formal lectures are not a central part of the process. Rather, the skills required of the lecturer centre on group facilitation, managing group dynamics, and ensuring that the task is completed in order to achieve the module outcomes. The facilitator checks that the students have understood the information they have collected and encourages critical thinking through open questioning.

There are a number of perceived advantages to EBL. The student centred nature of the approach promotes active learning with improved understanding and the generic skills and attitudes required for future practice are developed (Wood, 2003). Because all students are actively involved, the approach is motivating and students are able to build upon existing knowledge. Albanese and Mitchell (1993) suggested that medical students trained within a PBL curriculum found the course more nurturing and enjoyable. Developments of critical thinking, self-direction in learning and communication skills are further claims for PBL (Randle, Barker & Wilson, 2004).

Reflection is a central tenet of nurse education and seen as an essential component of professional practice (Barker, 2005). Reflection on practice through the trigger material is an integral part of EBL. With the emphasis on equality in learning and reflection as a central tenet, EBL appears to offer an appropriate method of preparing mental health nurses to engage in thoughtful, caring practice.

EBL is not without its problems, previous educational experience, learning styles, group dynamics and facilitations styles can all impact negatively on the process. Woods (2003) identifies practical drawbacks to this approach. More staff are needed to facilitate group processes than are required in traditional "lecture" style and there is a possible drain on library resources when many students need access to resources simultaneously. However advocates argue that with careful planning and appropriate preparation of students and teachers, EBL is more effective in preparing students for 21st Century health care than traditional approaches.

SERVICE USER INVOLVEMENT IN STUDENT NURSE EDUCATION

Current published research into service user involvement in nurse education is in its infancy but studies that have been undertaken have revealed some positive results (for example Wood & Wilson-Barnett, 1999). Students exposed to user involvement were less likely than others to use jargon and more able to empathise with clients' experiences of distress, less likely to use defensive "distancing" and more likely to take an individualised approach to assessment and interventions with clients. Positive changes in students' attitudes have been found, such as an increased awareness of the need to listen to the users' perspective and the need to reflect on their practice. Post-training attitudes have been found to be significantly more positive towards service users for those participants trained by a consumer, with the use of consumers as trainers being consistently evaluated positively. In Toronto, an evaluation of the impact of training for Community Rehabilitation Workers (CRWs) conducted five months after service users had been involved in a discussion on partnership issues revealed that the CRWs had made significant changes to their practice, including making more of an effort to ensure joint decision-making.

Mental health service user involvement in classroom work at The University of Nottingham, School of Nursing is well-established, comprising mainly of one or two hour sessions in each semester during which service users provide input alongside a lecturer to meet the module outcomes identified in the curriculum. The service users, giving students the benefit of their experiences of mental health issues and services, employ a range of teaching methods such as didactic teaching, discussion and group work. Students are given some opportunity to ask questions, but there is no formalised opportunity to discuss the extent to which they put into practice their specific learning from the service users.

COMBINING SERVICE USER INVOLVEMENT AND EBL

As identified, emerging research suggests that involving mental health service users in the classroom with student nurses has beneficial effects. However there is a growing belief that rather than service users simply "telling their story" there is a need to adopt more focused approaches. Within EBL concerns have been raised that written scenarios do not allow the service user's "voice" to emerge (Kenny & Beagan, 2004). Thus the combining of these two approaches seemed a logical progression in the development of positive learning experiences for students.

We had experience of facilitating EBL sessions with the students and we also had contact with a group of service users. However there appeared to be no available literature related to such endeavours to combine the two in nurse education. McAndrew and Samociuk (2003) have described the involving of service users in reflective approaches, but this did not involve the enquiry aspect of EBL. Dammers et al. (2001) outline the use of real patients in medical PBL approaches. Medical students, in a primary health care setting, prepared a summary of the patient's problems for use in the PBL process. What we proposed was somewhat different in that service users were to participate in the EBL process in the classroom with the mental health nursing students. In this way the service users were directly involved in the students' learning, becoming active partners in the learning process.

STUDENT AND SERVICE USER PREPARATION

The first year of the Diploma in Nursing programme is half theory, half practice with five discrete practice experiences. The students are allocated to a seven week mental health placement, followed by three, four week placements; one in each of the alternative branches of nursing (adult, learning disability and child). They complete the first year with a further seven weeks mental health inpatient placement. It was decided to introduce this approach to students as they commenced their final year one mental health placement. It was felt that their experience of EBL approaches up to this point would allow them to fully engage with the initiative and their previous clinical experience would provide them with a basis from which to ask mental health related questions. During clinical placement time, three school based days are allocated for what is identified as practice based learning; two days at the beginning of placement to prepare students for their experience and one at the end for reflection and consolidation. It was this practice based learning time that was to be used.

The two service users involved had previous experience of speaking in a classroom setting. One service user had a teaching certificate and the other had undergone preparation in presentation skills on the Training for Trainers course, a local initiative aimed at providing service users with the skills and confidence to engage in education activities (Hanson[1] & Mitchell, 2001). The authors and service users met prior to day one of the EBL process in order to prepare them for their role. The EBL process was explained and expectations clarified. The number of students and their prior knowledge and experience was also explained. As the students were about to be placed in in-patient settings, the service users were asked to prepare to discuss their own experiences of in-patient care. As is the norm in preparing service users for classroom work, reassurances were given in relation to confidentiality. It was stressed that personal information need only be revealed if they felt comfortable in so doing, and the service user's right to refuse to answer any questions was emphasised. A fee was agreed for three sessions. A letter was sent to the service users confirming our discussion and the terms of agreement.

---

[1] Now Rush, co-author of this paper.

Box 24.1   Summary of the EBL Process

Day 1

Morning

1.1 Facilitators and service users meet group of 26 students.
1.2 Introductions made and facilitators explain the process.
1.3 Group divides into 2 with 13 students, 1 service user and 1 facilitator.
1.4 During the morning service users describe their experiences of in-patient care.
1.5 Students ask questions and service users respond.
1.6 Students identify areas for further study, based upon the service user's input.
1.7 Facilitator writes student ideas on flip chart.
1.8 Students agree on who will research which topic.

Afternoon

1.9 Students gather the information as agreed.

Day 2

Morning

2.1 Students continue to gather information.

Afternoon

2.2 Students present and discuss their findings with service user and facilitator.
2.3 Students write action plans for their placements using information gained
       through EBL with the service user.

Day 3

3.1 Students return from 7 weeks in practice.
3.2 Students discuss with service user and facilitator, their experiences and actions
       in practice.

Overall the experience was a positive one for all involved and illuminating for the facilitators. As identified in Box 24.1, following introductions and an explanation of service users' involvement in the EBL process, the student group divided into two with thirteen students, one service user and one facilitator in each group. The service users talked to the students about their experiences as patients on acute admission wards and identified some helpful, and some not so helpful, responses from nurses. Anecdotal evidence suggests that if service users describe their experiences (positive and negative) in a way that enables the students to feel that they can make a difference in practice, then students respond in positive ways. If students are made to feel that they are to blame for service users' negative experiences, they are likely to feel disillusioned and may respond negatively to service user input. As the service users in these sessions had been prepared in presentation skills, they were able to discuss their experiences in ways which the students found helpful.

Box 24.2   Topics Chosen by Students for Further Study

- Section 2 of the Mental Health Act
- Support groups; carer support
- Psychotropic medication
- Hearing voices
- The referral process
- Admission process
- Crisis intervention services
- Schizophrenia
- Coping strategies

All students participated in the process and the service users appeared relaxed. Small working groups have the advantage of enabling all students to participate in the discussion and are less daunting for the service user than speaking to larger groups. When the service users invited questions, the students were at first hesitant. The facilitators initially acted as role models, asking questions and exploring issues. Thereafter, the students appeared to relax and the questions "flowed", leading to an in-depth discussion on the experience of mental disorder, mental health services and the nurse's role. Both service users brought material to assist the students' learning, which was incorporated into the discussions. Following discussion and questions to the service user, the students identified the topics they wished to pursue (see Box 24.2). Having agreed on how the work would be distributed, the students pursued their own study for the afternoon and the following morning.

On the afternoon of Day 2 the students presented to, and discussed their findings with their peers, the service users and the facilitator in each group. This allowed the service users "voice" to be added to the professional and academic literature presented by the students, encouraging them to consider issues from different perspectives.

The students spent the final hour of the day writing action plans, using the information they had gained through the EBL process to direct their learning whilst on placement. The role of the facilitator at this point in the process was to encourage the students to make links between the service user input and the forthcoming placements. For example, the students would not necessarily meet patients in practice that had the same psychiatric diagnosis as the users in the classroom. However issues relating to hospital admission and the need to build rapport, offer genuine respect and support were emphasised as being transferable to any practice area.

On their return from practice, the students talked with the service users and facilitator about their learning in practice. It was clear that the students had used the information gained from Days 1 and 2 to focus their learning. So, for example, one student talked about referrals between nursing teams and this led to a discussion on various forms of communication. Another spoke about support services available to older people with mental health problems. With the facilitation of the lecturer, the students made links between their previous reading, the users' information and their recent practice.

EVALUATION

Evaluation is considered to be essential in maintaining the quality of, and facilitating improvements in, educational programmes and can take many forms. Dixon (1996) identifies four levels of evaluation. At level one, evaluation tends to take the form of gauging student satisfaction with a particular teaching session or programme and is usually captured on evaluation forms completed by students. This is part of every day teaching practice and is non-intrusive in nature. At level two evaluation check whether participants' knowledge has changed; level three seeks to establish whether learning is applied to practice; and level four estimates the value of the training for an organisation.

The approach to evaluation in our project was at level one. Level one evaluation is useful to programme planners as it identifies what students liked/disliked about the content so that changes can be made if necessary. Thus such an approach allowed us to uncover the students' views as to the appropriateness of our teaching strategy and identify any necessary changes before moving on to other forms of evaluation. As such the evaluation is a work in progress, which has the potential to be extended to consider more fully the outcomes of EBL and service user involvement on student nurses' practice.

Twenty six students provided written evaluations of their experiences of service user involvement in the EBL process. Box 24.3 identifies the questions asked. The questions identified were designed to address some of the concerns raised earlier relating to whether service user involvement would make the EBL process move valid in allowing the service user voice to come through, the impact of service user involvement on student's learning and to explore if there were other ways of enhancing the student experience.

The students' written and verbal comments provide convincing evidence that involving service users in the process of EBL was a worthwhile enterprise. The students found the sessions thought provoking and provided a more rounded view of issues, identifying:

> Listening to actual experiences of service users makes it more real.

> The involvement of a service user improved the EBL in general, in that it felt more relevant and it was interesting to get the views of someone who has experience with the mental health service.

Certainly it appeared to be a motivating experience with students asserting:

> Makes you want to make more of an effort and be more involved as you know that the service user is sharing their personal experiences with you.

> I enjoyed this EBL more than the others we have done . . . I also found it good to be able to research on my own and then bring my findings together with the group.

Box 24.3 Evaluation Questions

1. How does this experience of EBL compare with other modules using this approach?
2. How does the involvement of a service user impact on the experience of EBL?
3. What did you like about the experience?
4. How could the experience be improved?

The notion that service users provide a meaningful view point, readily accessible to students was highlighted

> The experience and knowledge brought forward by a service user puts things into perspective and understandable.

> Highlights practice-theory. The service user's true experience facilitates learning better than reading a book or journal article, which may highlight what "should" happen rather than what "does" happen.

One of the prime objectives of EBL is to enable students to access different perspectives and the involvement of service users appeared to enhance this. One student commented:

> It gives an insight into areas to research that would not otherwise be aware of through textbooks/journals or own research.

The reflective aspect was also enhanced:

> Was excellent to gain an insight into how a person feels about mental health services as this can be reflected on and improved, how we as students can improve services that we will end up working in.

For some this was an inspiring experience,

> It felt easier and more valuable than simply reading a trigger . . . it reminds you of why you have chosen this branch – inspiring to see improvement in the patient's experience of health and illness.

> It gave me insight into how to reflect my own thoughts, given me ideas how to improve myself and the care I may give.

The notion of working in partnership was also highlighted:

> It was an enjoyable interactive session which took down all the barriers of "stigma"/"patient/nurse". All equal adults working together collectively.

> I enjoyed being able to work in a smaller group and exchange ideas.

In terms of improving the experience over all the students felt that the format worked and asked for "More of the same". Some identified that they would have liked more time to explore issues. As the whole group discussed their experiences, students were interested to hear what the service user in the other small group had said:

> It would be interesting if we could have compared with the other group if both users were willing to share the experience.

> Being able to spend more time asking questions – perhaps seeing the other service user the same day and seeing their point of view also.

DISCUSSION

This project set out to combine two tried and tested learning methods and evaluate the students' experience of these approaches. Overall, we consider the EBL with service users to be a success, based upon the student evaluations and the service users' verbal expressions of satisfaction on their own input. We acknowledge however that a number of factors enabled the positive responses to the exercise. Firstly, the small groups were appreciated by the students, enabling everyone to contribute to the discussion. The facilitators had experience of using EBL, working with service users and facilitating groups. Time was given to support the service users before, during and after each session.

Involving service users appeared to strengthen the EBL process and also added an inspirational factor that had not been present for the students when involved with triggers that did not include a "real" person. Whilst this project focused on student nurses, there is clearly potential to combine service user involvement with EBL in programmes for other professional groups. This approach is now being implemented across the five sites of our School of Nursing with student nurses undertaking adult, child and learning disabilities programmes, as part of their insight into care in the mental health sector. It is planned to evaluate the student experience further.

Involving service users in EBL ensures they are part of the learning process and addresses some of the criticisms leveled at course planners who bring service users into the classroom only to tell their stories. Anecdotally, the service users involved in this project found the experience engaging and satisfying. They spoke of feeling actively involved in the students learning process and being able to contribute to this at a deeper level than when "telling their story". The aspect of the service users experience is something that warrants further consideration.

CONCLUSION

Two learning methods were combined successfully in one School of nursing to provide an alternative way of learning. We hope we have also provided inspiration for other health and social care colleagues to involve services users in a focused and active way through the use of Enquiry-based learning.

ACKNOWLEDGEMENTS

The authors would like to thank the service users and student nurses that participated in the EBL sessions at the University of Nottingham, School of Nursing.

REFERENCES

Albanese, M.A. & Mitchell, S. (1993). Problem-based learning: A review of the literature on its outcomes and implementation Issues. *Academic Medicine, 68*(1), 52–81.
Barker, J. (2004). Reflection in mental health nursing. Chap. 9 in Tate, S. (ed) *The Development of Critical Reflection in the health professions.* Occasional Paper 4. London: Learning and Teaching Support Network.
Dammers, J., Spencer, J. & Thomas, M. (20001). Using real patients in problem-based learning: students' comments on using real as opposed to paper cases. *Medical Education, 33,* 27–35.
Department of Health (2001). Involving Patients and the Public in Healthcare: A Discussion Document. London: Department of Health.
Dixon, M.N. (1996). New Routes to Evaluation. *Training and Development Journal.* May 82–85
Grandis, S., Long, G. & Glasper, A. (2003). *Foundation Studies for nursing: using enquiry-based learning.* Basingstoke: Palgrave MacMillan.

Hanson[2], B. & Mitchell, D.M. (2001). Involving mental health service users in the classroom: a course of preparation. *Nurse Education in Practice*, *1*, 120–126.

Kenny N. P. & Beagan B. L. (2004). The patient as text: challenge for problem-based learning. *Medical Education*, *38*(10), 1071–1079.

McAndrews, S & Samociuk, G.A. (2003). Reflecting together: developing a new strategy for continuous user involvement in mental health nurse education. *Journal of Psychiatric and Mental Health Nursing*, *10*(5), 616–621.

Price, B. (2001). Enquiry-Based Learning: an introductory guide. *Nursing Standard*, *15*(52), 45–52.

Randle, J. Barker, J. & Wilson, S. (2004). Implementing problem-based learning: findings from one higher education institution in the United Kingdom. *Asian Journal of Nursing Studies*, *7*(2), 64–70.

Wood, D. F. (2003). ABC of learning and teaching in medicine Problem based learning. *British Medical Journal*, *326*, 8 February, 328–330.

Wood, J. & Wilson-Barnett, J. (1999). The influence of user involvement on the work of mental health nursing students. *NT Research*, *4*, 257–270.

---

[2] Now Rush, co-author of this paper.

CHAPTER 25

Promoting Emotional Development Through Using Drama in Mental Health Education[1]

Yolanda Wasylko and Theo Stickley

The use of performing arts in learning is incredibly powerful and allows a level of engagement which you cannot achieve in more traditional teaching methods.

(Drabble, 2001)

INTRODUCTION

Mental health students experience a duality of education as they move in and out of class and practice environments seeking to understand the perceptual realm of the service user and testing out skills shared by peers or role models. Methods used to facilitate growth in class may become the foundation for helping others in the practice setting. Essentially, mental health education is about learning practice in a safe environment in order to become a safe practitioner through enhanced performance. It is not only cognitive and behavioural changes that occur but also a powerful affective internal dialogue (reflective practice) that influences role development (Landy, 1993). Busy teachers, however, may not have enough contact with students to establish a trusting relationship in order to promote these values. Such contact between the students and their lecturers is essential in order for teachers to model the worker-client relationship. Also, traditional teaching environments may inhibit students' potential to effectively learn the fundamental skills of mental health practice. With increasing pressures to recruit and educate students for mental health practice, group sizes are growing which further mitigates against effective learning as diverse teaching methods become limited. Theories of mental disorder may be adequately communicated

---

[1] This chapter contains extracts from an earlier published version: Wasylko Y. & Stickley T. (2003) Theatre and Pedagogy: using drama in mental health nurse education. *Nurse Education Today*, 23(6), 443–448 and used with the permission of Elsevier Publishing.

Teaching Mental Health. Edited by Theo Stickley and Thurstine Basset.
Copyright © 2007 John Wiley & Sons, Ltd.

via didactic teaching method and cognitive development may be achieved by enquiry based learning. However, the affective development of the humanistic skills and attitudes essential for mental health practice (respect, empathy and positive regard), may be best facilitated through an experiential methodology with workable group sizes (Rogers, 1951). Using drama in mental health education is one way of allowing students to feel valued and at the centre of their learning. Students may become active participants rather than passive observers (Schatzberg, 1974).

EMOTIONAL INTELLIGENCE THROUGH DRAMA IN THE CLASSROOM

It is widely held that personal development, including self-awareness is essential for the maintenance of a healthy therapeutic relationship especially within mental health practice, (Wash, 1995; Dexter & Burnard, 1999). However, although considered essential for counselling and psychotherapy training this appears absent from mental health education for example in mental health nursing. Some may argue that rather than merely promoting self-awareness; we need to nurture emotional intelligence in the educational system (Goleman, 1996). We invite the reader to turn to Chapter 13 in this book that is devoted to the concept of emotional intelligence in mental health education. The idea of emotional intelligence has been popularised by Daniel Goleman in his book "Emotional Intelligence" although it is not a new concept. Mayer and Salovey whose research in the 1980's concluded with their findings that emotional intelligence is an actual intelligence that can be nurtured and tested as is intelligence normal associated with IQ. They propose that emotional intelligence comprises the perception, identification, assimilation, using and understanding of emotions. Goleman (1996) argues that emotional intelligence contains a range of emotional skills and personality traits namely, self-awareness, self-management, social awareness and social skills. Following Goleman's argument, emotional intelligence is essential for mental health workers for personal development. Intrinsic to personal growth is the willingness to self-disclose; however, mental health practice culture may prohibit the expression of practitioner vulnerability. In mental health education, there is little demand upon self-disclosure, and professional training usually strives to suppress and hide psychological wounds, and discourages self-revelation (Brandon, 1999). In reality, every mental health worker is a feeling human being; it would be unnatural for professionals not to be personally moved by the impact of working with people with mental health problems. It should be natural, right and proper for mental health workers to feel vulnerable, express their feelings to their peers and supervisors and receive appropriate support for those expressed feelings. The use of drama in education can facilitate this process.

Using drama in education intrinsically implies personal involvement. It is normal for students to allow right brain activity and in some senses, allows them to "drop their guard" and take the opportunity for genuine self-expression. One outcome may well be expression of individual vulnerability. By contrast, on occasions, some may experience moments of great insight. Teachers who themselves have trained in therapies develop their own ways of responding to the array of emotions expressed in the classroom, however it is essential for them to be clear of their boundaries within the role. We need to be aware of our responsibility to keep the group feeling safe but at the same time seize the moment to influence inter-dependence between emotional intelligence and professional education. These approaches however, require a high level of self-awareness and facilitation skills on the part of the tutor. We would emphasise the need for the tutors themselves to receive supervision for this kind of teaching which ultimately impacts upon individual's lives.

Using drama in mental health education is a form of dialogue. Students are permitted to be themselves in a safe environment and it is hoped this would permeate into their practice. Education is not therapy but learning is therapeutic; it is necessary for mental health students to grow emotionally in the process of their education. Among other personal attributes, it is the essential quality of empathy that results from this emotional growth. For a client however, learning is a by-product of therapeutic working, what is common to both is the growth experience. Given the depth of working in this way we acknowledge the potential for teachers to "therapise" students in order to meet our needs for practice. There is a need for teachers to practice outside of the classroom, not only to get these needs met but to also maintain the links and skills of the profession.

HISTORICAL BACKGROUND TO THE USE OF DRAMA IN EDUCATION

Where civilisation has existed so has the expression and interpretation of life through theatrical performance; from ancient Greek tragedies to medieval morality plays, from Shakespeare to pantomime. The very words "Folklore", "Fairy Tale", "Greek Tragedy" or "Shakespeare Play", conjure an image of content. A metaphor is immediately conveyed to the perceptual realm of the receiver. If a person is open to experience, this metaphor has powerful impact potential (Jones, 1996). The historical impact of theatre has been the engagement of the audience with the inherent message of the production. This "dialogue" with the audience became all but lost in the modernist, twentieth century type performance that virtually marginalised those watching. For instance, the importance of "Mother Courage" by Brecht was that the audience understood the message of Capitalism rather than becoming involved with the action on stage. Hence, actors would be stage props such as trees in order to "alienate" the audience from emotional content (Landy, 1993; Willett & Manheim, 1995). This more passive experience of theatre has created what Boal (1992) called "monologue". He believed that when dialogue is lost, oppression ensues. All human beings are conditioned to communicate through dialogue and that the oppression experienced in theatre – the observing audience – was a representation of the larger drama of social oppression being acted out in twentieth century Western society. In an effort to transform theatre from the "monologue" of performance into a "dialogue" between audience and stage, Boal experimented with many kinds of interactive theatre and developed the Theatre of the Oppressed. This exemplified power relationships and used various forms of theatre workshops and performances which aimed to meet people's need for dialogue, critical thinking and, furthermore, fun.

Another influencing factor in the development of drama as an educative tool was the work of Jacob Moreno. As his psychoanalytical psychotherapy practice progressed, he rejected the authority of the psychoanalysts' position and originated the practice of psychodrama. Moreno realised that people could not always articulate past experiences but they could act them. The pre-verbal ability to act, he believed, was a more accessible skill than the ability to articulate verbally. Psychodrama in turn gave rise to drama therapy that gained widespread recognition as a healing and growth phenomena (Goldman & Morrison, 1984). Healing and growth intrinsically implies a process of learning, whether about self, past experiences, others or the world. It was only a matter of time before drama found its way into the classroom as an educative tool. The use of drama in education recognises the power positions of teachers in relation to students and minimises oppression in their relationship (Freire, 1970). This potential for oppression can be paralleled in the wider arena of mental health care.

DRAMA PRINCIPLES AS EDUCATIONAL TOOLS

Drama in education should not be used in a vacuum or in isolation. Rather, it has to be inter-dependent with philosophies of teaching and learning. Learning that incorporates drama needs to be genuinely interactive with the teacher as facilitator. The educational and therapeutic philosophy that supports drama in education needs to be essentially humanistic, one that may provide the necessary and sufficient conditions for personal growth. As a facilitator, the teacher also needs to be a role model and not just paying lip service to creative approaches for the sake of being trendy or popular, but needs to provide the essence of what is being taught through their attitude and approach.

Any teaching session that involves drama needs a warm up, work out and wind down, similar to an aerobic exercise class. The warm up may include the teacher demonstrating to students about the dynamics of being together in the classroom. Simple movement activities can be introduced. These are generally perceived as fun and non-threatening. Some visual expression can be used such as drawing themselves on a large piece of paper and talking to each other about their self-image. The subject of relationships and relationship building can be easily introduced through narrative or role-play. Video and DVD can be useful in looking at the way people behave in social situations. Scenes from plays may be viewed with the sound turned down so that students are asked to interpret the action by observing non-verbal communication. Critical discussion can be developed with prompts such as: *what might she have been feeling then? Who do you think they were talking about? What might have preceded this scene?* Students could be asked to explore potentially different responses to certain expressions of feeling they see on film clips. They should be encouraged to experiment with potentially *nice verses nasty* responses. It is better to make mistakes and experience shock in the classroom than out in the practice area. Drama allows mistakes to be made and explored in the safety of the classroom.

For teachers wanting to experiment with and use drama in the classroom, it is recommended that they receive specialist training and experience and subscribe to a philosophy of experiential learning.

Often, the best result in drama and learning is when it is woven spontaneously into a lesson to illustrate a point. Drama can be used in conjunction with other creative methods such as drawing, visualising, story telling and using counselling skills. During the course of a lesson, however, students need to know when the activity is *playing* and when it is for real. Each activity requires its own boundaries. Whilst creative sessions may be *therapeutic* for a student, the teacher should take caution against providing *therapy* for the students. It could be said that unsolicited *therapising* by the experienced facilitator is abuse.

Just as facilitators use counselling skills but do not counsel so then can facilitators use drama principles but not always have purist drama in the classroom. Even the driest subject can be brought to life through drama. For example, a teacher may be required to teach about the health and safety of the taught environment. This could be brought to life by walking around the building and discussing the environment from different people's perspectives. Issues such as the organisation of the environment and risk assessments can become creative and fun. All lessons have the potential for being interactive and imaginative. Drama in education is not a staged artificial play, not a rehearsal for a way of being but a way of learning to be.

The benefits of drama in education occur over time and are not immediately perceived by participants. The *fun* of drama as the potential strength of its appeal to students is also its weakness. In a world where research emphasises empirical evidence, where technology distracts from engagement with real people in real roles (Brun et al., 1993; Cox, 2001) many student nurses may initially be resistive. Sometimes this will be due to not wanting to appear foolish, at other times due to the fact that they are not used to creative right brain expression. Teachers should not approach role-play or scenario development expecting all students to participate freely. Although all should be invited, some may find seemingly extrovert activities too challenging. Similarly, sensitivity is called for when introducing themes, for example if exploring the subject of "Motherhood and Mental Health" instead of asking students to think about *"your mother"* I was to say *"someone like a mother"* (Landy, 1993, p. 35). If I stick with *"your mother"* and the student's mother is seriously ill or recently died I risk inflicting emotional pain. True, some anxiety and pain is necessary for learning and as Brun et al., (1993) noted happiness could only achieved through suffering and discomfort is therefore part of learning.

The power of the metaphor to invoke individual symbolism cannot be denied and for some using drama as an educationally therapeutic tool poses ethical difficulties. We accept the covert therapeutic gain of any facilitated experiential session and that that students have consented to be in the classroom and that by virtue of relationship, qualification or whatever that students trust the teacher. But if during a session the power of the method overwhelms, we need consent to act in a different role in order to remain therapeutic without providing therapy. For example, a student who becomes distressed in class may exit with a friend close behind; another, on the other hand, may choose to remain. To ignore the hurt is insensitive and not a good "caring" role model for students to develop their practice. Educationally the facilitator needs to assist in alleviating short-term distress without engaging in long-term therapeutic work. Most mental health teachers possess counselling qualifications so the latter would not be beyond their skill repertoire but therein lies the danger, the boundary of therapy and education. The naturalness of practice versus the need of the moment. Unsolicited assistance is ethically unacceptable. If the only way of help I know at such times is to "freeze", "double" or "two chair" the action, we fail to de-role the student and serve only to stick a plaster over an uncovered hurt. In fact the individual that remains in class may well be expecting assistance from the collective response of peers and not from the facilitator alone. This leads onto psychological concepts of secondary gain and reinforcement that are not for process in this text. Suffice to say that group dynamics as with any group will need to be considered. Clearly as powerful as drama is for education it is a not *only* but *also* (Greenhalgh, 2001).

The use of "real life" scenarios turns the audience into actors. Furthermore, members of the audience (class) become fully involved in the process as director, and alternating as actors in the different roles. The method applies creativity to potentially any given situation. An event can be recreated and brought to life giving an opportunity to reflect upon the incident or event. The participants can then review the event from a new perspective. This process facilitates new learning by experience.

Drama facilitates active learning because it:

- engages the imagination;
- stimulates emotions;
- stimulates right brain activity;
- provides a safe context for exploring alternative actions and interventions;
- offers a fresh perspective on problems;
- provides a framework to facilitate change;
- explores a range of possible outcomes;
- helps individuals to resolve unresolved feelings and thoughts. (Jennings, 1987).

SKILLS DEVELOPMENT

Drama can be a valuable tool for the development of empathy and for reflective practice. Although the development of empathic understanding is considered an essential component for therapeutic relationships (Rogers, 1951), it is as much needed in relation to colleagues and relationships external to work. Rogers introduced the concept of empathy as a fundamental component of the therapeutic relationship more than half a century ago. Whilst recognising the later developments in terms of research and the development of empathy as a therapeutic intervention, we accept that Rogers' definition of empathy has remained the cornerstone of the therapeutic relationship in mental health practice. The key activity of empathic understanding is the ability to step into the shoes of another whilst retaining one's own identity and personal boundaries. The use of drama in the classroom is the perfect medium for the teaching of empathy as it can increase the student's non-verbal "reading" of others (Andersen-Warren, 1995). An example of an empathy exercise may include instructing the students to walk around the room on the sides of their feet. After a few minutes, they stop and are asked to share their perceptions of what they have done. Some recognise the pain, others the stigma attached to being looked at by their peers, and others begin to appreciate how the elderly or disabled may feel. Asking group members to remove their shoes and place them in the middle of the circle can extend this exercise. Students are then invited to try on one another's shoes (bearing in mind that some may find this whole exercise too gross to contemplate!). As they walk around the room, they literally find out what it is like in another's shoes. This hilariously uncomfortable exercise powerfully communicates the complexity of developing empathic understanding.

Another stage of empathic learning is to invite students to illustrate individual clients in front of their peers. Whereas role-play from a typed script may feel daunting, to mimic a client with whom they have been working is much easier. As the student acts the part of the client, several things happen at once; after the initial giggling, the student can become liberated in the role. Fellow students very quickly respect the efforts of the individual "actor" and a more serious atmosphere descends as all present are apparently moved by the client's reality being brought into the classroom. When the student de-roles and shares what it was like to be the client, it is usually evident that the student experiences some new insight into the client's world and perceptions, as well as their own. Although it may be difficult to measure the emergence of empathy because of the exercise, students generally positively evaluate the importance of this learning experience. Because the experience is so intrinsically meaningful, it automatically becomes the focus for the student's reflection.

Reflective practice is advocated in mental health practice to enhance and develop the profession. Whilst there is some excellent new literature on reflective practice there is little that considers the potency of using drama as a tool for reflection. One example of how drama might be used is the implementation of forum theatre in the classroom. A student is invited to relate a critical incident from practice, or indeed imagine an anticipated scenario (e.g. "starting a new placement on Monday"). All the students are invited to participate in the exercise. The person who is relating the story becomes the "director". The teacher retains the role of facilitator throughout the session. Furniture is arranged in order to represent the ward or community location. Each student is allocated a part in the "play". The group acts out the scene as described by the director. Anybody has the right to freeze the action at any time especially if they feel distressed or disturbed by the proceedings. The director will encourage the actors to stick with the recalled or anticipated events although improvisation is essential and, at times, extremely effective. During the frozen moments, the facilitator may intervene in order to stimulate thinking, feeling and discussion. Examples of facilitator interventions may include:

- "What was that like when she came in?"
- "How did you feel when he said that?"
- "With him standing there, how do you feel?"
- "What would help right now?"

It is remarkable that once the students are involved in the process, they evidently fully engage with the method. Students apparently enjoy the process and are quick to speak out about what is good or otherwise in relation to the scene or role they playing.

When students freeze the action and request some kind of change, the facilitator will ask how the change has affected their roles. It is normal to swap roles so that every student may get a sense of what it is like to experience the role of the other, or introduce two people with various facets of the one role, "the double" (Leverton, 1977; Jennings, 1987). The process encourages the participants to offer their own opinions as to how conflicts could be resolved or to listen to solutions of other members of the audience. If there are too many students for the exercise then they will become audience and take it in turns to step outside of the action and offer feedback about the experience. Thus, the audience is not passive but remains alert to the emotional content of the scenario. However, if the group is too large, they may look to the teacher for direction or response instead of interacting with each other. The teacher may then be seen as in control (Daines & Graham, 1988). Similarly, some people find it difficult to talk in large groups and smaller group sizes encourage quieter members to feel safe enough to engage (Bligh, 1971).

Following such activities, it is always necessary to allow time for the students to de-role and wind down from the demands of performing and to fully assimilate the impact of the work. This is part of the drama and does not substitute an evaluation of the entire session. An example of a winding down exercise is an adaptation of the fishbowl. Four or five students sit in a small circle facing one another. The rest of the group is seated in a circle surrounding the "fish bowl". The inner group (on stage) begin a discussion regarding the focus of the session. The students on the outside (off stage) are invited to replace students on the inside as and when they think they need "rescuing" either due to a sensing that somebody is being angry or upset or by a student thinking that they have a meaningful contribution to the discussion. It is essential during this wind down stage that students do not challenge or argue and that the discussion is discursive and constructive. What this process achieves by way of skill development is that it develops non-judgemental listening and conflict resolution skills because the student can recognise their subjective and objective selves. Thus continuing the emotional development necessary for mental health practice.

EXAMPLES OF THE USE OF DRAMA IN A CURRICULUM

In planning a curriculum that incorporates drama, such sessions sit most comfortably with experiential learning components of interpersonal skills training. The following examples are based upon a group of sessions called "Factors affecting listening and responding". The outlines and exercises are presented without their accompanying educational introductions, learning outcomes and resource materials. The rationale presented for each stage of the sessions focuses on drama and drama principles as a medium for learning. It can be assumed that some sort of theoretical input will support every session either appropriately before or after the workshops. The term *patient* is used as a universal symbol rather than selecting one of the other terms that in some quarters are seen as controversial. The aim of each session is:

- To increase the student's self awareness.
  Rationale: any individual aware of their own personal cognitive, affective and behavioural response potential is likely to manage practitioner to patient interactions more skilfully.
- To develop the student's insight into the interdependent effect of behaviour.
  Rationale: individuals who seek to understand the meaning of behaviours in context rather than in a purely theoretical sense will not only demonstrate empathy but also be open to self-exploration.
- To explore the student's own potential to professionally interact with some degree of self-satisfaction.
  Rationale: constructive self-analysis will improve confidence and self esteem. Students who feel "just good enough about themselves that they want to do more" will be motivated toward improved practice.
- To nurture reflective practice.
  Rationale: lifelong learning requires the student to continue development without a facilitator or a safe environment.

LISTENING SKILLS

A series of exercises form the main working phase of these workshops is now presented through various scenarios. For example, a worker and a depressed person, a teenager who self harms, somebody hearing voices. The facilitator prepares individuals that are working in pairs. Hence, only the people playing "tutor" or "student", "worker" or "patient" know how they are to be. The exercises begin with the here and now, the reality of tutor and student together. As these exercises become more intrusive to personal space and the inner sanctum of self, the facilitator must remain vigilant and balance timing. Inadequate time and discomfort will continue with limited learning, too long and uncomfortable laughter takes over with learning blocked. The people in need (student or patient) will feedback first. The facilitator asks questions like "what happened?" "what did that feel like?", "what was it that was not . . . ?", "what would have made it better?", "what did you want to happen?". Students that shrug the exercise off or present thoughts instead of feelings do not need coaching too soon. Even given that people have different learning styles, most students in time will gain from drama as an educative tool. Furthermore, some may say that "snapshot" exercises such as these are not "drama" but "role play" however, role-play *is* drama. Drama seems to be the "grown up" title now used in education to get away from the stigma and damage done by tutors who, years ago, believed they could read a book on role-play, get students to join in, everyone would remain safe and everyone would learn. The paradox of the tutor as facilitator for active learning given the degree of required skill means that even diminutive snapshot exercises are by no means *easy*. The exercises can be adapted for other sessions such as "giving and receiving supervision" or "assertiveness".

The influence of non-verbal communication on perceived listening cannot be overestimated. Demonstrating lack of interest by poor attention or the over indulgence of too much attention may serve to silence the student and increase anxiety which may in turn at best lead to poor attempt, at worst lead to avoidance altogether. Both ways serve no mutual benefit so whilst being professional may at first seem aloof or distant in the end it is the most gratifying way for both parties. Initially facilitators may need to assist students to transfer such principles to practice. Continued "spelling it out" would in the long term be detrimental to individuals reflecting for themselves.

THE CAROUSEL EXERCISE

This is suggested for use with groups of no more than twelve people. This exercise can be used for exploring attitudes in the development of helping skills such as needed in counselling or supervision. For a group of twelve, six chairs are placed facing outward forming a centre of a circle. A further six chairs are placed opposite the original six but facing inward. The six people sat in the inner circle remain static whereas those forming the outer circle rotate clockwise. Those in the centre are the helpers. Those rotating around the outer circle represent the needy. Rotations need to be either at three or five-minute intervals depending on the intensity of working required. The facilitator acts as timekeeper and supervisor. Both helpers and "patients" are briefed in separate groups. The patients leave the room. The helpers are instructed to behave as themselves. However, with more senior and/or experienced students the facilitator may "plant" a rogue helper (see Box 25.2). The patients can be assigned or elect differing roles from a predetermined list (see Box 25.1). The list is situation dependent and based on events that students are likely to encounter in practice (the examples listed below are in no particular order and include student suggestions requirements). Also, topics on the list can be determined by degree of difficulty. The exercise can be video recorded to provide both subjective and objective feedback. If this is the case feedback rules need to be followed. For example, the individual being discussed must feedback first, questions to that person begin with the word "what" so as not to elicit defensive or purely cognitive answers but develop personal insight and if someone wishes to focus on an apparent behaviour, they must use "I" statements, such as *"when I said . . . , I noticed that you seemed to pull back. What was that about?"* The potential intensity of this exercise needs to be remembered and a wind down exercise followed by debrief is essential. A group sculpture is another option. Following feedback, the group devise and form a human sculpture entitled *"this is us"*. This can be pre-meditated in that they sit in groups and have five minutes to decide and plan what to do and then do it. However, this could re engage other processes and may best suit group theory of group dynamics sessions. As a wind down, we advocate spontaneity whereby people just "latch on" and shape themselves into *"this is us"*. The group sculpture helps students re-group to reality following their separateness as helper and patient. Touch is a *"grounding"* experience. Overtly requesting students to touch one another on the arm may be seen as forcing the issue and is not without peril for there are those who may violently recoil from the use of touch for reasons located in their past, such as having experienced childhood sexual abuse.

Box 25.1.   Potential Ideas for use with Carousel Exercise

- Anticipation anxiety about placements or assignments
- Talk non-stop
- Silence
- Hostility
- Person with learning difficulties wants to get married/wants to have sex/is head banging
- Child is dying
- Prospective mutilating surgery
- Addiction
- Anorexia
- Suicidal intent/self harm
- Having experienced theft
- Having experienced rape
- Having murdered (with or without factors crime of passion/just flipped/pre menstrual tension, etc)
- Swearing/language barriers
- HIV Aids (Haemophilia)
- Homosexuality
- Sexual activity – Oral/Outdoors/Age related
- Pregnancy
- Prostitution
- Getting old
- Smacking a child
- Child abuse – Verbal/physical/sexual
- Offspring via different fathers
- Terminal illness aged 30

Box 25.2.   Ideas for the Rogue Helper

- Talks about themselves
- Non responsive
- Being overly religious
- Being angry
- Demonstrate different cultural values
- Being judgemental
- Being over-emotional
- Being disinterested

ASSERTIVENESS TRAINING

Assertiveness training is probably the most obvious fodder for the use of drama as an educational tool. In fact so popular that in the UK Andrew Sachs televised a whole series entitled "Assert yourself" and documentaries on remedial drama have used assertiveness as an example. Exercises used to assist people with developing assertiveness skills in healthcare need to be supported by theory input either before or after the workshops. Maximum numbers are suggested as twenty. Known warm up activities such as standing in non-verbal angry postures or shouting "yes" or "no" at one another may be used. Students are asked to complete a questionnaire. They are asked to answer ten questions that commence with the stem "*It bothers me to/when . . .*" and ten questions that commence with the stem "*I feel safe when . . .*" Novice students may need each stem completing and an agree/disagree on a Likert scale. In pairs, students then discuss what this says about their assertiveness. Secondly, in groups of five or six they each recall and reflect on a personal or professional situation when they did not perceive their response as assertive. Each group elects one to enact using psychodrama principles. Students elect which roles they initially want to play but the scenario is run at least twice in order to allow the protagonist (main player) to obtain differing views. Furniture within the classroom is used as props and arranged to suit. The scenario selected will reveal levels of felt safety and/or motivation in the groups. For instance, nearing Christmas one student group elected to help a colleague to not eat her mother's Christmas pudding, which she disliked. After she had acted being mother in the kitchen, and being dad listening to mum moan and sister still living at home, she decided that Christmas pudding was not vital in the grand scheme of things and that she would be selfish to refuse. However, a colleague asked "*what's that about then?*", she then replied "*anything for a quiet life*" and so began a journey of self discovery on the basis of what the group had seen as something which would originally be "*a laugh*".

CONCLUSION

The concept of using drama in education is consistent with the humanistic and person-centred philosophy of Carl Rogers (Rogers, 1994). Rogers believed in the individual's personal power for healing and learning. Drama as a learning medium can be empowering and promote personal growth. The students' experiences and subsequent reflections guide the session and act as a facilitator, Because of the empowering nature of the use of drama in nurse education, optimally, it promotes personal development, self-awareness and potentially, professional efficacy. At the very least, it can enhance conflict management and communication skills (Riseborough, 1993; Lancee et al., 1995). The focus on hearing clients' and carers' stories whether for history taking, assessment or relationship building has recently received greater emphasis in health care (Staricoff, 2004). It is clear that practitioners need the skills not only to elicit such information but to appreciate what it must feel like to be interviewed and to reveal such personal information. The use of drama in education enables the student to develop emotional intelligence and to be able to develop empathy. By learning what it must feel like to be in another's shoes, the student automatically treats the person with the respect and understanding required for mental health practice. In a health and education system that is becoming increasingly technologically determined, it is proposed that mental health students can benefit from greater right brain activity in the classroom. The use of drama in the classroom enables the student to experiment with different roles and promotes increased empathy. We recognise the lack of research evidence in this area and merely offer our thoughts from years of experience of using drama in the classroom. We consider that an essential quality in the teacher/student relationship is the ability to nurture. We argue that the freedom to play *(freedom to learn)* is vital to personal growth. Using drama with students may well evoke powerful feelings that need attending to. Teachers may not (and should not) provide therapy but should be prepared to point students in the right direction when appropriate. There is potential for confusion of roles here and teachers have a responsibility for professional conduct and maintaining of professional boundaries. Similarly, teachers need to work within their competency and receive training in the use of drama if they are to utilise the medium.

REFERENCES

Andersen-Warren, M in Mitchell S. (ed) (1995). *Dramatherapy: Clinical Studies*. London: J Kingsley.

Bligh D.A. (1971). *What's the use of Lectures?* London Univ. Teaching Methods Unit.

Boal, A. (1992). *Games for Actors and Non-Actors*. London: Routledge.

Brandon, D. (1999). A Necessary Madness: The Role of the Wounded Healer In Contemporary Mental Health Care. *Mental Health Care, 21*(6), 198–200.

Brun, B., Pederson, E.W. & Runberg, M. (1993). *Symbols of The Soul: Therapy and Guidance Through Fairy Tales*. London: Jessica Kingsley.

Burnard, P. (1999). *Counselling Skills for health Professionals*. Cheltenham: Stanley Thornes.

Cox, K. (2001). Stories as Case Knowledge: Case Knowledge as Stories, *Medical Education, 35*, 862–866.

Daines, J. & Graham, B. (1988). *Adult Learning Adult Teaching*. Nottingham Department of Adult Education, University of Nottingham.

Dexter, G & Wash, M. (2nd edn) (1995). *Psychiatric Nursing Skills*. London: Chapman & Hall.

Drabble, M. (2001). http://www.palspathfinder-trent.org.uk/forumtheatre.html.

Freire, P. (1970). *Pedagogy of the Oppressed*. London: Penguin Books.

Goldman, E.E. & Morrison, D.S. (1984). *Psychodrama: experience and process*. Iowa: Kendall.

Goleman, D. (1996). *Emotional Intelligence*. London: Bloomsbury.

Greenhalgh, T. (2001). Storytelling Should Be Targeted Where It Is Known To Have Greatest Added Value, *Medical Education, 35*, 818–819.

Jennings, S. (ed) (1987). *Drama Therapy*. London: Routledge.

Jones, P. (1996). *Drama as Therapy. Theatre as Living*. London: Routledge.

Landy, R.J. (1993). *Persona and Performance: the Meaning of Role in Drama, Therapy and Everyday Life*. London: J Kingsley.

Lancee, W.J., Gallop R., McCay E. & Toner, B. (1995). The relationship between nurses limit-setting styles and anger in psychiatric inpatients. *Psychiatric Services*, June, *46*(6), 609–613.

Leveton, E. (1977). *Psychodrama for the Timid Clinician*. New York: Springer Pub. Co.

Riseborough, R. (1993). The use of drama in health education, *Nursing Standard*, *7*(15–16), 30–32.

Rolfe, G., Freshwater D. & Jaspers, M. (2001). *Critical Reflection for Nurses*. Basingstoke: Palgrave MacMillan.

Rogers, C. (1994). *Freedom to Learn*. New York: MacMillan College Inc.

Rogers, C.R. (1951). *Client-Centred Therapy*. Boston: Houghton & Mifflin.

Schatzberg, A.F. (1974). The use of Psychodrama in the Hospital Setting. *The American Journal of Psychotherapy*, *28*(4), 553–565.

Staricoff, R. (2004). *Research report 36. Arts in health: a review of the medical literature*. London: Arts Council England.

Willett, J. and Manheim, R. (eds) (1995). *Life of Galileo, Mother Courage and her Children*. London: Methuen.

CHAPTER 26

Work-based Learning: A Model for the Future

Alan Beadsmoore and Thurstine Basset

Work-based learning is a learning process which focuses University level critical thinking upon work (paid or unpaid) in order to facilitate the recognition, acquisition and application of individual and collective knowledge, skills and abilities, to achieve specific outcomes of significance to the learner, their work and the University

(Garnett, 2005).

INTRODUCTION

Work-based learning has a long history and is well established in many forms of vocational education and training, for example in apprenticeships. Within health and social care education and training work-based learning comprises a major component of the learning undertaken in the preparation for professional practice in areas such as nursing, social work and medicine and in continuing professional development activities (Rounce & Workman, 2005a). However there are varying terminologies in use and often confusion about the different forms that work-based learning can take. Are we, for example, talking about learning that takes place in situ at work, learning that is for the purpose of improving effectiveness at work, or learning that is achieved through the actual activity of work?

In this chapter we want to present a particular model of work based learning in higher education developed at Middlesex University in the National Centre for Work Based Learning Partnerships. Through partnerships with external organisations, using the process of academic accreditation, the university is offering an innovative approach to teaching and learning in mental health and opening up opportunities for mental health workers to develop their capabilities and gain recognition for their learning.

WHY WORK-BASED LEARNING?

Mental health workers, along with all other health and social care professionals, are facing rapid changes in their working practices through service reorganisations, modernisation, new technologies and new models of practice. The development of person centred, comprehensive, integrated mental health services requires workers who are capable of working effectively in a variety of settings and in constantly changing circumstances. Therefore mental health workers need to develop and build on a repertoire of knowledge and skills whilst at the same time developing the capability to apply such knowledge and skills in different settings and circumstances.

Capability is becoming an increasingly important concept in mental health practice (Sainsbury Centre for Mental Health, 2001). It is based on the recognition that workers not only require specific skills but also a broader range of characteristics that constitute effective and reflective practice in mental health. Stephenson (1998) defines capability as an integration of knowledge, skills, personal qualities and understanding used appropriately and effectively. It can be observed in a person's ability to:

- take effective and appropriate action;
- explain what they are about;
- live and work effectively with others;
- continue to learn from their experiences as individuals and in association with others, in a diverse and changing society.

A key outcome for the education and training of mental health workers is to enable individuals to progress towards becoming such a capable practitioner. In the last decade mental health education, particularly in professional education, has come to be dominated by a model of practice that sees development of knowledge, skills and attitudes as being grounded in the experience of care and reflection on practice. The workplace is seen as the main resource for learning that provides the worker with the opportunity to develop their practice.

Thus work-based learning provides a powerful model to achieve the development of capability in mental health work. Dewar and Walker (1999) have identified a number of factors emphasising the potential of work-based learning in education and training:

- promoting learning that is practice driven;
- encouraging the practitioner to learn how to apply theoretical knowledge in their practice;
- encouraging the practitioner to identify and implement change in their practice;
- providing an opportunity for the practitioner to develop reflective and other transferable learning;
- involving the individual in eliciting and articulating the implicit knowledge acquired through experience, which underpins their practice.

A useful distinction is to be made between work-based learning as a mode of study and as a field of study (Armsby & Costley, 2005). Work-based learning as a mode of study is probably the commonest sense in which learning at work is understood and the predominant form within which such learning takes place. It covers activities such as work experience, sandwich courses and practice placements. At higher education levels it is perhaps better to consider this as *work-related* learning where practical experience is being used to aid the learning of the theory.

As a field of study *work-based* learning refers to learning from the activity of work itself. Learners remain in the workplace and undertake activities that focus on experiential learning and reflection on underpinning knowledge. These activities form a basis for the development of work-based projects within an applied practical context. It is about the knowledge and understanding needed to be an effective person in a particular work role and the concern is with application and the theory behind it rather than being theory-led. Thus theory, and reflection in a working context, follows the practice.

Individuals reflect upon learning and seek new knowledge in practice and programmes of learning are derived from the needs of the workplace and the learner rather than controlled by a curriculum set by the university. These applied reflective experiences in the workplace are designed to enable learners to develop new insights and may result in greater understanding, fresh approaches or the ability to reach new solutions in the work environment (Nikolou-Walker & Garnett, 2004).

Work-based learning programmes as a field of study usually share a number of characteristics (Boud et al., 2001):

- A partnership between a university and an external organisation.
- Learners are employees or have some type of formal relationship with an external organisation, and this can include self-employment and voluntary work.
- Learning programmes are derived from the needs of the workplace not the requirements of a university curriculum. The learners work is the curriculum.
- Learners start a programme after identifying their learning achievements to date and plan the subsequent programme based on what they want to further achieve. Each programme is therefore customised to the individual learner and will start at a different point.
- Major components of work-based learning programmes are projects in the workplace.
- The university assesses the learning outcomes of programmes against a framework of standards that is trans-disciplinary and not subject specific.

All work-based learning programmes at Middlesex University include most of the above characteristics and are built around four stages:

STAGE 1: RECOGNITION AND ACCREDITATION OF LEARNING (RAL)

This involves the development and presentation to the university of a portfolio of evaluated prior learning including previous accredited or certificated learning. This prior learning is assessed and forms part of a Work-based Learning Studies qualification. A distinctive feature of work-based learning is the opportunity to build upon the learning already achieved from work, education and training. RAL is a dynamic process of recognising, analysing and reflecting upon learning to date. After assessment for accreditation, such learning may form a substantial component of a customised work based programme, and consequently reduce the overall length of time of the qualification.

STAGE 2: PLANNING WORK-BASED LEARNING

This involves designing a personal Work-based Learning Studies programme in negotiation with the employer/sponsor and the university, and includes an individual learning agreement containing a proposed study plan and project ideas.

STAGE 3: PROJECT DESIGN

This includes developing a proposal for a real-life work-based project. Activities at this stage include examining research methodologies, action research, designing a research proposal, objectives, methods and instruments, and the ethics of work-based research.

STAGE 4: PROJECT IMPLEMENTATION

The final stage involves major project work that offers individuals the opportunity to create new professional knowledge and innovate within their working environment. Typically projects include exploration of aspects of service systems, policies and procedures, training approaches, team working or internal communications. However, within designated criteria, work-based projects can take almost any form appropriate to an individual or organisation's interests. Work-based projects, or parts of projects, may be undertaken individually or as part of a group, with work-based students on the same or different study levels.

As Boud et al. (2001) suggest, such work-based learning programmes offer a range of flexible models based on a trans-disciplinary approach with no subject content in the conventional sense. This is because work-based learning can be applied to any subject area that involves work, and it is difficult to think of areas of human activity that do not.

Assessment of learning then centres on the knowledge and abilities required to be successful as a work-based learner within the context identified by the individual and the organisation. The role of the university is to provide and apply generic rather than subject specific assessment criteria that takes account of the holistic interpretation given to "work" and based on broad descriptions of learning.

This flexible nature of work-based learning means that customised programmes of study can be constructed; partnership programmes, individual programmes, and programmes that build in accreditation of prior and experiential learning that include taught modules from in or outside of the university.

WHAT IS ACCREDITATION?

Accreditation is the name given to the formal mechanism for the recognition of learning that is achieved outside of the university's main academic programme. It uses the university's academic framework to evaluate and quantify such learning in terms of credit points at a particular level (Rounce & Workman, 2005b).

Academic accreditation is not a new phenomenon in the UK. It does however remain a controversial one. Although since its introduction from the USA in the 1970's it has become established in an increasing number of universities, it is primarily used as APEL (accreditation of prior experience and learning) to support admissions processes and to justify advanced standing against specific modules or learning units. However at Middlesex University the development of Work-based Learning as a field of study and a subject area in its own right has enabled widespread uptake of accreditation of individuals' learning and it has been embedded into Work-based Learning programmes at all academic levels.

This recognition of learning achieved outside of the university is important for the personal and professional development of individuals and also respects and values the contribution that such people may bring to the university. It provides quality assurance for external organisations of the learning outcomes and assessment of their educational and training activities. The university gains from the opportunity to develop links with other education and training providers, possible leading to "top up" awards, as in the example from the Richmond Fellowship below, or even the development of joint programmes.

The use of a clear accreditation framework enables the university to work not just with individuals but to extend that work to external organisations in order to assess learning and consequently award both the level and amount of academic credits. This has become particularly important in the areas of health and social care in recent years where there is much investment in education and training in order to enable staff to develop the skills and knowledge necessary for a modern service (Department of Health, 2001).

The following examples outline the way accreditation has been used by three different organisations to develop mental health education and training ranging from an organisation's multi-module programme to small single course run by and for mental health service users.

EXAMPLE 1: RICHMOND FELLOWSHIP DIPLOMA IN COMMUNITY MENTAL HEALTH

Background

The Richmond Fellowship, which was founded in 1959, is a national organisation offering a range of supported housing, registered care, employment schemes and other services (including advocacy, nursing homes, day centres, drug/alcohol dual diagnosis treatment and family assessment).

Over a number of years, the Fellowship had built up a good reputation for its training services, which were provided both in-house for its own workers as well as externally for mental health workers from other organisations. Training had traditionally been delivered as a series of consistently well-evaluated short courses, attendance at which increased the knowledge and skill base of workers. These courses were, however, largely un-accredited and there was little option for students to be assessed.

In 1999, the Fellowship took the decision to approach Middlesex University to develop a diploma in community mental health. It had increasingly realised the importance of accredited qualifications linked to career development pathways and statutory requirements such as care standards. As an NVQ assessment centre the Fellowship were already committed to the achievement of competence-based qualifications for their own staff, but also recognised the need for there to be "life beyond NVQ" and specific avenues for continuing professional development.

The Fellowship decided to work with Middlesex University not only because of their good reputation as an innovator in mental health education but also because they shared their perspective on the importance of work-based learning in this field.

After accreditation in 2000, the Diploma started in 2001. Four cohorts of students had completed the diploma by 2005. The diploma was then up-dated and re-accredited for the fifth intake of students.

Developing the Diploma

The accreditation process was itself extremely useful as it helped the Fellowship clarify what they were trying to achieve. It moved them away from the approach of starting from a broad knowledge of the areas that should be covered and developing a curriculum based on this.

Instead they felt able, and indeed were encouraged by Middlesex University, to move towards a more strategic approach of setting learning outcomes in the key areas to be covered and then working out how students could be facilitated to meet these outcomes and how they could show through the assessment process that the outcomes had been met.

The Students

The students undertaking the Richmond Fellowship diploma are employed by various voluntary sector mental health organisations, including those providing services specifically for Black service users, by housing associations, private/independent residential care homes, NHS trusts, by the Probation Service and by Social Services. The majority of students are from workplaces outside the Richmond Fellowship, with a small number of students working for the Fellowship itself.

This wide and diverse spread is also reflected in job titles such as: housing support organiser, support work co-ordinator, proprietor, assistant manager, team leader, mental health support worker, nursing assistant, project worker, project manager, carer's health and support officer and resettlement officer. These are the sort of people that the Department of Health have indicated as potential STR (Support, Time and Recovery) workers.

This diversity of work situations is a strength for the course. Motivation and interest levels are high among students and the majority of students are paying a significant proportion, if not all, of the course fees themselves.

The Diploma – Content

The diploma consists of six modules each accredited at 20 credits (HE level 2):

1. The reflective and capable mental health practitioner.
2. Human development and understanding mental health and distress.
3. Communication skills and approaches in mental health work.
4. The service user experience.
5. Holistic assessment and individual planning.
6. Contemporary issues and future development for the capable practitioner.

The teaching team brings together a mix of trainers, some already with close links with the Richmond Fellowship, with others independent of any specific organisation. The module leader is responsible for writing the handbook for their module. In addition to a full description of the module and the materials that are needed for the five training days per module, these handbooks describe work-based activities that students are encouraged to pursue in their day-to-day work.

All modules contain very contemporary material. Module 4 "The service user experience" is perhaps the most unusual as it was planned and is run entirely by service user trainers. When it was first delivered, it was the only one of its kind in the UK. The module was developed initially from a small workshop of service users. Peter Campbell, the module leader, now works closely with one other service user/survivor trainer to plan and deliver the module. There is involvement of a service user group in the delivery of the module. The module leader is also the first marker for the assignment.

Involving service users from the start in this way has also paved the way for other service users to be involved as trainers on two of the other modules. The first external examiner also came from a service user background.

Learning Outcomes

The overall learning outcomes for the whole diploma are for students to be able to:

- describe and analyse core values and principles that underpin mental health work and demonstrate how these values and principles are applied in their work;
- demonstrate a reasoned understanding of key knowledge in areas such as mental health policy, models for mental health and distress, human development, approaches in mental health work, the service user experience, mental health legislation, holistic assessment and care planning;
- work in a reflective and anti-oppressive way, empowering and enabling service users, and using communication, care planning and intervention skills within an overall team approach;
- critically analyse their working practice and manage themselves in the workplace, making good use of support and supervision;
- describe their personal and professional development plan based on their reflective learning on the Diploma and within the context of the capable mental health practitioner.

Assessment

Assignments are academic in nature but contain within them the importance of work-based knowledge and learning. They include:

- 2,000-word personal account, with reference to a reflective diary, on the use of reflection in learning together with a learning plan for the diploma (first module of the diploma);
- 2,000-word essay on the capable mental health practitioner;
- 15-minute presentation on communication skills, backed up by a 2,000-word account on the use of communication skills;
- various 3,000 or 4,000 word essays or case studies;
- personal and professional learning and development plan as a capable practitioner (last module of the diploma).

Great efforts have been made to make even the more academic essays have a strong work-based focus, so that they all have marking criteria in relation to evaluation by the student as to how both themselves and their work team put the theory from the module into practice, together with potential changes to practice.

EXAMPLE 2: HARINGEY USER GROUP RESEARCH PROJECT

Background

This programme is a response to both the need to engage service users more actively in their local services, and the need to improve the experience of mental health care locally. The programme aims to provide mental health service users with an opportunity to develop skills, knowledge and experience in research and evaluation methods and to develop work experience through their involvement in part-time project based work.

This programme is supported by two local NHS trusts: Barnet, Enfield and Haringey Mental Health Trust, and Haringey Teaching Primary Care Trust in the following ways:

- The trusts have agreed to pay for the full costs of accreditation, including annual quality monitoring fees, and fees for individuals submitting their work for accreditation.
- In commissioning current and future projects from the service user research group.
- In providing representatives to sit on steering groups for all relevant projects.

The participants include people from Haringey Mental Health Service User Group and other mental health service user groups affiliated with the two local trusts.

The programme includes the following elements:

- Research workshops that comprise a combination of presentations and group tutorials in order to develop the theoretical knowledge and skills required of participants and the practical application of these to their research projects.
- Group supervision sessions that follow on from the research workshops. Here participants work together on specific aspects of the project work that have been previously introduced in the workshops (e.g. designing questionnaires and interviews, role playing interviews, designing spreadsheets, analysing results).
- The project work itself comprises a large proportion of the time commitment of the programme. Here participants carry out various research tasks across all stages of the research process (from preparation to data collection and analysis, to report writing and presentations).
- In addition, to apply for individual accreditation, participants also carry out independent learning activities for the writing up of their individual assignments. Group and individual tutorials support this individual component of the programme.

The programme is supported by a collection of learning materials for the research workshops, other references, and a participant's guide to the assignment.

Syllabus Content

- Designing and developing ideas for research and evaluation projects.
- Ethical issues for research and evaluation of mental health services.
- Project planning and management (e.g. writing proposals; obtaining permissions and approvals, including Local Research Ethics Committee approval).
- Specific research methods – as relevant to the chosen research project (e.g. questionnaire design and development; designing and conducting semi-structured interviews; carrying out an audit project).

- Specific methods of data analysis – as relevant to the chosen research project (e.g. database design and development; using spreadsheets; quantitative analysis; qualitative analysis).
- Writing up and presenting the research.

Learning Outcomes

On successful completion of the programme, participants should be able to:

- Identify and contribute to key stages in the planning and development of research/evaluation projects.
- Outline the main ethical issues for research and evaluation in mental health services.
- Utilise specific research skills relevant to the chosen research/evaluation project.
- Develop data analysis skills, relevant to the chosen project.
- Communicate research findings in an appropriate manner.
- Demonstrate insight into own research work and its implications for practice/service development.
- Reflect on and appraise personal learning.

Assessment

In addition to the group project work, individual participants may apply for accreditation of 20 credits (HE level 1) by submitting an individual assignment for assessment. This consists of two components:

- A portfolio demonstrating the areas of skills and knowledge developed through attending the programme and carrying out the related project work (2,000 word equivalent).
- An essay of 2,000 words, which describes and reflects the writer's experience of learning and development during the programme of training and research work experience.

EXAMPLE 3: BRENT RELAPSE PREVENTION PROGRAMME

Background

For the last five years a multi-professional team of health care professionals, service users and carers from Brent Mental Health services in North West London have been developing a new model of care for people with severe and enduring mental health problems. This new model of care, Relapse Prevention, is based on research and practice development conducted in the USA by Alan Marlatt (1998). The Relapse Prevention (RP) model is mainly used in the field of substance misuse or addictive behaviours and is primarily about the self-management of healthy and unhealthy behaviours. The wider application to other areas including mental health is becoming increasingly recognised as the model aims at developing and maintaining learning skills that empower service users. It places emphasis on service users continuing to recover in their own time and by maintaining healthy behaviours in the community reduce the use of admission to mental health inpatient units and the trauma involved for both the service user and their family/carer.

Following implementation of the RP model in the day care services, the decision was made to develop an education and training programme that would allow the mental health service to cascade this way of working through the development of a critical mass of capable people such that all mental health care in the area would be based on the Relapse Prevention model. The audience for the programme was to reflect the implementation model and the course is targeted at professionals, service users and carers, all of whom enrolled on the first and subsequent programmes. This is a major undertaking for the Trust and requires significant resources in time and funding.

In the first instance the programme team contacted the university with a view to gaining academic recognition of the programme. This was seen as desirable as it would aid the development of a coherent programme aimed at a particular level of achievement. Following discussions it became clearer to the programme team that the accreditation would have wider benefits through the quality assurance role of the university ensuring that the programme would have a recognisable quality standard. Additionally, whilst the programme team had developed a detailed syllabus, the work with the university enabled them to develop appropriate learning outcomes and a focused approach to assessment based on these outcomes.

The Programme

The programme aims to train mental health professionals, service users, carers and others in touch with the care and treatment of those with serious enduring mental health problems to improve practice and to support service users in the community to maintain a balanced life style. The model used is a combination of cognitive behavioural therapy and social learning theories, which will provoke thought, discussion and research at practice level. It will, in particular, help service users who are at risk of relapsing and use relapse prevention techniques to explore and help modify attitudes and behaviours to care and treatment and thus improve the risk of relapsing and improving benefits in practice.

The programme consists of nine study days and comprises a combination of lectures, seminars and tutorials in order to develop knowledge and skills to practice, including sessions led by service users. Group work to address personal relapse prevention goals is required (one hour per week in each study day). This provides participants with opportunities for improvement through reflection on aspects of the course to their individual clinical area. Completion of a portfolio is required – to include a reflective diary – of application of relapse prevention principles to the participant's own work with service users. Participants may apply on successful completion of the course for 20 credits (HE level 3).

Learning Outcomes

On successful completion of the programme, participants should be able to:

- have a critical understanding of the importance of the relapse prevention model and its practical application;
- be able to analyse the concepts used in relapse prevention;
- critically analyse the techniques used in relapse prevention;

- identify and select appropriate assessment scales, which can be used in relapse prevention;
- evaluate methods used in treatment concordance including medication issues;
- apply relapse prevention strategies in their own work with service users;
- evaluate their practice regarding the implementation of relapse prevention;
- critically reflect on their own role and attitudes regarding relapse prevention with service users.

An example of the content of a study day is session 4, which focuses on developing understanding of stress in relapse.

Session 4: Managing Stress/Mood

Objectives

At the end of this session you should:

- understand the role of stress related factors in relapse;
- understand the stressors that people with serious enduring mental health problems face in their everyday activities;
- understand the assessment of stress in coping responses;
- discuss the application of coping strategies in reducing stress as part of a lapse and relapse prevention plan with your work colleagues;
- evaluate your learning from this session.

Activities

- Overview of the definition of stress, anxiety and mood.
- Application of stress factors with severe and enduring mental health problems.
- Assessment of stress factors in coping responses.
- Interactive session. Group to identify stress situations, coping strategies and self efficacy.
- Co-ordinator's tasks. To identify key concepts of stress situations, coping strategies and self-efficacy.
- Defining key concepts.
- Integration of key concepts. How they combine into the structure of the model.
- Clinical application. Group discussion applying stress situations, coping strategies and self efficacy to chosen service user's case study.
- Summary.

Homework Assignments

- Review *last session assignment*.
- Cards to record stress situations, coping strategies and self-efficacy.

The success of the programme has lead to the development of two further accredited courses within Relapse Prevention; looking at medication issues and supervision for relapse prevention practitioners (each 20 credits at HE level 3). The next stage is for the participants to undertake a Work Based Learning Studies qualification at the university building on the learning already achieved through their accredited activity.

CONCLUSION

The examples illustrate how a partnership approach has enabled the different organisations and the university to construct programmes of education and training that are relevant to the workplace and the development needs of mental health workers. They embody the idea that there should be an equal partnership between mental health training organisations and higher education. This recognises that learning can no longer be viewed solely as the transfer of knowledge from a university to an individual but requires a qualitatively different approach to recognising how and where learning takes place. The examples also outline both the accessibility and flexibility of a work-based learning approach.

- Accessibility – the courses have created avenues for service users to become involved both as teachers and learners and overcome the barriers to service user involvement so often encountered in Higher Education (Basset, Campbell & Anderson, 2006). They also open up the opportunity for staff that traditionally may not have had access to learning or higher education to develop new skills and knowledge and gain recognition for this.
- Flexibility – work-based learning's trans-disciplinary approach cuts across traditional professional boundaries with the focus on mental health work rather than a specific profession/discipline's input to the work.

If the challenge of new ways of working within mental health (National Institute for Mental in England, 2006) is to be met and effective person-centred services achieved, then innovative learning programmes which enable all to develop the skills, knowledge and attitudes must be available. Work-based learning offers a model for such a future.

REFERENCES

Armsby, P. & Costley, C. (2005). Types of Work Based learning: what are they and what are the implications for assessment, in *Assessment and Evaluation in Work Based Learning*. Conference Proceedings Work based learning network of the University Association for Lifelong Learning: 21 and 22 March 2005, Edinburgh University.

Basset, T. Campbell, P. & Anderson, J. (2006). Service user/survivor involvement in mental health training and education: overcoming the barriers, *Social Work Education*, 25(4), 393–402.

Boud, D. Solomon, N. & Symes, C. (2001). New practices for new times, in D. Boud and N. Solomon (eds) *Work-based learning: A New Higher Education*. Buckingham: SHRE and Oxford University Press.

Dewar B.J. & Walker, E. (1999). Experiential learning: issues for supervision. *Journal of Advanced Nursing*, 30(6), 1459–1467.

Department of Health (2001). *Working Together, Learning Together*. London: HMSO.

Garnett, J. (2005). University Work Based learning and the knowledge-driven project, in K. Rounce & B. Workman (eds) *Work-based learning in Health Care: applications and innovations*. Chichester: Kingsham Press.

Marlatt, G.A. (1998). *Harm Reduction: Pragmatic Strategies for Managing High Risk Behaviours*. New York: Guilford Press.

National Institute for Mental Health in England (2006). http://nimhe.csip.org.uk/nww (accessed on 10 July 2006).

Nikolou-Walker, E. & Garnett, J. (2004). Work-Based Learning. A new imperative: developing reflective practice in professional life. *Reflective Practice*, 5(3), 297–312.

Rounce, K. & Workman, B. (2005a). Introduction to Work Based Learning in health and social care, in K. Rounce & B. Workman (eds) *Work-based learning in Health Care: applications and innovations*. Chichester: Kingsham Press.

Rounce, K. & Workman (2005b). Accreditation of organisational learning: experience in the health sector, in K. Rounce & B. Workman (eds) *Work-based learning in Health Care: applications and innovations*. Chichester: Kingsham Press.

Sainsbury Centre for Mental Health (2001). *The Capable Practitioner*. London: Sainsbury Centre for Mental Health.

Stephenson, J. (1998). The concept of capability and its importance in higher education, in J. Stephenson & M. Yorke (eds) *Capability and Quality in Higher Education*. London: Kogan Page.

CHAPTER 27

Information Technology: From the Classroom to the Workplace

Paul Linsley

INTRODUCTION

In the UK, the National Health Service (NHS) is set to undergo a technological revolution with the introduction of the National Programme for Information Technology (NHS Connecting for Health, 2005a). The Programme will be gradually phased in across England over the next six years, according to priorities and when NHS organisations are ready to implement them (NHS Connecting for Health, 2005). Similar programmes will be rolled-out across the other home countries of the United Kingdom following a similar time scale. This is the first time that such a project of this nature and scale has been undertaken in the world and the cost of implementation is currently estimated at 20 billion pounds.

The "value" of the National Programme is the range of benefits from the new systems that will be available to the NHS and its patients. These benefits range from the convenience to patients having a choice of consultant, location and time of treatment to efficiency gains for primary and secondary staff (NHS Connecting for Health, 2005b).

Delivering benefits to staff and patients will contribute to achieving NHS performance improvement goals against the "Standards for Better Health", National Service Frameworks and other service improvement initiatives. The installation of the Information Technology will be accompanied by significant changes to existing ways of working (Proctor, 2001). This is turn will have an impact on the way training and education for health care staff will be structured and delivered.

All improvement requires change. Changing the way things are done, changes in processes and in the behaviour of people and teams of people (Garside, 1998). Implementing the National Programme will invariably have a fundamental effect on the organisation and the way people work. Whether it is anticipated or not, the implementation of an information system in an organisation involves the mutual transformation of the organisation by the technology, and of the system by the organisation (Drazen et al., 1995; Berg, 1999; Kaplan, 2001).

This is a two-way process. On the one hand, the technology will affect the distribution and content of work tasks, change information flows and affect the visibility of these works tasks and information flows. Because of this, it will also change the relationships between groups of health care professionals and other staff. Electronic patient records, for example, inevitably change recording practices, and raise questions about who will get access to whose data, under which conditions. Such changes inevitably trigger subtle (and sometime not to subtle) social and political processes about who gets to fill in what parts of the record, who "owns" what information and who gets to check on whose work (Groth, 1999; Glaser & Hsu, 2003).

Likewise when faced with change of this kind organisations will respond differently. The response is likely to be influenced by the past experience of managers and by wider social and political processes in the organisation (Johnson & Scholes, 1989). Educational establishments, such as universities and centres of higher education will need to be alert to such changes and organisational manoeuvring in order to respond and meet practice expectation and more importantly to support staff and students in clinical practice. Increased effort will be needed to support the complex roles that workers undertake as part of mental health practice and ensure that they contribute to the knowledge development, dissemination and adoption efforts of the respective professions.

THE CHALLENGE

As healthcare becomes more knowledge intensive, workers are challenged to manage clinical information effectively and keep abreast of professional knowledge (Snyder-Halpern, Corcoran-Perry & Narayan, 2001). Rapid proliferation of new knowledge, expanding professional practice expectations and changing practice environments require that practitioners become lifelong learners capable of constantly reflecting on and modifying their practice. Mental health education needs to take stock of this and embrace and make use of information technology (IT) learning media to help workers make use of these demands (Clarke, 2004).

Historically, there has been an absence of education and training specifically designed for the mental health care worker within the clinical setting (NIMHE, 2003). Educational programmes have largely been delivered by professional educators remote from the practicalities of the workplace. This is being challenged however with the increase in modern technology and the opportunities that this provides (NIMHE, 2003). Small-scale implementations in health communities have enabled technology to be effectively tested in situ and for a number of issues to be addressed. Learning from these implementations is informing the wider implementation of systems, which is set to increase dramatically in the coming years. As part of this process there is a commitment to ongoing engagement with educationalists and frontline staff to ensure that maximum benefit can be derived from the technology whilst ensuring that the educational programmes being delivered meet the needs and requirements of patients, as well as staff.

Educational strategies need to focus on the long-term development of an information culture, and not as in the past, on short-term training designed simply to get people using computer and information systems (Ballard, 2001). In turn, these training strategies should be fully integrated and co-ordinated with organisational and mainstream educational programmes of learning. Work based learning is an approach that allows practitioners to learn from their work in a structured manner, test out changes in practice and to be highly reflective and reflexive. It enables practitioners to become more in control of their learning and can form whole or part academic awards. Using modern technology to assist in the development and delivery of training and education could bring benefits to a number of practice areas.

Ideally, workers should be able to engage with computers as a process of their work and develop their own interpretation of the information provided by computers in order to construct their own meaning of that information for use in clinical practice (Glaser & Hsu, 1999). To this end computers should be seen as an integral part of and not something separate to, clinical practice if they are to make a worthwhile contribution to the work of those that use them (DOH, 2001).

In the UK, computers are already used within the National Health Service; although their use is often limited and stand-alone (Proctor, 2001). Nursing Information Systems or Patient Administration Systems are used for keeping nursing records for individual patients. These are designed to move data rapidly through complex institutions, providing support for admission, discharge and transfer of patient details (NHS Connecting for Health, 2005c). Systems have also been developed that encompass administrative duties and non nursing tasks; these are largely involved in data collection and analysis and are used on a verity of levels, from planning the ward duty rota, through to audit and quality control. There would seem to be a general recognition that computers and information technology have the potential to play an even bigger part in improving the functioning of clinical environments, particularly with regards to the enhancement of communication, service delivery, access to health information and the education of staff and patients (Connecting for Health, 2005a, 2005b, 2005c).

However, detailed customisation is needed for any service (Checkland & Holwell, 1998). This is not in technical detail about planning or software but rather in defining the operational tasks and educational support that computers should undertake, and allow the implementation of systems that will actually match what it is they do, to what is required of them by those in clinical practice. Psychiatric services have long been an afterthought in the implementation of main hospital systems, or lip service has been given to the speciality by the addition of unsatisfactory "bolt on" mental health modules (Glover, 1996). This is turn has made the introduction of computer and information technology difficult to achieve with mental health nursing staff.

In addition to this mental health nurses and information technology can be perceived as having relationship difficulties. Mental health nurses focus their interventions from a humanistic platform that on the surface of consideration is at odds with the mechanistic image of information technology utilisation. Indeed, when reviewing mental health nursing textbooks and literature, the use of information technology as an intervention is singularly absent with the issues of relationship formation and interpersonal relating dominant. Subsequently, mental health has little evidenced foundation to view computers and the related skills to use them as being part of the nurse-user relationship constructs so valued by nurses and users alike.

Nurses will need to become computer literate if for no other reason than the fact that computers are not going to go away and will be part of their everyday professional life. It is also likely that nurses will embark on further studies and research which will require the use of computers as information seeking tools and for word-processing and data analysis. Those mental health nurses not actively seeking additional qualifications are still required to maintain contemporary knowledge and to incorporate evidenced based practice into their daily user interventions. Accessing data base information is not only important but essential.

E-LEARNING

At present, computerised educational and knowledge based resources are provided in a variety of formats that range from general online resources, such as clinical practice guidelines and clinical textbooks, to more sophisticated educational and knowledge based systems delivered in support of formal qualification and career development (Pare & Elam, 1998).Perhaps the best known of these is e-learning, a concept that is increasingly being promoted as a means of bridging the gap between formal educational establishments and the clinical practice environment (Yates, 1996).

E-learning refers to the use of Internet technologies to deliver a broad array of solutions that enhance knowledge and performance (Rosenberg, 2001). It includes the use of a variety of media and techniques for learning, including text, sound, graphics, photography, animation, video, email, discussion forums, chat rooms, virtual meetings or tutorials, simulations and much more. The interactive nature of the Internet means that, unlike many previous educational technologies, the educator can adapt the material and offer support while the course is in progress, rather than just relying on the material embedded within the technology itself (as for example with a CD ROM). Work is currently underway to extend this mode of delivery by making use of hand held devices such as Personal Digital Assistants (PDA's) and cell phones. This new, mobile form of education is called, unsurprisingly, m-learning (Kruse, 2004).

The flexibility that such technology offers is fundamental to its success, in particular the freeing up of staff time. By introducing e-learning into the clinical environment means that staff can access learning materials at a time suitable to them. Significant blocks to the release of staff for education and training are overcome as is the cost incurred in sending staff on courses (Taylor, 1995). The portability of laptops, for example, allows the clinician to not only study in their work environment but at home or on the bus. Work based learning of the kind described here is an approach that allows the clinician to learn from their work in a structured manner, test out changes in practice and to be highly reflective and reflexive. It enables participants to become more in control of their learning and can form whole or part of academic awards (National Research and Development Centre, 2003).

E-learning is not without its difficulties however. This mode of delivery challenges to achieve the flexibility to meet the needs of a variety of clinicians at different stages of their personal and professional development while equally, promoting humanistic skills and attributes from a technology base. At present, learning applications tend to be sealed micro-worlds with little integration into the real world (DOH, 2001). These tend to follow a similar pattern of design for a tutorial or narrative with questions of comprehension placed either during or at the end of each session. These learning applications can have inbuilt notebooks, reference materials, calculations and final tests. The primary learning activity tends to be the consumption of the content for the purpose of regurgitation during the final test. What is needed is greater interaction with the student through the available technological applications.

While rote learning and memorisation may have a place within the learning process, learning is not something that is external to the learner nor is it solely a practice of grafting knowledge and understanding onto a learner (Robotham, 1999). Rather, learning is ideally a function of understanding, thinking actively about materials, their structure and relationships (Entwistle, 1998). Students should be encouraged to develop their own interpretation of information through interactivity and hence construct their own meaning. These learning principles reflect the needs of most adult learners who are self-directive, relatively independent and need to focus their learning on individual life issues (Goodsir, 1978).Consequently, health practitioner learning becomes an experiential approach to individualised challenges that subsequently allows the learner to autonomously pursue relevant learning. Personal autonomy becomes both part of the health practitioner-directed learning process and a desired goal of the process (Kreber, 1998). Technology based learning can be shown here as supporting humanistic aspects of practitioner education through the process of allowing them the freedom to access, process and reflect upon information when and how they choose, dependent of the needs of the learner at the time.

It is not enough to think that the "navigation" itself will give the learner control and that this will automatically translate into intrinsic motivation and empowerment (Salmon, 2003). Clinicians should be encouraged to engage in learning activities with the intention of understanding or seeking meaning, and not memorisation as the focus or objective of their learning. Mental health practice requires both instrumental and communicative learning to encompass the task orientated and critically reflective components of effective care (Chase, 1997). Communicative learning utilises speech, art and writing to promote an understanding of the meaning of ideals and values of others (Mezirow, 1996). Incorporating web-based communication to facilitate rational discourse, central to communicative learning, not only offers another communication modality but also a modality that exports discourse from local geographical confines into vast pools of informed, rational and reflective professional others. Memorisation, learning information that can be reproduced, is associated with poor learning outcomes whereas students that are engaged with the intention of understanding or seeking meaning are associated with higher quality learning outcomes (Entwistle & Ramsden, 1983; Watkins, 1983).

The simple transfer of text or other learning material into hypertext/hypermedia has no use as a primacy of the learning experience, as it only allows the user to follow predefined pathways and does not take full advantage of the technological platform; it is merely repackaging (Diller, 1995). Students need to do more than access or look for information as the main function primary of their learning experience, but should be enabled to examine, perceive, interpret and experience information (Brookfield, 1987).Interactive media only provide opportunities for users to learn to visualise and understand complex relationships in ways that are not possible on other media. One possible solution to this might be to change the primacy of learning experience to heuristic activities that trigger and encourage the student to seek meaning by accessing various disparate media and informational resources (Koppi & Chaloupka, 1997).

The ability to adapt a computer system to meet the needs of all its users whilst delivering the essential information to support the worker in practice must be one of the fundamental aspects of health information technology (Anderson et al., 1995). Ideally, practitioners should be able to engage with computers as part of their work and develop their own interpretations of the information provided by computers in order to construct their own meaning of that information in clinical practice (Drazen et al., 1995). To this end computers should be seen as an integral part of and not something separate from, clinical practice if they are to make a worthwhile contribution to the work of those that use them. Current provision of in-patient care often lacks responsiveness to the individual problems, strengths and needs of service users, with many aspects of patient care being standardised, from care planning to group interventions and individual work. The aim of such educational programmes should be to create flexible learning opportunities, using the technology available, within a framework of priorities for the development of the required skills, knowledge and attitudes needed to improve the effectiveness and acceptability of clinical care. Health practitioners and those that they care for must be involved in the development of such educational packages. A primary reason why e-learning fails to transform clinical practice is that they are frequently developed away from the area that they seek to serve. In order to overcome this problem, the recruitment of staff and service users has been undertaken in the development of courses and training material.

THE ROLE OF THE TUTOR/E-MODERATOR

Web-based learning also impacts upon the role of the tutor or to give them their proper name, e-moderator (Kruse, 2004). The demands of having technological expertise and utilisation skills divest teacher roles from the imparting of knowledge toward managing knowledge and promoting conceptual discourse. Educators are required to produce resources, printed course material and computer generated materials suitable for a wide variety of learners whilst also providing opportunities for learners and courses that require social interactivity to promote learning (Weller, 2002). While professional peer support can be readily available for most problems arising from traditional classroom teaching, this is reduced when technological expertise is a requirement. Administrative support is also required in the form of assistance from technicians, budget allocations and workload redistribution (Link & Scholtz, 2000).

Potential advantages in this role-change exist in the changed relationship between students and tutor. Adult learning requires a reduction of the power differential between tutor and student (Mezirow, 1996). Removing the tutor from the front of the classroom and into a shared communication modality addresses power differentials and also reflects healthcare curricula and practice where issues of equal partnership between worker and service users are central. In this respect the use of information technology to diminish the teacher-learner differential also reflects what is being sought in the practitioner-client relationship. To achieve this requires a great deal of work and effort on the part of the tutor. E-learning is not something that can be put together one night and delivered the next day. It is time consuming, challenging and sometimes very frustrating, but tutors who make a success of it also find it personally enriching and professionally very satisfying and fulfilling. Many tutors also enjoy the challenge of making learning active and practical and fun.

There are practical advantages in students being able to turn the tutor on or off, for example greater choice about when to engage with education, and being able to avoid travel and parking costs. Students with disabilities benefit from improved access. Students who are struggling or unmotivated, however, are not detected easily and the technology medium can be experienced as cold or unemotional (Burgstahler, 1997). These educational concerns are offset by how technology based learning can enhance the joining of practice and theory with the entire intake group being able to communicate with tutors whilst on placement rather than waiting for a campus based practice learning day. Students generally find this a non-threatening way to discuss ideas and engage in discourse. This makes e-learning a powerful method for promoting group reflective practice (Christianson, Tiene & Luft, 2002). Organisational considerations such as presumed savings associated with computer based learning and the reduced need for valuable classroom space are balanced with initial high costs in equipment and training tutors who are still required to provide guidance to students (Malloy & DeNatale, 2001).

Such approaches represent a departure for many educators, but this also applies to many students, who have often been schooled in the traditional "chalk and talk" approach. This could result in both frustration and resentment on the part of the student. Much of the focus can be centred on the approach itself rather than the topic in question. In this respect educators have a duty to both structure courses so as to minimise such feelings, for example by giving clear indications as to what is expected from students and offer ongoing support and guidance during group work. It may be necessary to consider the level of the students, so that more radical approaches are reserved for more experienced learners (Malloy & DeNatale, 2001). Similarly, the degree to which any approach is implemented can vary. There are courses with very strong constructivist or resource-based approaches, which do not provide any material to the students, whereas others may offer a specific database or set of materials, along with more guidance. When dealing with any educational technology there is a strong link between the pedagogy and the possibilities of the technology itself. Many of the approaches to teaching can be combined successfully within one course using e-learning. This not only means that each can be used where it is best suited, but also makes for an interesting course. The danger is that students feel they have just become comfortable with one approach when a new one is thrust upon them, which can be disruptive.

Sharpe, (2003) identifies some typical worries for online students that include the following: students may become unclear about the purpose of the activity and/or what is expected of them; they may be apprehensive or unsure about what roles the tutor will take on; e.g. who will respond and when there may be uncertainty about using the systems, e.g. handling threads and multiple discussions and data bases. Students may worry about poor typing, spelling and the permanency of messages. Students may feel isolated and not know how to ask for help.

The educator's function is to firstly create the learning opportunities and then guide students through these, while allowing the students to be active in the learning process. This is quite a fundamental shift for many educators, and it has been suggested by Salmon (2003) that it is one that rather undermines the ego of some. This is significant as the e-learning medium is not suited to being dominated by one individual, but rather it is the technology that facilitates communication from all participants. Invariably the personal tastes and beliefs of the tutor will have an influence on the way the course is constructed and run as will the needs and resources of the institute that the tutor works for.

Innovators within traditional courses have embraced the concept and have often produced creative and high quality material to supplement their existing courses. But these individuals are in a minority; most nurse educators will not become developers or supporters of such technology unless considerable time and resources are dedicated to supporting this activity. Staff who are sent on "generic" workshops designed to improve their use of computer assisted learning technologies may complain afterwards that they still do not know where to start and feel the time was not well spent. For all these reasons, staff training should be tightly targeted and be offered on a project by project basis.

Developing e-learning applications is a lengthy and skilled process. The cost of hardware and software, and telephone line charges, often prove a more important barrier to accessing web-based materials and programmes than the course organisers assume initially. The amount of training needed to become comfortable with specialised software packages is often underestimated; students on a course that relies heavily on computer work may spend most of their first term getting to grips with the technology. Few students learn all the essential skills at the onset of the course. Rather they tend to use "just in time learning" – that is, most of them make no attempt to get to grips with a feature of the software until they actually need to use that feature. This suggests that too much initial training may not be popular or effective.

Tutors will also need a degree of political "nous" in order to understand the point of view of the various stakeholders (Groth, 1999). Organisational managers may have a different perspective from the tutor and there may well be different, and possibly conflicting, interests within and between organisations. However, if an initiative is to develop and succeed, these differences have to be worked with in the interests of the project. Accommodating more positively different points of view and working with available resources can lead to local innovation and lead to new forms of provision.

There are particular challenges in designing and delivering programmes that need to be multidisciplinary, relevant and accessible for nurses and other disciplines such as social workers and medical staff. Nursing, like these other professions, involves decision making based upon the best available evidence. There has been an explosion of knowledge and information in health care in the past decades. Patient care has become complex, resulting in increased specialisation in all health care professions, and in-depth exploration of issues by each specific profession. However, this means that no one health care provider can meet all the complex needs of a patient and his/her family. With increasing specialisation, learners have fewer opportunities to interact with either disciplines and professions, immersing themselves more and more in knowledge and culture of their own professional group. Even the geographic locations of the schools within a university limit possible inter-professional interactions. E-learning is one way of breaking down these barriers by collaborative working. By acknowledging and valuing the differences between professions courses can be developed in which students can interact through a virtual community, sharing ideas and knowledge through social discord and learning.

However, whatever course is pursued, it will inevitably be influenced by those that are running it. This will be balanced by the needs of the students and the requirements of the course in terms of qualification and outcome. When good teaching and learning happen, the student becomes the focal point and the positive results that education should have become the common goal of all members of the educational team. E-learning activities should therefore put the student and their needs foremost; be interactive and engaging; supported by relevant, accessible resources; integrated into the course and its assessment; and link theory to practice. This can be ensured by considering the student at the planning and policy level through to monitoring and evaluation. As part of the monitoring process each student can be tracked and progress expressed in the form of graphs and written information; a feature of many off the shelf teaching packages (e.g. WebCT). Laurillard (2000) stresses that for higher level learning, dialogue must take place at both a theoretical level and practical level. This not only enables students to link theory with practice, but also enables the e-moderator to evaluate whether or not he or she has set appropriate tasks for the student.

One of the major characteristics of the model is the way in which the student and e-moderator interacts. In face-to-face teaching, many of these interactions are so spontaneous and intuitive that they can be overlooked in the design of technology educational systems. Therefore Laurillard made these interactions explicit. Technology can support these interactions in the following ways:

- Narrative – e-moderators" conceptions are made accessible to students and vice versa.
- Interactive – the e-moderator provides feedback to students based on the outcomes of tasks students undertake. In addition the e-moderator uses this information to revise what learning has occurred and, if necessary, change the focus of the dialogue (adaptive)
- Communicative – the moderator supports processes where the students discus and reflect upon their learning. The e-moderator and student agree learning goals and task goals, which can be achieved using "productive" media, such as online presentations.

Learners need to make consistent decisions based independently on applying a series of rules and guidelines. They need to reach collaborative decisions together through negotiation and discussion. Learners need to be able to analyse material for technical and aesthetic concerns, content and historical influences. Material studied within an electronic medium needs to relate to the wider world and these links need to be made specific. This can be done by either by applying a set of predefined criteria to the material studied or by establishing criteria for the critical evaluation and analysis of what is being taught.

If practitioners are to embed new learning and skills into their routines and make changes in the way they work, then adequate support and supervision is essential to making this happen. Without it, the use of new skills and learning may well be compromised. Informal supervision is often a significant form of support to ward based practitioners and education, and this should be recognised as a useful and important part of course development. However, more formalised approaches should complement these arrangements. Just because a module may be run over the web, it does not negate the support that a student is entitled too and time for this important activity should be incorporated in planning stage.

A CHECKLIST FOR DEVELOPING AN E-LEARNING ACTIVITY

Lastly there needs to be a means of evaluating the instructional design. Whether evaluating your own instructional design efforts or those of your training vendor, a yes to all of the following questions is evidence of a high quality instructional design programme:

- Does the programme immediately capture one's attention when it is run?
- Does the training programme explain its relevance to learners? Does it answer the student's question, "What's in it for me?" Ask how the student might experience their progress through the learning activity, from start to finish.
- Are learning objectives presented near the beginning of each lesson?
- Are learning objectives specific and observable?
- Is the presentation of content made interesting with a variety of media or through an engaging treatment?
- Does the programme provide a variety of interactive exercises beyond simple multiple-choice questions?
- Are learners given the opportunity for frequent practice?
- Is feedback immediate and specific? What opportunities are there for feedback to students on their progress?
- Clarify how students will be supported in their learning.
- How have issues of accessibility been accommodated within the design of and preparation of the materials? How does the design proactively accommodate diversity within the student body?

- Who will teach/tutor on the activity? What additional skills/facilities might the staff need?
- How much of the technology incorporated in the plan is already available and accessible to the clinical practice area?
- Does the programme include a post-test or other final assessment? Can the learning process through the activity be related to the final assessment to the understanding of the student?

(Adapted from Kruse, K. (2004). Checklist: Evaluating Instructional Design for e-Learning.)

Applications for information technology utilisation expand into other areas other than education and learning. Technology that offers advantages to mental health workers and service users will offer additional incentives for use and engagement. Setting up web sites for integrated mental health programmes with links to individual teams can inform all service stakeholders on issues such as access, staff profiles, services, operational issues such as hours of operation and specific team roles. Additional links to relevant health sites can also be incorporated. Access can be graded so that staff can utilise the same web site for sharing knowledge and in-house learning, particularly useful in rural and mixed urban/rural areas of service delivery. It is important to remember that e-learning is an idea and like all good ideas it needs to be sold and the benefits highlighted.

CONCLUSION

It is important that in order for e-learning to take place within the clinical environment practitioners and service users are taken on board right from the beginning. Collaboration is required to develop effective opportunities for learning using electronic media. There must also be a commitment to expanding the resources required for running such educational support systems. A successful health education system needs to match its environment in relation to technical, social and organisational factors; these latter ones including the perceptions of key stakeholders. Too often, such programmes are developed in isolation away from the clinical setting based on policy and procedure. Educational systems of the kind described above make imperative an understanding of practitioner decision making and the client experience. Presenting information in a form understandable to practitioners, as an active first person encounter of the type they would engage in practice, provides a means for comprehending knowledge through service delivery and personal and practice development. E-learning cannot function in isolation but should be part of an overall strategy of learning designed to reflect the needs of practitioners and in turn service users. The purpose is to make learning activities an experience with information where content delivery is not the primary experience but is secondary to the use of new and existing knowledge within the clinical setting.

REFERENCES

Anderson J.G., Aydin C. & Jay S.J. (1995). *Evaluating Health Care Information systems*. London: Sage.

Ballard, E. (2001). Taking control of information, *Nursing Management*, 8(2), 10–15.

Berg, M. (1999). Patient Care information Systems and Healthcare Work: A Sociotechnical Approach. *International Journal of Medical Information*, *55*, 87–101.

Brookfield, S.D. (1987). *Developing critical thinkers: Challenging adults to explore alternative ways of thinking and acting*. San Francisco: Jossey-Bass.

Burgstahler, S. (1997). Teaching on the Net: What's the difference? *Technological Horizons in Education Journal*, April, 61–64.

Chase, S.K. (1997). Charting critical thinking: Nursing judgements and patient outcomes. *Dimensions of Critical Care Nursing*, *16*, 102–111.

Checkland, P.B. & Holwell, S. (1998). *Information, Systems and information Systems*. Chichester: John Wiley & Sons, Ltd.

Christianson, L. et al. (2002). Web-based Teaching in Undergraduate Nursing Programs, *Nurse Educator*, *27*, 276–282.

Clarke, S. (2004). *Acute Inpatient Mental Health Care: Education, Training & Continuing Professional Development for All*. London: Department of Health Publications.

Drazen, E.L., Metzger, J.B., Ritter, J.L. & Schneider, M.K. (1995). *Patient Care information Systems: Successful Design and Implementation*. New York: Springer.

Department of Health (2001). *"Building the Information Core – Implementing the NHS Plan"*. London: Department of Health.

Diller B. (1995). Don't repackage – redefine [Available] www.Hotwired.com

Entwistle, N.J. (1998). Improving teaching through research on student learning. In J.J. F. Forest (ed) *University teaching: International Perspectives*. New York: Garland, pp. 73–112.

Entwistle, N. & Ramsden, P. (1983). *Understanding Student Learning*. London: Croom Helm.

Garside, P. (1998). Organisational context for quality: lessons from the fields of organisational development and change management. *Quality in Health Care*, *7*(Suppl), S8–S15.

Glaser, J.P. & Hsu, L. (1999). *The Strategic Application of Information Technology in Healthcare Organisations*. Boston: McGraw-Hill.

Goodsir, W.W. (1978). Knowles' term "Andragogy" and its implications for adult education, *Australian Journal of Adult Education*, *18*, 10–18.

Groth, L. (1999). *Future Organisational Design: The Scope for IT-based Enterprise*. Chichester: John Wiley & Sons, Ltd. .

Johnson, G. & Scholes, K. (1989). *Exploring Corporate Strategy: Text and Cases*. London: Prentice Hall International.

Kaplan, B. (2001). Evaluating informatics applications: social interactionism and call for methodological pluralism, *International Journal of Medical Information*, *8*(2), 194–198.

Koppi, A. & Chaloupka, M. (1997). Heuristic contextual action works best. *ASCILITE*, December 1997. http://www.ascilite.org.au/conferences/perth97/papers/Koppi/Koppi.html [Accessed 30.08.2005].

Kreber C. (1998). The relationship between self-directed learning, critical thinking , and psychological type, and some implications for teaching in higher education, *Studies in Higher Education*, *23*, 71–87.

Kruse, K. (2004). e-Learning Alphabet Soup: A Guide to Terms. [Available] e-LearningGuru.com. www.e-Learningguru.com [Accessed 30.08.2005].

Malloy, S.E. & DeNatale, M.L. (2001). Online Critical Thinking: A Case Study Analysis, *Nurse Educator*, *26*, 191–197.

Mezirow, J. (1996). Contemporary paradigms of learning, *Adult Learning Quarterly*, *46*(3), 158–172.

Link, D.G. & Scholtz, S. (2000). Educational Technology and the Faculty Role: What You Don't Know Can Hurt You, *Nurse Educator*, *26*(6), 274–276.

National research and Development Centre (2003). *Using laptop computers to develop basic skills: a handbook for practitioners*. London: NRDC Publications.

NHS Connecting for Health (2005a). *Better information better health*. London: NHS.

NHS Connecting for Health (2005b). *A guide to the National Programme for Information Technology*. London: NHS.

NHS Connecting for Health (2005c). *Making the Connection*. London: NHS.

NIMHE (2003). *Expert Briefing – post-qualifying mental health training* London: Department of Health.

Pare, G. & Elam, J.J. (1998). Introducing information technology in the clinical setting. *International Journal of Technology Assessment in Health Care, 14*(2), 331–343.

Proctor, P.M. (2001). Information and Communications Technology: Nursling's future role, *Japanese Journal of Nursing Research, 34*(3), 73–80.

Robotham, D. (1999). *The Application of learning style theory in higher education teaching.* University of Wolverhampton.

Rosenberg, M. (2001). *eLearning.* London: McGraw-Hill.

Salmon, G. (2003). *Bang on the door. . . New technologies and E-learning.* Nottingham University, School of Nursing Conference.

Sharpe, R. (2003). *Designing activities for online learning.* Oxford Centre for Staff and Learning Development.

Snyder-Halpern, R., Corcoran-Perry, S. & Narayan, S. (2001). Developing Clinical Practice Environments: Supporting the Knowledge Work of Nurses. *Computers in Nursing, 19*(1), 45–52.

Taylor, J.C. (1995). Distance education technologies: The fourth generation, *Australian Journal of Education Technology, 11*(2), 1–7.

Yates, F. (ed) (1996). *Creative Computing in Health and Social Care.* Chichester: John Wiley & Sons, Ltd.

Watkins, D.A. (1983). Depth of processing and the quality of learning outcomes, *Instructional Science, 12*, 49–58.

Weller, M. (2002). *Delivering Learning on the Net.* London: Routledge Farmer.

CHAPTER 28

Therapy Training Online: Using the Internet to Widen Access to Training in Mental Health Issues

Chris Blackmore, Emmy van Deurzen and Digby Tantam

INTRODUCTION

This chapter examines the role of the internet in mental health training and examines what can be learnt from the experience of SEPTIMUS, a new E-based psychotherapy training programme.

In one study, we report on a comparison of eLearning and face-to-face training. In another study, we outline our response to an evaluation of the programme which suggested that the learning materials should be redesigned to increase the potential for collaborative learning. We measure the impact of this change in course culture by comparing a battery of outcomes at the end of years 1 and 2. We also include an analysis of one country where the collaborative learning model was not adopted, and this serves as a control.

THE INTERNET AND MENTAL HEALTH

As the internet continues to become a more significant and ever-present part of every-day life, there is growing evidence that mental health interventions over the internet are effective. Much of the research on computer-based programmes has focused on anxiety disorders (Newman, 1997). Randomised controlled trials in delivering online interventions for depression (Christensen, Griffiths et al., 2004) and anxiety disorders (Richards, 2002; Kenardy, 2003) have shown that the internet can be used effectively. And when surveyed, online patients seemed happy with the treatment they receive (Ainsworth, 2002). There have been increasing numbers of empirical reports utilising online therapy, with every one of these empirical studies showing significant improvements for those treated using online therapy (Griffiths, 2003). In terms of training for psychotherapy students, recent research

Teaching Mental Health. Edited by Theo Stickley and Thurstine Basset.
Copyright © 2007 John Wiley & Sons, Ltd.

(Blackmore, 2005) suggests that in comparative studies, eLearning fares very well compared to traditional face-to-face methods of teaching psychotherapy theory.

eLEARNING IN EUROPE

Whilst electronic approaches to theoretical learning ("eLearning") have been rapidly expanding in the last decade, they have not had a major impact on the field of mental health training until relatively recently. This may have been due to the view that the internet was not suitable for training students in a field which is practice-based and relies heavily on both verbal and non-verbal communication. Furthermore, the ambitions of some of the eLearning protagonists have proved over-optimistic. The demise of expensive learning collaborations like the UK eUniversity and "Fathom", a partnership between several prestigious universities and the British Library, have created a backlash against the feasibility of eLearning. Studies suggest that eLearning is not just limited by the availability of the internet. Statistics published by Internet World Statistics (http://www.internetworldstats.com/stats4.htm, updated 23.7.05) indicate that 36.8 % of the 731 million people in Europe have access to the internet, and that the proportion is higher in the European Union (48.1 %) and higher still in the UK (59.8 %), making it the fifth most internet-connected European Union country, after Sweden, Denmark, Finland and the Netherlands, and the seventh in the world.

However, it is not internet access that limits the use of the internet for eLearning, but the perception of the value of eLearning compared to face-to-face learning. In a "Eurobarometer" survey carried out by the University of Cologne on behalf of the European Centre for the Development of Vocational Training, 18,000 European Union citizens were interviewed, of whom 80 % thought that life-long learning was important, but only just over a half were confident in using a computer (65 % of male and 52 % of female respondents). Only 17 % of respondents had recently taken courses, or thought of taking courses, at schools, universities, or colleges; only 31 % of people have taken part in some form of education in the past year; and only 12 % would consider distance learning. Even fewer would consider using the internet for collaborative learning (Chisholm, 2004). This is a reflection of a general phenomenon in internet development – new ideas and new programmes are quickly taken up by a minority of "early adopters", but then take much longer to be adopted by the majority of web users.

There is increasing evidence from early meta-analyses of eLearning versus traditional learning to show that on cognitive measures such as performance, learning, and achievement, students in eLearning classes perform at least as well as those in "face-to-face" classes (Sonner 1999; Spooner 1999; Schoech 2000). Research on satisfaction is not so clear – Carr (2000) found online instruction in psychology to be effective, but not satisfying, while Johnson et al. (2000) found that students in a face-to-face course held slightly more positive perceptions about the instructor and overall course quality than those in an eLearning course, although there was no difference between the two course formats in several measures of learning outcomes. However, when like-for-like methods are compared, i.e. the same courses delivered by the same teachers in either eLearning or traditional formats, the differences in student performance and satisfaction disappear (Broudo, 1997). Russell (1999), from a research bibliography of 355 research reports, summaries and papers, finds "no significant differences" in student outcomes between alternate modes of education delivery. eLearning is no less effective than traditional learning and, for potential students who are too distant from training centres or who have family or other commitments that prevent them from attending, may be the only available kind of learning.

The research suggests that distance students seem to learn as much as students receiving traditional face-to-face instruction so long as three conditions are met:

- the method and technologies used are appropriate to the instructional tasks;
- there is student-to-student interaction;
- there is regular and appropriate tutor-to-student feedback (Moore, 1990; Verduin, 1991).

SEPT AND SEPTIMUS

Against the background of eLearning described above, a series of action research projects on eLearning funded by grants from the European Commission have been conducted in recent years. The SEPT project (Tantam, 2001) showed that access to psychotherapy training for those who are in most need is restricted in many European countries. Therefore the SEPTIMUS project was designed to widen accessibility to psychotherapy training by increasing access for students who live in geographically isolated areas, who have family/work commitments or who have a disability. SEPTIMUS is a one year psychotherapy training programme blending theoretical instruction and tutoring delivered by eLearning methods with supervision, therapy, and practical experience delivered face-to-face and local to one of the 16 participating training centres, located in eight European countries – Austria, Czech Republic, Ireland, Italy, Poland, Portugal, Romania and UK.

The SEPTIMUS units were aimed at mental health professionals, primarily counsellors and psychotherapists, but also social workers, teachers, psychiatric nurses, doctors and the police. The first three units were developed and available to students in 2002–3 and 2003–4. The subsequent three units have been made available to students in five countries from 2004 onwards as part of a SOCRATES ERASMUS project. The units available are as follows:

1. Well-being and mental health.
2. Existential and human issues.
3. Conflict management.
4. An overview of different methods of psychotherapy and personal change.
5. Ethics, culture and discrimination.
6. Development through the life cycle.

Each unit consisted of 10 weeks' worth of study, and each week, students are required to:

(a) read between five and 10 pages of online course material;
(b) follow up on any of the many hyperlinks to related internet sites;
(c) respond to at least three of the questions at the bottom of each page by posting an answer onto the discussion forum;
(d) respond to other students' and tutors' postings on the discussion forum;
(e) complete three online multiple choice questions about that week's material;
(f) attend the one hour chatroom with fellow students and tutors to reflect upon that week's materials and the points raised in the discussion forum postings.

At the end of each unit, a 3,000 word assignment is required on that unit's topic.

To date, over 200 students have studied on the programme, from over 20 different countries worldwide. Application data of the original research group confirms that over half (N = 61) of SEPTIMUS students had been previously prevented by an external factor from applying for a psychotherapy course, giving the following reasons:

Table 28.1 Factors that have prevented previous applications for psychotherapy training

	Child-care (%)	Distance from training centre (%)	Lack of practical experience (%)	Lack of qualifications (%)	Finance (%)	Other (%)
eLearners (n = 61)	19.7	55.7	31.1	19.7	55.7	13.1

Comparisons of eLearners with attending learners suggest that distance from training institute has been a significant barrier in the past.

Furthermore, when asked how often they would be able to visit their nearest training institute, 78 % (N = 45) of attending students could visit their training institute at least weekly, but 49 % of SEPTIMUS students (N = 61) considered that they could only realistically visit their training institute monthly or even less.

Thus SEPTIMUS has widened accessibility to mental health training in Europe, particularly for those who live long distances from training institutes.

COMPARISON OF SEPTIMUS WITH FACE-TO-FACE PSYCHOTHERAPY LEARNING

In order to measure student satisfaction and performance for the eLearning course, upon finishing one of the three units of study, each student was required to complete a 32-item questionnaire, submissible online. This asked them to detail their levels of satisfaction with and time spent on various aspects of the programme. 156 students from across the eight project countries returned data. To compare eLearning and face-to-face learning, 61 students who were taking comparable, but traditional attending courses in three of the participating training institutes (in Romania, Ireland and UK) were given an adapted 32-item questionnaire. For example, E-learners were asked "How much do you think the course material helped you to understand this area?" whereas face-to-face learners were asked, "How much has looking at course texts helped you to understand this area?" Students were required either to give a score of 1 to 5 on the Likert scale, or to give durations in hours/minutes.

RESULTS

The answers from the two groups of students were statistically analysed as shown in the tables below:

Table 28.2   Distance of home from nearest training institute

	Average distance from home to nearest training institute
eLearners (n = 106)	116 Km
attending students (n = 56)	44 Km

Table 28.3   Frequency with which training institute could be visited

	2 × per week (%)	1 × per week (%)	1 × per 2 weeks (%)	1 × per 4 weeks (%)	less often (%)
eLearners (n = 124)	16.9	15.3	18.5	30.6	18.5
Attending students (n = 58)	48.3	29.3	17.2	1.7	3.4

Table 28.4   Student feedback data comparing satisfaction levels between SEPTIMUS (2002–4) and comparable face-to-face psychotherapy training courses (2003–4)

	Means for face-to-face learning methods (n = 61)	Means for eLearning methods (n = 156)	Mann-Whitney sig
Satisfaction with course materials (1–5)	2.63	3.82	MW = 2119.000, p < 0.0001
Satisfaction with tutor (1–5)	3.13	3.65	MW = 3374.000, p < 0.0001
Satisfaction with class discussions/discussion forums (1–5)	2.92	3.15	MW = 6843.500, p = 0.839
Understanding of whole unit (1–5)	3.72	3.81	MW = 6357.500, p = 0.315

Table 28.5   Student feedback data comparing time spent on SEPTIMUS (2002–4) and comparable face-to-face psychotherapy training courses (2003–4)

	Means for face-to-face learning methods (n = 61)	Means for eLearning methods (n = 156)	T-test sig
Time on course materials (hours/week)	2.82	4.52	t = −4.830, p < 0.0001
Time with tutor (hours/week)	1.73	1.17	t = 2.350, p = 0.024
Time on class discussions/discussion forums (hours/week)	1.81	1.32	t = 1.670, p = 0.096
Time on assessment (hours/week)	2.30	1.90	t = 0.861, p = 0.396

When comparing the e-learners (n = 156) with traditional learners (n = 61), the results were as follows:

Satisfaction levels

- There is strong statistical evidence of greater satisfaction of eLearning students with regard to the course material and tutor (both p<0.0001).
- The data does not provide enough evidence of different levels of satisfaction between the two groups with regard to the discussion forums (p = 0.839) and understanding of topic (p = 0.315).

Time

- There is strong statistical evidence of eLearning students spending more time on the course material (p < 0.0001).
- There is strong statistical evidence of face-to-face students spending more time with their tutors (p = 0.024).
- The data does not provide enough evidence of different amounts of time being spent between the two groups with regard to the discussion forums (p = 0.096) and assessments (p = 0.396).

In summary, E-learners were more satisfied with the course material and tutors than face-to-face learners. E-learners spent longer on the course materials than face-to-face learners, but less time with tutors. Other differences noted between the two groups were not statistically significant in this instance.

COLLABORATIVE LEARNING

In response to an evaluation at the end of the 2002/3 year of study, it was recommended that the learning materials be redesigned to increase the potential for collaborative learning to take place. Collaborative learning is defined by Gokhale (1995) as "an instruction method in which learners at various performance levels work together in small groups toward a common goal"; the active exchange of ideas within small groups increases interest and promotes critical thinking (Gokhale, 1995). Collaborative learning involving the joint construction of meaning through interaction with others can be characterised by a joint commitment to a shared goal (Littleton, 1999; Lewis, 2000). Perhaps because of the positive experiences with collaborative learning methods in face-to-face scenarios (Slavin, 1996), they were an obvious candidate for use in this eLearning situation.

To promote collaborative learning, the box at the end of each page was redesigned to promote use of discussion forum and collaborative learning practices by asking, for example:

> Can you remember the first time that you gained an awareness of death as a child? Post a message to your discussion forum tutorial group, and remember to respond to others' messages.

Each student was invited to start a discussion thread with their answers, and students were then required to read and respond to one another's postings. Tutors would also respond to these postings, so that long threads, leading from the initial student's response, could develop over time. Case histories were linked to various pages each week and specially produced video material was made available where appropriate.

By directing students to the discussion forum at particular points in their study and with a particular task to complete, we were implementing behaviour rules for structuring dialogues, known as "co-operation scripts" (Dansereau, 1988; Webb, 1996). In addition, as feedback from learners showed that tutor support got the lowest rating of learner satisfaction in every country and it is well known that effective tutors are essential for distance learning programmes to be successful (Duggleby, 2000; Salmon, 2000), a more effective tutor training e-session was designed and implemented for the 2003–4 intake.

COMPARISON OF SATISFACTION LEVELS (WITHIN YEARS) IN COUNTRIES WITH OR WITHOUT COLLABORATIVE LEARNING

The data suggest that for 2002–3, the differences between the seven countries (without CL) and country P (no CL) were not significant for *satisfaction with understanding of topic*, *satisfaction with course materials* and *satisfaction with tutor*, but there was a significant difference between them in terms of *satisfaction with discussion forums*, i.e. even before the implementation of collaborative learning, there was significant difference between satisfaction with discussion forums between the two groups.

The data suggest that for 2003–4, the differences between the seven countries (with CL) and country P (no CL) were not significant for *satisfaction with understanding of topic*, *satisfaction with course materials* and *satisfaction with tutor*, but there was a significant difference between them in terms of *satisfaction with discussion forums*, i.e. this difference

Table 28.6 Learner data from feedback questionnaires comparing satisfaction levels between seven countries without CL and country P (non CL) for 2002–3 learner groups

	2002–3				
	Mean satisfaction in seven countries without CL (n = 163)	Standard deviation	Mean satisfaction in country P (no CL) (n = 163)	Standard deviation	Mann-Whitney U
With understanding of topic	3.87	0.59	3.78	0.49	MW = 1875.000 $Z = -.740$ p = .459
With course materials	3.86	0.66	3.70	0.63	MW = 1794.500 $Z = -1.076$ p = .282
With tutor	3.51	0.98	3.76	0.59	MW = 1836.000 $Z = -.896$ p = .370
With discussion forums	3.19	0.97	2.32	1.15	MW = 1183.000 $Z = -3.673$ p = .000

Table 28.7 Learner data from feedback questionnaires comparing satisfaction levels between seveb countries with CL and country P (non CL) for 2003–4 learner groups

	2003–4				
	Mean satisfaction in seven countries with CL for (n = 163)	Standard deviation	Mean satisfaction in country P (no CL) (n = 163)	Standard deviation	Mann-Whitney U
With understanding of topic	3.83	0.82	3.48	0.70	MW = 727.500 Z = −1.640 p = .101
With course materials	3.89	0.80	3.31	0.79	MW = 4807.500 Z = −2.291 p = .022
With tutor	3.81	1.05	3.49	0.48	MW = 5805.000 Z = −.429 p = .668
With discussion forums	3.45	1.02	2.33	0.95	MW = 3266.000 Z = −5.064 p = .000

between groups in terms of satisfaction with discussion forums remained after the introduction of collaborative learning. In fact, the difference between the two groups increased from 2002–3 to 2003–4.

COMPARISON OF TIME SPENT ON STUDIES IN COUNTRIES WITH OR WITHOUT COLLABORATIVE LEARNING

The data suggest that for 2002–3, the differences between the seven countries (without CL) and country P (no CL) were not significant for *time spent on course materials*, but there was a significant difference between them in terms of *time spent on discussion forums*, i.e. students were spending significantly longer in the discussion forums in the seven countries without CL compared to country P. Data for *time spent with tutor* was not available.

The data suggest that for 2003–4, there was a significant difference between the seven countries (with CL) and country P (no CL) for *time spent on course materials*, but there was no significant difference between them in terms of *time spent online with tutor* and *time spent on discussion forums,* i.e. students using collaborative learning methods spent significantly less time in direct contact with their tutors.

COMPARISON OF SATISFACTION LEVELS (BETWEEN YEARS) IN COUNTRIES WHERE COLLABORATIVE LEARNING WAS IMPLEMENTED

The data suggest that when comparing 2002–3 (without CL) and 2003–4 (with CL), the differences between the seven countries were not significant for *satisfaction with understanding of topic* and *satisfaction with course materials*. There was a significant difference between the two groups in terms of *satisfaction with tutor* and *satisfaction with discussion forums*, i.e. students reported significantly higher levels of satisfaction with their tutor and discussion forums as a result of implementation of collaborative learning.

The data suggest that when comparing 2002–3 and 2003–4 for country P (no CL), the differences were not significant for *satisfaction with understanding of topic, satisfaction with course materials, satisfaction with tutor or satisfaction with discussion forums*, i.e. there was no significant change in their satisfaction. This suggests that any changes in the other countries' satisfaction levels was indeed due to the implementation of collaborative learning.

Table 28.8 Learner data from feedback questionnaires comparing time spent on course between seven countries without CL and country P (non CL) for 2002–3 learner groups

	2002–3				
	Mean hours/week per learner in seven countries without CL (n = 163)	Standard deviation	Mean hours/week per learner in country P (no CL) (n = 163)	Standard deviation	t-test
On course materials	5.04	2.52	4.20	2.03	t = 1.708 df = 159 sig = .090
Online with tutor	*	*	*	*	t = * df = * sig = *
On discussion forums	1.07	0.78	0.46	0.45	t = 5.699 df = 76.205 sig = .000

*removed in the split half reliability calculation.

Table 28.9 Learner data from feedback questionnaires comparing time spent on course between seven countries with CL and country P (non CL) for 2003–4 learner groups

	2003–4				
	Mean hours/week per learner in seven countries with CL for 2003–4 (n =)	Standard deviation	Mean hours/week per learner in country P (no CL) (n = 163)	Standard deviation	Mann-Whitney U
On course materials	4.43	2.13	3.24	1.71	t = 2.147 df = 139 sig = .034
Online with tutor	1.06	0.71	1.25	0.26	t = −1.027 df = 135 sig = .306
On discussion forums	1.52	1.17	3.43	4.53	t = −1.516 df = 12.173 sig = .155

Table 28.10 Learner data from feedback questionnaires comparing satisfaction levels on course for seven countries without CL (2002–3) and seven countries with CL (2003–4)

	2002–3		2003–4		
	Mean satisfaction in seven countries without CL (n = 163)	Standard deviation	Mean satisfaction in seven countries with CL for 2003–4 (n =)	Standard deviation	Mann-Whitney U
With understanding of topic	3.87	0.59	3.83	0.82	MW = 7816.000 Z = −.184 p = .854
With course materials	3.86	0.66	3.89	0.80	MW = 7912.500 Z = −.576 p = .564
With tutor	3.51	0.98	3.81	1.05	MW = 6766.500 Z = −2.523 p = .012
With discussion forums	3.19	0.97	3.45	1.02	MW = 7085.500 Z = −1.978 p = .048

COMPARISON OF TIME SPENT ON COURSE (BETWEEN YEARS) IN SEVEN COUNTRIES WHERE COLLABORATIVE LEARNING WAS IMPLEMENTED

The data suggest that when comparing 2002–3 (without CL) and 2003–4 (with CL), the differences between the seven countries were significant for *time spent on course materials* and *time spent on discussion forums*, i.e. in 2003–4 students reported significantly less time on course materials and significantly longer in discussion forums when compared to 2002–3. This was very likely to be as a result of implementation of collaborative learning. Data for *time spent with tutor* was not available.

COMPARISON OF TIME SPENT ON COURSE (BETWEEN YEARS) IN COUNTRY WHERE COLLABORATIVE LEARNING WAS NOT IMPLEMENTED

The data suggest that when comparing 2002–3 and 2003–4 for the country where CL was not implemented, the differences between the two year groups were not significant for *time spent on course materials*. There was a significant difference between the groups for *time spent on discussion forums*. This change occurred in the opposite direction to the change seen in the other countries, and is likely to have been as a result of tutoring practices in that country rather than any changes in the course itself (which did not change between years in country P). Data for *time spent with tutor* was not available.

SUMMARY OF RESULTS

Using the country where CL was not implemented as a control, it is possible to state that when comparing the 2002/3 learners (n = 163) with 2003/4 learners (n = 142):

Table 28.11 Learner data from feedback questionnaires comparing satisfaction levels on course in country P for 2002–3 and 2003–4 learner groups.

	2002–3		2003–4		
	Mean satisfaction in country P (no CL) (n = 163)	Standard deviation	Mean satisfaction in country P (no CL) (n = 163)	Standard deviation	Mann-Whitney U
With understanding of topic	3.78	0.49	3.48	0.70	MW = 205.000 Z = −.999 p = .318
With course materials	3.70	0.63	3.31	0.79	MW = 186.500 Z = −1.395 p = .163
With tutor	3.76	0.59	3.49	0.48	MW = 202.000 Z = −1.063 p = .288
With discussion forums	2.32	1.15	2.33	0.95	MW = 232.500 Z = −.356 p = .722

Table 28.12 Learner data from feedback questionnaires comparing time spent on course for seven countries without CL (2002–3) and 7 countries with CL (2003–4)

	2002–3		2003–4		
	Mean hours/week per learner in seven countries without CL (n = 163)	Standard deviation	Mean hours/week per learner in seven country with CL for 2003–4 (n =)	Standard deviation	t-test
On course materials	5.04	2.52	4.43	2.13	t = 2.103 df = 254 sig = 0.036
Online with tutor	*	*	1.06	0.71	t = * df = * sig = *
On discussion forums	1.07	0.78	1.52	1.17	t = −3.548 df = 207.620 sig = .000

*removed in the split half reliability calculation.

Table 28.13 Learner data from feedback questionnaires comparing time spent on course in country P for 2002–3 and 2003–4 learner groups.

	2002–3		2003–4		
	Mean hours/week per learner in countries P (no CL) (n = 163)	Standard deviation	Mean hours/week per learner in country P (no CL) for 2003–4 (n = 163)	Standard deviation	t-test
On course materials	4.20	2.03	3.24	1.71	t = 1.608 df = 44 sig = 0.115
Online with tutor	*	*	1.25	0.26	t = * df = * sig = *
On discussion forums	0.46	0.45	3.43	4.53	t = −2.360 df = 12.102 sig = 0.036

*removed in the split half reliability calculation.

Satisfaction levels

- There were no significant differences in *satisfaction with course materials* (which did not change) or in learners' perceived *understanding of the topic* between the cohorts.
- The second cohort of learners were significantly more satisfied with their *tutor* and with their *discussion forum* compared to the first cohort

Time

- The second cohort spent significantly *less* time reading the *course material* than the first cohort.
- The second cohort spent significantly *more* time than the first cohort in the online *discussion forums*.
- Data for *time spent with tutor* was not available for the 2002–3 cohort, so it was not possible to make any comparisons between the year groups.

The data analysis of the country P which did not implement CL suggests that the changes brought about between the years 2002–3 and 2003–4 were indeed as a result of the instigation of a collaborative learning model.

Whilst there may have been other factors involved, such as increase in tutoring ability and in the type of student recruited, it seems likely that the implementation of collaborative learning, particularly via the discussion forums, resulted in the second cohort of learners being significantly more satisfied with their *tutor* and with their *discussion forum* compared to the first cohort. It was our understanding that students who had this experience of collaborative learning were also more satisfied with their learning on the course.

FUTURE TRENDS

The future for mental health training looks sure to rest increasingly on embracing the new technologies which are ever more important in people's day-to-day experience. With the geopolitical implications of the European Union becoming increasingly important, freedom to move and work will bring pressure to bear on training organisations to work towards unification of standards between countries. In psychotherapy, this process is likely to rely on the European Certificate of Psychotherapy which is already beginning to allow practitioners to move around Europe with valid certification of their competence to practice anywhere within the EU and looks now set to become the official minimum standard of psychotherapy training across Europe. Along with this new physical mobility will come an increasing reliance on mobile technologies to remain connected to one's families, friends and colleagues. Similarly, these mobile technologies will be used more and more for therapeutic purposes. However, face-to-face mental health work is unlikely to decrease, and the experiential element of training will for the foreseeable future remain a face-to-face activity, though here too new experiments are imaginable.

CONCLUSION

The findings of the SEPTIMUS project, and the experience of tutors, suggests that eLearning is a valuable tool for delivering course material. As with other subject areas, eLearning allows psychotherapy students to work through the course material at their own pace and provides a wealth of supplementary material for them to access. It allows the course material to come alive by being much more interactive – as well as reading the core text, students can find and follow hyperlinks in a way that is much harder to do with books. The course also provides the opportunity for detailed discussion in the form of discussion forums and chatrooms, both of which also provide a permanent record which can be reviewed at any point. This is not the case in conventional training where it can be harder to record interactions in seminar and tutorial discussions. In addition, the Virtual Learning Environment (VLE), along with careful interventions by tutors, facilitated the development of what McLellan calls a "virtual learning community" (VLC) (McLellan, 1998). Tutors were particularly keen to use Schrage's Model of Collaboration (Schrage, 1991) which involves developing virtual communities by emphasising collaboration:

> Collaboration is the process of shared creation: two or more individuals with complementary skills interacting to create a shared understanding that none had previously possessed or could have come to on their own (1991, p. 40).

The results of this study suggest that students valued tutors' input highly and that it helped them to engage with the course material, even though the actual amount of time spent with tutors as rated by students was less than in face-to-face teaching. There may be certain characteristics of the online tutor-student interactions which led to this finding. Online interactions often occurred in small groups of no more than six students. This afforded the interactions with a sense of intimacy. Furthermore, tutors would often respond directly to an individual's posting by replying to a message in a discussion forum thread, for example, and this response would generally occur within one or two days of a student posting their contribution. So it seems as though students felt that the tutors were responsive to them, both in terms of immediacy and intimacy. In short, students felt that the tutors (as well as fellow students) were genuinely interested in their contributions. Joinson and Banyard (2002) comment, "it has long been argued that the internet has a disinhibiting effect on users (Joinson, 1998) which may encourage users...to disclose more health-relevant information about themselves than they would face-to-face (Joinson, 2001)". It is possible that this tendency for the internet to be disinhibiting and to facilitate self-disclosure had a beneficial effect on the tutor-student relationship. Bearing this in mind, there might be ways in which face-to-face teachers can adapt their practice with students to Capitalize on some of the potential utilised in eLearning contexts.

eLearning has been found to be useful in ways specific to mental health issues. Tutors have found that the set-up of the VLE, the development of a VLC and the Model of Collaboration have encouraged students to be much more open and honest about their own personal experience and actively understand the relevance of their own experience to the process of psychotherapy. They have also been able to connect this to the theoretical material on offer through the webpages. This is an extremely valuable situation because mental health students by necessity must be able to examine their own personal experience and relate it to the theory so that they can respond appropriately to clients who may present with some of these same issues. This kind of self-exploration is a vital component of any mental health training, but usually the experiential and theoretical elements remain fairly separate. Through the e-learning the two have been brought together and integrated. Course tutors report that the eLearning model as used in this project has been extremely successful in helping students to feel able to discuss personal material in a safe and considered way, and that this kind of openness has happened much more often than during traditional mental health training. It should be noted that the linking between experience and the meaning of this experience in theoretical terms together with its relevance to therapeutic practice is the main gain of this approach as we have discussed elsewhere (Blackmore, van Deurzen & Tantam, 2005).

Discussion forums, like correspondence chess, offer the possibility of interacting with others at a time, place, and pace of one's choosing but they also provide some of the communicative pressure of a chat. They can be used synchronously, and then perform similarly to other IRC chat programmes like MSN messenger, or it can be a bit more like an exchange of emails. This produces a different quality of discussion than the chatroom. Replies can be more considered, hyperlinks can be added to messages, and images or documents attached. There is time for reflection. In our experience, the discussion forum is the most visited page in an educational site. It is an opportunity for students to comment on what they are being taught, and to share their own ideas. Discussion forums facilitate the application of what has been hailed as a new philosophy of teaching, which is variously termed constructivist, collaborative (in this paper), or cognitivist (after Vygotsky) and contrasted with traditional objectivist, didactic, or behaviourist methods. Collaborative teaching gives the learner greater control over their own learning, including control over their learning environment.

In conclusion, there are aspects of many training courses, and this is perhaps particularly true of mental health training, where face-to-face contact is essential. For example, mental health trainees need to be engaging in regular supervised psychotherapy, and both the sessions themselves and the supervision are best done in person. There is increasing interest in therapy over the internet, but it is not envisaged that a therapist could complete their training without spending significant amounts of time with clients in a face-to-face situation. Indeed,

European regulations governing accreditation of psychotherapy do not currently accept on-line therapy as a substitute for face-to-face therapy. Therefore, the preferred model for the foreseeable future of this course will be blended learning, where much of the theoretical element of a course can usefully be delivered from distance, and where certain significant interactions still occur in person. The findings of this study suggest that eLearning is a valuable tool for delivering mental health theoretical material, primarily due to its flexible and interactive nature. Course materials can be accessed at any time, and webpages provide a huge amount of potential further reading material. From the application data submitted by students, it is clear that eLearning has widened access to psychotherapy training, and the results of the project point to its considerable potential for the future in this subject area, especially as part of a blended learning programme.

REFERENCES

Ainsworth, M. (2002). ABC's of "Internet Therapy": E-therapy history and survey. http://www.metanoia.org

Blackmore, C., van Deurzen, E. & Tantam, D. (2005). A comparative evaluation of eLearning versus traditional "face-to-face" teaching methods in a psychotherapy training programme. *Encyclopedia of Virtual Communities and Technologies*. E.S. Dasgupta, George Washington University, USA.

Broudo, M., White, M., Rodenburg, D., Arseneau, R., Chalmers, A., Wright, J. et al., (1997). The Effectiveness of Interactive Multimedia as an Instructional Aid for Learning Basic Clinical Skills and Knowledge. In *Advances in Medical Education*. New York: Kluwer Academic Press, pp.1 321–326.

Carr, S. (2000). Online psychology instruction is effective, but not satisfying, study finds. *Chronicle of Higher Education*, *46*(27), A48, 2/5.

Chisholm, L., Larson, A. & Mossoux, A.-F. (2004). *Lifelong learning: citizens' views in close-up. Findings from a dedicated Eurobarometer survey*. Luxembourg: Office for Official Publications of the European Communities.

Christensen, H., Griffiths, K. M. et al. (2004). Delivering interventions for depression by using the internet: randomised controlled trial, *British Medical Journal*, *328*(7434), 265–276.

Dansereau, D.F. (1988). Cooperative learning strategies. In C. E. Weinstein, E. T. Grntz & P. A. Alexander (eds), *Learning and Study Strategies: Issues in Assessment, Instruction, and Evaluation*. San Diego: Academic Press, pp. 103–120.

Duggleby, J. (2000). *How to be an Online Tutor*. Aldershot: Gower.

Gokhale, A.A. (1995). "Collaborative learning enhances critical thinking." *Journal of Technology Education*, *7*(1), 22–30.

Griffiths, M.C.G. (2003). "Online therapy: implications for problem gamblers and clinicians." *British Journal of Guidance and Counselling*, *31*(1).

Johnson, S.D., Aragon, S.R., Shaik, N. & Palma-Rivas, N. (2000). Comparative analysis of learner satisfaction and learning outcomes in online and face-to-face learning environments, *Journal of Interactive Learning Research*, *11*(1), 29–49.

Joinson, A. & Banyard, P. (2002). Psychological aspects of information seeking on the Internet, *Aslib Proceedings*, *54*(2) 95–102.

Kenardy, J., McCafferty, K. and Rosa, V. (2003). Internet-delivered indicated prevention for anxiety disorders: a randomized controlled trial, *Behav Cognit Psychother. 31*, 279–289.

Lewis, R. (2000). *Human activity in learning societies*. Invited paper. In Proceedings of the International Conference on Computers in Education ICCEI/CCAI 2000, Learning Societies in the new Millennium (eds S.S-C. Young, J. Greer, H. Maurer and Y.S. Chee), pp. 36–45. Taiwan: National Tsing Hua University.

Littleton, K.H.P. (1999). Learning together: Understanding the processes of computer-based collaborative learning. *In Collaborative learning; cognitive and computational approaches*. P. Dillenbourg (ed). London: Elsevier Science, pp. 20–30.

McLellan, H. (1998). The internet as a virtual learning community, *Journal of Computing in Higher Education, 9*(2), 92–112.

Moore, M.G.T., Thompson, M.M., with Quigley, A.B., Clark, G.C., & Goff, G.G. (1990). The effects of distance learning: A summary of the literature. Research Monograph No. 2. University Park, PA: The Pennsylvania State University, American Center for the Study of Distance Education. (ED 330 321).

Newman, M. G., Consoli, A. & Taylor, C.B. (1997). Computers in assessment and cognitive behavioral treatment of clinical disorders: Anxiety as a case in point. *Behavior Therapy, 28,* 211–235.

Richards, J. C. and Alvarenga, M.E. (2002). Extension and replication of an internet-based treatment program for panic disorder. *Cognit Behav Ther* (31), 41–47.

Russell, T.L. (1999). *The "No Significant Difference" phenomenon.* Raleigh: North Carolina University.

Salmon, G. (2000). *E-Moderating – The Key to Teaching and Learning Online.* London: Kogan Page.

Schoech, D. (2000). Teaching over the Internet: Results of one doctoral course. *Research on Social Work Practice, 10,* 467–487.

Schrage, M. (1991). *Shared minds: The new technologies of collaboration.* New York: Random House.

Slavin, R.E. (1996). Research on cooperative learning and achievement: What we know, what we need to know. *Contemporary Educational Psychology, 21*(1), 43–69.

Sonner, B. (1999). Success in the capstone business course – assessing the effectiveness of distance learning, *Journal of Education for Business, 74* (4), 243–248.

Spooner, F., Jordan, L., Algozzine, B. & Spooner, M. (1999). Student ratings of instruction in distance learning and on-campus classes, *Journal of Educational Research, 92,* 132–141.

Tantam, D. et al. (2001). The survey of European Psychotherapy training, *International Journal of Psychotherapy, 6*(2), 141–227.

Verduin, J. R. C. & Clark, T. A. (1991). *Distance education: The foundations of effective practice.* San Francisco: Jossey-Bass.

Webb, N.M.P. & Palincsar, A.S. (1996). Group processes in the classroom. *Handbook of Educational Psychology.* D.C. Berliner and R.C. Calfee (eds). New York: MacMillan, pp. 841–873.

CHAPTER 29

Teaching and Learning in the Future

Theo Stickley and Thurstine Basset

INTRODUCTION

In drawing this book to a close, we reflect upon the themes presented and consider how mental health education needs to develop in the future. In order to do this we re-examine some of the influences that have shaped contemporary thinking in mental health education. For it is our assertion that the shape of the future often lies in the vision of those who created the foundations. Every society will have its share of people with mental health problems. Society needs practitioners that can on the one hand weep with those that weep, and on the other provide hope, encouragement, therapy and the kind of relationship that can bring about lasting change. It is the role of the educator to provide an education that is built upon firm foundations.

It is hoped that the chapters offered in this book not only give examples of good practice in mental health education but also communicate methods and approaches rooted within core values. What is intrinsic to each chapter is the sense of shared core values. In this final chapter we examine the nature of these core values.

CORE VALUES IN MENTAL HEALTH EDUCATION

A number of chapters in this book are about service user involvement in one form or another. The current emphasis upon involvement may alter, but the meaning behind it remains. Mental healthcare is provided in an intrinsically political arena. As with any national institution, power struggles are inevitable. These struggles are perhaps more significant in the history of psychiatry with enforced treatment and abuse, notably in the asylum era. There is a history of how service users relate to statutory services in terms of positions of power. In the UK, the process of de-institutionalisation from the asylums and the subsequent perceived failure of community care in the late 1980's and early 1990's, has given rise to the service user movement. During this period a number of initiatives became evident across the country: Patient's Councils emerged, advocacy groups were funded by statutory health authorities. Service user involvement became both expected and demanded by service providers and service users. Service users joined together and nominated representatives to serve on management committees of the newly formed mental health NHS trusts. Apparently, for the first time, mental health service users had their say. As mental health service users began to have their voices listened to, so many voices spoke out in a radical way, which was highly critical of existing services. Some, such as the founder members of *Survivors Speak Out*, did not wish to be branded as service users but survivors; survivors not only of the effects of mental illness but moreover, the effects of being the recipients of mental health *care*, or rather, *having been through the psychiatric system.*

At times, service user groups have gratefully accepted the opportunity to represent service users' views in high places. Furthermore, advocacy organisations have trained service users in the language, politics and discourse of service providers in order to be heard. In recent years however, there have been those who have proposed not merely involvement in the statutory agenda, but rather, partnership working. How can service users (those technically considered by society as "mad", therefore irrational) work in partnership with those who hold institutional power? In the fullness of time it might be seen that the concept of service user involvement has been created by the dominant discourse, that reinforces the power/knowledge position of that discourse and it is only by applying theories of emancipation and liberation that genuine change may be wrought for the position of the service user in relation to psychiatry. There are opportunities to develop new models and approaches that go beyond involvement and that are genuinely emancipatory for people who use mental health services. The PINE project and the delivery of Psychosis Revisited, both described in this book, hopefully illustrate such models in mental health education. Ultimately, the core value expressed through service user involvement in education is the need to transfer power from those who have traditionally been regarded as experts to those who are in reality experts by their own experiences in life. Furthermore, it is this shift in role and power that enables students to engage with learning about mental health on an emotional as well as an intellectual level. Our emphasis upon developing skills of critical reflection and deeper learning enables students to learn by seeing the whole subject of mental health from a more meaningful perspective. It is our role and responsibility to promote caring practice through both emotional and intellectual understanding. Thus, mental health education is inseparable from values that inform teaching and learning.

VALUES BASED TEACHING AND LEARNING

There is much in the way of educational philosophy that supports the core values espoused in this book. For it is how the teacher communicates with the student that models the values of mental health practice. An educational approach that ignores the individual student's learning style, resources, social influences or goals becomes overly didactic and disempowers the student and inhibits learning. Thus, it might be said to be paternalistic. It is here that we would like to draw parallels with people diagnosed as mentally ill. In both cases, the professional holds the knowledge and the power (Foucault, 1971) and autonomy is suppressed. Marton and Saljo (1976) would identify this method of teaching as promoting a "surface" approach to learning. This involves the student memorising facts and concepts without analysis or reflection of their meaning. This, in opposition to a "deep" approach to learning which relates previous knowledge to new knowledge within the wider context and promotes the synthesis of arguments through analysis and reflection (Ramsden, 1992).

Mezirow (2000) suggests that individuals can be transformed through a process of critical reflection in his theory of transformative learning. This is strongly applied to contemporary mental health education by Dawn Freshwater in this book. Influences on the theory include Paulo Freire (1972) and constructivist thought. Paulo Freire describes the process of conscientisation, by which adults achieve an awareness of both the socio-cultural reality which shapes their lives and their capacity to transform that reality through action upon it. Constructivism is the assumption that meaning exists within ourselves rather than in external forms. Catalysts for transformative learning are "disorienting dilemmas", situations that do not fit one's preconceived notions. These dilemmas prompt critical reflection and the development of new ways of interpreting experiences. In this way, transformative learning involves reflectively transforming the beliefs, attitudes, opinions, and emotional reactions that constitute our meaning schemes.

According to Mezirow (2000), the role of the educator is to help the learner focus on and examine the assumptions that underlie their beliefs, feelings and actions and assess the consequences of these assumptions. They should identify and explore alternative sets of assumptions and test the validity of assumptions through effective participation in reflective dialogue. This will involve the learner becoming more reflective and critical and more open to the perspectives of others by being less defensive and more accepting of new ideas. Educators may help others, and perhaps themselves, to move towards a fuller and more dependable understanding of the meaning of our mutual experience.

Rogers Carl (1994) made significant contributions to the field of adult education, with his experiential theory of learning. Rogers maintained that all human beings have a natural desire to learn. He defined two categories of learning: meaningless, or cognitive learning (e.g., memorising multiplication tables) and significant, or experiential (applied knowledge which addresses the needs and wants of the learner).

According to Rogers, the role of the teacher is to facilitate experiential learning by setting a positive climate for learning, clarifying the purposes of the learner, organising and making available learning resources, balancing intellectual and emotional components of learning and sharing feelings and thoughts with learners but not dominating. As for the personal growth and development of the student, Rogers suggests that significant learning takes place when the subject matter is relevant to the personal interests of the student. He maintains that learning which is threatening to the self (e.g., new attitudes or perspectives) is more easily assimilated when external threats are at a minimum as learning proceeds faster when the threat to the self is low. Finally self-initiated learning is the most lasting and pervasive.

A Strengths Approach

A further principle is the recognition of the importance of the relationship between the individual who uses mental health service and the person, in the eyes of the service, responsible for their care. Rapp (2006) describes the relationship process as the client testing the worker's promises, interests, and sincerity that leads to confidence building in the relationship which replaces scepticism. The client then becomes reaffirmed as a person with assets and valid aspirations which leads to goals becoming more ambitious, communication more honest, and assistance more accessible. The final principle is the belief that people who use mental health services can continue to learn, grow, and change. This principle is based upon maintaining hope within the relationship and ensuring the term "can do" is at the heart of every process (Rapp, 2006).

The principles outlined above can be applied to the teaching of all mental health workers and represent a parallel to the educational theories presented by Carl Rogers. The implementation of these principles will firstly involve asking the students to identify goals they feel would be valuable to them to have achieved by the end of any teaching session. This reflects the first principle of strengths outlined above as it will allow the teacher to ascertain the student's current level of knowledge along with their aspirations for future knowledge. This shifts the responsibility of learning away from the teacher and towards the student and requires the teacher to adopt the role of facilitator. The notion of two-way questioning between teachers and students is reminiscent of the emphasis placed upon dialogue by Freire (1972). Dialogue, he argued, involves respect and directly confronts the power/knowledge discourse identified by Foucault. Freire rejected the idea that teachers were superior, pouring from their jug of knowledge into the students' empty cups. Students are regarded as creative, intelligent and able to give as much as they receive in the educative process. Freire proposed transcendence between teachers and students. In part, this is to occur as learners develop their consciousness as adults.

This method of teaching will require the teacher to be confident in their awareness of the teaching environment and how to facilitate the acquisition of the required resources that is in line with the second principle of strengths. This is a direct challenge to the belief that the teacher should hold all the answers which once given, should not be questioned by the student. The student will have the opportunity to discover new principles and apply them through analysis and self-reflection.

The process of allowing the students the freedom to direct the process of learning reflects the student's right to determine the form and substance of their education. This will result in a teaching that is tailored to the individual needs of the group rather than the need the teacher has to regurgitate their knowledge on the subject. The benefit of this is to prevent the teacher from asking too much of the students which may impact negatively on their confidence and future learning. By adopting an approach that promotes student self-determination, a partnership begins to build between the student and the teacher. The teacher is able to work on behalf of the students and the students' goals and learning outcomes become the focus of the learning. This does not suggest however that the teacher should adopt a passive stance in the teacher/student relationships. The focus is upon partnership therefore each party should have equal power that reflects another principle of the strengths perspective. The combination of these factors will help to create an atmosphere which will promote the empowerment of the student and teacher. In doing so the session becomes motivating which encourages the student to learn, grow and may also influence a change in their perception of the professional/service user relationship.

CONCLUSION

Having been involved in mental health services for many years, we conclude that the medical model of care on its own has little to offer the person in terms of hope, meaning to life and a sense of recovery. That is why much of this book focuses upon methods and approaches that are holistic. Mental health practitioners desperately need to have a greater sense of the needs of people in society, and not simply to regard people as biologically ill entities. Care needs to shift away from a traditional medical model of care to one that acknowledges the individual and the influence of their social world. It is the recovery movement that offers an alternative to the current preoccupation with pathology and negative aspects of people and society and is more about hope and rebuilding lives. Practitioners of the future need to focus upon people's aspirations, their qualities, hopes, wishes and upon their personal resources to realise their goals.

At the time of writing in the UK, there are various shifts taking place that will inevitably affect the mental health workforce of the future. One of these shifts is towards inter-professional learning, and the other is towards greater partnership working with the non-statutory sector. Both of these shifts indicate a broadening of the focus of mental healthcare provision away from a narrow medical model approach. It is true that nurses are by far the largest professional group that provides mental healthcare. We would also encourage and welcome developments of the mental health workforce away from professionalised roles such as nursing and to roles that are more generic. For as long as mental healthcare delivery remains largely with nurses, so it remains largely intertwined with the medical model.

The same argument applies to the environments that people are offered when seriously distressed. An acute ward of a psychiatric unit is often the last environment that a person in distress would want. Whilst we acknowledge there are times that people need some form of physical containment, this need not necessarily have to be in a ward in a hospital. A more homely environment would be welcomed by all. Whilst we do not lament the demise of the old Victorian hospitals, many at least provided gardens, recreational activities and opportunities for doing something meaningful. Many of our acute wards these days are stark noisy places, often with no grounds or gardens and situated in heavily built up areas.

We do not shy away from the political responsibility that lies in the hands of educators. Where there is bad practice and institutional failure, educators have the responsibility to challenge and speak out. As more and more people may be put off "whistle-blowing" for fear of recrimination, often it is only the educators that are in a position to challenge failures in care provision.

We may be accused of being idealistic in our assertion for more humanistic approaches to mental health education. For, it could be argued that in the *real world* we need to prepare our students for the reality of the medical model of care and all that it entails. In return, we would argue that the cycle of ignorance needs to be broken at some point and it is the role of the educators to educate according to their own intrinsic values and not to simply provide canon fodder for the service providers. Approaches to mental healthcare need to change. We argue that this change needs to take place both in practice and in the classroom. The learners of today are the leaders of tomorrow.

REFERENCES

Foucault, M. (1971). *Madness and Civilization.* London: Tavistock.
Freire, P. (1972). *The pedagogy of the oppressed.* London: Penguin.
Marton, F. & Saljo, R. (1976a). On qualitative differences in learning I: Outcome and process. *British Journal of Educational Psychology, 46,* 4–11.

Mezirow, J. (2000). *Learning as transformation: critical perspectives on a theory in progress.* San Francisco, Jossey-Bass.

Ramsden, P. (1992). *Learning to Teaching in Higher Education.* London: Routledge.

Rapp, C.A. (2006). The Strengths Model. (2nd edn) New York: Oxford University Press.

Rogers, C.R. (1994). *Freedom to Learn* (3rd edn) New Jersey: Merrill.

Index